A REVIEW OF FIFTY PUBLIC UNIVERSITY

HONORS PROGRAMS

with additional reviews of five

REGIONAL PUBLIC UNIVERSITY HONORS PROGRAMS

©Copyright 2014 Public University Press

ISBN: 0692314865
ISBN 13: 9780692314869

APRIL 2015

CONTENTS

CONTENTS

REGIONAL PUBLIC UNIVERSITY HONORS:

Cover photo of French House, home of the LSU Honors College, courtesy of Louisiana State University Office of Communications and University Relations.

The first edition of *A Review of Fifty Public University Honors Programs,* published in 2012, was in many ways a "first draft" attempt to evaluate most of the major public university honors colleges and programs in the nation. We have learned a lot since then, much of it because of that first attempt.

In late 2011, we began contacting Honors Deans, Directors, and staff affiliated with the first group of fifty honors programs that we hoped to review. Although several programs were unresponsive, much of what we planned to use was available in the public domain, especially information about the curriculum requirements for honors completion--our key metric. Accordingly, we went on with the project and, eventually, publication in April 2012.

After maintaining contact with as many honors professionals as possible and establishing additional contacts in that community, we came to realize that our initial focus on the *quantity* of credits required for honors completion overlooked the many nuances of honors curricula, including a sometimes confusing classification of courses. The major premise behind our emphasis on curriculum requirements was and remains sound: the greater the honors course requirements, the greater the opportunities to study with students of high ability, take smaller classes with engaging professors, discover research mentors, and develop the confidence and skills to compete for prestigious scholarships. But in focusing on the number of credit hours we did not give sufficient attention to the range, type, size, and availability of honors course sections.

Another important learning experience came with this second round of evaluations. By branching out to programs of public universities beyond the flagships, we observed that many of them had excellent honors programs and colleges but that our previous emphasis on the number of prestigious scholarships (Rhodes, Truman, Goldwater, Fulbright, etc.) won by students was skewing our overall evaluations too much in favor of "public elite" universities. In addition, although most of these awards are won by honors students, not all of them are. As a result, we reduced the weight of prestigious scholarships as the second edition work moved forward. Please see the section on "Methodology" for further discussion.

For this edition, we contacted 77 honors programs that were potential candidates for review, and received 53 responses. After preliminary reviews, we decided to rate 44 programs that responded and another six that did not. These six are the subjects of "external reviews" based on public information. (We are also reviewing, but not rating, an additional five public honors programs housed in "regional" universities, based on their formal responses; this has been an exciting process that has brought home to us the value that honors programs can have for universities of any type or size.) Therefore, of the 55 total reviews in this edition, 49 are based primarily on program responses.

Our special thanks to the many honors professionals around the nation whose thoughtful responses to our questionnaire and continuing feedback made this book possible. We hope you find our in-depth profiles of all the above programs to be of significant use as you consider you college options. Please contact the editor@publicuniversityhonors.com if you have questions about this publication.

Best wishes,

John Willingham, Editor

3

The second edition of *A Review of Fifty Public University Honors Programs* is very different from its predecessor. The first edition, published in 2012, combined numerical rankings with relatively short narrative profiles of each honors college or honors program. The numerical rankings relied on honors-specific data and university-wide data, not the best possible approach but the only one available at the time. The numerical ("ordinal") rankings across multiple categories that we presented in the first edition separated programs by as little as .01 on a scale of 100. This time around, we have abandoned numerical rankings in favor a "mortarboard" rating system (instead of 3, 4, or 5 stars or other symbols, think mortarboards--the more there are, the better the ranking). More about those mortarboards later...

Why did we decide not to use numerical rankings this time? The decision was difficult because many readers and college junkies like us love to keep up with the often minor changes in the *U.S. News, Forbes, Times Higher Ed, Kiplinger,* and *Washington Monthly* rankings. Ultimately, we concluded that *any* numerical rankings, however interesting they may be, are so subjective that claiming distinctions based on statistical variations as little as .01 or even 1.0 out of 100.0 actually creates differences where they do not exist in any meaningful sense. It is far more realistic, we believe, to use large amounts of data, which we do have this time around, but not to claim that the data can do more than suggest *groups* within which multiple programs can be placed.

Yet like all rankings and ratings, those in his book are to some extent subjective. After three years of research, the editor reviews the data and then decides what *he thinks* the best use of it will be to produce fair and accurate ratings. In the case of evaluating honors programs, the hardest tasks are finding rating categories that can each be applied to a broad spectrum of programs and then deciding how much weight to assign each category. A wonderful article in *The New Yorker* by Malcolm Gladwell, in the February 14, 2011 issue ("The Order of Things: what college rankings really tell us"), puts the problem this way:

"A ranking can be heterogeneous...as long as it doesn't try to be too comprehensive. And it can be comprehensive as long as it doesn't try to measure things that are heterogeneous." In other words, one can rank many differing entities using very few criteria, or one can rank a few highly similar entities using many criteria.

Public university honors colleges and programs are certainly diverse, but despite occasional protestations from the honors community that there is too much diversity in the programs to permit any comprehensive evaluation, we have attempted to do so, with great care in the selection of our criteria. We hope you will agree that honors curriculum, range of courses, class sizes, graduation rates, staff ratios, honors benefits, and an accurate record of winning prestigious awards are indeed applicable to all major honors programs, especially from the perspective of parents and prospective students.

As noted in the Introduction, we will use mortarboard images (e.g. 🎓 🎓 🎓 $^{1/2}$) to illustrate the ratings for each honors program or college. The highest rating in a category is five mortarboards, and possible ratings in most categories are 5, 4.5, 4.0, 3.5, and 3.0. The Perception category (see below) reaches down to a rating of 2.0 because of the greater variability in the national university rankings upon which it relies.

Overall Rating--is based on the sum of all ratings in the categories below, except for Perception.

Perception--is based on the ranking of the **university as a whole** among public universities as listed in the 2014 *U.S. News Best Colleges* report. The purpose of this category is to give readers a very general idea whether the honors program is better, the same, or perhaps not as good as the perception of the university within which it functions. Please bear in mind that the better the *U.S. News* ranking, the more difficult it is for an honors college or program to have a rating that equals or improves on the magazine ranking. That we use the *U.S. News* rankings to illustrate Perception does not mean that we see those rankings as definitive; it is only in recognition of the influence of the rankings on public perception.

Curriculum Requirements--is a measure of the number of honors course credits that are required for "honors completion" of the curriculum, and it carries the most weight in our system. This is not a qualitative metric, as it does not measure the quality or range of honors courses but only the quantity of credit hours, as a percentage of the total credit hours required for university graduation.

Range and Type of Honors Courses--is the **most subjective** of our categories, as only part of it is based on the raw number of honors sections. The other part is subjective because in addition to the number of course sections, we evaluate the range, depth, and types of honors classes. Class type can include **honors-only seminars and colloquia** (colloquia are similar to seminars, but the topics may be more general, the discussions may be more frequent, or the instructors may vary as the sub-topics do); **honors-only classes in the specialized disciplines**, e.g., math, physics, English, psychology; **mixed sections** (also called add-ons, stacked sections, embedded sections), in which honors and non-honors students attend the same lecture class but honors students also attend smaller breakout sections, usually called discussion sections, or complete extra assignments for honors credit; and **honors contract courses** (also known as options, conversions), regular non-honors classes that typically lack any honors designation in advance but do require an honors-approved contract between the student and instructor who agree on extra assignments for honors credit. (Please see "Choosing an Honors Program: Twenty Questions to Ask.")

Within the discussion of the Range and Type of Honors Courses, we usually say whether the honors college or program is a **core program, a blended program, or a department-based program.** (Please see "Honors Programs by Type.") The **core honors programs** usually offer a range of quality colloquia and seminars that meet university Gen Ed requirements in area topics such as humanities, math and science, social sciences, and fine arts. Honors students usually benefit from much smaller Gen Ed classes as well as the challenge of engaging other students of similar high ability. Sometimes core honors programs offer little in the way of upper-division honors courses, and they may or may not require an honors thesis. It is generally more difficult for a core program without upper-division courses or requirements to achieve a high rating in the Range and Type of Honors Courses category, though there are certainly exceptions. **Blended honors programs** feature a strong selection of core Gen Ed seminars and colloquia along with a good range of departmental and upper-division honors classes. They often require an honors thesis. Finally, **department-based honors programs** usually offer few or no seminars and colloquia but do list many sections of lower- and upper-division honors classes in the academic

5

disciplines. Department-based programs are also likely to require an honors thesis. **Range and Type of Honors Courses is the most complex category and also one of the most important.**

Average Honors Class Size--The average includes mixed and all-honors sections. Please see the "Methodology" section for a detailed explanation.

Adjusted Graduation Rate--The purposes of this rating are (1) to show the six-year graduation rate for first-year honors *entrants*—not for honors completers; (2) to compare the honors graduation rate with that for the university as a whole; and (3) to compare the honors program graduation rate with the overall average graduation rate for all 50 programs.

Ratio of Staff to Students--A straightforward measure based on program responses to our survey questionnaire, the rating also shows the program ratio of staff to students in relation to the overall average ratio for all 50 programs.

Honors Housing--One of the most controversial rating categories, honors housing is important to a lot of parents and prospective students. Some honors professionals argue that honors perks, such as special dorms and priority registration, only serve to confer an "elite" status on honors students by setting them apart from non-honors students. But our ratings do favor programs that have designated honors housing. Suite-style, air-conditioned rooms with shared baths are rated higher than basic double rooms with hall baths; and residence halls with locations that are convenient to classes and dining facilities are also rated higher. Our preference for suite-style rooms is also somewhat controversial because many educators believe that the more communal atmosphere of the traditional corridor dorms is especially beneficial to first-year students who often have few friends on campus and benefit from more socialization early on.

Priority Registration--Sometimes referred to as "early registration," this honors perk is very popular among students, although some honors programs do not offer it for the same reason that honors housing is not made available or because priority registration can become the main or even only reason that honors students continue in a program whose overriding goal is strictly academic. Priority registration can come in several forms: early registration for all classes in all years; for honors classes only; for all classes after or before a certain year; and in yet other forms.

Curriculum Requirements (35 pts)--For each program, we (1) determine the highest level of honors completion, (2) determine the minimum number of credits required to fulfill the requirements for that level, (3) calculate a small percentage credit for the number of STEM (especially engineering) graduates from the university,* (4) take the total raw number derived from the previous steps, (5) divide that number by the total credit hours required for graduation (120 for semester, 180 for quarter), and (6) scale the number to a highest value of 35. (Scaled data may also be adjusted.)

*Developing an extensive honors curriculum in a university with a high proportion of engineering students is difficult for honors programs (absent generous endowments) because those universities must allocate so many of their resources to science and engineering equipment, labs, and instruction. Engineering students are also hard-pressed to take very many honors classes in addition to the demands of their majors. These factors work in general to limit the honors curricula in many of these universities. The small proportional adjustment that we make for all programs is an attempt to even the playing field just a bit for those that operate in the context of a STEM-heavy university.

Range and Type of Honors Courses (12.5 pts)--Using the data we received from respondents about the number and type of class sections *and* reviewing the class schedules for every university, we (1) determined the number of honors seminars and other honors-only classes and the number of departmental honors sections; (2) classified the programs as core, blended, or department-based; (3) reviewed the number of sections by discipline; (4) assigned a numerical score to (a) the interdisciplinary component, based on the number and range, and to the departmental component based on the same; (5) averaged these scores; and (6) scaled the raw average to a highest value of 12.5.

Class Size (12.5 pts)--For honors-only sections, we counted the total enrollment, but we did not count tutorials, thesis, labs, and break-discussion sections, only the enrollment for the main class sections. For mixed (stacked, add-on, embedded) sections with more than one student, we counted the total enrollment up to 99; enrollments of 100 or more were divided by two, with a minimum value of 100; the single largest mixed section was omitted along with listed mixed sections with only 1 or 0 honors students. Why did we count the total honors enrollment in large all-honors classes but divide the large mixed sections by two? The mixed sections often have very few honors students, so rather than count only honors students in these large classes (misleading) or count the total enrollment (also misleading), we discounted the size. The raw data was not scaled but separated into quintiles with point values.

Adjusted Graduation Rates (12.5 pts)--Using the six-year graduation rate for honors entrants, whether or not they completed the honors program, would have essentially tied this metric to selection criteria--if you set the bar really high, a lot of the students you admit will graduate. So we did the following: (1) used the six-year honors entrant graduation data submitted by respondents and scaled it to a value of 12.5; (2) determined the percentage of difference between the six-year grad rate of honors entrants and the six-year grad rate for the university as a whole; (3) scaled that difference value to a highest value of 12.5; and (4) averaged the two scaled values to a single raw number with a maximum value of 12.5. In the end, we wanted to give equal value to the six-year honors rate in its own right and to the extent of improvement that rate represented over the grad rate of the university as a whole.

Honors Housing (10 pts)--We evaluated the room configurations, locations, amenities, and dining options of honors residence halls and then assigned maximum values as follows: (1) assigned a base value of 4.0; (2) added a maximum of 1.5 points for location, with possible scores of .5, 1.0, or 1.5, using campus maps for every residence hall; (3) added a value for air conditioning, maximum of 1.0; (4) assigned three possible scores for room configurations=1.5 for suite; 1.0 for corridor with in-room sink; .5

for corridor and hall baths, no sink; (5) assigned three possible scores for dining=1.5 for inside the residence hall or quad; 1.0 for "close" within a half mile or less; and .5 for inconvenient, using campus maps for this score; (6) added .5 for on-site laundry, which almost everyone received. The maximum score is 10.0.

Staff Ratio (7.5 pts)--To determine the ratio, we took (1) the current honors student enrollment number submitted by honors respondents and (2) divided that number by the total number of honors staff, as listed on the response. The result was scaled to a value of 7.5.

Prestigious Awards (7.5 pts)--(1) We used raw totals for the entire history of the following: Rhodes, Marshall, Gates Cambridge, Churchill, Truman, Udall, and Goldwater; (2) we used raw totals for three years of Fulbright Student, Boren, and NSFGRG awards (2011--2013 inclusive); and (3) a percentage of Gilman awards during the same period.. These totals were scaled to a maximum value of 7.5. **This is the only metric we use that is not *entirely* honors specific. The totals are for the universities as a whole, not for the honors program or college only, although many and in some cases most of the awards are won by honors students. We use the data because we believe highly-talented prospective students should have an idea how well the program and university perform in this area.**

Priority Registration (2.5 pts)--Full or partial credit of up to 2.5 points was possible only if priority registration was a formal feature of the honors program and not a benefit resulting from a university merit scholarship.

As we noted in the previous section on "Ratings Definitions," honors colleges and programs fall into three basic types: core, blended, and departmental. **Core programs** typically emphasize honors interdisciplinary seminars in the first two years; these courses often count for university Gen Ed requirements. **Blended programs** also offer interdisciplinary courses and usually meet Gen Ed requirements with honors courses as well, but they also offer or require a significant number of more specialized departmental honors courses. **Department-based honors programs** rely mostly on discipline-specific honors classes and offer few or no seminars. Department-based programs are more likely to be decentralized. Please understand that there are additional differences within these fairly broad types: some core programs have 10-20 department-based classes, for example, and many blended programs lean toward more seminars or toward more department-based classes. Several department-based programs at least offer first-year seminars. **Each program type has advantages:** core programs are likely to have smaller classes with a higher percentage of interdisciplinary courses; blended programs have a good mix of classes; department-based programs often allow students to focus early on honors in the major. **Several programs of each type are also rated very highly, at 5.0 and 4.5.**

Core Programs

Kentucky, Maine, North Carolina State, Oregon, UC Irvine, UT Austin, Utah, Vermont, Washington, Washington State

Blended Programs

Alabama, Arizona State, Auburn, Colorado State, Connecticut, Delaware, Florida State, Illinois, Indiana, Iowa, LSU, Massachusetts, Minnesota, Mississippi, Missouri, North Carolina, Oklahoma, Oklahoma State, Oregon State, Purdue, Rhode Island, Rutgers, South Carolina, Temple, Texas Tech, UCLA.

Department-Based Programs

Arizona, Arkansas, Clemson, Georgia, Kansas, Miami, Michigan, Ohio University, Penn State, Tennessee, Texas A&M, University at Albany, Virginia, Wisconsin.

Here are some figures that illustrate the differences between honors colleges and honors programs:

1. Size–The 25 honors colleges under review have an average enrollment of 1,900 students, versus the average enrollment of 1,492 in the 25 honors programs.

2. Staff–Honors colleges have more staff members per student. In honors colleges, the ratio of students to honors staff is 141.7. In honors programs, the ratio is 162.4. It is possible that honors programs have more indirect staff support from, say, the Dean of Undergraduate Studies, but the ratios above are based on actual honors staffing figures in 2013-2014.

3. Structure–The additional staff at honors colleges appears to contribute to the higher percentage of a "blended" honors structure at honors colleges. By a **blended structure**, we mean that there are both honors-only seminars (often interdisciplinary in nature) offered solely by the honors college, along with many honors classes focused primarily on specific academic disciplines. Fourteen of the 25 honors colleges fall into this category, versus 12 of the 25 honors programs. Six honors colleges have a **department-based** honors structure, while eight honors programs feature this more decentralized structure. This means that, speaking in general terms only, honors programs might be more appealing for students who are more focused on their majors and less interested in the broader approach typical of most seminars.

A relatively small number of colleges and programs have a **core** structure. The core programs are almost exclusively based on a set of honors seminars and colloquia designed to offer interdisciplinary perspectives on the humanities, social sciences, math and science, and fine arts. Often, these courses count for and replace the Gen Ed courses taken by non-honors students. Honors core programs may or may not require an honors thesis. Most do not offer a lot of upper-division or department-centered courses. Five honors colleges are based on the core model, and so are five honors programs.

4. Average Honors Class size–Honors colleges have a better ratio of students per class section, using data from the Spring 2014 term. (For colleges on the quarter system, we use a formula to equalize quarter sections with semester sections.) What honors colleges and programs say about having smaller classes is mostly true: Honors colleges average about 19.8 students per section, and honors programs about 22.5 students per section for all honors courses. Please know, however, that both honors colleges and honors programs have some large classes, typically in the sciences. They offset the size of the main course sections by offering multiple small all-honors discussion sections and labs that are attached to the main lecture section but meet at different times. We did **not** count discussion sections or labs in calculating class size, only the main class sections.

5. Contract Courses--There is disagreement about the relative value of contract courses. Clearly, such classes do not require all-honors enrollment or staffing and can be accomplished without reducing the "credit" a given professor receives for teaching larger classes, the only difference being that the honors student under contract does extra work for honors credit. Contract classes are therefore extremely cost-effective for the university. They can also be a boon for some honors students, who find that they can in fact get into that hard class they need to graduate, even if it's not an all-honors class. On average, honors colleges allow 7.0 contract credit hours, and honors programs allow 8.9 contract credits toward honors completion. (Some colleges and programs, however, allow up to 30 hours of contract credit.) **It is very**

important for prospective students to gain an understanding of the types of courses that can be counted as honors credit.

6. Big Fish in the Pond–Using a formula that compares average (mean) honors test scores for honor students to average test scores for students in the university as a whole, and students in the top quarter of the university as a whole, we find that there is a greater gap between students in honors colleges and their non-honors classmates than there is between students in honors programs and the non-honors students in their universities. So, based on test scores alone, honors college students have a somewhat higher chance of being regarded as the "smart kids" on campus.

7. Honors Housing–Here, although there are many exceptions, honors colleges tend to offer more amenities such as suite-style dorms. One reason for discrepancies in housing is that many prominent public universities have made a conscious decision not to contribute to the "big fish" perception and do not provide separate honors housing at all. In this group are UCLA, Illinois, and Wisconsin, all of them honors programs rather than colleges.

Please bear in mind that these statistics describe general characteristics of honors colleges and honors programs. There are many honors programs, especially, that mirror all of the features associated with honors colleges.

We have noticed that many students apply to prominent public universities and then, almost as an afterthought, begin to wonder if the honors program at University A makes that school a better choice than regular admission to the higher-ranked University B.

A far better way to look at honors is to evaluate programs in some depth at the earliest stages of the college application process. Otherwise, students realize too late that the honors application or scholarship deadline has passed and find themselves searching for anecdotal evidence with little time to spare.

Honors colleges and programs differ greatly in size, quality, curricula, housing, overall philosophy, and financial aid opportunities. Working through the maze of differences can be a daunting prospect, especially when time is an issue. When it comes to honors programs, many of the most important questions can be answered only by consideration of those all-important "details." Below are twenty steps that should be very useful in helping you make the best decision:

1. Match <u>basic</u> admission requirements with your test scores, GPA, and essays.

2. Request <u>actual average</u> enrollee statistics. These may vary greatly from basic (minimum) requirements. In general, honors students will have average test scores 6-10% higher than the 25th percentile of accepted students for the university as a whole. The 25th percentile scores are available from *U.S. News* and other sources. If there is a wide gap between the basic and average stats, and your stats are much closer to the basic stats, then you can probably find a better option. Even so, if the admissions requirements are more holistic and less stats-driven, you may be fine.

3. Determine the size of the honors program (mean size in major public universities is ~1,700, but programs may be as small as 140 or as large as 6,000).

4. Ask the fish-to-pond question: Are honors students big fish in a small pond or is the pond full of sizable fish? The more selective the university as a whole, the bigger all the fish. Some parents and prospective students might prefer an honors program that stands apart on campus, while others might like a program that is more expansive. Perhaps if you are not sold on the overall quality of the university, you might choose a program that stands apart; if you think the university as a whole has a strong student body or you simply prefer a non-elitist atmosphere, you might like the more expansive program.

5. Assess the quality of the city, surrounding area, and climate.

6. Determine the curriculum requirements as a percentage of graduation requirements. Generally, the number of honors hours should be at least 25% of the total required for graduation.

7. Determine the number of honors sections per semester/quarter.

8. Evaluate the reputation of university in preferred or likely areas of study.

9. Ask whether there are special research opportunities for undergrads **and if an honors thesis is required.** Some students find that completing the honors thesis is a burden, while others recognize how valuable it can be for applications to graduate or professional school and for employment prospects.

10. Ask about staff size, the number of advisers, and availability to students, as well as special freshmen orientation programs.

If the above check out, then:

1. Ask about the number of honors sections, <u>by discipline</u>, per semester or quarter and try to verify; determine the average enrollment in honors seminars and sections. The average class size can vary greatly among honors programs, from fewer than 10 students per class to more than 35. Most seminars and all-honors sections should have around 25 students or fewer, although in almost every case you will find that there are a few large classes, notably in first-year sciences and economics. Some honors programs have few or no honors courses in certain disciplines.

2. Ask about the <u>types</u> of honors sections: all-honors <u>seminars</u>; all-honors sections offered by honors <u>or</u> a department; "mixed" sections of honors and non-honors students; and the percentage of honors contract/option/conversion courses per average student at time of graduation.

<u>Mixed sections</u> may be small or, more often, large sections that can have more than 100 total students in 3-4 credit hour courses. Of these students, maybe 10-20 could be honors students, who then meet for one hour a week (rarely, two hours a week) in separate "discussion" or "recitation" sections. These sections can be led by tenured professors but are typically led by adjunct faculty or graduate students. Ask how many sections are mixed, and of these, ask how many of the main section classes are large.

<u>Contract courses</u> are regular–and often larger–sections with both honors and non-honors students, mostly the latter, in which honors students contract with the instructor to do extra work. While most programs have some contract courses, they are generally more prevalent in large honors colleges and programs. There are advantages and disadvantages associated with contract courses. They can speed graduation, offer more flexibility, expand the influence of honors in the university as a whole, and foster contacts with mentoring faculty. But their quality and size may vary greatly.

3. Ask about tuition discounts, scholarships, continuing financial aid, including special recruitment of national merit scholars.

4. Determine if there is priority registration for honors students and, if so, type of priority registration.

5. Research the types of special honors housing for freshmen <u>and</u> upperclassmen, if any, including basic floor plans, on-site laundry, suite or corridor-style rooms, air-conditioning, location of nearest dining hall, proximity of major classroom buildings (especially in preferred disciplines), and availability of shuttles and other transportation on campus. <u>If there is no special honors housing, it is often a sign that the honors program does not want to foster the big fish in a small pond atmosphere. The absence of priority registration may be an additional sign.</u>

6. Research the study-abroad opportunities; most universities have a separate division for study-abroad programs. Sometimes there are special opportunities for honors students, including financial assistance.

7. Ask about the presence and involvement of advisers for prestigious scholarships, such as Goldwater, Rhodes, Marshall, Truman, etc., and program success in achieving these awards.

8. Ask about additional fees for participation in honors **and ask about the percentage of honors "completers."** These are honors students who actually complete all of the honors requirements and graduate with some form of honors. There are many programs that have completion rates as low as 25% and a few with completion rates higher than 80%. (This is different from the graduation rate from the university, which, for freshmen honors entrants, is anywhere from 75%–99% after six years.)

9. Now, try to assess the quality of the honors program versus quality of university as a whole.

10. VISIT the college if you have not done so and try to question current honors students. Some of the information mentioned above can only come from a personal visit or be learned after a student has been accepted.

Editor's Note: *This post appeared on our website and has received so many views that we are including it in the* Review *for easy reference. The figures are current as of Fall 2014, using the most recent National Merit data from 2013:*

After comparing National Merit Scholarship awards for both 2012 and 2013, it is clear that the number of university-sponsored NMS awards is declining, with colleges spending $1 million less on NMS sponsorships in 2013 than in the previous year. The number of colleges sponsoring any merit scholars also declined, from 193 to 186.

(The actual figures are $21.9 million in 2012 and $20.9 million in 2013.)

But while the total number of college-sponsored awards declined from 4,553 to 4,302 in one year, and the total dollar amount also fell, the average college NMS award in 2013 was a few bucks higher than in 2012–$4,858 versus $4,801. **The net result: fewer finalists are receiving almost exactly the same amount of money in college support.**

Although the drop in support may not appear to be dramatic, it is surprising how many colleges previously known for their NMS sponsorships have made some severe cuts (see below).

On the corporate sponsorship side, however, the total dollar amount is the same for both years–$19 million. This money came from 248 corporate sponsors in 2013, up just 4 from the previous year. **The best news about corporate sponsorships is that they averaged about $18,200 in 2013.** This amount is almost identical to the average award the previous year, so at least corporate sponsorships are not declining.

About 3.5 million students take the PSAT during their junior year in high school, at the latest, and of these approximately 8,000–9,000 may be selected as winners of national merit scholarships. Another 50,000 reach "commended" status, and about 15,000 are "semifinalists."

But the ground rules for allocating institutional (college) funds for merit scholars have changed significantly over the last few years. With declining state support and rising costs, along with concerns about providing financial assistance to students who may not have a clear need for it, many elite public and private universities no longer use their own funds for national merit scholarships.

All of the Ivy League universities have stopped matching or funding national merit scholarships, although they continue to enroll large numbers of winners because of the prestige of the institutions. Ivy League schools also, as a rule, provide generous financial support based on actual need, making them an excellent choice for most of the applicants they admit. The mean SAT scores for many of these schools are likely significantly higher than the mean score nationwide on the PSAT (converted to SAT).

Nowadays, winners of merit scholarships whose families fall into that broad range of being moderately well to do but not comfortably well off need to know which universities still place a premium on National Merit Scholars. The universities that continue to recruit NM scholars typically do so because (1) they want to compete with the Ivies for the best students and/or (2) they want to raise the profile of their undergrads so that national rankings will show a higher degree of selectivity.

Most of the highly-ranked private universities that continue their relationship with the National Merit Scholarship Corporation fall into category (1) above. Foremost among these are the University of Chicago with 314 merit scholars (173 of them with university sponsorship); USC with 245 merit scholars (192 with USC support); Northwestern with 249 scholars (183 with school support); Washington University St. Louis with 202 scholars (157 with university sponsorship); and Vanderbilt with 260 scholars (194 with university support). Of these, each of the last three has increased college support–Vanderbilt dramatically–and all of the others have reduced their support even though they remain leaders overall.

A longer list of public universities appears below.

All of these excellent private universities are willing to take the heat for funding non- need-based students based on merit alone at a time when the inequities of scholarship funding have led to a greater emphasis on allocating funds mostly or entirely on a need-based scale.

Again, for many families, that trend is a good one; but for families with incomes in the mid six figures, for example, the ability to qualify for need-based aid may be negligible while the pinch on the family budget is still significant.

Many public elites have joined the Ivies in not providing their own funds to match or pay entirely for merit scholarships. Among these schools are all the UC campuses, UT Austin, and the University of Washington. Michigan and Virginia also appear to have stopped using their own funds for merit scholarships based solely on the PSAT. At these universities, merit scholars may still receive assistance but it will not be in the form of merit matching funds or totally funded merit scholarships. These and other universities may also have non-need-based scholarships for valedictorians.

The University of Wisconsin only funds 5 merit scholars a year, and these must be need-based.

Below is a list of public universities that continue to match or fund National Merit Scholars, regardless of need, and that had 25 or more merit scholars in 2012. We will list the university, followed by the total number of merit scholars in the 2012 report, followed again by the number of those scholars that also received school support based on the merit scholarship. Then we do the same for merit scholars in the same universities in 2013.

If there is a steep decline in the total number of merit scholars from 2012 to 2013, that probably means that corporate sponsorships are not filling the void left by the decline in university sponsorships. If there are more total college sponsorships in 2013, then that means that the university may have decided to "double down" and take advantage of the void left by others.

As a general rule, the higher the number of school-supported merit scholars, the greater the recruitment is for merit scholars.

Alabama (2012): 241 total merit scholars, 208 with school funding; **2013: 123 total, 111 with university funding**

Oklahoma (2012): 194 merit scholars, 160 with school funding; **2013:** 173 total, 151 with university funding

Minnesota (2012): 143 merit scholars, 114 with school funding; **2013:** 135 total, 107 with university funding

Florida (2012): 136 merit scholars, 116 with school funding; **2013:** 20 total, **none with university funding**

North Carolina (2012): 136 merit scholars, 101 with school funding; **2013:** 37 total, **none with school funding**

Texas A&M (2012): 136 merit scholars, 113 with school funding; **2013: 150 total, and 126 with university sponsorship**

Georgia Tech (2012): 119 merit scholars, 91 with school funding; **2013: 161 total, and 128 with university sponsorship**

Arizona State (2012): 97 merit scholars, 75 with school funding; **2013: 119 total, and 102 with university sponsorship**

UC Berkeley (2012): 90 merit scholars, none with school funding; **2013:** 109 total, none with university sponsorship

Arizona (2012): 81 merit scholars, 69 with school funding; **2013:** 68 total, 58 with university sponsorship

Kentucky (2012): 70 merit scholars, 54 with school funding; **2013: 95 total,** 75 with university sponsorship

Central Florida–67 merit scholars, 57 with school funding; **2013:** 60 total, 54 with university sponsorship

Illinois (2012): 64 merit scholars, 40 with school funding; **2013: 85 total, 64 with university sponsorship**

UT Dallas–63 merit scholars, 56 with school funding; **2013: 89 total, 70 with university sponsorship**

Auburn–62 merit scholars, 50 with school funding; **2013:** 67 total, 55 with university sponsorship

Maryland (2012): 61 merit scholars, 46 with school funding; **2013:** 54 total, 40 with university sponsorship

Indiana (2012): 59 merit scholars, 44 with school funding; **2013: 66 total, 54 with university sponsorship**

Ohio State–57 merit scholars, 41 with school funding; **2013: 18 total, none with university sponsorship**

UT Austin (2012): 57 merit scholars, none with school funding; **2013:** 67 total, none with university sponsorship

Georgia (2012): 51 merit scholars, 42 with school funding; **2013:** 55 total, 42 with university sponsorship

Michigan (2012): 46 merit scholars, none with school funding; **2013:** 56 total, none with university sponsorship

Nebraska (2012): 46 merit scholars, 38 with school funding; **2013:** 51 total, 41 with university sponsorship

Clemson (2012): 42 merit scholars, 23 with school funding; **2013:** 37 total, **32 with university sponsorship**

South Carolina (2012): 41 merit scholars, 34 with school funding; **2013**: **54 total, 44 with university sponsorship**

Ole Miss (2012): 40 merit scholars, 28 with school funding; **2013:** 39 total, 36 with university sponsorship

Michigan State (2012): 39 merit scholars, 33 with school funding; **2013:** 38 total, 28 with university sponsorship

LSU (2012): 37 merit scholars, 33 with school funding; **2013:** 41 total, 33 with university sponsorship

Cincinnati (2012): 37 merit scholars, 28 with school funding; **2013:** 26 total, 22 with university sponsorship

Arkansas (2012): 35 merit scholars, 31 with school funding; **2013:** 34 total, 27 with university sponsorship

Iowa State (2012): 35 merit scholars, 30 with school funding; **2013:** 38 total, 27 with university funding

Missouri (2012): 29 merit scholars, 26 with school funding; **2013: 11 total, 11 with university sponsorship**

Houston (2012): 27 merit scholars, 24 with school funding; **2013:** 25 total, 24 with university sponsorship

Editor's Note: *The post below received even more views on our website, so we are including it in the* Review *as well.*

To qualify for a National Merit Scholarship, the PSAT must be taken in the student's junior year of high school. Some parents may not be aware that there is no single nationwide score on the PSAT that will qualify a student to become a NMS semifinalist, a critical preliminary step on the way to becoming a finalist and then perhaps a merit scholar.

Semifinalists emerge from the top 3-4% of students (50,000 or so) taking the test, by virtue of the PSAT score alone. The top 3-4% of students earn "commended" status, and there is a national uniform score for commended students=203 for 2014, higher than in the past. (See below for SAT equivalent.) Semifinalists, on the other hand, account for only a bit more than 1% of all students, or about 16,000 nationwide.

From these students, the merit scholar foundation, using state allocation levels, selects about 15,000 to become finalists; and from this group, about 9,000 are actually selected as merit scholars, based on both PSAT and SAT scores and a letter of recommendation from the high school principal. Therefore, many students who meet the semifinalist thresholds listed below do not go on to become finalists or merit scholars (two different things, though for some schools being a finalist is sufficient to earn support). We speculate that meaningful improvement on the SAT, taken in the spring of the junior year, relative to the PSAT score from the preceding October, may help in identifying students who go beyond finalist status and become merit scholars.

Each state has its own threshold PSAT score, which is the baseline for students to be considered as semifinalists in a given state. The scores vary widely, from 201 in West Virginia to 224 in the District of Columbia and New Jersey (see below). Converted to SAT (two-part) scores, there is an estimated difference of 154 points between the SAT scores required in West Virginia and those required in the District of Columbia and New Jersey.

The mean of state minimum semifinalist PSAT 2015 scores is 212.2, down slightly from the 2014 average of 214.1. The 2015 average score converts to an SAT score of 1422.

(To obtain an approximate conversion of PSAT to SAT, you can multiply the PSAT by 10.0= SAT three-part score; and then multiply by 0.67 to obtain the two-part SAT score.)

Estimated PSAT Minimum Semifinalist Scores, and estimated SAT Equivalencies, 2015, by State:

Alabama	207	1387
Alaska	210	1407
Arizona	213	1427
Arkansas	206	1380

California	222	1487
Colorado	213	1427
Connecticut	220	1474
Delaware	215	1441
D.C.	224	1501
Florida	211	1414
Georgia	215	1441
Hawaii	214	1434
Idaho	211	1414
Illinois	215	1441
Indiana	212	1420
Iowa	207	1387
Kansas	213	1427
Kentucky	210	1407
Louisiana	208	1394
Maine	212	1420
Maryland	221	1481
Massachusetts	223	1494
Michigan	210	1407
Minnesota	215	1441
Mississippi	207	1387
Missouri	209	1400

Montana	206	1380
Nebraska	209	1400
Nevada	208	1394
New Hampshire	212	1420
New Jersey	224	1501
New Mexico	210	1407
New York	218	1461
North Carolina	212	1420
North Dakota	201	1347
Ohio	213	1427
Oklahoma	206	1380
Oregon	217	1454
Pennsylvania	216	1447
Rhode Island	212	1420
South Carolina	209	1400
South Dakota	203	1360
Tennessee	212	1420
Texas	218	1461
Utah	208	1394
Vermont	213	1427
Virginia	219	1467
Washington	219	1467

West Virginia	201	1347
Wisconsin	208	1394
Wyoming	204	1367
Commended	201	1347
Outside U.S.	224	1501
U.S. Territories	201	1347

Although we are not ranking honors colleges and programs in numerical order, the summary below provides average (mean) overall results for the 50 programs that we rated, and additional data.

Size of Honors Colleges/Programs:

Average size of all colleges/programs=1,714

Largest of all 50 colleges/programs=~5,500

Smallest of all 50 colleges/programs=230

Curriculum Requirements:

Average number of honors credit hours required for program completion=28.2 semester hours

Required honors credit hours as a percentage of total credits required for graduation=23.5%

Highest credit hour completion level of the 50 colleges and programs=45

Lowest credit hour completion level of the 50 colleges and programs=18

Honors Course Range and Type:

Average number of honors sections classified as seminars, colloquia=24.3

Average number of honors sections classified as departmental honors=69.1

Percentage of honors sections classified as seminars=26.1%

Percentage of honors sections classified as departmental=73.9%

Honors Class Size:

Average number of honors students per section, including mixed sections=21.2

Highest average honors class size=37.7

Lowest average honors class size=10

Honors Graduation Rate (6-year), Freshman Entrants, not Honors "Completers":

Average reported or estimated honors 6-year graduation rate=89%

Highest average reported or estimated honors 6-year graduation % rate=99

Lowest average reported or estimated honors 6-year graduation % rate=75

Ratio of Honors Students to Honors Staff:

Average number of honors students to honors staff person=159.8

Highest average number of honors students to staff=352.9

Lowest average number of honors students to staff=30.7

Score out of 10 on Honors Housing (No designated honors housing=default score of 6.00)

Highest housing scores on scale of 10.00=10

Lowest housing scores on scale of 10.00=6

Test Scores:

Average (mean) two-part SAT for enrolled students in all 50 programs=1378.8.

Lowest average (mean) two-part SAT score=1235

Highest average (mean) two-part SAT score=1508 (estimated)

Ranking Data for Academic Departments: For business and engineering, the rankings are of the undergraduate programs; for all other departments, the rankings are of graduate programs.

Much of our data is unique and is therefore not available in any other publication or online. Some of these unique data elements include:

- Actual average SAT or ACT test scores of enrolled honors students and the actual high school GPAs of the enrolled honors students in 85% of the 55 public honors programs rated or reviewed; statistical estimates of the non-responding programs' average test scores and high school GPAs
- Comparative statistics on the number of prestigious scholarships won by each national university
- Actual honor class sizes from 85% of the 55 public honors programs rated or reviewed
- Actual honors graduation rates from 85% of the 55 honors programs
- Comparative information about the honors residence halls (or lack thereof) designated by all 55 honors programs, including room configurations, amenities, and nearest dining facilities
- Ratios of honors students to administrative staff, all 55 programs
- Summaries of the honors completion/graduation requirements of all 55 programs
- Descriptions of the types of honors courses offered by each program, along with examples of seminar and departmental honors course descriptions
- National Merit scholarship information, including PSAT and SAT test score equivalencies

In each of our profiles of public honors programs in national universities, there is a section titled "Prestigious Awards" that provides a summary of the awards earned by undergraduates and graduates of the universities as a whole. The awards that we track include the Rhodes Scholarship, Marshall Scholarship, Gates Cambridge Scholarship, Truman Scholarship, Churchill Scholarship, National Science Foundation Graduate Research Fellowships, Fulbright Student Scholarships, and Boren Scholarships, most of which are for college upperclassmen or graduates. Undergraduate awards include the Goldwater Scholarships, Udall Scholarships, and Gilman Scholarships.

It is a great honor for an undergraduate or graduate to win a prestigious award, and many of the awards lead to further success in graduate school and public life. Below are brief descriptions of each award.

Boren Scholarships provide $20,000-$30,000 to U.S. undergraduate students, including freshmen, to study abroad in areas of the world that are critical to U.S. interests and underrepresented in study abroad, including Africa, Asia, Central & Eastern Europe, Eurasia, Latin America, and the Middle East. The countries of Western Europe, Canada, Australia, and New Zealand are excluded. The GPA requirement is 3.50, with a relevant background and language ability.

Churchill Scholarships are valued at approximately $45,000 for 9-12 months of study at Cambridge University. Eligibility requires at least a bachelor's degree and a 3.70 GPA; however, the average GPA is closer to 3.90. Students in the STEM disciplines and public health are eligible. Only 14 scholars are chosen each year.

Fulbright Student Scholarships are for graduating seniors or graduates who are selected to study or teach overseas. The award has a value of up to $25,000 for one year. Depending on whether the recipient is teaching English or conducting research, the GPA requirements vary from 3.40 to 3.90.

Gates Cambridge Scholarships are the most generous awards we track, currently valued at about $84,000 for up to three years of graduate study at Cambridge University. Successful candidates must have at least a 3.80 GPA and be graduating seniors or graduates. Although many Gates Cambridge Scholars are STEM students, the award is not restricted to scholars in the STEM disciplines. About 95 scholars are chosen annually from more than 4,000 candidates.

Gilman Scholarships allow students of limited means and students in underrepresented disciplines to study or participate in internships abroad. The average value is $4,000. Required GPA is 3.20 to 3.50.

Goldwater Scholarships are perhaps the most prestigious undergraduate awards. They are valued at $7,500 per year, and successful candidates are outstanding students in the STEM fields with a GPA of 3.80 and higher. There have been a few two-time winners. A university may nominate up to four candidates a year. About 300 scholars are chosen each year from among thousands of sophomore and junior candidates.

Marshall Scholarships are extremely prestigious awards granted to about 40 American graduating seniors in all majors each year. Scholars currently receive approximately $28,000 per year to study at one of scores of universities in the United Kingdom, usually for two years, but sometimes for three years. A large number of Marshall Scholars study at the universities of Cambridge and Oxford; the University of London (King's College, University College, Imperial College); and the London School of Economics and Political Studies (LSE). The GPA requirement is 3.80 and higher.

National Science Foundation Graduate Research Fellowships are awarded to 900-1,000 students annually to fund three years of graduate study in a STEM field or a social or behavioral science discipline. Fellows receive $10,500 for each of the three years. A minimum GPA of 3.70 and very high GRE scores are required.

Rhodes Scholarships remain the best-known and most prestigious of all awards, in addition to being the oldest. Each year 32 Americans are chosen to study for two (and sometimes three) years at the University of Oxford, in all majors. The dollar value of the award is similar to the value of the Marshall Scholarship, and the minimum GPA requirement is also 3.80.

Truman Scholarships are awarded to juniors at participating U.S. universities who want to go to graduate school in preparation for a career in public service (government or the nonprofit and advocacy sectors). The minimum GPA requirement is 3.80. Awardees receive $2,000 to complete their undergraduate education and $12,000 a year for two years of postgraduate study.

Udall Scholarships provide $5,000 toward tuition for undergraduates interested in environmental, sustainability, or planning issues, or for Native Americans focusing on health care or tribal policy. Only 50 awards are granted each year.

NAME: UNIVERSITY OF ALABAMA HONORS COLLEGE

Date Established: 2003

Location: Tuscaloosa, Alabama

University Full-time Undergraduate Enrollment: 25,430

Honors Enrollment: approximately 5,500-6,000 (mean enrollment of 50 programs is 1,714); the largest honors college or program on one campus, when all four components of the college are included. Most students are enrolled in the University Honors Program (3,000-3,500).

Review/Admissions Category--II: Programs with **average SAT scores of 1343--1382 for enrolled students**. *The following test scores and class rank are **estimates only.***

Estimated average (mean) score for enrolled honors college students in all four programs=1358-1368; *estimated* ACT average=31.

The **minimum** requirements for admission to the University Honors Program are SAT 1250 *or* ACT 28 *and* high school GPA 3.5. National Merit and National Achievement Scholars receive automatic admission.

Admission to the Computer-based Honors Fellows, SAT 1350, ACT 32; but the average scores are SAT 1480, ACT 33; high school GPA 4.35.

Admission to International Honors, SAT 1250, ACT 28; high school GPA 3.5.

Admission to University Fellows, SAT 1400, ACT 32; high school GPA of 3.8.

Honors Programs in Admissions Category II (average SAT scores of 1343-1382): Alabama, Delaware, Florida State, LSU, Massachusetts, Missouri, North Carolina State, Ohio University, Temple, Purdue, UCLA, Utah, Vermont, and Wisconsin.

Administrative Staff: The Honors College has 17 full-time employees.

FOR ALL "MORTARBOARD" RATINGS BELOW, A SCORE OF 5 IS THE MAXIMUM AND REPRESENTS A COMPARISON WITH ALL 50 HONORS COLLEGES AND PROGRAMS:

PERCEPTION* OF UNIVERSITY AS A WHOLE, NOT OF HONORS: 🎓🎓 🎓🎓

OVERALL HONORS RATING: 🎓🎓🎓🎓

Curriculum Requirements: 🎓🎓🎓

Class Range and Type: 🎓🎓🎓🎓🎓

Class Size: 🎓🎓🎓🎓¹ᐟ²

Adjusted Grad Rate: 🎓🎓🎓🎓

Ratio of Staff to Students: 🎓🎓🎓

Priority Registration: Yes. Honors College students have the highest registration priority. Entering freshmen may sign up for the first summer orientation sessions on a first come, first served basis. After the first semester, all Honors College students are able to register before all other students, each semester.

Honors Housing: 🎓🎓🎓🎓¹ᐟ²

Prestigious Awards: 🎓🎓🎓🎓

*Perception is based on the university's ranking among public universities in the 2014 U.S. News Best Colleges report. Please bear in mind that the better the U.S. News ranking, the more difficult it is for an honors college or program to have a rating that equals or improves on the magazine ranking.

Curriculum Requirements (3.0): For the University Honors Program, students are required to earn at least eighteen hours of Honors credit, including at least six hours of Honors Foundation courses, and graduate with an overall GPA of at least 3.3. There is **no thesis requirement.**

The Computer-based Honors Experience requires completion of two specialized honors computer science courses and four 3-credit projects "combining the student's research and computer applications." Students must graduate with an overall GPA of 3.3. No thesis is required.

The International Honors Program requires 9 hours of coursework with an international focus along with 12 hours of foreign language. Students must graduate with a 3.3 GPA. No thesis is required.

University Fellows:

Freshman year—"Seminars to explore issues of servant leadership, personal development, project development and implementation, and civic engagement; Black Belt Experience in May, wherein Fellows partner with local initiatives, programs, and individuals in Perry County, Alabama and implement projects that address challenges of systemic poverty."

Sophomore year—"Seminars to explore issues of leadership in the community, including a series of exposures to the practical and multi-faceted aspects of being a good citizen; participate in significant contributions both individually and collaboratively in an effort to connect idea development with the creation of positive action."

Junior year—"Receive individualized assistance and support for career options and post-undergraduate opportunities; active and ongoing research and correspondence with key figures in their field of interest, including pertinent professional conferences; peer Mentors and committee chairs for UFE Committees in the planning and implementation of key events, programs and initiatives."

Senior year—"Distinguish themselves in their fields of study through published or presented articles, research, or related productive materials; reflect their work in a four-year culminating Portfolio; teach one-hour Honors College seminar courses on a topic of their choosing. No thesis is required."

Contract courses: Only six credit hours can be earned through honors contract courses, so most honors credits come from all-honors classes.

Range and Type of Honors Courses (5.0): The **Alabama Honors College is undoubtedly a national leader in the number and range of honors courses offered to students**. It is an excellent example of a blended program, one with a wide variety of seminars *and* a full range of departmental honors courses. In the Spring of 2014, we counted 76 honors seminars, with an average enrollment of 15-22 students. Included are three freshman seminars on International War Crimes, a whole series on Honors and the Fine Arts, and about forty 3-credit seminar sections with historical, cultural, and interdisciplinary emphases. They include Finding Financial Freedom; Mentoring Entrepreneurs; Heroes, Faith, Justice; Religion & Politics; Representations of the Human; Mindset of War. Others are of particular interest to aspiring physicians and lawyers: The Legal Process, Legal Writing, and Introduction to Clinical Medicine. Another seminar bears this intriguing title: Taking on Tough Issues. There is yet another series of about 15 interdisciplinary STEM/Business sections, each awarding 1.5 credit hours.

The impressive course offerings continue with the many **departmental honors** sections that are available. When it comes to classes in English composition and English and American literature, the honors college lineup is one of the best in the nation. The same is true of the courses in the computer-based honors program. Often the list of economics sections is minimal in honors programs, but Alabama honors has nine sections of macro- and micro-economics, averaging only 32 students or so, a low class size for econ sections. There are relatively few large sections, but classes in accounting and intro biology are likely to be among them. Some chemistry and physics classes may have 50-70 students, but, again, these numbers are all lower than average for science sections. Honors calculus sections are present, but only two were offered in the Spring of 2014.

Average Class Size (4.5): We estimate the **average class size for Alabama honors to be 19.7,** including the larger departmental class sections mentioned above. Again, the average for the honors college classes (offered by the college, not through departments) is more in the 15-18 range. (The overall class size for the 50 colleges and programs under review in this edition is 21.2 students.

Adjusted Graduation Rate (4.0): The AGR is not simply the six-year graduation rate of students in the honors college who graduated from the university **(88.3%),** whether or not the students completed the honors program ("honors completers"). It also reflects the extent to which the honors graduation rate from the university is higher than that for the university as a whole. The **university-wide rate is 67%,** yielding the 4.0 AGR for the college. The average six-year **honors graduation rate for all 50 programs** under review **is 89%.**

Ratio of Staff to Honors Students (3.0): Our estimate is that there is 1 staff member for every **323.5** students. (Mean ratio for all 50 programs is 1 staff member for every 159.8 students.)

Honors Residence Halls (4.5): "Living-Learning Communities allow students to have access to educational programs and extra-curricular activities exclusive to the Honors College. Starting in the Fall 2013, the Honors community will include the entire Ridgecrest community, including North, South, East, and West, which will only be available to members of the Honors College. These coed living-learning facilities form the center of the University's tightly-knit Honors community.

"These buildings feature 4-bedroom suites with private bedrooms, 2 bathrooms, a living/dining area, and a kitchenette. The kitchenette has a full-size refrigerator, microwave, and cabinet space. The bedrooms feature height-adjustable beds with extended twin mattresses."

"In addition to the benefits of living with other Honors College students, faculty residents in each dormitory further increase the value of such an opportunity." Faculty-in-residence programs offer social events and serve as informal advisors for students living in those dorms.

Prestigious Awards (4.0): Alabama students have been strong competitors when it comes to winning the highly coveted undergraduate Goldwater Scholarships for outstanding promise in the STEM fields. Many of the 35 Goldwater Scholars have been students in the honors college. The UA performance in achieving prestigious postgraduate awards is most evident in the 14 Truman Scholarships awarded to its graduates.

Continuation Requirements: 3.30 GPA; also the minimum required for graduation with honors.

Academic Strengths: The strongest departments at UA are business administration, English, and business-related majors such as marketing.

Undergraduate Research: "The McWane Undergraduate Research Fellowship awards up to $1,500 for students engaged in a research or creative project with a mentoring faculty member. These awards provide support for students who plan to be involved in a research or creative effort that is individual or collaborative. Scholarship recipients will verify their eventual participation in the proposed research endeavor and submit a one-page description of the research project to the Honors College." The Honors College does not require a thesis for any program, although the Computer-Based Honors Program has substantial experimental/lab requirements.

Study Abroad: The University of Alabama offers a variety of summer and interim overseas study programs that allow students to travel with a group of UA students and study under the direction of a UA professor. Scholarships ranging from $500 -$1,500 are available for some students who study abroad.

UA's summer programs have recently been offered in Australia, Austria, Belgium, China, Dublin, Ecuador, England, France, Ghana, Greece, Guatemala, Iceland, Italy, Japan, Korea, London, Mexico, Oxford, Spain, Sweden, Turkey, Vietnam, and other locations.

"An exchange program is a direct link between The University of Alabama and an overseas partner institution. UA has many exchange programs that allow students to continue their academic courses while studying overseas.

"These competitive programs are open to all qualified students who have studied on the UA campus for at least one semester. Students chosen as exchange participants pay regular UA tuition and spend one semester or year abroad. UA holds exchange relationships with universities in the following countries: Australia, Austria, Belgium, China, Denmark, England, France, Germany, Italy, Japan, Korea, The Netherlands, and Wales."

Financial Aid: The University of Alabama ranked first among public universities nationwide in the enrollment of National Merit Scholars for 2012, with 241 scholars in the fall 2012 freshman class, of which 208 were sponsored by the university. That ranking also placed UA fourth among all universities in 2012. Only the University of Chicago, Harvard and the University of Southern California enrolled more National Merit Scholars that Fall. However, in 2013 total Merit Scholar enrollment fell to 123, with 111 receiving university sponsorship—in line with a national trend of declining university support.

At a time when many public "elites" are not providing university funding for National Merit Scholarships, the University of Alabama still does so, for 208 of the 241 scholars listed above. The school is one of only seven in our review to fund, in some cases, tuition, room, and board—the famous but disappearing "full ride," or something approaching it. **The university is a leader in both the amount of funding it provides per merit scholar and the total number of scholars it supports.**

Degree of Difference (Honors students/non-honors students): 2.70 on a scale of 5. Some parents and prospective students might prefer an honors program that in many ways stands apart on campus, while others might prefer a program that is more expansive. The rating here tries to provide an indication of where a given honors program is on the stand apart/expansive spectrum. The rating is based on the difference between (1) the average SAT scores for enrolled honors students and (2) the average test scores for all students in the university as a whole *and* for students with scores at the 75% level or above. A score of 3.5 or higher indicates a high degree of difference. A score of 3.2 to 3.49 indicates a relatively high degree of difference. Finally, a score below 3.2 indicates a modest difference. **Please keep in mind that neither the high nor low selectivity of an honors program determines how effective the program is; this rating is merely "cultural" and *not* qualitative.**

NAME: UNIVERSITY OF ARIZONA HONORS COLLEGE

Date Established: 1962 as a program; 1999 as a college.

Location: Tucson, Arizona

University Full-time Undergraduate Enrollment: 28,210

Honors Enrollment: 4,507 (Fall 2013); mean enrollment of all 50 programs is 1,714.

Review/Admissions Category--I: Programs with **average SAT scores of 1235--1342 for enrolled students**. The average (mean) score for enrolled honors college students is 1306, and the ACT average is 29.2. The average high school GPA is 3.81.

"We use an index to admit students that uses regression analysis to predict academic success at UA (as measured by 1st year GPA) based on factors of high school preparation (test scores, grade point average, and strength of curriculum taken [AP/ IB courses, college level courses, Honors courses, accelerated courses]. **We also have an essay question that taps into motivation.** Students also can submit a teacher recommendation, new test scores, and 7th semester transcripts and additional information for a holistic review."

Honors Programs in Admissions Category I (average SAT scores of 1235-1342): Arizona, Arizona State, Arkansas, Colorado State, Iowa, Maine, Mississippi, Oklahoma State, Oregon, Oregon State, Rhode Island, Texas Tech, University at Albany, and Washington State.

Administrative Staff: The Honors College has 27.625 full-time equivalent employees.

FOR ALL "MORTARBOARD" RATINGS BELOW, A SCORE OF 5 IS THE MAXIMUM AND REPRESENTS A COMPARISON WITH ALL 50 HONORS COLLEGES AND PROGRAMS:

PERCEPTION* OF UNIVERSITY AS A WHOLE, <u>NOT</u> OF HONORS: 🎓🎓🎓

OVERALL HONORS RATING: 🎓🎓🎓 1/2

Curriculum Requirements: 🎓🎓🎓🎓

Class Range and Type: 🎓🎓🎓🎓

Class Size: 🎓🎓 1/2

Adjusted Grad Rate: 🎓🎓🎓 1/2

Ratio of Staff to Students: 🎓🎓🎓 1/2

Priority Registration: Yes. Honors freshmen and sophomores register with UA seniors. Honors juniors and seniors register with military veterans and NCAA athletes, the very first group of students on campus who are eligible to register.

Honors Housing: 🎓🎓🎓🎓

Prestigious Awards: 🎓🎓🎓🎓🎓

*Perception is based on the university's ranking among public universities in the 2014 U.S. News Best Colleges report. Please bear in mind that the better the U.S. News ranking, the more difficult it is for an honors college or program to have a rating that equals or improves on the magazine ranking.

Curriculum Requirements (4.0): Graduation with honors requires the completion of 30 hours of honors credits. Included in the 30 hours is a six-hour thesis. Of the 30 total hours, up to 12 may be earned by taking honors contract courses, which allow honors students in regular sections to contract with the instructor to do extra work.

Graduation with honors from the College of Engineering requires the completion of 30 hours, but, of those 30 hours, only 17 hours are in honors courses, including up to six hours by contract. There is no thesis requirement, but 7 credit hours must be in earned in engineering design courses.

Honors graduation from the Eller College of Management Entrepreneurship requires the completion of 21 credit hours, 12 of which may be earned in contract classes (no more than 6 hours in lower division contract classes). In addition, there is an honors capstone project that counts for another 9 credit hours.

The Honors College also has a First Level Honors Award (essentially for two years of honors work), which requires completion of 15 credit hours.

Contract courses: As noted above, up to 12 credit hours can be earned through honors contract courses, about average for larger programs.

AP/IB credit: Advanced placement credits do **not** replace honors courses.

Range and Type of Honors Courses (4.0): The Honors College offered more than 200 honors sections in the Spring of 2014, of which about 16 sections were honors seminars. We classify the college as being primarily a **department-based program** with fewer than 20% of the honors courses being offered by the college rather than the academic departments.

The seminars include four sections of advanced analytical writing and thinking, along with two sections each of Tradition and Culture, Thinking Critically about New Media, and Cultures of Surveillance. Most of these seminars have fewer than 25 students enrolled, some as few as 15.

By far, most of the honors classes are centered in the academic departments, and many are in mixed sections that may be large. The main reason is that the university as a whole, in adopting a revised Gen

Ed curriculum, mandated that all Gen Ed classes (typically offered in the first two years) must have an honors accommodation. In practice, this means that honors students are folded into often large regular sections and then required to do extra work for honors credit, much like an **honors contract course** but on a more regular, systematic basis.

The result of this university policy is that honors "add-on" classes in art history, fine arts, oceanography, economics, geography, geosciences, linguistics, computer science, management, physiology, and others have enrollments that exceed 200 total students (honors and non-honors, mostly the latter). Yet some of the several econ sections are in the 30-50 range, more typical of honors programs. Other departmental honors sections have enrollments in the 18-40 range. Only one math section (calculus) was offered in the Spring of 2014--but most notably **the honors courses in physics are among the best, if not the best, of all the programs under review**. The courses cover Newtonian physics, relativity, computational physics, theoretical mechanics, quantum physics, and introduction to electricity and magnetism. Although some of the physics lecture classes are large, discussion sections are small, only 11 students. There is a lack of history sections, at least in the Spring of 2014, but a good selection of English classes.

Average Class Size (2.5): That so many UA honors classes are offered in large mixed sections results in an average class size higher than in most programs, probably 35-50 students; however, **there are 29 honors stand-alone seminars and departmental classes that have an average enrollment of 22 students**. (The overall class size for the 50 colleges and programs under review in this edition is 21.2 students.

Adjusted Graduation Rate (3.5): The AGR is not simply the six-year graduation rate of students in the honors college who graduated from the university **(82.9%)**, whether or not the students completed the honors program ("honors completers"). It also reflects the extent to which the honors graduation rate from the university is higher than that for the university as a whole. The **university-wide rate is 61%,** yielding the 3.5 AGR for the college. The average six-year **honors graduation rate for all 50 programs** under review **is 89%.**

Ratio of Staff to Honors Students (3.5): Our estimate is that there is 1 staff member for every **163** students. (Mean ratio for all 50 programs is 1 staff member for every 159.8 students.)

Honors Residence Halls (4.0): Honors students can choose to live in one of two Honors residence halls or from 20 other halls on campus. Statistics show that 90% of Honors students live in a residence hall their first year and almost 40% remain on campus in subsequent years.

"Árbol de la Vida is the largest and newest Honors hall comprised of five buildings connected by bridges. Its green design, cutting edge technology and modern design make it one of the most desired places to live on campus," the Dean reports. "This hall has many smart, sustainable features, like solar-heated water, low-flow water fixtures, smart thermostats, 'green' outlets, and passive water harvesting. Community is built in the many common spaces including study rooms, living rooms, recreation and media center, exercise spaces and gathering places indoors and out. Honors classes and Honors advising are also offered on-site.

"Yuma Hall is listed on the National Register of Historic Places and features the classic red brick tradition of UA campus. Its location in the historic north area of campus is close to the Eller College of

Management, College of Engineering, College of Fine Arts and Memorial Student Union. Inviting community spaces include sunken living room, kitchen, multi-media study space, recreation room and large patio. Yuma hall was the first Honors hall and this close-knit community celebrated its 25th anniversary as Honors housing in 2013.

Prestigious Awards (5.0): UA students are among the best nationally in winning each type of prestigious undergraduate award that we track: Udall Scholarships, Goldwater Scholarships, Boren Scholarships, and Gilman Scholarships. These are awarded, respectively, for scholarship work or travel related to Native American studies or environmental sciences, STEM research, study in a foreign country with relatively few American student-visitors, or studying abroad for students with limited means.

UA students also rank at or above the median among the 50 public universities under review in the achievement of prestigious postgraduate awards, and among the top 10 when it comes to being awarded Rhodes Scholarships, with a very impressive total of 24. They are also far above the median in winning Gates Cambridge Scholarships, National Science Foundation Graduate Research Fellowships, and Fulbright Student Scholarships.

Continuation Requirements: 3.50 GPA.

Academic Strengths: One of the major strengths of the university is its outstanding faculty. The average national ranking of 15 academic departments is about 38, meaning that almost all major disciplines are recognized as being among the top 50. Particularly strong are earth sciences (7), sociology (20), business (22), biology (34), physics and economics (both 36), and chemistry (38).

Undergraduate Research: More than 65% of honors students participate in serious academic research by the time they graduate. **The thesis requirement** for the main graduation option contributes to this high percentage.

"The First Year Project is a one-unit experience for students in the second semester of their first year. Students work with a faculty mentor to complete a research project of their own design and present their findings at a research expo. The projects are judged by Honors faculty and current students with prizes given in design, common reading, analytical research, lab/field experience, applied research/ community project and creative expression.

"The Undergraduate Research Grant program awards small grants (up to $1,500 each) for summer research for students entering the sophomore, junior or senior years. 35-45 grants are awarded annually ($50,000-$65,000). Abstracts are published and students present their research at the Honors Research Expo.

"Small grants are available to support student travel to conferences and professional meetings where they are presenting research and travel, supplies and other costs associated with Honors thesis research."

Study Abroad: The Honors College offers five study abroad programs where students can study for a summer, semester or year in another country. **The most popular is the Honors Trip, a tale of two cities, where students earn 6 units of Honors humanities credits in locations such as London/ Paris or New York/ Rome.** Summer study also includes a 4- week archaeology experience on the Greek island of Paros that earns 6 units of anthropology and 6-week adventure in Namibia studying conversation biology and ecology. Exchange relationships enable students to earn Honors credit while studying at the National University of Singapore or University of the Armed Forces in Munich, Germany.

The Honors College offers $75,000 annually in study abroad scholarships to help students from all backgrounds attain international experience. The university also has scholarship opportunities that many Honors students receive; all National Scholars can receive $1500 toward study abroad. The Honors College sponsors a study abroad photo contest with prizes in five categories.

The University of Arizona has a total of 186 study abroad programs that students can choose among. Thirty-four are agreements with international universities where the student enrolls directly and credits transfer to UA. Fifty are faculty led experiences, many of which are summer programs that span the globe. Another 25 are agreements with organizations that provide study abroad to a variety of institutions; these programs, like Semester at Sea, typically transfer as elective credit. There are 76 exchange relationships with international universities and 4 other programs that involve international internships.

Financial Aid: The University of Arizona offers $35.8 million in need based financial aid and $18.7 million in merit-based scholarships annually. Nearly all Honors students receive merit based scholarships and one quarter qualify for the federal Pell grant program.

The Honors College provides approximately $370,000 in need based aid to help Honors students meet the costs of fees and another $55,000 annually in scholarships from donors.

In addition to the research grants and study abroad scholarships described above, the Honors College offers a number of scholarships to assist students make the most of their Honors education. Professional development grants cover expenses such as summer language institutes, test preparation courses and fees, application fees, travel to job/school interviews, professional clothing, and certification exam fees. The Honors College provides $60,000 in internship scholarships so that students can gain valuable career-related experiences.

The university continues to sponsor 58 of the 68 National Merit Scholars in 2013, down somewhat from the previous year in line with a national trend.

Degree of Difference (Honors students/non-honors students): 3.25 on a scale of 5. Some parents and prospective students might prefer an honors program that in many ways stands apart on campus, while others might prefer a program that is more expansive. The rating here tries to provide an indication of where a given honors program is on the stand apart/expansive spectrum. The rating is based on the difference between (1) the average SAT scores for enrolled honors students and (2) the average test scores for all students in the university as a whole *and* for students with scores at the 75% level or above. A score of 3.5 or higher indicates a high degree of difference. A score of 3.2 to 3.49 indicates a relatively high degree of difference. Finally, a score below 3.2 indicates a modest difference. **Please keep in mind that neither the high nor low selectivity of an honors program determines how effective the program is; this rating is merely "cultural" and *not* qualitative.**

NAME: BARRETT, THE HONORS COLLEGE, AT ARIZONA STATE UNIVERSITY

Date Established: 1988

Location: Tempe, Arizona

University Full-time Undergraduate Enrollment: 49,945

Honors Enrollment: 4,800 (mean enrollment of all 50 programs is 1,714).

Review/Admissions Category--I: Programs with **average SAT scores of 1235--1342 for enrolled students**. The actual average (mean) score for enrolled Barrett students is 1310, and the ACT average is 29. The average high school GPA is 3.85.

"Students are required to have at least one letter of recommendation as part of their Barrett application, though two are strongly encouraged, with at least one being from a teacher or professor. A third letter may also be submitted if it contains substantive information or a unique perspective not present in the first two letters. As one example, a student may choose to submit two letters of an academic nature and a third letter that speaks to an extracurricular activity (e.g. from a coach, organization advisor, employment supervisor, etc.).

"A Barrett application will not be complete and cannot be moved into evaluation until all letters of recommendation have been received. It is the responsibility of the prospective student to ensure a complete application is on file by the appropriate deadline. An incomplete application will be remanded to the next deadline pool for evaluation."

Honors Programs in Admissions Category I (average SAT scores of 1235-1342): Arizona, Arizona State, Arkansas, Colorado State, Iowa, Maine, Mississippi, Oklahoma State, Oregon, Oregon State, Rhode Island, Texas Tech, University at Albany, and Washington State.

Administrative Staff: The Honors College has a staff of 58.

FOR ALL "MORTARBOARD" RATINGS BELOW, A SCORE OF 5 IS THE MAXIMUM AND REPRESENTS A COMPARISON WITH ALL 50 HONORS COLLEGES AND PROGRAMS:

PERCEPTION* OF UNIVERSITY AS A WHOLE, NOT OF HONORS: 🎓🎓 1/2

OVERALL HONORS RATING: 🎓🎓🎓🎓🎓

Curriculum Requirements: 🎓🎓🎓🎓🎓

Class Range and Type: 🎓🎓🎓🎓🎓

Class Size: 🎓🎓🎓🎓 1/2

Adjusted Grad Rate: 🎓🎓🎓🎓^1/2

Ratio of Staff to Students: 🎓 🎓🎓🎓🎓

Priority Registration: Yes, students register for **all** courses, honors and otherwise, with the first group of students during **each** year they are in the program.

Honors Housing: 🎓🎓🎓🎓🎓

Prestigious Awards: 🎓🎓🎓🎓🎓

*Perception is based on the university's ranking among public universities in the 2014 U.S. News Best Colleges report. Please bear in mind that the better the U.S. News ranking, the more difficult it is for an honors college or program to have a rating that equals or improves on the magazine ranking.

Curriculum Requirements (5.0): Freshman entrants must complete 36 honors credits out of 120 hours required for graduation. Barrett is generous in the number of contract courses it allows for honors credit, up to 24 credit hours, but at least 12 hours of the 36 total required must be in regular honors classes. Although a lot of Barrett students contract for at least one course per term, the amazing range of regular honors classes available to them would seem to make contract courses only a way to explore graduate or specialized classes rather than a necessary means of meeting the completion requirements. **A six-hour thesis is also required**.

Contract courses: As noted above, up to 24 credit hours can be earned through honors contract courses, higher than average for larger programs. But, in practice, 18 credit hours must be in regular honors classes or thesis, so any contract class credits above 18 (of the total 36-hour completion requirement) would be in addition to the completion requirement.

AP/IB credits are not counted as replacements for honors courses.

Range and Type of Honors Courses (5.0): Barrett is an outstanding example of a **blended honors program,** where a large number of quality seminars are complemented by an impressive selection of courses in the academic disciplines. It is truly rare to find such an array of courses along with the small classes and excellence that Barrett provides. The honors Dean reports that "almost all departments at the university offer 'honors courses' that are only for honors students but that grant departmental (i.e. major) credit. Also, all honors courses are taught as seminars, so there is no difference between an 'honors course' and an 'honors seminar', though we do have 'honors lab sections'. Each semester in 2014, there are between 290 and 300 honors courses offered (we have already listed for registration our fall 2014 courses) throughout the university, and 240 more courses each semester have listed themselves as offering 'honors contracts'. Just listing themselves as offering an honors contract does not mean that other courses in the same departments will *not* give an honors contract if asked, just that the 240 are advertising that they do. *Each year, over 1700 ASU faculty 'teach' honors students when you combine faculty offering courses, contracts and overseeing undergraduate theses."* Even without counting lab sections, tutorials, and thesis classes, we counted more than 200 honors sections, of which more than half were Honors College ("HON") classes. Of these, more than 80 were sections of the signature seminar titled "The Human Event." Almost all of these were the second half of the course, since we looked only at the Spring 2014 term. Here are the **course descriptions for the Human Event seminars**, which do in fact average about 19 students each:

The Fall course is "a discussion of landmark texts in human social and intellectual development, with emphasis on critical thinking and argumentative writing, from earliest recorded human ideas to approximately 1600 CE." Enrollment is restricted to Barrett students. The Spring course is a continuation, with the chronological period changing to approximately 1600 CE to the present. Prerequisite: [first semester course] with a 'C' or better.

The impressive string of honors seminars doesn't end with The Human Event series, however. There are four seminars on the History of Ideas, a series on Deductive Logic, Leadership, and Industry Structure, and another series with course titles that promise an enriching experience: Nature in Context: the Eco-critical Imagination; Science and Sexuality; Supernatural as Natural--the Origins of Religion and Human Evolution; Philosophers, Poets, and Revolutionaries; and our favorite, **The Big(gest) Questions.**

The classes centered in the departments have only honors students, hence their designation of "Honors Only" classes in the class schedule. All-honors departmental sections are rare in honors programs that have as many classes as Barrett; most programs must use mixed sections with both honors and non-honors students to provide sufficient breadth in courses. Of these discipline-specific classes, the smallest in terms of class size are probably the seven English composition sections, averaging about 16 students each. The biology sections are also small, especially in comparison to most of those offered in honors programs. (It was something of a surprise not to find an honors chemistry lecture section.) There are at least five math sections, two in physics, four in psychology, two in political science, and seven in journalism and communications. The management sections average about 46 students—but this is a very low number relative to most honors section in management.

Another interesting series is the "Project Excellence" course offerings that allow some Barrett students to take classes in the university law school. Usually only 1 to 4 honors students enroll in any one of these sections: Law, Science, and Technology; Public Health Law and Ethics; Sports Law; Watergate's Legacy; Foreign Relations Law; and Real Estate and Business Evaluation.

Average Class Size (4.5): The average honors class size at Barrett is 18.28 students, including the classes centered in the academic departments, an impressively low figure given the size of the honors college. True, some of the pressure in regular classes is reduced because of the semi-formalized honors contract courses available. But as we noted above, our view is that the contract courses are more of an enhancement than they are a convenient or subordinate method to earn honors credits. The overall class size for the 50 colleges and programs under review in this edition is 21.2 students.

Adjusted Graduation Rate (4.5): The AGR is not simply the six-year graduation rate of students in the honors college who graduated from the university **(estimated at 87%)**, whether or not the students completed the honors program ("honors completers"). The AGR also reflects the extent to which the honors graduation rate from the university is higher than that for the university as a whole. The **university-wide rate is 57%,** yielding the strong 4.5 AGR for the college. **Barrett also reported that the graduation rate from the honors program, i.e., the percentage of Barrett students who**

completed the honors curriculum along with the required thesis, is an extraordinarily high 85%. The average six-year **honors graduation rate for all 50 programs** under review **is 89%.**

Some honors research indicates that actual honors completion levels are extremely low, in the range of 25% to 40%. This is one possible reason that some programs do not require an honors thesis for completion.

Ratio of Staff to Honors Students (5.0): Our estimate is that there is 1 staff member for every **82.8** students. (Mean ratio for all 50 programs is 1 staff member for every 159.8 students.)

Honors Residence Halls (5.0): Here, we will let the Dean of the Honors College discuss the housing at Barrett:

"We are the only university in the nation with our own entire 9-acre, $140 million, 600,000 square feet honors campus at Tempe, complete with everything a private college campus would have, besides things like the university health service and the student recreation center. On top of this, we have Barrett living communities on all four of ASU's campuses in the Phoenix Valley, though the one described just above is at Tempe, the biggest campus of ASU. Each of the other three Barrett communities--at the ASU West, ASU Downtown Phoenix, and ASU Polytechnic campuses --have honors headquarter space with classrooms, computer labs, advising offices, social lounges, conference rooms and faculty offices.

"Also at each of the other campuses, there is separate honors housing that is usually several floors or wings of a larger residential hall that also houses non-honors students. Each of these housing units has a dining hall, laundry, AC, kitchens at least 'down the hall,' honors lounges, **a choice of suite-like rooms that are co-ed by hall** but not by room and have special honors RAs (or 'CAs' as we call them at ASU). *We require honors students to live on campus in honors residences at all four of ASU's Barrett campuses and communities for two years.*"

Prestigious Awards (5.0): ASU students rank 1st in the number of Udall Scholars among all public universities with 30 and 1st in Boren Scholarships, for work and study in foreign countries where the U.S. presence is underrepresented. ASU is tied for 8th among public universities in Goldwater Scholars with 54, awarded for outstanding promise in the STEM fields. University students also do well in the Gilman Scholarship competition, which assists students of limited means with study-abroad funding.

With respect to prestigious postgraduate awards, ASU is tied for 7th among public universities in the number of Marshall Scholars, with 16. ASU students are among public university leaders in winning Fulbright Student Scholarships and National Science Foundation Graduate Research Fellowships. Finally, ASU students have won an impressive 19 Truman Scholarships.

Continuation Requirements: 3.25 GPA.

Academic Strengths: While *U.S. News* uses a methodology that penalizes almost all large public universities listed in the magazine's annual college rankings--especially Arizona State--there is ample evidence of a very strong academic community at ASU. Interestingly, the magazine's own rankings of graduate departments show that of 15 major academic departments at ASU, **the average departmental ranking is better than 50 among all "national" universities public and private.** ASU has seven departments that are ranked better than 50: earth sciences (17), education (24), business (27), economics and psychology (both 36), engineering (43), and physics (48).

Undergraduate Research: Again, from the Barrett Dean: *"The thesis ends up being an automatic driver of student research for each honors student."* Accordingly, since 85% of Barrett students are honors completers who finish their theses, all such completers are seriously engaged in research. "Barrett has a full-time person in an office of Internships and Research Experiences that arranges both for any honors student who asks," the Dean reports, "and in ten years at Barrett and ASU I am not aware of any honors student who has wished to do the kind of formal 'lab-type' research this kind of question is usually getting at who has not found that kind of research to do."

Study Abroad: "Barrett has its own summer study abroad courses each summer, taking approximately 200-250 students on 3 to 6 trips each summer. The trips go all over the world--Paris and the Loire, London/Dublin/Edinburgh, Spain, Costa Rica, China and Indonesia, Greece and Italy are the most recent in the last two years. The trips are led by Barrett faculty, take only Barrett students, and the students get credit for two full honors courses on each trip since they both take the courses and visit the countries that are the subjects of the courses in each case. In addition to these trips, there are over 30 summer study abroad trips from ASU open to all students each summer, and honors students can take those too, gaining honors credit for courses taught on those trips by completing an honors contract during the trip.

"We have close to $200,000 per year in scholarship funds, given out on a need basis, to help send students on these trips from all socioeconomic backgrounds.

"We have formal exchanges with the National University of Singapore each academic year during which around four students from each institution comes to the other for a semester."

Financial Aid: The financial aid office of ASU handles all scholarships, including those for honors students. ASU gives out many levels of merit aid, and then of course has need-based aid. "95% of Barrett students have merit aid, but 40% *also* have need-based aid *on top of* their merit aid." The merit aid is dispensed using a formulaic combination of high school GPA, rank in class, and ACT or SAT scores, and is "tiered" as you would expect by decreasing dollar amounts as this combination decreases. The **university also has national scholar awards *uncapped in number* that are the same amount for National Merit, Hispanic and Achievement Scholars.** These appear to be mostly in the form of tuition offsets rather than "full ride" scholarships, although a combination of National Merit and other awards would be even more generous. ASU had 97 National Merit Scholars in 2012, and 75 of those received university sponsorship. **In 2013, the university increased is sponsorships to 102 out of 119 total merit scholars—this in spite of a national decline in university sponsorships.**

Degree of Difference (Honors students/non-honors students): 3.21 on a scale of 5. Some parents and prospective students might prefer an honors program that in many ways stands apart on campus, while others might prefer a program that is more expansive. The rating here tries to provide an indication of where a given honors program is on the stand apart/expansive spectrum. The rating is based on the difference between (1) the average SAT scores for enrolled honors students and (2) the average test scores for all students in the university as a whole *and* for students with scores at the 75% level or above. A score of 3.5 or higher indicates a high degree of difference. A score of 3.2 to 3.49 indicates a relatively high degree of difference. Finally, a score below 3.2 indicates a modest difference. **Please keep in mind that neither the high nor low selectivity of an honors program determines how effective the program is; this rating is merely "cultural" and *not* qualitative.**

NAME: UNIVERSITY OF ARKANSAS HONORS COLLEGE

Date Established: 2002. Preceded by Arts & Sciences honors program (1954) and College of Business honors program (1997).

Location: Fayetteville, Arkansas

University Full-time Undergraduate Enrollment: 17,799

Honors Enrollment: approximately 2,903 (mean enrollment of 50 programs=1,714).

Review/Admissions Category I: Programs with **average SAT scores of 1235--1342 for enrolled students**. Actual average (mean) score for enrolled students at Arkansas Honors College=1284; ACT average=30.1. The mean High School GPA for entering honors students=4.003. The minimum requirements for admission are SAT 1240; ACT 28; high school GPA 3.5 (3.75 for Walton College of Business).

Honors Programs in Admissions Category I (average SAT scores of 1235-1342): Arizona, Arizona State, Arkansas, Colorado State, Iowa, Maine, Mississippi, Oklahoma State, Oregon, Oregon State, Rhode Island, Texas Tech, University at Albany, and Washington State.

Administrative Staff: The Honors College has 17 full-time employees.

FOR ALL "MORTARBOARD" RATINGS BELOW, A SCORE OF 5 IS THE MAXIMUM AND REPRESENTS A COMPARISON OF ALL 50 HONORS COLLEGES AND PROGRAMS:

PERCEPTION* OF UNIVERSITY AS A WHOLE, NOT OF HONORS: 🎓🎓$^{1/2}$

OVERALL HONORS RATING: 🎓🎓🎓🎓$^{1/2}$

Curriculum Requirements: 🎓🎓🎓🎓

Class Range and Type: 🎓🎓🎓🎓

Class Size: 🎓🎓🎓🎓🎓

Adjusted Grad Rate: 🎓🎓🎓🎓

Ratio of Staff to Students: 🎓🎓🎓$^{1/2}$

Priority Registration: Yes, honors students have priority registration for **all** courses, in the form of being able to register with the class ahead of them.

Honors Housing: 🎓🎓🎓🎓

Prestigious Awards: 🎓 🎓 🎓 🎓[1/2]

*Perception is based on the university's ranking among public universities in the 2014 U.S. News Best Colleges report. Please bear in mind that the higher the U.S. News ranking, the more difficult it is for an honors college or program to have a rating that improves on the magazine ranking.

Curriculum Requirements (4.0): The honors college coordinates the honors programs in the J. William Fulbright College of Arts and Sciences; the Fay Jones School of Architecture; the College of Education and Health Professions; the Sam M. Walton College of Business; the College of Engineering; and the Dale Bumpers School of Agricultural, Food, and Life Sciences. The credit hours required for honor s completion vary significantly, with the College of Arts and Sciences and the School of Architecture having the most extensive requirements, **33-36 hours in Arts and Sciences and 38 hours in Architecture**. Business honors requires 17 credit hours, engineering 12 credit hours, and education/health professions 24 hours. The Bumpers School requirement is 15 credit hours. There is an **honors thesis** requirement for **all honors students.**

AP/IB credit is allowed in all honors programs, in substitution for up to six credit hours, and the **AP test score** requirement is 5.

Range and Type of Honors Courses (4.0): We classify the honors college as a **department-based program**, meaning that it offers a relatively small number of interdisciplinary seminars with most classes centered in the academic departments. Of the more than 160 honors sections in the Spring of 2014, only eight were honors seminars.

As part of an inspired and creative effort to develop the best seminars and courses possible, the Honors College has since 2006 provided up to $25,000, on a competitive basis, to each of 30 faculty teams for developing interdisciplinary, problem-focused honors courses for junior and senior honors students. These courses run the gamut and include:

- Visualizing the Ancient Roman City [digitizing the built environment of Ostia and Pompeii] (Classics, Architecture, and Computer Science),
- The Darwin Course (Science Education, Law, Biology, Physics, English, Philosophy Political Science, Anthropology, and History)
- Integrating Nanotechnology into Honors Education (Physics, Chemistry/Biochemistry, Chemical Engineering, and Biological Engineering),
- Music, Language and Thought (Music, Philosophy, and Psychology),
- Childhood Obesity: Context and Prevention (Human and Environmental Science and Agricultural Economics),
- Cultivating Interprofessional Collaboration to Improve Health Outcomes (Nursing, Social Work, and Psychology),
- Community Development in a Global Context: An International Service Learning Course [in Belize] (English, Social Work, Economics, Agricultural Economics, Biology, and Civil Engineering).

Most of these courses have served as a catalyst for even more scholarly activities of faculty and students. The Community Development course has led to the creation of a second service learning study abroad program in Mozambique and has laid the groundwork for additional international service learning programs, some in collaboration with the Clinton Foundation and Clinton School of Public Service in Little Rock, Arkansas.

The departmental classes are comprehensive, except that in the Spring of 2014 we found no listings for honors math sections and only an independent study option in political science. (Note: it is not unusual for honors programs to offer a wider range of classes in the Fall.) On the other hand, there was a strong selection of chemistry and chemical engineering sections, and at least four physics sections. Almost unique among honors programs, the college also offered honors classes in geology and geography. At least seven anthropology sections were listed, an excellent range for an honors program. Three sections of honors econ were available, each with about 45 students. The college and its affiliated college honors programs only occasionally utilize honors contracts or mixed classes, so most honors classes are just that—all honors.

Average Class Size (5.0): The college reports that the overall honors class size is a very impressive 14.6 students, but as noted above a few sections may be as large as 38-45 students. (The overall class size for the 50 colleges and programs under review in this edition is 21.2 students.)

Adjusted Graduation Rate (4.0): The AGR is not simply the six-year graduation rate of students in the honors college who graduated from the university (**84%**), whether or not the students completed the honors program ("honors completers"). It also reflects the extent to which the honors graduation rate from the university is higher than that for the university as a whole. The **university-wide rate is 60%**, yielding the 4.0 AGR for the college. (The college reports that the university graduation rate for students who never participated in honors is only 52%.) The average six-year **honors graduation rate for all 50 programs** under review **is 89%**.

Ratio of Staff to Honors Students (3.5): Our estimate is that there is 1 staff member for every **170.8** students. (Median ratio for all 50 programs is 1 staff member for every 159.8 students.)

Honors Residence Halls (4.0*): Honors freshmen may be assigned to the newly-remodeled Hotz Honors Hall (400 students) or to Maple Hill East (42 students) or Northwest Quad (99 students). Following is a summary from (now retired) Honors College Dean Robert C. McMath:

"Hotz Honors Hall, home to Honors College freshmen, is newly renovated and features small study rooms and open study spaces, a home theater, presentation rooms, a kitchen, a covered patio, and a music room. In addition to the communal activities created through the close proximity of the honors students, Honors College graduate assistants initiate special programs and events to enhance the intellectual and social community in the hall. Honors faculty members are invited for monthly programs focusing on undergraduate research and publication. The 'Pizza and Professor on the Patio' sessions cover an eclectic array of topics. Small interest groups and networking opportunities among peers and upper class honors students abound. Recent activities include upper class mentor panels, live streaming of athletic events, a tessellated mural painting, the Olympic Ceremonies celebration with a nod to Russian cuisine and culture, the building of gingerbread structures during the holidays, and many more diverse and unique events specifically targeted to our freshmen.

"We also offer on-campus housing spaces for both upperclassmen and freshmen honors students in the Northwest Quad (Buildings A and C, 135 students), Futral Hall (99 students), and for freshmen in Maple Hill East. Though these spaces will serve a smaller number of students, we provide programs featuring faculty interaction, continued upperclassmen mentoring, service and social opportunities, and close proximity to other Honors College events on campus such as current events discussions, book clubs, tips on thriving throughout the upperclassmen years, and other ways to create a more enriching honors experience."

*Hotz is a wonderful addition to the campus and Honors College, and a big improvement over the previous honors dorm. The 4.0 rating is not higher because our housing methodology awards points for suite-style dorms and other amenities. Hotz has corridor-style rooms with traditional baths serving multiple rooms on a floor. Many honors educators believe that, while suite-style and apartment-style rooms are desirable in the eyes of parents and prospective students, once students are on campus they frequently prefer the more collegial atmosphere of the traditional dorm styles.

All of the honors dorms are air-conditioned, with on-site laundry. The closest dining facility for all the dorms is Northwest Quad Dining Hall, close to Hotz Hall and not far from Maple Hill East.

Prestigious Awards (4.5): U of A has a very strong record of winning prestigious awards, especially Goldwater Scholarships (48) for undergrads in STEM fields, and Marshall Scholarships (7), all of which are indicative of achievement at the highest level. U of A was named a Truman Scholarship Honor Institution in 2002, and U of A students have won 18 Truman Scholarships. The university also has 10 Rhodes Scholars.

The Office of Nationally Competitive Awards (ONCA), founded by Dr. Suzanne McCray, became part of the Honors College at its inception. Dr. McCray is a founder and past-president of the National Association of Fellowship Advisors and has published three volumes of NAFA conference proceedings and an additional book, *All In: Expanding Access through Nationally Competitive Awards* (2013). Dr. McCray was Associate Dean of the Honors College until 2010, when she became Vice Provost of Enrollment Services. ONCA moved with her, but it remains closely linked to the Honors College, and **almost all U. of A. students who compete for the awards listed above are honors students.**

Continuation Requirements: 3.50 GPA; also the minimum required for graduation with honors.

Academic Strengths: The nationally ranked departments at U of A are the Walton College of Business and the Fay Jones School of Architecture. The Dale Bumpers College of Agricultural, Food and Life Sciences, and the College of Engineering also have national recognition.

Undergraduate Research: 100% of honors students who complete the program complete a thesis in their field of study consisting of traditional research or other forms of creative work which is directed by a professor and, in most of the colleges, evaluated by a faculty committee. **In 2013, the Honors College provided over $743,000 from its own endowment in support of undergraduate research, including over $427,000 in student stipends and $316,000 in faculty mentor funds, and $10,000 in conference travel not covered by other funds.** Students also received research funding from fellowships and scholarships, State Undergraduate Research Fellowships, and NSF REU grants.

The Honors College has a formal program for its required undergraduate research component, and the individual honors programs provide support for their particular academic areas. Students are guided by faculty to: a) develop a project proposal, b) select a committee, c) learn basic and intermediate (and often up to graduate level) research methods, d) engage in faculty-led and mentored research, e) submit a thesis, f) present their research in a public forum and, ultimately, g) defend their thesis. Students must reach milestones throughout the process, such as forming a committee before completing 65 credit hours, to ensure that they are kept on track for completion by their final semester of study.

Study Abroad: "Most of our undergraduates from Arkansas have never before traveled outside the United States. For many, the necessity of working to help fund their education precludes extended study abroad. The strategy of our university for study abroad, which the Honors College fully supports, is to make extended programs available and affordable for those who can take advantage of them, while at the same time providing maximum support to those for whom short-term programs are the only option. In 2013, with funds from the 2002 Walton Foundation gift that helped create the Honors College, we provided $597,523 in study abroad grants."

The University of Arkansas owns an educational center in Rome, which accommodates its own students in several fields of study and also students from other Southeastern Conference universities. The U. of A. has active exchange programs with 22 universities in Austria, Denmark, United Kingdom, France, Germany, Italy, Spain, Sweden, Mexico, Japan, China, South Korea, and Australia, with others in the works in African and Latin American nations.

Financial Aid: Each year the Honors College awards up to 90 fellowships to entering freshmen that provide each student with $50,000 to $70,000 over four years, plus non-resident tuition, if applicable.

Beginning in Fall 2015, all Honors College Fellowships will offer $70,000 over four years. For programs with degree plans of more than four years, extra semesters of funding may be available. The fellowships are renewable annually based on academic performance and personal conduct.

Most honors students who do not win a fellowship receive other merit-based scholarships offered through the Office of Academic Scholarships. These range from scholarships providing $10,000 per year, renewable for four or five years (depending on course of study), to one-time awards of $1,000.

The university is still very **friendly to National Merit Scholars**, despite a national trend to the contrary, and funds 27 of 34 merit scholarships from university resources, providing very high tuition relief.

Degree of Difference (Honors students/non-honors students): 2.2 on a scale of 5. Some parents and prospective students might prefer an honors program that in many ways stands apart on campus, while others might prefer a program that is more expansive. The rating here tries to provide an indication of where a given honors program is on the stand apart/expansive spectrum. The rating is based on the difference between (1) the average SAT scores for enrolled honors students and (2) the average test scores for all students in the university as a whole *and* for students with scores at the 75% level or above. A score of 3.5 or higher indicates a high degree of difference. A score of 3.2 to 3.49 indicates a relatively high degree of difference. Finally, a score below 3.2 indicates a modest difference. **Please keep in mind that neither the high nor low selectivity of an honors program determines how effective the program is; this rating is merely "cultural" and *not* qualitative.**

Testimonials:

Prof. Gisela Erf--"I have always enjoyed working with honors students and introducing them to all aspects of scientific research. Honors students bring a level of excitement, curiosity and interest to a project that is captivating. Some may need more personal attention and mentoring than others, but all are eager to learn and determined to have this real-life research experience. There are few more rewarding moments in my job than when students, who just months ago knew very little about research, have taken ownership of their project and are discussing approaches and future research directions."

Honors grad--"Studying abroad free of charge was another benefit of being an honors student. I studied abroad three times, and each trip was fully funded by Honors College study abroad grants. I would not have been able to travel without this help, and my situation was not unusual. Prior to graduation I pursued a Gates Cambridge scholarship, and for months my scholarship advisors met with me weekly to assess and edit my application and eventually organized six mock interviews and offered extensive coaching that made me calm and ready for the actual interview. **Now that I am at Cambridge and speak with other students about their undergraduate experiences, I realize how unique and valuable the U of A Honors College is.** It is rare and special to receive these extensive opportunities that can open up so many doors for students even after their undergraduate career is over."

NAME: THE HONORS COLLEGE AT AUBURN UNIVERSITY

Date Established: 1979, Honors Program; 1998, Honors College

Location: Auburn, Alabama

University Full-time Undergraduate Enrollment: 19,799

Honors Enrollment: 1,940 (mean size of all 50 programs is 1,714)

Review/Admissions Category IV: Programs with **average SAT scores of 1417 or higher for enrolled students**. The **average** (mean) SAT score for enrolled Auburn honors students is 1417, and the ACT average is 32. The average high school GPA is 4.19; the average (mean) high school class standing is the 94th percentile (median is 98th percentile).

Minimum Admission Requirements: SAT 1290, ACT 29; high school GPA 3.75.

Honors Programs in Admissions Category IV (average SAT of 1417 and higher): Auburn, Clemson, Georgia, Illinois, Kansas, Michigan, Minnesota, North Carolina, Rutgers, South Carolina, UT Austin, Virginia.

Administrative Staff: The Honors College has a staff of 12.

FOR ALL "MORTARBOARD" RATINGS BELOW, A SCORE OF 5 IS THE MAXIMUM AND REPRESENTS A COMPARISON WITH ALL 50 HONORS COLLEGES AND PROGRAMS:

PERCEPTION* OF UNIVERSITY AS A WHOLE, NOT OF HONORS: 🎓 🎓🎓[1/2]

OVERALL HONORS RATING: 🎓🎓🎓🎓

Curriculum Requirements: 🎓🎓🎓🎓[1/2]

Class Range and Type: 🎓🎓🎓[1/2]

Class Size: 🎓🎓🎓🎓[1/2]

Adjusted Grad Rate: 🎓🎓🎓🎓

Ratio of Staff to Students: 🎓🎓🎓[1/2]

Priority Registration: Yes, honors students have priority registration for **all** courses, in the form of being able to register with the class ahead of them.

Honors Housing: 🎓🎓🎓🎓 1/2

Prestigious Awards: 🎓🎓🎓 1/2

*Perception is based on the university's ranking among public universities in the 2014 U.S. News Best Colleges report. Please bear in mind that the better the U.S. News ranking, the more difficult it is for an honors college or program to have a rating that equals or improves on the magazine ranking.

Curriculum Requirements (4.5): The honors completion requirement is substantial, and the ways students can meet it are many. "Students must complete 30 hours of Honors-level credit selected from the following types of Honors courses: Honors University core courses, Honors Departmental courses, Graduate-level courses in the major field of study, Honors Study and Travel courses, Honors Seminars, Honors Research Seminars, Honors Contract courses, and Honors Participation courses." All students must complete at least one of the following Senior Year Honors Experiences: Departmental Capstone Course (credit hours vary by department); Honors thesis in the major department (6 credit hours); or three graduate courses in the student's major.

In addition, there are some limits on the number of courses that can be taken in some of the categories listed above:

Graduate Courses--9-12 hours of graduate work can be counted towards honors completion, **and "these hours may count towards both the student's undergraduate and graduate degrees at Auburn University."**

Study Abroad--Course credit for one study-abroad experience may be counted.

Honors Seminars--A maximum of two regular seminars and one research seminar may count toward honors completion.

Contract courses--There is no stated limit on the number of contract courses (please see the introductory section titled "All about Honors Classes") that may be counted toward completion. A contract course at the college is a core course "that cannot be taken as Honors because of a scheduling conflict or lack of an Honors version" or a course that is needed to complete a curricular requirement outside of honors completion.

Honors Participation Courses--Students may earn 1 credit each for as many as three Participation courses. This classification of courses includes Honors Freshmen Exploration, Honors Lyceum, Honors Book Club and Honors Forum. **Honors Freshman Exploration** classes provide insights and practical skills related to study abroad, course registration, campus activities and participation, and service learning. The maximum for **Honors Lyceum** (1 credit each) is two courses. These include spirited discussions of current events, controversial issues, and international affairs. **Honors Forum** allows honors students to earn up to two credits (1 hour each) by attending 10 lectures, films, or performances pre-approved by the college. Students write reflective essays after each event. **Honors Book Club** participation is also limited to two total credits and requires reading and detailed discussion of 2-3 books.

AP/IB credits are **not** counted as replacements for honors courses.

Range and Type of Honors Courses (3.5): Auburn, like several honors colleges and programs, offers more sections in the Fall than in the Spring. It is possible that our focus on the Spring term has had a relatively negative impact on our assessment of the classes offered at Auburn because their Fall offerings may be disproportionately greater in comparison to the Spring classes. With about nine 3-credit seminars in the Spring along with about 39 other honors sections, the Auburn Honors College could be called a blended program or a discipline-specific program—on the cusp so to speak—but the feel is more that of a blended program with some interesting seminars and a substantial if not extensive array of departmental honors classes.

The flexibility of the honors completion requirements, outlined above, means that relatively few formal honors sections may be sufficient to serve a sizable program. If a student can gain lots of honors credit through honors contracts, by taking graduate courses, and through the 1-hour Honors Participation courses, then there is less need to offer a large number of honors sections. Whether this approach is in the best interests of the student depends on the student. The rigor of most graduate courses is not much in doubt, so meeting the completion requirements by taking those is an advantage. Some of the formal honors sections, especially the writing and world literature seminars, are another strong option. So are the small philosophy classes. Honors contract courses always depend on the relationship between the student and the instructor and the extra effort each is willing to contribute.

The departmental sections are strongest in math and science: four sections of the former and eight of the latter, more than most programs offer. The science sections include classes in biology, chemistry, and physics. Economics is fairly well represented with two small sections--and most honors econ classes run larger at other universities. In addition, there is one section in political science.

Missing from the Spring list are honors classes in psychology, anthropology, sociology, which are offered in the Fall, and foreign languages. The absence of foreign language sections is not unusual, however.

Average Class Size (4.5): The average honors class size at Auburn Honors College is 19.8 students, with very few really large classes involved. Some of the 1-credit Honors Participation sections might have a large number of enrollees, but class size in these is of less importance than it is in 3- or 4-credit hour classes and seminars. (The overall class size for the 50 colleges and programs under review in this edition is 21.2 students.)

Adjusted Graduation Rate (4.0): The AGR is not simply the six-year graduation rate of students in the honors college who graduated from the university **(estimated at 86%),** whether or not the students completed the honors program ("honors completers"). The AGR also reflects the extent to which the honors graduation rate from the university is higher than that for the university as a whole. (The **university-wide rate is 68%,** yielding the 4.0 AGR for the college.) The average **honors** six-year **graduation rate for all 50 programs under review is 89%.**

Ratio of Staff to Honors Students (3.5): Our estimate is that there is 1 staff member for every **161.7** students. (Mean ratio for all 50 programs is 1 staff member for every 159.8 students.)

Honors Residence Halls (4.5): Honors students can live in Aubie Hall, a large 300-bed facility located in the newer community called the "Village." The units are configured in "super suites" shared by four students. The suites consist primarily of four single bedrooms, two bathrooms and a common living/dining area. Rent includes all utilities including basic TV cable and wireless internet service.

"Each bedroom in the Village is furnished with an extra-long (80") twin bed, study desk and chair, chest of drawers, and closet. The living/dining areas are furnished with a sofa and side chair, dining table with 2 chairs, microwave, fridge, sink, and counter and cabinet space. There is a laundry facility and common kitchen in each residence hall. Residents receive their mail and pick up packages at a centrally located mailroom in the Village."

Honors students can also live in any one of the four residence halls in the "Upper Quad": Broun, Harper, Little, and Teague. They are air conditioned, and convenient dining facilities are located in Foy Hall and the Student Center.

"All Quad rooms are configured in suites consisting of two double rooms (two students per room) connected by a bathroom. There are a very limited number of single rooms available. Quad rooms are furnished with an extra-long (80"), bunkable twin bed, study desk and chair, chest of drawers, and closet for each resident. Rent includes all utilities including basic T.V. cable and wireless internet service. Washers and dryers are located in a laundry facility centrally located in the Quad Center."

Residents receive their mail and packages at the mailroom located in that building as well. "Members of the Honors College are not automatically placed in an Honors Hall. They must be guaranteed on-campus housing and request placement in an Honors Hall. While there is no guaranteed placement in an Honors Hall, University Housing is usually able to accommodate the majority of requests. Only Honors College students may live in the Honors Halls in the Village and Upper Quad: therefore, Honors students who request roommates who are not members of the Honors College will not be considered for placement in an Honors hall."

Prestigious Awards (3.5): The University's strongest performance in this category is in winning undergraduate Goldwater Scholarships for outstanding promise in the STEM fields. Auburn scores above the mean in the number of students who have won the generous Gates Cambridge postgraduate awards for students at Cambridge University.

Continuation Requirements: Cumulative 3.4 GPA for honors completion.

Academic Strengths: Engineering and business are the strongest academic colleges at Auburn. The agriculture-related programs are also highly regarded.

Undergraduate Research: The Office of Undergraduate Studies has an Undergraduate Research Program and offers year-long, semester-long, and summer competitive fellowships. Fellowships can be conducted on campus or off campus in locations such as national or specialized laboratories. Year-long fellowships begin in the summer and extend through the spring semester. One-semester fellowships can be conducted in any semester. Length of fellowship offered varies by college/school.

Honors student Chris Bartel, a chemical engineering student working with Dr. Mark Byrne, is working on a project to reduce the discomfort often associated with wearing contact lenses. "The primary research objective is to engineer a therapeutic contact lens to controllably release comfort molecules thereby developing a technology with the potential to limit the discomfort felt during lens wear. An additional benefit is reducing protein and lipid deposition to the lens, leading to a healthier lens and a healthier eye."

For honors student Madeline Moore, the goal is to develop a testing environment (a "media") for a bacterium that can destroy plants by forming a film inside the water-conducting xylem vessels which nourish the plants. Madeline is working with plant pathologist Dr. Leonardo De La Fuente. "The definition of a media that reproduces natural growth conditions for this bacterium is important because it will allow for a better understanding of the infection process inside the plants."

(Chris and Madeline are both Undergraduate Research Fellows.)

Study Abroad: "In an effort to provide Honors students with a holistic college experience, the Honors College has created a study and travel program. This program includes both domestic and international trips, some being the capstone of HONR 3087, Honors Study and Travel. Other experiences include alternative break travel, for students who would like to experience immersion in a culture other than their native."

Recent honors study-abroad trips have been to Greece, Turkey, Germany, and Costa Rica.

Other travel opportunities exist within the U.S. Leonard E. Jordan II, a student in the College of Science and Mathematics, writes that in "the spring of 2012, I had the pleasure of traveling with Dr. Harris and Mrs. Mattox to Washington, DC in a small group with other Honors College students. We toured the [Defense Intelligence Agency] and learned about the Agency itself as well as the important tasks assigned to the various employees. In addition to this, we were also able to tour the Capitol as well as the rest of the city. I was able to visit the graves of Thurgood Marshal and John F. Kennedy in the Arlington Cemetery, learn the metro system in order to explore the city, and visit some good friends at Howard University who were able to show me more about the city than I could have discovered on my own."

Financial Aid: National Merit Finalists and National Achievement Finalists receive a National Scholars Presidential Scholarship:

- **Tuition for four years for Alabama residents, currently valued at $34,368 ($8,592 per year),or $80,000 over four years for non-residents ($20,000 per year)**
- $1,000 technology stipend in the first fall semester
- $2,500 enrichment experience stipend available for one semester after the second year of study at Auburn for study abroad or undergraduate research
- On-campus housing stipend for one year, valued at $7,200
- University stipend for four years at $4,000 to $8,000 ($1,000 to $2,000 per year), depending on eligibility as determined by National Merit Scholarship Corporation and financial need as determined through completion of the Free Application for Federal Student Aid (FAFSA).

In 2013, Auburn had 67 merit scholars, and 55 of these were sponsored by the university, an increase over 2012 despite a national trend of declining university sponsorship.

Spirit of Auburn Scholarships are **awarded to Alabama resident students** from October to February, based on academic achievement as demonstrated by standardized test scores and high school GPA. These four year, renewable scholarships are awarded at three levels: Presidential, Founders, and University. Students must be accepted for admission, complete the scholarship application and have the minimum ACT or SAT score and high school GPA requirements to receive consideration. Minimum test scores required for consideration at each level do not include the writing score.

Presidential Scholarship

- Requires a 32-36 ACT or 1400-1600 SAT score <u>and</u> a minimum 3.5 high school GPA for consideration.
- Awarded at tuition for four years and a $1,000 technology stipend the first fall semester.

Founders Scholarship:

- Requires a 30-31 ACT or 1330-1390 SAT score <u>and</u> a minimum 3.5 high school GPA for consideration.
- Awarded at tuition for four years.

University Scholarship

- Requires a 28-29 ACT or 1250-1320 SAT score <u>and</u> a minimum 3.5 high school GPA for consideration.
- Awarded at $12,000 over four years ($3,000 per year).

Degree of Difference (Honors students/non-honors students): 3.09 on a scale of 5. Some parents and prospective students might prefer an honors program that in many ways stands apart on campus, while others might prefer a program that is more expansive. The rating here tries to provide an indication of where a given honors program is on the stand apart/expansive spectrum. The rating is based on the difference between (1) the average SAT scores for enrolled honors students and (2) the average test scores for all students in the university as a whole and for students with scores at the 75% level or above. A score of 3.5 or higher indicates a high degree of difference. A score of 3.2 to 3.49 indicates a relatively high degree of difference. Finally, a score below 3.2 indicates a modest difference. **Please keep in mind that neither the high nor low selectivity of an honors program determines how effective the program is; this rating is merely "cultural" and not qualitative.**

NAME: CALHOUN HONORS COLLEGE, CLEMSON UNIVERSITY

Date Established: 1962

Location: Clemson, South Carolina

University Full-time Undergraduate Enrollment: 15,643

Honors Enrollment: 1,341 (mean size of all 50 programs is 1,714)

Review/Admissions Category IV: Programs with **average SAT scores of 1417--1521 for enrolled students**. The **average** (mean) SAT score for enrolled Clemson honors students is **1453**, and the ACT average is **33**, making it **one of the most selective public honors programs in the nation**. The average high school class rank is the 97th to 99th percentile.

Minimum Admission Requirements: SAT 1320, ACT 30, high school class rank, 90th percentile.

Honors Programs in Admissions Category IV (average SAT scores of 1417-1521): Auburn, Clemson, Georgia, Illinois, Kansas, Michigan, Minnesota, North Carolina, South Carolina, Rutgers, UT Austin, and Virginia.

Administrative Staff: Calhoun Honors College has a staff of 8.

FOR ALL "MORTARBOARD" RATINGS BELOW, A SCORE OF 5 IS THE MAXIMUM AND REPRESENTS A COMPARISON WITH ALL 50 HONORS COLLEGES AND PROGRAMS:

PERCEPTION* OF UNIVERSITY AS A WHOLE, NOT OF HONORS: 🎓🎓🎓🎓

OVERALL HONORS RATING: 🎓🎓🎓🎓 1/2

Curriculum Requirements: 🎓🎓🎓🎓 1/2

Class Range and Type: 🎓🎓🎓🎓 1/2

Class Size: 🎓🎓🎓 1/2

Adjusted Grad Rate: 🎓🎓🎓🎓 1/2

Ratio of Staff to Students: 🎓🎓🎓🎓

Priority Registration: Yes, honors students register for **all** courses, honors and otherwise, with the first group of students during **each** year they are in the program.

Honors Housing: 🎓🎓🎓🎓🎓

Prestigious Awards: ♟ ♟ ♟[1/2]

*Perception is based on the university's ranking among public universities in the 2014 U.S. News Best Colleges report. Please bear in mind that the better the U.S. News ranking, the more difficult it is for an honors college or program to have a rating that equals or improves on the magazine ranking.

Curriculum Requirements (4.5): The requirements for the most basic level of honors completion **(General Honors)** are at least six honors courses of 3 or more credit hours each. Students must make an A or B in each course counted toward completion. General Honors essentially fulfills the university's Gen-Ed requirements through honors classes.

The college works very closely with academic departments to coordinate and track honors students pursuing departmental honors. The credit hours required for departmental honors vary from 6-12 hours. The reason is that some departments require research seminars or other coursework *and* an honors thesis.

"Normally, **Departmental Honors** is completed during your junior and senior years. To be considered for any Departmental Honors program, you must have a cumulative GPA of 3.40 or higher and the approval of your department, which may take into consideration such factors as your maturity and motivation."

Honors completion at the **highest level (General Honors plus Departmental Honors)** typically requires approximately 31 credit hours, but many students take more honors courses than required.

AP/IB credits are **not** counted as replacements for honors courses.

Range and Type of Honors Courses (4.5): Although we classify the honors college as a **department-based** program because of the large number of departmental honors sections, the number and variety of honors seminars gives the program a nice balance. Of the 16 honors seminars offered in Spring 2014, we liked these best: Technology, Culture, and Design; Free to Choose; Wisdom of the Ages; The Great War; The Cinema of Adolescence; The Abyss—Humanism, Modernity, and the Examined Life; and our favorite, **The Nature of Infinity.**

The college goes out of its way to make sure that there are as many honors sections in the academic departments as possible, including a large number of advanced courses in the sciences and engineering, including electrical and computer engineering. There were five sections of accounting, four of economics--a strong showing--and four sections of management. The college offered five sections of honors calculus. Most impressive was the presence of ten physics sections in Spring 2014. And then there were seven classes in microbiology and three more in biochemistry, several of them advanced. What we did not find was an honors class in political science, but there were four honors seminars taught by political science faculty.

Average Class Size (3.5): In order to make so many departmental courses available for honors credits, especially in the sciences, the college has accepted the need to mix honors students with non-honors students in many of these sections. In addition, some of the sections are large, with one general biology section numbering 166 total students, 20 of them in honors. The largest sections are mainly those in biology, biochemistry, and microbiology--but, again, the trade-off here is that there are more courses to choose from than there would be if only all-honors sections were offered. The many physics sections, on the other hand, are actually smaller than average, with a few in the 15-20 student range. **The enrollment levels in the seminar classes, such as The Nature of Infinity, average only 12.6 students.** The overall **average class size is 28.3**, compared to the average class size of 21.2 among all 50 programs under review.

Adjusted Graduation Rate (4.5): The AGR is not simply the six-year graduation rate of students in the honors college who graduated from the university **(95%),** whether or not the students completed the honors program ("honors completers"). The AGR also reflects the extent to which the honors graduation rate from the university is higher than that for the university as a whole. (The **university-wide rate is 82%**, yielding the 4.5 AGR for the college.) The average **honors** six-year **graduation rate for all 50 programs under review is 89%.**

Ratio of Staff to Honors Students (4.0): Our estimate is that there is 1 staff member for every **149.0** students. (Mean ratio for all 50 programs is 1 staff member for every 159.8 students.)

Honors Residence Halls (5.0): Clemson freshmen are required to live on campus, and honors students are fortunate that the Holmes Hall Honors Living/Learning Community (McCabe and Holmes Halls) is set aside for honors students, including upperclassmen. The rooms are all suite-style with connecting baths and air-conditioned. There are no less than three kitchens available for student use. The Harcombe Dining Hall is nearby.

The Honors Director tells us that in addition to the more than 300 Honors students who live in this LLC, "the entire Honors community has access to the **Honors Academic Activities Center** located in Holmes Hall. This 2,500-square foot space provides lounges, meeting and study space, classrooms, a kitchen, and other amenities (coffee and printing) that Honors students can access 24/7. Honors staff and Honors RA's hold regular drop-in advising hours in this space as well.

"Also, the Honors LLC benefits from a **Faculty in Residence** who lives in an apartment in the LLC and provides mentoring and advising throughout the year and coordinates educational enrichment programs, such as book and current event discussions."

The college website notes that new honors students "may request a roommate or suitemates for the Honors LLC ONLY if both/all students are admitted to Honors, and ONLY if both/all students have submitted the required University Housing application and properly requested each other as roommates/suitemates."

Prestigious Awards (3.5): Clemson students do especially well in winning prestigious Goldwater Scholarships for undergraduates studying in the STEM fields, in accordance with the school's proud tradition of excellence in those subjects. The university has few winners of prestigious postgraduate scholarships, however, with the exception of National Science Foundation Graduate Research Fellowships. The Office of Major Fellowships was not created at the university until 2006. **Since the 2007-2008 academic year, Clemson students have won 17 Goldwater Scholarships, including at least two every year, one of the strongest showings among all universities under review.**

Continuation Requirements: Cumulative 3.4 GPA for honors completion.

Academic Strengths: The leading academic departments at Clemson are business, engineering, computer science, and economics.

Undergraduate Research: "Most departmental Honors programs feature undergraduate research as an essential component" the Calhoun Director reports. "In addition, many Honors students participate in undergraduate research through Clemson's **Creative Inquiry Program**; some of these creative inquiry groups consist wholly or predominantly of Honors students."

The Creative Inquiry and Undergraduate Research website says Clemson students can "take on problems that spring from their own curiosity, from a professor's challenge or from the pressing needs of the world around them. Team-based investigations are led by a faculty mentor and typically span two to four semesters. Students take ownership of their projects and take the risks necessary to solve problems and get answers.

"Topics are boundless. Students often find themselves presenting their work at national conferences, fielding questions from professionals. This invaluable experience produces exceptional graduates. Our Creative Inquiry participants develop critical thinking skills, learn to solve problems as a team and hone their communication and presentation skills."

There are almost 300 student research projects already under way, and the program goal is to reach at least 1,000.

The Honors College also funds Educational Enrichment Travel Grants (EETG), which "are designed to fund life-changing educational experiences that take place away from Clemson and outside of the classroom. These experiences may be internships, foreign study, public service projects or other significant undertakings that are consistent with a student's educational, career and/or personal goals. (Study-Abroad **courses** will not be funded through EETGs…**Priority will be given to proposals that, in the judgment of the review committee, show promise for contributing to a strong and potentially successful application for an extramural fellowship. Such fellowships include, but are not limited to, the Rhodes, Marshall, Truman, Mitchell, Goldwater and Udall scholarships, and Fulbright Grants.**"

Note: Although study-abroad courses, which provide credit hours, cannot be funded through EETGs, *research* abroad can receive such funding.

Study Abroad: "The Honors College features a summer study abroad program in Brussels, Belgium, and specialized programs for selected students in Brussels, Belgium, and Strasbourg, France, and in locations chosen on an annual basis."

The Brussels program includes two honors courses taught in English by Belgian professors. In one course, students learn about the origins, development and contemporary role of the European Union. Interactions with European Union officials give students a first-hand understanding of the issues facing the 26-member EU. The other course examines the history and cultural traditions of Belgium, including its historic reputation as "Europe's battlefield."

Both courses count toward the Honors College General Honors requirement.

"The program features numerous excursions to historically significant cities and sites, including Bruges, known as the 'Venice of Northern Europe,' and the great art cities of Ghent and Antwerp. A popular feature of the program is a bike tour through the World War I battlefields in western Belgium. One weekend is open for personal travel, with popular destinations being Paris, Amsterdam and London."

Financial Aid: In addition to **the National Scholars Program, which provides full scholarships to the cost of tuition, fees, room, board and books**, Honors students at Clemson University are eligible for numerous merit scholarships. In-state students in Honors who are also designated as Palmetto Fellows by the state of South Carolina receive the $2,500 Palmetto Pact Scholarship, and many receive the prestigious $2,500 Presidential Scholarship as well. Out-of-state Honors students usually qualify for an award of between $7,500 and $17,500 annually--depending on test scores, high school performance and financial need.

In 2012-2013, the university had 41 National Merit Scholars; 23 received funding from the university. The National Scholars Program (not necessarily for National *Merit* Scholars, although some surely qualify) is a wonderful opportunity for any highly talented freshman, and it is only open to students accepted to the honors college. "Selection to the NSP is highly **competitive. Approximately 40 applicants are invited to compete for an invitation to join the NSP each year, out of more than 1,000 Calhoun Honors College applicants.** A successful candidate will present, through his or her written record, personal interview and participation in other National Scholars Weekend activities:

- a documented record of academic excellence, as reflected in SAT or ACT scores and the high school transcript,
  - **between 2000 and 2012, the nearly 500 finalists invited to compete for an invitation to the NSP have presented an average SAT of 1500 (verbal/critical reading and math) or an average ACT of 34, and a class rank in the top 1% (51% were ranked number 1 in their high school class);**
- a documented record of intellectual curiosity and engagement;
- a detailed record of the depth and significance of his or her most meaningful extra- and co-curricular activities, including leadership, service and research experiences;
- meaningful, thoughtful and informed responses to essay and interview questions; and
- outstanding and detailed letters of recommendation.

"Due to the small size of the National Scholars Program, the selection committee must make difficult choices from among many highly qualified candidates at both the Finalist and Scholar stages of the process."

Degree of Difference (Honors students/non-honors students): 3.36 on a scale of 5. Some parents and prospective students might prefer an honors program that in many ways stands apart on campus, while others might prefer a program that is more expansive. The rating here tries to provide an indication of where a given honors program is on the stand apart/expansive spectrum. The rating is based on the difference between (1) the average SAT scores for enrolled honors students and (2) the average test scores for all students in the university as a whole *and* for students with scores at the 75% level or above. A

score of 3.5 or higher indicates a high degree of difference. A score of 3.2 to 3.49 indicates a relatively high degree of difference. Finally, a score below 3.2 indicates a modest difference. **Please keep in mind that neither the high nor low selectivity of an honors program determines how effective the program is; this rating is merely "cultural" and *not* qualitative.**

Testimonials:

Honors student—"**Holmes Hall itself was an experience I will never forget. Living in a community of high achievers and in one of the finest on-campus dormitories, I had never felt more inspired to be my best.** For the first time, I was entirely surrounded by some of the most impressive people of my age. Their achievements and their goals motivated me to do better and to excel in the classes I was taking. We all shared similar goals, and we lived in a top-notch space in which we could fulfill them."

Honors student—"My Honors experience has provided me with **amazing opportunities that would otherwise not have been available, for instance: backpacking in Alaska, researching in South Africa, attending formal and informal discussions in the Holmes basement, seeing concerts at Brooks, taking classes with like-minded, driven individuals, living in Holmes, building relationships with professors, and so much more.**

Honors Alum—"From principles of aesthetic philosophy to the role of clergy in American society, the knowledge I've gained is vast and varied. And while some of this knowledge may not directly relate to my chosen field of study, it serves as the foundation for a rich liberal arts education—something Clemson prides itself on being able to offer. **I firmly attribute my acceptance to the University of Oxford for graduate study and my overall success to an undergraduate education characterized by diverse thought.**"

Honors faculty—"So, instead of a classroom with ~250 students, **the Honors College setting of ~25 students provided an atmosphere where we could have detailed discussions about genetics and explore science in a way that is not possible in the large didactic classroom.** Additionally, the smaller setting allowed me to get to know the students, both as scholars and people, at a level that is not possible in bigger lecture halls."

Honors faculty—"The content of an honors and a non-honors class might be identical, but **in the honors class the students will do the readings more carefully and come to class with questions of their own. The result is the sort of true intellectual exchange where everyone in the room is engaged and actually learning (including the professor).**"

NAME: UNIVERSITY HONORS PROGRAM, COLORADO STATE UNIVERSITY

Date Established: 1957

Location: Fort Collins, Colorado

University Full-time Undergraduate Enrollment: 21,193

Honors Enrollment: 1,500 (mean size of all 50 programs is 1,714)

Review/Admissions Category I: Programs with **average SAT scores of 1235--1342** for enrolled students. The *estimated* average (mean) test scores for honors enrollees at Colorado State are SAT 1324-1344, ACT 30. The *estimated* average high school GPA is 3.85.

Minimum admission requirements: We have no information about minimum scores and GPA requirements.

Honors Programs in Admissions Category I (average SAT scores of 1235-1342): Arizona, Arizona State, Arkansas, Colorado State, Iowa, Maine, Mississippi, Oklahoma State, Oregon, Oregon State, Rhode Island, Texas Tech, University at Albany, and Washington State.

Administrative Staff: The Honors Program has a staff of 5.

FOR ALL "MORTARBOARD" RATINGS BELOW, A SCORE OF 5 IS THE MAXIMUM AND REPRESENTS A COMPARISON WITH ALL 50 HONORS COLLEGES AND PROGRAMS:

PERCEPTION* OF UNIVERSITY AS A WHOLE, <u>NOT</u> OF HONORS: 🎓🎓🎓

OVERALL HONORS RATING: 🎓🎓🎓$^{1/2}$

Curriculum Requirements: 🎓🎓🎓$^{1/2}$

Class Range and Type: 🎓🎓🎓🎓$^{1/2}$

Class Size: 🎓🎓🎓🎓$^{1/2}$

Adjusted Grad Rate: 🎓🎓🎓🎓

Ratio of Staff to Students: 🎓🎓🎓$^{1/2}$

Priority Registration: Yes, but we do not have exact details.

Honors Housing: 🎓🎓🎓🎓$^{1/2}$

Prestigious Awards: 🎓🎓🎓¹ᐟ²

*Perception is based on the university's ranking among public universities in the 2014 U.S. News Best Colleges report. Please bear in mind that the better the U.S. News ranking, the more difficult it is for an honors college or program to have a rating that equals or improves on the magazine ranking.

Curriculum Requirements (3.5): The honors program has a modest completion requirement of 23 credit hours for Track 1 and 17 credits hours for Track 2. Track 1 is mostly a **core honors program,** and Track 2 is a decentralized **departmental honors program.**

Track 1 (University Honors Scholar) requires 16 credits in honors-only seminars at different class levels; 3 credits in a sophomore-level departmental course; 3 credits in an upper-division departmental course; 1credit of pre-thesis preparation; and a 3-credit honors thesis. The departmental classes may or may not be honors-only, depending on the department, and may also be earned through a contract between the honors student and the instructor.

Track 2 (Discipline Honors Scholar) is often the choice of students who have completed their Gen Ed requirements at CSU or elsewhere and want to add rigor to the upper-division courses in their majors. A total of 17 credits are required (16 for transfer students): A 1-credit honors orientation course (not required for transfers); 12 honors credits in the major; a 1-credit thesis preparation course; and a 3-credit honors thesis. Six of the 12 departmental honors credits may be in honors contract classes.

AP/IB credits: It might be possible for some of the Track 2 course requirements to be met through AP credit, but we could not confirm this.

Range and Type of Honors Courses (4.5): The UHP offers an excellent selection of Honors Scholar seminars, and they are honors-only classes. We counted 29 seminars in Spring 2014, and many of them appear to be offered in Spring 2015 as well. Overall, the UHP is a **blended program.**

Two seminars are titled **Move It!** "There will be opportunities to experience 'the fullness of developing our physical potential' and discovering the stories of ourselves in movement as we understand 'the fullness of the sacred gift of life.' This class will explore how everyday movement forms have evolved throughout history to present day and possible contributions not only to a variety of cultures but to individual experience."

Our favorites include **The Story of Stuff;** Vietnam & America: An Introduction; **Tell Me a Story: Finding and Creating Meaning in our Lives;** two sections of Gender in our Lives; **and Art is Politics, Politics is Art.**

In **The Story of Stuff**, students "examine the results of living in an affluent society and the epidemic of stress, overwork, waste, and indebtedness caused by dogged pursuit of the American Dream." In **Tell Me a Story,** students are taught to be mindful about the stories that shape their lives by exploring "the nature and function of stories as they are manifested in such narratives as myths, dreams, tragedy and comedy, autobiography, and politics. In doing so, we will focus on three general questions: Why do we need stories at all? Why do we need the 'same' story over and over? Why do we always need more stories?"

The title of **Art is Politics, Politics Is Art** is emphasized in the seminar description: "Politics is an art, not a science; all art is political. The central thesis of the course is that politics and art are drama, and we will explore the implications of that metaphor [by] drawing on political speeches and documents (e.g. Lincoln's 'Gettysburg Address,' Martin Luther King Jr.'s 'I Have a Dream' speech, excerpts from Marx's *Communist Manifesto*, film and TV documentaries, etc.)."

The upper-division seminars are outstanding as well. Lincoln reappears in **America and the Civil War,** a senior honors seminar. "'Any understanding of this nation has to be based on an understanding of the Civil War... it defines us.' These are the words of the eminent Civil War historian, Shelby Foote, and they form the premise for this course. The consequences of the Civil War, both good and ill, are all around us."

Construction of the Self in Arts and Sciences explores "three views of this most essential of human traits-- the biological, the philosophical, and the literary. Literature and philosophy have for centuries probed at the surface and the cavities of self. Biology, our teachers have told us, couldn't care a whole lot less about the nature of the human self. But as we will see in this course, biological and medical sciences, though less overtly, are also steadily changing the way we view our selves.

It is somewhat difficult to quantify the **departmental honors courses** because many of them do not carry the honors designation; but in tandem with the excellent seminars, the departmental honors sections that are identifiable are best in biological sciences: two sections of biochemistry, five of biology, three of microbiology, four in life sciences, and two in anatomy. Two honors math sections and an honors physics section are additional offerings in the math/science line. We found one honors chemistry lab section. Outside of the sciences, there was at least one designated honors section in English, finance, management, engineering, computer science, marketing, psychology, and sociology. The scarcity of formal departmental honors courses in the humanities is offset by the many honors seminars with a humanities focus.

Average Class Size (4.5): Our *estimate* is that the average *designated* honors class size is 17.1 students. Honors contract classes would in most cases be significantly larger. The overall average class size for the 50 colleges and programs under review in this edition is 21.2 students.

Adjusted Graduation Rate (4.0): The AGR is not simply the six-year graduation rate of students in the honors college who graduated from the university (*estimated at* **86.2%),** whether or not the students completed the honors program ("honors completers"). The AGR also reflects the extent to which the honors graduation rate from the university is higher than that for the university as a whole. The **university-wide rate is 63%,** yielding the 4.0 AGR for the college. The average **honors** six-year **graduation rate for all 50 programs under review is 89%.**

Ratio of Staff to Honors Students (3.5): Our estimate is that there is 1 staff member for every **300** students. (Mean ratio for all 50 programs is 1 staff member for every 159.8 students.)

Honors Residence Halls (4.5): Honors housing is certainly an asset to the UHP. **Only first-year honors students are allowed** to live in the Honors Residential Learning Community (HLRC) in the **Academic Village,** the newest residence hall at CSU. "The Academic Village is a state-of-the-art living learning environment that integrates classroom and experiential learning into the living area with programming space, seminar and meeting rooms, multi-media classrooms, and more. **It features hotel**

style rooms with private bathrooms. The village is also home to Rams Horn Dining and the engineering department.

Honors upperclassmen can live in Edwards Hall, also part of the HLRC, adjacent to the Village. The rooms are traditional doubles with shared hall baths. Both HLRCs are located in south campus, not too far from the landmark "Oval," and close to many academic buildings.

Prestigious Awards (3.5): CSU students have won 15 Goldwater Scholarships, awarded to outstanding undergraduates studying STEM subjects. University graduates have also won an impressive 5 Marshall Scholarships that provide generous funding for two years of graduate work in the U.K.

Continuation Requirements: 3.50 cumulative GPA for completion.

Academic Strengths: The strongest academic departments at CSU are chemistry, earth sciences, engineering, business, physics, math, and biology. CSU is also an excellent choice for pre-vet education, and **the veterinary school is ranked 3rd in the nation by *U.S. News.***

Undergraduate Research: CSU has a highly commendable **Undergraduate Research Honors Program.** Incoming first-year students must apply for admission by April 1 before their freshman year. During the first semester, students meet with an assigned faculty mentor for 3-6 hours a week while becoming familiar with university life and research opportunities. The URHP also sets up meetings where all URHP students can discuss ideas and develop their own research community.

In the second semester, students actually begin hands-on research, spending "between six and ten hours a week either working with your faculty mentor on a research project of your own design, or on a research team with other undergraduate and graduate students, lab technicians, postdoctoral fellows and faculty already engaged in a current research project."

"Opportunities for attending professional conferences and participating in seminars and symposia will also be provided. **During your participation in the Honors Undergraduate Research Scholars Program, you will present your research findings and results at the annual Celebrate Undergraduate Research and Creativity (CURC) Showcase held on the Colorado State University campus at the end of each spring semester."**

Study Abroad: Honors students are eligible for **honors enrichment awards**, which can be used for study abroad, internships, and volunteer projects in the U.S. and foreign countries. In recent years, honors students have won awards to work on environmental preservation and education projects in Catalina Island, CA; work with survivors of gender-based violence in Kenya; volunteer at the Best Friends Animal Society animal sanctuary in Kanab, Utah; participate in medical relief projects in India; volunteer with medical clinics in Guatemala; train at the Pasteur Institute in Paris; and intern with a U.S. Senator's office in Washington, DC.

Other awards have been used for course credit in Costa Rica, Australia, The Netherlands, Spain, Czech Republic, Japan, Great Britain, Italy, Chile, Hungary, and a Semester at Sea.

Financial Aid: "National Merit Finalists who list CSU as their first-choice institution with National Merit Corporation, National Hispanic Scholars, and National Achievement Scholars will automatically receive the **Presidential Scholarship.** This scholarship provides a $9,000 annual reward for the first year, renewable for six more semesters. **Students who score 1300 or better on the SAT (29 ACT) and have a high school GPA of at least 3.80 are also eligible for the Presidential Scholarship.**

Other merit scholarships include the **Provost's Scholarship,** valued at $7,000 a year. This award requires an SAT of at least 1230 (ACT 27) and a high school GPA of 3.60-3.79. The **Dean's Scholarship** requires an SAT of 1150 (ACT 25) and a high school GPA of at least 3.4. The value is $5,000 a year.

Degree of Difference (Honors students/non-honors students): 3.93 on a scale of 5. Some parents and prospective students might prefer an honors program that in many ways stands apart on campus, while others might prefer a program that is more expansive. The rating here tries to provide an indication of where a given honors program is on the stand apart/expansive spectrum. The rating is based on the difference between (1) the average SAT scores for enrolled honors students and (2) the average test scores for all students in the university as a whole *and* for students with scores at the 75% level or above. A score of 3.5 or higher indicates a high degree of difference. A score of 3.2 to 3.49 indicates a relatively high degree of difference. Finally, a score below 3.2 indicates a modest difference. **Please keep in mind that neither the high nor low selectivity of an honors program determines how effective the program is; this rating is merely "cultural" and *not* qualitative.**

NAME: UNIVERSITY OF CONNECTICUT HONORS PROGRAM

Date Established: 1964

Location: Storrs, Connecticut

University Full-time Undergraduate Enrollment: 26,021

Honors Enrollment: Approximately 1,853 (mean size of all 50 programs is 1,714)

Review/Admissions Category--III: Programs with average SAT scores of 1383--1416 for enrolled students. The mean average SAT score is 1414, and the mean ACT score is 32; the average high school graduation percentile is 96%.

Minimum Admission Requirements: "Admission to UConn Honors is based on a holistic review of applicants' academic and extracurricular records. While SAT and/or ACT scores, high school GPA, and class rank are considered as part of that competitive review, there are no minimum requirements."

Honors Programs in Admissions Category III (average SAT scores of 1383--1416): Connecticut, Indiana, Kentucky, Miami University, Oklahoma, Penn State, Tennessee, Texas A&M, UC Irvine, and Washington.

Administrative Staff: The Honors Program has a staff of 11.5 full-time equivalent employees, along with support from an additional 17 employees in the university's Enrichment Programs unit.

FOR ALL "MORTARBOARD" RATINGS BELOW, A SCORE OF 5 IS THE MAXIMUM AND REPRESENTS A COMPARISON WITH ALL 50 HONORS COLLEGES AND PROGRAMS:

PERCEPTION* OF UNIVERSITY AS A WHOLE, <u>NOT</u> OF HONORS: 🎓🎓🎓🎓

OVERALL HONORS RATING: 🎓🎓🎓🎓

Curriculum Requirements: 🎓🎓🎓🎓

Class Range and Type: 🎓🎓🎓🎓 1/2

Class Size: 🎓🎓🎓🎓

Adjusted Grad Rate: 🎓🎓🎓🎓

Ratio of Staff to Students: 🎓🎓🎓🎓

Priority Registration: Yes, honors students have priority registration for **all** courses, in the form of being able to register with the class ahead of them.

Honors Housing: 🎓🎓🎓¹ᐟ²

Prestigious Awards: 🎓🎓🎓

*Perception is based on the university's ranking among public universities in the 2014 U.S. News Best Colleges report. Please bear in mind that the better the U.S. News ranking, the more difficult it is for an honors college or program to have a rating that equals or improves on the magazine ranking.

Curriculum Requirements (4.0): UConn Honors has two completion awards--Sophomore Honors and Honors Scholar.

Sophomore Honors requires 16-18 credit hours within the student's first two years, the higher number being required for honors students who do not take a 1-credit First Year Experience Seminar.

Of the required hours, at least three honors credits must be earned in an Honors Core course. Students must also attend an honors thesis/research preparation workshop; attend at least five honors events and submit journal information on time; have a cumulative GPA of 3.40 or higher; and earn a grade of B- or better in any honors course or honors conversion (contract) to receive honors credit.

Graduation as an **Honors Scholar** requires completion of 12 credits at the 2000 level or above in departmental honors coursework, research, and thesis, plus an additional 3 credits that may be in any department at any level. At least three of these 15 credits must be in an honors or graduate course (not conversion, independent study, or thesis). Honors credit is only awarded when students earn a B- or better in an honors course or an honors conversion. Students must have earned a cumulative GPA of at least 3.40.

Up to 3 credits may apply to both Sophomore Honors and Honors Scholar completion, so the **minimum** number of honors course credits needed to earn both awards would be 28, including the **required honors thesis.**

AP/IB advanced placement credits cannot be used to replace required honors courses.

Range and Type of Honors Courses (4.5): We classify UConn Honors as a **blended program,** with an excellent selection of honors core seminars and perhaps an even stronger group of more specialized classes in the academic disciplines.

As for the core seminars, here are some of our favorites from Spring 2014: Literature and Civilization of the Jewish People; Nanoscience and Society; **Game Theory with Applications to the Natural and Social Sciences;** Gender and Science; **Economics, Nature, and the Environment;** Privacy in the Information Age; Global Environmental Politics; and **Anthropology through Film.**

About **Game Theory:** "Introduction to game theory examines applications in the natural and social sciences and technology, which may include electric power auctions, evolutionary biology, and elections. The course is an opportunity for students to begin to think strategically about many types of problems found in science, social settings, and even university life."

And **Anthropology through Film:** "This course introduces cultural anthropology through the medium of film. By studying and comparing the diverse experiences and viewpoints of people around the world, cultural anthropologists seek to explain why people in other societies hold beliefs and behave in ways that differ from our own. Cross-cultural comparisons also provide a fresh vantage point for studying our own society, making it possible to gain awareness of ideas and practices so basic to our personal experiences that they often seem natural."

Among the many exceptional features of the **departmental honors courses,** the number and range of **math sections** is remarkable: six sections of honors calculus, at different levels; and one each in differential equations, financial mathematics, and probability/stats. Even more surprising, in comparison with most honors programs, is that there are seven honors sections in the Foundations of **Engineering** *and* five more in electrical and computer engineering. Two sections in biology, two in molecular biology, four in biomaterials; four in general chemistry, another in organic chemistry, and two in chemical engineering round out an impressive sequence in the STEM fields. In view of all this, the presence of only one honors physics section seems minor.

The social sciences and humanities are also well-represented. There are six honors economics sections, two of them core seminars, and five anthropology sections, including one core class. The nine English sections of Literary Studies through Reading and Research sound especially rigorous, with their heavy emphasis on close readings of texts and an "emphasis on academic writing." History has only two sections—Modern Western Traditions and Gender and Sexuality in Modern Europe. (Of course, historical themes are very much present in many honors core classes.) The number of honors political science and psychology courses, popular not only for majors but also as electives, is much higher than average for the 50 programs under review.

Average Class Size (4.0): The average UConn Honors class has **22.4 students,** almost exactly the average size of 21.2 for all 50 programs under review.

Adjusted Graduation Rate (4.0): The AGR is not simply the six-year graduation rate of students in the program who graduated from the university **(92%),** whether or not the students completed the honors program ("honors completers"). The AGR also reflects the extent to which the honors graduation rate from the university is higher than that for the university as a whole. The **university-wide rate is 80%,** yielding a high AGR of 4.0. The average six-year **honors graduation rate for all 50 programs** under review **is 89%.**

Ratio of Staff to Honors Students (4.0): Our estimate is that there is 1 staff member for every **161.1** students. (Mean ratio for all 50 programs is 1 staff member for every 159.8 students.)

Honors Residence Halls (3.5): The UConn Honors staff has good news for the future: **"A new Honors residence hall is planned for fall 2017.** This new building will house the growing Honors freshman class and contain the Honors Program offices, additional academic and community spaces, and a dining hall."

This is an important and positive development for UConn Honors because **the university "has among the highest percentage of students living on campus of any public university in the nation.** Almost all Honors freshmen live in the Honors First Year Honors Residential Community in the Buckley-Shippee Complex, which also contains the Honors Programming and Events Office. After the first year, many (43%) Honors students choose to remain in Honors housing and participate in events and community activities at the other three halls. We have expanded our upper-class Honors housing options to respond to this demand."

The Honors First Year Community at **Buckley Hall** houses 451 honors students in traditional double rooms with hall baths. Buckley is not air conditioned (homes and business in the area do not require air conditioning during the Fall, Winter, and Spring, either) but it does have on-site dining and laundry facilities.

In response to demand, an honors community at **Shippee Hall**, immediately adjacent to Buckley Hall, was added in Fall 2014; it serves at least 50 additional honors students in rooms similar to those at Buckley Hall.

For **upperclassmen**, there are honors communities in **Brock Hall, Wilson Hall, and Connecticut Commons.** Brock offers corridor-style double rooms with hall baths for 150 honors students, while Wilson and Connecticut Commons offer suite-style rooms for another 142 and 341 students, respectively.

Prestigious Awards (3.0): As we have noted in our profile of another strong honors program (the Commonwealth Honors College of the University of Massachusetts), it is extremely difficult to get much traction in winning prestigious awards--Rhodes, Marshall, Goldwater, etc.--when your immediate neighborhood is home to some of the most elite private colleges and universities in the nation, if not the entire world. There are strong signs of change, however.

"Since 2005," the honors staff reports, "UConn Honors students have received two Marshall scholarships, twelve Goldwater scholarships, four Udall scholarships, and two Truman scholarships. During the same period, we have also had ten Goldwater honorable mentions, five Truman finalists, three Marshall finalists, one Rhodes finalist, one Mitchell finalist, one Gates Cambridge finalist, one Carnegie Junior Fellow finalist and one Udall honorable mention **who were Honors students."**

Continuation Requirements: 3.40 cumulative GPA

Academic Strengths: The average department at UConn ranks among the top 65-70 in the nation, among all universities public or private. Leading departments are education, business, psychology, sociology, English, history, and engineering--all ranked 65th or better in the nation.

Undergraduate Research: "Undergraduate research is a key aspect of UConn Honors, as all Honors graduates must complete an independent thesis project," according to honors staff. "The Honors Program works closely with the Office of Undergraduate Research (OUR), also part of Enrichment Programs, to develop our students' skills and opportunities in research, scholarship, and creative activity. OUR sponsors regular workshops, information sessions, seminars, and exhibitions of student work in order to engage the UConn community as a whole in conversations about undergraduate research.

"They also provide several funding opportunities for student research, scholarship, and creative work, including the innovative UConn IDEA Grant program that supports student-designed projects of all kinds, such as artistic endeavors, community service initiatives, entrepreneurial ventures, and research projects. **During the 2012-2013 academic year, OUR distributed over $330,000 to support undergraduate researchers.**

"Honors students are encouraged to plan their undergraduate research careers early, starting with a thesis workshop within their first two years. In addition to the resources and opportunities offered to all undergraduate researchers through OUR, Honors students may participate in programs like the **Life Sciences Honors Thesis Award or Holster Scholars.** The Life Sciences Honors Thesis Award helps defray the cost of laboratory supplies or other consumables used in thesis research in those fields; **in 2013, over $21,000 was awarded to support 28 Honors scholars.**

"Inspired by Robert Holster's own experiences as a member of the inaugural class of UConn Honors, the Holster First Year Project supports a small number of motivated Honors students in independent study projects during the summer following their first year. This program, along with research courses, internships, and opportunities in a variety of departments, exemplifies how undergraduate research and scholarship should be a developmental process throughout an Honors student's career, not simply a checkbox on a form."

Study Abroad: Again, here is a summary from honors staff: "Through its Office of Study Abroad, UConn offers over 300 programs for students seeking international experiences to enrich their education. Some of these are especially geared toward Honors students and earn Honors credit, including exchanges with University College Maastricht and University College Utrecht, both in the Netherlands, and National University of Singapore, as well as UConn faculty-led experiences in South Africa, Spain, Guatemala, and Armenia. UConn plans to join the Principia Consortium, which will offer our students an international Honors experience at the University of Glasgow.

"Honors students may also earn Honors credits through course conversion contracts while studying abroad. The contract may be between the student and the instructor at the international institution or between the student and a faculty advisor in the relevant UConn department. This allows Honors students to participate in any UConn Study Abroad experience--including over 20 exchanges through the Universitas 21 network of international research universities--without interrupting their Honors plans of study."

Financial Aid: According to UConn Honors, **96% of Honors first-year students at UConn receive at least one renewable merit scholarship.** These scholarships are administered through the Office of Undergraduate Admissions.

A few scholarship programs are specifically connected to the Honors Program, including automatic Honors admission for award winners. The Stamps Scholars Award connects recipients to a national network through the Stamps Family Charitable Foundation; the John and Valerie Rowe Health Professions Scholars Program provides opportunities to students from backgrounds underrepresented in the health fields; and the new STEM Scholars Award is a recent addition.

Degree of Difference (Honors students/non-honors students): 3.05 on a scale of 5. Some parents and prospective students might prefer an honors program that in many ways stands apart on campus, while others might prefer a program that is more expansive. The rating here tries to provide an indication of where a given honors program is on the stand apart/expansive spectrum. The rating is based on the difference between (1) the average SAT scores for enrolled honors students and (2) the average test scores for all students in the university as a whole *and* for students with scores at the 75% level or above. A score of 3.5 or higher indicates a high degree of difference. A score of 3.2 to 3.49 indicates a relatively high degree of difference. Finally, a score below 3.2 indicates a modest difference. **Please keep in mind that neither the high nor low selectivity of an honors program determines how effective the program is; this rating is merely "cultural" and *not* qualitative.**

NAME: UNIVERSITY OF DELAWARE HONORS PROGRAM

Date Established: 1976

Location: Newark, Delaware

University Full-time Undergraduate Enrollment: 15,899

Honors Enrollment: 1,568 (mean size of all 50 programs is 1,714)

Review/Admissions Category--II: Programs with **average SAT scores of 1343--1382 for enrolled students**. Actual average (mean) SAT three-part score for enrolled honors students is 2056, and the average ACT is 31 (high end of Category II). The average high school GPA is 4.05, top 5% of high school class.

Minimum Admission Requirements: "All admission decisions for the Honors Program are made by the undergraduate admissions office. Although there are no minimum test scores of GPA requirements, students must have a highly competitive profile. Students must specify their interest in applying to Honors and must submit an additional essay. SAT Subject Tests are strongly recommended."

"All averages and means are for the Fall 2013 admitted class. Admission decisions are made holistically, **placing the greatest importance on the academic curriculum and rigor of course selection, especially through the senior year. Emphasis is also placed on grades in core courses.** In addition to a careful review of the high school transcript and provided test scores, an assessment of all essays, letters of recommendation and extracurricular involvements is made."

Honors Programs in Admissions Category II (average SAT scores of 1343-1382): Alabama, Delaware, Florida State, LSU, Massachusetts, Missouri, North Carolina State, Ohio University, Temple, Purdue, UCLA, Utah, Vermont, and Wisconsin.

Administrative Staff: The Honors Program has a staff of 11.

FOR ALL "MORTARBOARD" RATINGS BELOW, A SCORE OF 5 IS THE MAXIMUM AND REPRESENTS A COMPARISON WITH ALL 50 HONORS COLLEGES AND PROGRAMS:

PERCEPTION* OF UNIVERSITY AS A WHOLE, <u>NOT</u> OF HONORS: 🎓🎓🎓🎓

OVERALL HONORS RATING: 🎓🎓🎓🎓

Curriculum Requirements: 🎓🎓🎓🎓🎓

Class Range and Type: 🎓🎓🎓🎓¹ᐟ²

Class Size: 🎓🎓🎓

Adjusted Grad Rate: 🎓🎓🎓🎓

Ratio of Staff to Students: 🎓🎓🎓🎓

Priority Registration: Yes, honors students register for **all** courses, honors and otherwise, with the first group of students during **each** year they are in the program.

Honors Housing: 🎓🎓🎓🎓

Prestigious Awards: 🎓🎓🎓🎓

*Perception is based on the university's ranking among public universities in the 2014 U.S. News Best Colleges report. Please bear in mind that the better the U.S. News ranking, the more difficult it is for an honors college or program to have a rating that equals or improves on the magazine ranking.

Curriculum Requirements (5.0): "All Honors students begin their Honors curriculum with a 3-credit Honors Colloquium and an Honors English Composition course in the first year. The Honors Colloquia are interdisciplinary courses offered in a wide variety of topics in the humanities, social science and sciences. Most other Honors courses are offered through departments. In addition to satisfying Honors Degree requirements, these courses can be used to fulfill University breadth and general education requirements as well as major specific requirements within a student's degree program." UD honors students can pursue one of four levels of completion:

Honors Degree with Distinction—Completion at this highest level "requires a 3.4 GPA and 30 total Honors credits, including coursework in the major and in Honors at the upper-level as well as an Honors capstone. The capstone requirement can be satisfied by taking a more specialized Honors capstone offered through the major department or by taking an interdisciplinary Honors Senior Seminar. **Students who earn the Honors Degree with Distinction complete the requirements for the Honors Degree as well as a 6 credit Honors senior thesis.**

Honors Degree—Completion is the same as for the Honors Degree with Distinction, 30 honors credits, except that the 6-credit **thesis is not required.**

General Honors Award—Completion does result in an honors degree, but an honors award granted after the sophomore year and completion of 18 honors credits, including the 3-credit colloquium and English honors composition course. To earn the General Honors Award, students must also participate in the Honors Freshman Living Learning Community. "Honors students typically complete 12 credits of Honors coursework in the first year, including a 3-credit Honors Colloquium and a 3-credit Honors freshman composition course. The General Honors Award requires an additional 6 credits of Honors in the 2nd year and a minimum GPA of 3.2 at the end of the 2nd year."

Honors Foreign Language Certificate--The UD honors program is **unique in awarding an honors certificate to students who complete 12 credit hours of honors foreign language** offered by the Department of Foreign Languages and Literatures.

AP and IB credits are **not** counted as replacements for honors courses.

Range and Type of Honors Courses (4.5): The honors program listed 217 honors sections in Spring 2014, but of these, perhaps two-thirds are honors "add-on" sections--classes large and small that have a mix of honors and non-honors students and require additional work for honors credit. Add-ons are similar to honors contract courses, but they are in fact more formalized and the instructors are familiar with and accustomed to developing and mentoring the work of honors students. As noted above, **UD Honors is almost exclusively a department-based honors program,** bearing some resemblance to Texas A&M Honors, which likewise has very few or no seminars. Such programs can be very effective and highly appropriate for students who want to hone in on their academic majors and preferred disciplines. The tradeoff, as noted elsewhere, is that in order to schedule so many honors sections in such a wide variety of disciplines, some of those mostly mixed sections will be large.

The sciences are well-represented, especially chemistry, one of the best departments at UD, along with chemical engineering. Classes in the former are small, and in the latter somewhat large, especially in systems and technical design. But the 10 English composition classes are only about 20 students each, and the excellent selection of history sections are about the same size. The many honors foreign language classes are also small, a bonus in these disciplines which are so often underrepresented in honors curricula. The required honors colloquia have only 24 or so students.

One of the major advantages of the UD approach is that there are numerous honors choices in the high-demand disciplines--chemistry (13 sections), economics (8 sections), psychology (5 sections), political science (3 sections), biology and physiology (4).

The range of honors courses, when add-ons are included, is remarkable, reaching to disciplines that are seldom or never listed with honors sections. Among these at UD are Latin, Greek, Japanese, chemical, mechanical, and electrical engineering, biomechanics, medical microbiology, and Chinese.

Average Class Size (3.0): Even though the average class size of **35.6** is high compared to most other programs under review, **61.5% of all honors classes, including add-ons, have fewer than 30 students per section. And the actual average class size of these 134 sections is only 18 students. In any given semester, probably fewer than 15% of honors students will find themselves in even one large honors-credit class.** The average honors class size is 21.2 among all 50 programs under review.

Adjusted Graduation Rate (4.0): The AGR is not simply the six-year graduation rate of students in the honors program who graduated from the university **(90%),** whether or not the students completed the honors program ("honors completers"). The AGR also reflects the extent to which the honors graduation rate from the university is higher than that for the university as a whole. The **university-wide rate is 80%,** yielding the 4.0 AGR for the college. The average six-year **honors graduation rate for all 50 programs** under review **is 89%.**

Ratio of Staff to Honors Students (4.0): Our estimate is that there is 1 staff member for every **142.6** students. (Mean ratio for all 50 programs is 1 staff member for every 159.8 students.)

Honors Residence Halls (4.0): UD Honors is exceptional in the number of residence halls that are assigned to honors students almost entirely or, in the case of upperclassmen, by floors. First-year honors students are expected to live on campus in the Louis L. Redding Residence Hall, except in the very rare cases when students from nearby communities commute to campus.

Redding Hall accommodates more than 400 first-year honors students. The rooms are traditional doubles with hall baths, all are air conditioned, and Russell Dining Hall is close at hand. Laundry facilities are on site. **Each floor has three study lounges.**

The Honors Director tells us that the "Freshman Honors living-learning community provides students the opportunity to study together, share their talents and interests, and participate in a variety of Honors co-curricular programs. **The first-year Honors experience is supported by Honors peer mentors (Munson Fellows) who guide students through their first year. The Munson Fellows are specially trained to assist with academic questions and registration**, and are event planners and community builders who give the Honors freshmen a complete living/learning experience."

Honors upperclassmen can choose to live in honors floors in one of five residence halls: Cannon, Brown, Harter, Sypherd, and Sharp. All five have traditional double rooms and hall baths; however, Cannon, Brown, and Harter are not air conditioned. Food service for all five upperclassmen residence halls (actually floors in each residence) is provided by Kent Dining Hall.

Prestigious Awards (4.0): The Honors Director tells us that UD "does not have a separate prestigious scholarships office. **Administration of the most prominent prestigious scholarships (Rhodes, Marshall, Mitchell, and Truman) is housed within the Honors Program**. The Honors Program Senior Associate Director is the official institutional representative for the Rhodes, Marshall, Mitchell, and Truman Scholarships. The Goldwater Scholarship is administered by the Office of Undergraduate Research, the Udall is administered by the Office of Service Learning, and the Fulbright is administered by the Institute for Global Studies.

"In fall of 2013 the University increased staffing support of prestigious scholarships through two new positions in the Honors Program-- an Assistant Director position and an Academic Program Coordinator position. The Assistant Director position has enabled the Honors Program to offer a 1 credit course entitled "Intellect and the Good Life" directed at students in the second year who are interested in pursuing prestigious scholarships."

UD students are well above the mean among students in the 50 universities whose honors programs we are reviewing when it comes to winning the prestigious and very important **Goldwater Scholarships (44 to date),** awarded to outstanding undergraduates pursuing STEM studies. UD students have also won 12 Rhodes Scholarships and a very **competitive number of Truman Scholarships—18 so far.**

Continuation Requirements: 3.40 cumulative GPA for Honors degrees; 3.20 for General Honors

Academic Strengths: The UD academic departments with the most national recognition among all universities public or private are education (37), engineering (53), chemistry (60), English (63), history (64), sociology (64), and psychology (67). **The undergraduate program in chemical engineering, however, is 10th in the nation among all universities, and the physical therapy program is ranked 2nd in the nation.**

Undergraduate Research: "Every UD college, department and research center provides opportunities for interested students to get their hands on the source of learning," according to the university's Undergraduate Research Program Office. "Approximately 1,000 students participate each year." As stated above, any UD student who graduates with an Honors Degree with Distinction must successfully complete a thesis, usually in the student's major field.

"Students interested in participating in research throughout the academic year generally go about doing so in two ways: as a volunteer or via and independent study. Many first-year students who are still adjusting to life on campus opt to begin their careers as researchers by volunteering for a faculty member: this type of research work allows for much greater flexibility with the work schedule and required time commitment." While students may not receive any official recognition for their initial work, **"volunteering at the start of a project can help you to get an idea of whether or not you are really interested in** a particular project, and you can then work more fully on it in the future."

Financial Aid: "All freshmen admitted to the University of Delaware's Honors Program are offered a merit scholarship," the Director says. "The merit awards range from $1,000 per year to a full scholarship that covers tuition, room, board and fees, and includes a book stipend and enrichment funds. **Merit Awards are offered irrespective of financial need. Awards for non-residents are larger than residents as a result of the tuition difference.** The University also sponsors the Distinguished Scholars program, which allows the strongest Honors applicants each year to compete for named awards. These awards range from full tuition to full funding for all expenses including a stipend for an enrichment activity.

"All admitted freshmen are also eligible for verified need-based aid. Students are eligible for federal funding, including the Pell grant, work study, and both subsided and unsubsidized loans. UD also has institutional aid and provides need-based grants to eligible Honors students. **"UD will meet the cost for all in-state Honors students up to the cost of the bill minus all federal aid including loans. Total loan costs for a resident will not exceed 25% of total cost of a degree."**

Several departments also have institutional aid available, which is distributed based on talent or academic interest. "Music scholarships require an audition."

Degree of Difference (Honors students/non-honors students): 2.89 on a scale of 5. Some parents and prospective students might prefer an honors program that in many ways stands apart on campus, while others might prefer a program that is more expansive. The rating here tries to provide an indication of where a given honors program is on the stand apart/expansive spectrum. The rating is based on the difference between (1) the average SAT scores for enrolled honors students and (2) the average test scores for all students in the university as a whole *and* for students with scores at the 75% level or above. A score of 3.5 or higher indicates a high degree of difference. A score of 3.2 to 3.49 indicates a relatively high degree of difference. Finally, a score below 3.2 indicates a modest difference. **Please keep in mind that neither the high nor low selectivity of an honors program determines how effective the program is; this rating is merely "cultural" and *not* qualitative.**

FLORIDA STATE UNIVERSITY

NAME: FLORIDA STATE UNIVERSITY HONORS PROGRAM

Date Established: We do not know. *This is an external review, meaning that we are reporting what we know about the program without having received information from the program staff.*

Location: Tallahassee, Florida

University Full-time Undergraduate Enrollment: 28,733

Honors Enrollment: *Estimated* 1,500-2,000 (mean size of all 50 programs is 1,714)

Review/Admissions Category--II: Programs with **average SAT scores of 1343--1382 for enrolled students**. *Estimated* average (mean) three-part SAT score for enrolled honors students is 2050, and the estimated average ACT is 31. The *estimated* average high school GPA is 4.3.

Minimum Admission Requirements: "The opportunity to join the Honors program is based on the evaluation of your entire record, including the strength of your academic curriculum, which was submitted to the University during the general admission process."

Honors Programs in Admissions Category II (average SAT scores of 1343-1382): Alabama, Delaware, Florida State, LSU, Massachusetts, Missouri, North Carolina State, Ohio University, Temple, Purdue, UCLA, Utah, Vermont, and Wisconsin.

Administrative Staff: The Honors Program has a staff of 6.

FOR ALL "MORTARBOARD" RATINGS BELOW, A SCORE OF 5 IS THE MAXIMUM AND REPRESENTS A COMPARISON WITH ALL 50 HONORS COLLEGES AND PROGRAMS:

PERCEPTION* OF UNIVERSITY AS A WHOLE, NOT OF HONORS: 🎓🎓🎓$^{1/2}$

OVERALL HONORS RATING: 🎓🎓🎓$^{1/2}$

Curriculum Requirements: 🎓🎓🎓

Class Range and Type: 🎓🎓🎓🎓

Class Size: 🎓🎓🎓🎓

Adjusted Grad Rate: 🎓🎓🎓🎓

Ratio of Staff to Students: 🎓🎓🎓

Priority Registration: **Yes,** honors students have "the privilege of being able to register at the same time as seniors" in the university.

Honors Housing: 🎓🎓🎓🎓🎓

Prestigious Awards: 🎓🎓🎓¹ᐟ²

*Perception is based on the university's ranking among public universities in the 2014 U.S. News Best Colleges report. Please bear in mind that the better the U.S. News ranking, the more difficult it is for an honors college or program to have a rating that equals or improves on the magazine ranking.

Curriculum Requirements (3.0): The basic honors completion requirement at FSU is 18 credit hours in honors courses or an equivalent amount of credits including honors departmental research and thesis.

Of special interest to many prospective students are the programs for Honors Legal Scholars and Honors Medical Scholars, both designed for highly qualified honors students who want to earn **automatic admission to the FSU Law or an opportunity for a 7-year BS/MD degree sequence.**

"Honors Legal Scholars gain experience and knowledge through volunteer and educational activities as well as social gatherings. They are given pre-professional advising, meet with professors, observe classes, and shadow current students in the College of Law." Successful honors completion earns automatic law school admission at FSU.

Honors completion does not bring automatic admission into the College of Medicine, but "FSU Honors Medical Scholars who successfully complete the program and pre-medical requirements will be eligible to apply to the FSU College of Medicine through the early decision process. **The program allows eligible students to pursue a Bachelor of Science degree of their choice. In some cases it may be possible to finish the undergraduate and M.D. degrees in seven years depending on college credits earned before enrollment at FSU."**

Here are the two basic options for honors completion:

Honors Finisher: "Students must earn eighteen honors points, which are usually honors credits earned through coursework. These eighteen honors points must include a minimum of nine semester hours of honors coursework (honors sections of regular courses, honors seminars, the honors colloquium, honors-augmented courses). The remainder of the eighteen honors points can be earned through any combination of further honors coursework including honors Directed Individual Study (DIS), graduate classes, or Honors in the Major work (also known as honors thesis)."

Honors in the Major: "Students who finish the Honors in the Major program must complete six or more credits hours of honors thesis work and successfully defend their thesis. A student who finishes eighteen credit hours of honors coursework that **includes** completion of the Honors in the Major (nine to twelve hours coursework plus six to nine hours of thesis) is given special recognition at the awards ceremony and has both distinctions described here noted on their transcripts."

AP and IB credits: We did not receive this information, nor could we find it in our searches.

Range and Type of Honors Courses (4.0): FSU Honors is a **blended program** that combines a significant number of interesting seminars with a good range of more specialized courses in the major academic disciplines.

We counted about 20 seminars for Spring 2014, including these favorites of ours: **Religion and Capitalism;** Music, History, and Culture in London; Defining Moments and Identities: From the Persian Wars to September 11; Human Nature and Philosophy; and Exploring Racial Inequality in the U.S.

Let's take a look at **Religion and Capitalism:** "As Adam Smith is often quoted on this point: 'It is not from the benevolence of the butcher, the brewer, or the baker that we expect our dinner, but from their regard to their own self-interest.' Of course, the issue is not quite as simple as all that. For example, both *financial credit* and its doppelganger, *financial debt,* fundamentally depend upon relationships of *trust* and *promise-keeping.* Indeed, there is a sense in which *money* itself is nothing but a *token of trust.* **This seminar will explore how the manifold tensions between trust and self-interest have been negotiated throughout American history."**

About **Human Nature and Philosophy:** "This is a course on competing philosophical views about human nature. The 'persistent issue' it addresses is also a contemporary issue, because it is the single most fundamental issue any of us face: How should I live? What shape does a properly led life take? Socrates recommended a particular approach to this question, and philosophers have been pursuing it ever since. The course is designed, in part, to familiarize you with some of the central issues and figures in philosophy through the study of one of Western philosophy's most active and important periods, i.e., the 'modern' (sometimes, "early modern") period (roughly 1600 -1800 AD)."

As for **departmental honors courses,** they are not necessarily plentiful, but they do cover most of the bases with the exception of political science, a discipline for which we found no honors sections in Spring 2014. English and history each had three 3-credit sections, and there were two 1-credit courses in the humanities. Psychology and religious studies each had two honors sections. The three honors math sections were in advanced calculus. The sciences were present in the form of one section of biology, five in chemistry (including organic chemistry), and one in physics. There were four sections of economics, better than average for this popular subject. Honor students could also select one of three communications courses in public speaking.

Average Class Size (4.0): All we could do was *estimate* the average honors class size: **20 students per section.** (This could be as many as 25 per section, however.) The average class size is 21.2 among all 50 programs under review.

Adjusted Graduation Rate (4.0): The AGR is not simply the six-year graduation rate of students in the honors program who graduated from the university **(*estimated at* 89.3%),** whether or not the students completed the honors program ("honors completers"). The AGR also reflects the extent to which the honors graduation rate from the university is higher than that for the university as a whole. The **university-wide rate is 75%,** yielding the 4.0 AGR for the program. The average six-year **honors graduation rate for all 50 programs** under review **is 89%.**

Ratio of Staff to Honors Students (3.0): Our estimate is that there is 1 staff member for every **258.5** students. (Mean ratio for all 50 programs is 1 staff member for every 159.8 students.)

Honors Residence Halls (5.0): Honors students may live in Landis Hall or Gilchrist Hall, both featuring suite-style double rooms with a connecting bath. The halls are coed but gender-separated by suite. Both residences are air conditioned. Laundry is on site. **All residents must purchase one of the Seminole Dining meal plans.** There are several options and a wide variety of campus dining venues to choose from, some national chains and others local.

Prestigious Awards: (3.5) For the last three years, FSU has been recognized as a leader producer of Fulbright Student Scholars, a highly-competitive award to outstanding students selected to study or teach abroad. By our count, FSU students have won 24 Fulbright Scholarships during that period. FSU undergraduates have also won 20 Goldwater Scholarships, and university graduates have won 5 Rhodes Scholarships and an equal number of Truman Scholarships.

Continuation Requirements: 3.20 cumulative GPA

Academic Strengths: FSU has a highly respected faculty, with four departments ranking in the top 50 among all universities public or private. These include sociology (39), political science (40), education (44), and physics (48). Other especially strong departments at FSU are chemistry, psychology, and economics.

Undergraduate Research: "The *Undergraduate Research Opportunity Program* (UROP) offers a rare opportunity for you to partner with our excellent faculty as research assistants. Students in UROP work closely with faculty and peers, receive mentorship and training in the UROP Colloquium class, and present their contributions in the Spring Research Symposium. UROP aims to enhance the academic culture of our student body, helping them to achieve their academic, personal, and career goals, and better contribute to the world."

First- and second-year undergraduates can qualify for the two-semester program, regardless of major. Only about 250 students are accepted to the highly competitive program.

Study Abroad: FSU ranks 20th among all major universities in the number of students who study abroad.

The university offers Global Scholars Travel Award stipends on a need basis, assisting students in participating in FSU's Global Scholars program "who may not otherwise be able to take part due to financial obstacles."

Recipients will receive a stipend of up to $2,000 (up to $3,250 in some cases) to cover expenses associated with participating in FSU's Global Scholars Program. "Funds may be used for general program costs, living expenses, and/or travel."

Financial Aid: The university is making a concerted effort to recruit some of the most outstanding first-year students in the nation. The Presidential Scholars Honors Program serves the top 25 students enrolled in the FSU Honors Program.

"We are very excited about launching this new scholarship program," said Dean of Undergraduate Studies Karen Laughlin. "It invests in undergraduate students who have extraordinary potential to be the transformational leaders of their generation and makes a clear statement about the university's commitment to recruiting and supporting students who are critical and innovative thinkers."

Presidential Scholars must attend group meetings in the Honors, Scholars, and Fellows house "in which they will build connections and provide peer mentorship and review." The scholars receive a $4,800 scholarship per year, or waived out-of-state tuition for non-Floridians. Scholars may also receive additional funding valued up to $12,500 for activities "that will enrich their experience at Florida State," such as research, study abroad, or service-based programs and internships.

The university also offers the following merit awards:

University Freshman Scholarship

- A $9,600 scholarship distributed over four years. Recipients are selected from the best freshman students admitted to the University based upon high school grades and test scores.

Tuition Reduction Scholarships:

- **Full Out-of-State Tuition Waiver**
  Awarded to a limited number of non-Florida freshmen based on academic merit. The total amount of this award is a 100% reduction (waiver) of the out-of-state portion of tuition (approximately $14,444 based on 30 semester hours for the academic year). The waiver amount is only applied toward tuition and does not include other fees, nor does it apply toward study-abroad programs.

- **Partial Out-of-State Tuition Waiver**
  Awarded to a limited number of non-Florida freshmen based on academic merit or special talent. The total amount of this award is a 50% reduction (waiver) of the out-of-state portion of tuition (approximately $7,222 based on 30 semester hours for the academic year). The waiver amount is only applied toward tuition and does not include other fees, nor does it apply toward study-abroad programs.

Degree of Difference (Honors students/non-honors students): 2.86 on a scale of 5. Some parents and prospective students might prefer an honors program that in many ways stands apart on campus, while others might prefer a program that is more expansive. The rating here tries to provide an indication of where a given honors program is on the stand apart/expansive spectrum. The rating is based on the difference between (1) the average SAT scores for enrolled honors students and (2) the average test scores for all students in the university as a whole *and* for students with scores at the 75% level or above. A score of 3.5 or higher indicates a high degree of difference. A score of 3.2 to 3.49 indicates a relatively high degree of difference. Finally, a score below 3.2 indicates a modest difference. **Please keep in mind that neither the high nor low selectivity of an honors program determines how effective the program is; this rating is merely "cultural" and *not* qualitative.**

NAME: UNIVERSITY OF GEORGIA HONORS PROGRAM

Date Established: 1960

Location: Athens, Georgia

University Full-time Undergraduate Enrollment: 24,514

Honors Enrollment: 2,250 (mean size of all 50 programs is 1,714)

Review/Admissions Category IV: Programs with **average SAT scores of 1417 or higher for enrolled students**. The **average** (mean) SAT score for enrolled Georgia honors students is 1462, and the ACT average is 32.7, **among the highest of all programs under review**. The average high school GPA is 4.07.

Minimum Admission Requirements: SAT 1400, ACT 31.

Honors Programs in Admissions Category IV (average SAT of 1417 and higher): Auburn, Clemson, Georgia, Illinois, Kansas, Michigan, Minnesota, North Carolina, Rutgers, South Carolina, UT Austin, Virginia.

Administrative Staff: The Honors Program has a staff of 20.

FOR ALL "MORTARBOARD" RATINGS BELOW, A SCORE OF 5 IS THE MAXIMUM AND REPRESENTS A COMPARISON WITH ALL 50 HONORS COLLEGES AND PROGRAMS:

PERCEPTION* OF UNIVERSITY AS A WHOLE, NOT OF HONORS: 🎓🎓🎓🎓 1/2

OVERALL HONORS RATING: 🎓🎓🎓🎓 1/2

Curriculum Requirements: 🎓🎓🎓🎓 1/2

Class Range and Type: 🎓🎓🎓🎓 1/2

Class Size: 🎓🎓🎓 1/2

Adjusted Grad Rate: 🎓🎓🎓🎓

Ratio of Staff to Students: 🎓🎓🎓🎓 1/2

Priority Registration: Yes, honors students register for **all** courses, honors and otherwise, with the first group of students during **each** year they are in the program.

Honors Housing: 🎓🎓🎓🎓

Prestigious Awards: 🎓🎓🎓🎓[1/2]

*Perception is based on the university's ranking among public universities in the 2014 U.S. News Best Colleges report. Please bear in mind that the better the U.S. News ranking, the more difficult it is for an honors college or program to have a rating that equals or improves on the magazine ranking.

Curriculum Requirements (4.5): The Georgia Honors Program has three completion options, all of which require nine honors courses but differing thesis and GPA requirements:

Graduation with **Honors**--The nine courses must have 3-4 credits, except that three 1-credit seminars may count for one of the nine courses. The three 1-hour classes are the only honors courses that can be taken for a Satisfactory/Unsatisfactory grade. At least three of the nine courses must be upper-division or graduate level and may include thesis, independent research, or internship courses, but a thesis is not required for this option. **Graduation requires a cumulative GPA of 3.4 and an honors GPA of 3.3.**

Graduation with **High Honors**--Again, nine courses are required, but in addition, students must complete 3-4 credit hours in undergraduate research and another 3-4 credit hours by writing a thesis or finishing an internship of equivalent credit. For this option, **graduation requires a cumulative GPA of 3.7 and an honors GPA of 3.5.**

Graduation with **Highest Honors**--The most rigorous option, graduation with highest honors carries the same course requirements as graduation with high honors, except **the cumulative GPA must be at least 3.9 with an honors GPA of 3.5.**

AP/IB credits are **not** counted as replacements for honors courses.

Range and Type of Honors Courses (4.5): The Georgia Honors Program is an outstanding example of a **department-based honors program**, although in Spring 2014 there were 11 Introduction to Honors 1-credit seminars along with 25-30 departmental honors seminars, also 1-credit courses.

According to the Director, the Introduction to Honors courses provide a "key aspect of peer mentoring...facilitated by a team of peer Honors Teaching Assistants (HTAs), who are supervised directly by the Honors Director. This course is one important component of a multifold first-year experience, which also includes an Honors Program Convocation. The...course serves as an introduction to the Honors Program and is required of all Honors students during their first semester [and] introduces students to campus life by surveying university and Honors philosophy, expectations, policies, and procedures. It explores the range of events and services offered on campus and through the Honors Program, including study abroad and internship support, as well as scholarships and undergraduate research opportunities."

One of the ways honors students can earn course credit is through **honors options, or "honors contract" courses.** This option, as we have noted elsewhere, can be an important one if it provides honors credit for a non-honors course section that is necessary for the individual's major or for exploration of some area that lacks honors sections. **What we especially like about the Georgia approach to honors options is that the honors "contracts" are limited to three,** and each must be in an upper-division course, thereby preventing the overuse of contracts while ensuring that they are advanced. The honors program offers an impressive range of departmental classes, although we did not find in Spring 2014 an honors section in physics. Yet there is an abundance of classes to choose from. From statistics to music, philosophy (four sections) to accounting (eight sections), the range is impressive. Four in economics, six in English composition, two literature survey courses, four in history, five in psychology. Both geography and geology, both seldom present in honors programs. Only two math sections in Spring 2014, and two more in chemistry. Also present are four sections of Spanish and one of French--and honors language classes are rare. Business classes are more in evidence as well: four in marketing, three in finance, and four more in management.

Average Class Size (3.5): The average honors class size at UGA is about 27.6 students, with several really large class sections, including the aforementioned business-related classes, accounting among them. Some of these are well over 100 students total--but all of them have honors breakout sections that meet for one or two hours a week in addition to the large lectures. Once again we say it: the advantage of department-based honors programs is that they almost always have a large number of honors classes (or at least classes with both honors and non-honors students that can be taken for honors credit), but more likely than not, these department-based programs are also more likely to have, on average, larger class sizes and fewer all-honors seminars and interdisciplinary classes. The Georgia honors program is similar to the Texas A&M program in this respect, although the range of honors courses at UGA includes many more sections in the humanities. Both are mostly all about the academic disciplines and the mastery thereof.

But on a percentage basis, 76% of the 122 classes offered by Georgia honors in Spring 2014 had an average enrollment of only 15.5 students. So while class size is important…it is probably not all that important if around three-quarters of the honors classes are small, as well as being made up solely of honors students. (A similar situation prevails in many other programs that have several really large mixed sections.) The average class size among all 50 programs in the review is 21.2 students.

Adjusted Graduation Rate (4.0): The AGR is not simply the six-year graduation rate of students in the honors college who graduated from the university **(estimated at 91.5%),** whether or not the students completed the honors program ("honors completers"). The AGR also reflects the extent to which the honors graduation rate from the university is higher than that for the university as a whole. (The **university-wide rate is 82%,** yielding the 4.0 AGR for the college.) The average **honors** six-year **graduation rate for all 50 programs** under review **is 89%.**

Ratio of Staff to Honors Students (4.5): Our estimate is that there is 1 staff member for every **112.5** students. (Mean ratio for all 50 programs is 1 staff member for every 159.8 students.)

Honors Residence Halls (4.0): "Myers Hall serves as the Honors magnet residence hall at UGA. This beautifully renovated hall is home to 250 first-year Honors students, affording them the opportunity to live and study in a learning community of like-minded peers. An Honors satellite academic advising office is also conveniently located in Myers Hall.

"The Honors Program as a whole is housed in the historic Moore College building, which serves as the administrative and cultural home of the Honors Program."

Myers has 85% corridor rooms and hall baths, along with 15% suite-style rooms with connecting baths. The residence hall is air-conditioned, has on-site laundry **on every floor**, and is notable for **having a kitchen area on each floor.** The Myers location is excellent—and the dining options are remarkable. Snelling and Oglethorpe are convenient, yes, but here's the best news: "UGA Food Services has participated in the Loyal E. Horton Dining Awards program (the gold standard for national recognition in this area) for 25 years, receiving a national record of 68 Horton awards since 1987."

Prestigious Awards (4.5): UGA is a national leader in winning prestigious undergraduate awards (both Udall and Goldwater Scholarships), especially in recent years. Even more important for our readers is the fact that Georgia honors students are frequently among the winners--almost certainly in greater proportion than in almost any other program. Surely much of the success in winning 47 Goldwater Scholarships is attributable to the university's Center for Undergraduate Research Opportunities (CURO), which is closely affiliated with the honors program (see below). The Director tells us that "in the past 20 years **all of the UGA recipients of the scholarships [that the editor tracks], excluding the Fulbright Student awards, were Honors students, save one Udall recipient.** Honors students do quite well with the Fulbright Student scholarship, but we also have some non-Honors recipients, as well as graduate student recipients." UGA students are also well above the mean in winning Boren Scholarships for international study. In the postgraduate category, UGA students (almost all of them honors students) rank among the public university leaders in winning Rhodes (23), Gates Cambridge (6), Marshall (6), Truman (17), and Fulbright Scholarships.

Continuation Requirements: Cumulative 3.40 GPA (but see also the completion GPA requirements above).

Academic Strengths: UGA has at least five academic departments ranked in the top 50 nationally among all universities public or private led by the business school, ranked 27th. Others in the top 50 are education (43), biology and sociology (both 46), and political science (48). Ranked in the 50's are chemistry, English, history, math, and psychology.

Undergraduate Research: Here is what the Director has to say about the renowned research program for undergraduates:

"The Center for Undergraduate Research Opportunities (CURO) is an initiative that was launched in the late 1990s through a grant from the Fund for the Improvement of Postsecondary Education. It was institutionalized in 2000, housed in the Honors Program, following a commendation by the Southern Association of Colleges and Schools for its 'contributions to excellence in undergraduate education.' Though it is still administered by the Honors Program, CURO is now open to all undergraduates at UGA without regard to discipline, major, or GPA. Through CURO, students can begin undergraduate research as early as their first semester and can continue for up to four full years. CURO operates primarily through faculty-mentored research courses, but it also offers a range of other opportunities, including a summer research fellowship program; an annual undergraduate research symposium; an online student research journal; and a specialized undergraduate research scholarship to support students from underrepresented groups.

"CURO research courses are faculty-mentored and individualized syllabi are facilitated for each student. Students can become involved with an existing research project, or they can ask faculty mentors to oversee projects of their own design. Thus, students can choose their own research agenda to fit their own professional and academic goals, yet pursue it under faculty guidance.

"As a leading indicator of the positive impact that CURO has provided for these students, it is the case that **since the inception of CURO, every recipient from UGA of a Udall, NSF, or Goldwater scholarship has participated in CURO (as is the case as well with recipients of Rhodes, Marshall, Mitchell, and Gates Cambridge scholarships)."**

Study Abroad: "The Honors Program annually supplies travel-study funding to students holding one of two academic scholarships it administers--the Foundation Fellowship and Ramsey Honors Scholarship (see section IX below)--amounting to approximately $550,000 per year," the Director reports.

"In addition, the Honors Program annually awards stipends to support study abroad by additional Honors students through its Honors International Scholars Program (HISP). The majority of HISP awards are earmarked for travel to Asia, Latin America, and Africa. A number of awards, however, can be granted for travel elsewhere, especially to students traveling abroad for the first time or who demonstrate significant financial need. **In 2014, more than 60 Honors students will receive HISP support, totaling more than $220,000 (at an average award of $3,500 per student).**

"In sum, the Honors Program annually provides combined funding in excess of $770,000 to Honors students conducting travel-study. They have used this funding to participate in traditional university-sponsored study abroad programs; university-to-university exchanges; intensive language-training institutes; internships; and public service projects.

"UGA as a whole is well-recognized for its support of study abroad. The University of Georgia was ranked 15th among all U.S. institutions of higher education in the 2013 Open Doors report on the number of U.S. students studying abroad. UGA had 1,991 students (almost 14 percent of whom were Honors students—a total of 275 in all) who studied abroad for academic credit in the 2011-2012 academic year....The majority of UGA students participate in one or more of approximately 100 faculty-led programs around the world, including programs at **UGA's year-round residential centers in Oxford, England; Cortina, Italy; and in the Monteverde region of Costa Rica. (All first-year Foundation Fellows study at Oxford University and live in the UGA house there.)** Others enroll in semester or year-round exchanges at one of UGA's 50 exchange partners abroad or join external programs. In addition to traditional classroom-based programs, study abroad opportunities also include service-learning, lecture, fieldwork, internship, and laboratory experiences."

Financial Aid: The Honors Director: "Approximately 85% of UGA students are in-state and are eligible for the HOPE Scholarship (http://osfa.uga.edu/hope.html). A full 100% of in-state Honors students carry this scholarship (selection criteria ensure this). Many out-of-state Honors students carry other scholarships, such as the Charter Scholarship, awarded by the UGA Admissions Office.

"In addition to these broad scholarships, the Honors Program administers three internal scholarship programs: (1) the Foundation Fellowship (which approximates the full cost of attendance and supplies a generous set of enrichment funds to support study abroad, internships, undergraduate research, etc.), awarded to a total of about 90 Honors students; (2) the Ramsey Honors Scholarship (which offers approximately 75% of the financial support of the Foundation Fellowship), awarded to between 20 and 30 total Honors students; and (3) the CURO Honors Scholarship, which supplies a $2,000 annual stipend (on top of other awards) to 40 Honors students from underrepresented groups, who specialize in undergraduate research.

"In addition to these scholarships, there are several other funding opportunities for students through the Honors Program, including the HISP awards mentioned above, as well as Honors Internship programs in New York City, Washington, DC, and Savannah, GA (which supply stipends of $3,000 to $4,000); the Ash Service Award (a $3,000 stipend); and the Crane Leadership Scholarship (a $1,000 award).

"It should be noted that the majority of these funding opportunities are directly attributable to the fact that the Honors Program has its own, very active fundraising office."

Also very much worth noting is that UGA actually increased the number of National Merit Scholars in 2013 and maintained its level of university sponsorship, despite a national trend of declining university support of National Merit Scholars.

Degree of Difference (Honors students/non-honors students): 3.60 on a scale of 5. Some parents and prospective students might prefer an honors program that in many ways stands apart on campus, while others might prefer a program that is more expansive. The rating here tries to provide an indication of where a given honors program is on the stand apart/expansive spectrum. The rating is based on the difference between (1) the average SAT scores for enrolled honors students and (2) the average test scores for all students in the university as a whole *and* for students with scores at the 75% level or above. A score of 3.5 or higher indicates a high degree of difference. A score of 3.2 to 3.49 indicates a relatively high degree of difference. Finally, a score below 3.2 indicates a modest difference. **Please keep in mind that neither the high nor low selectivity of an honors program determines how effective the program is; this rating is merely "cultural" and *not* qualitative.**

NAME: CAMPUS HONORS PROGRAM, THE UNIVERSITY OF ILLINOIS URBANA-CHAMPAIGN

Date Established: 1986

Location: Urbana-Champaign, Illinois

University Full-time Undergraduate Enrollment: 31,118

Honors Enrollment: Approximately 500 (mean size of all 50 programs is 1,714)

Review/Admissions Category IV: Programs with average SAT scores of 1417 or higher for enrolled students. The CHP uses ACT scores, and the actual average **(median) ACT is very high, at 34.** This converts to an SAT score of approximately 1500. High school rank/GPA varies with the Academic Index (see below).

NOTE: Enrolled students in the CHP are referred to as Chancellor's Scholars. "There are also honors programs in every college (these individuals are referred to as 'James Scholars'), and in many departments. The James Scholar Programs range from a few dozen students (for example, the College of Media and the College of Fine and Applied Arts) up to the College of Engineering and College of Liberal Arts James Scholar Programs, which usually number more than 1,000." **Students *can* be Chancellor's Scholars and James Scholars if they are accepted by both programs.**

The **minimum** requirements require some explanation, and CHP staff provided excellent information for this and every other inquiry. "The Campus Honors Program has minimum ACT and **Academic Index** scores (AI, an assessment of high school grades combined with factors related to the high school) for each college....These change every year, and are adjusted on a college by college basis, to ensure that the broadest representation of student applications are received for review; **the CHP minimum is generally in the low-30's for ACT.**

"What is much harder to show is that our admissions criteria focus on a student's *desire* to do honors--which is much harder to encapsulate. In our admissions process, we look for genuine enthusiasm and a wide array of interests, as shown by the personal statement and activities (both breadth and depth, as well as leadership); we also do a limited reference check. Each application is pre-screened (a student application with a perfect ACT or SAT but with no activities does not move forward), and then each application is reviewed by multiple readers."

Honors Programs in Admissions Category IV (average SAT of 1417 and higher): Auburn, Clemson, Georgia, Illinois, Kansas, Michigan, Minnesota, North Carolina, Rutgers, South Carolina, UT Austin, Virginia.

Administrative Staff: The CHP has a staff of 4.5 full-time employees.

FOR ALL "MORTARBOARD" RATINGS BELOW, A SCORE OF 5 IS THE MAXIMUM AND REPRESENTS A COMPARISON WITH ALL 50 HONORS COLLEGES AND PROGRAMS:

PERCEPTION OF UNIVERSITY AS A WHOLE, **NOT** OF HONORS: 🎓🎓🎓🎓^1/2

OVERALL HONORS RATING: 🎓🎓🎓🎓**

Curriculum Requirements: 🎓🎓🎓^1/2

Class Range and Type: 🎓🎓🎓^1/2

Class Size: 🎓🎓🎓🎓^1/2

Adjusted Grad Rate: 🎓🎓🎓🎓^1/2

Ratio of Staff to Students: 🎓🎓🎓🎓^1/2

Priority Registration: Yes, Chancellor's Scholars register first (with students with disabilities and athletes), by order of number of hours previously earned.

Honors Housing: N/A

Prestigious Awards: 🎓🎓🎓🎓🎓

*Perception is based on the university's ranking among public universities in the 2014 U.S. News Best Colleges report. Please bear in mind that the better the U.S. News ranking, the more difficult it is for an honors college or program to have a rating that equals or improves on the magazine ranking.

The CHP would easily have an overall rating of 4.5 mortarboards if (1) it required more credit hours for program completion, and (2) it provided a designated residence hall for CHP students. **Some of the outstanding universities in the original Big Ten are notably reluctant to set their honors students apart from other students by way of offering too many forms of preferential treatment. UW Madison is the clearest example, but Minnesota and Michigan, even though both offer honors housing, do not offer priority registration. The same goes for Indiana's Hutton Honors College and Iowa honors. The CHP does offer priority registration, but has taken a firm position in the past about not providing separate honors housing out of respect for the overall quality of the UIUC student body. The highly selective UT Austin Plan II Honors Program and the even more selective SAS Program at Rutgers are two more that do not offer priority registration, probably for similar reasons. The result is that all of these fine programs take at least a small hit in our ratings because of the absence of one or more honors "perks," which are generally popular with parents and prospective students.

Curriculum Requirements (3.5): What is said above about the reluctance of honors programs to confer overt elite status on their students does not alter the fact that Chancellor's Scholars at UIUC are among the most elite students in the nation (based on test scores and other qualifications), and probably rank in the top 1% of students at UIUC. Given the option that these highly talented students can also participate in other honors programs that have their own requirements, and the rigorous demands of most UIUC majors, the basic completion requirements for CHP itself are designed to be modest.

"Required CHP coursework is concentrated in the freshman and sophomore years, when students take intensive and specialized versions of general education courses," according to the CHP Director. "At the junior and senior level, when students are necessarily involved in their majors, they are required to take one advanced CHP seminar. In short, our emphasis is on fundamental principles and interdisciplinary connections, because the CHP is directed at students who desire an undergraduate education that is broad and general as well as professionally specialized.

"It is as important to understand what CHP is not, as to understand what it is. CHP courses represent additional opportunities for academically gifted and adventurous students; they are not an alternative curriculum. **Basically, they provide an honors-quality way of satisfying general education requirements for graduation and of helping students to discover the interrelations between their own discipline and other disciplines.** Nor does CHP supplant or conflict with departmental honors programs. In consultation with their departmental academic advisors, Chancellor's Scholars develop their own combination of regular and CHP courses. **Accordingly, most of the courses our students take are regular University offerings."**

We estimate that CHP completion requires approximately 18-19 credit hours, including 12-13 in CHP seminars and another 3 credits in a capstone seminar.

AP/IB credits are **not** counted as replacements for CHP courses.

Range and Type of Honors Courses (3.5): As the new Director emphasizes, the CHP is mostly about the honors seminars the first year or two, and a few thereafter. Of these, our favorites are Approaches to Peace (political science); Children, Communication, and Language Issues (speech and hearing science); Probability and the Real World (math); **Books Matter, Book Matters (CHP);** World Food Economy; and **The Woman Reader in British Fiction.**

The CHP **Capstone Seminars** in Spring 2014 were The War to End all Wars: World War I, which, tragically, only led to the horrors of World War II and the Holocaust; and Bioethical Issues.

In **The War to End all Wars,** students examine "the origins, brutality, and legacy of the war and its political, cultural, and scientific consequences in an interdisciplinary fashion. **World War I changed the face of modern civilization by uprooting its certainties and augmenting its horrors.** The course will explore this break in fundamental expectation in three ways, (1) by exploring the cultural and political impact of World War I on the twentieth century; (2) by investigating the experience of the war in the years 1914-1918, from its origins to its unforeseen but deadly escalation into the most catastrophic event known until then in modern history; and (3) by analyzing the cultural artifacts by which contemporaries made sense of the cataclysm."

The **departmental honors seminars and classes** may be relatively few, including those that are not specifically CHP courses, but the math sections, especially, were excellent in Spring 2014, including one section of calculus II, two more in calculus III, two in abstract algebra, a class in advanced analysis, and **a math capstone class in analysis, algebra, and geometry that studies "matrix Lie groups from an algebraic, geometric and analytic viewpoint.** The course provides an elementary introduction to Lie groups at an advanced undergraduate level."

History offers two honors sections: a course in historiography and another in research and methodology, both pointing to departmental honors in history. Psychology also offers two sections, one in experimental methods and contemporary research, and the other a seminar that poses this question: **Is Humanity Doomed or Thriving?** We wanted to tell you the answer but could not find the course description. One economics class and one more political science class were offered in Spring 2014.

Biology at UIUC is actually two departments: **Integrative Biology (IB) and Molecular and Cell Biology (MCB).** Both have their own honors tracks that can offer many additional science courses for both James Scholars and Chancellor's Scholars. Here we should say that Chancellor's Scholars who find either of these honors concentrations appealing should probably become James Scholars as well, because the two concentrations specifically provide credit for James Scholars. **In some cases (see below), Chancellor's Scholars may need to complete the IB or MCB core classes as well as science classes required by the CHP.**

"Integrative" biology means "that the emphasis is on how different parts of biological systems interact with one another." Only 20 IB honors students are chosen out of each freshman class in the Spring semester to participate in the **IB Honors Concentration**, and they must have already earned at least a 3.0 GPA during the preceding Fall, including the completion of general chemistry. Classes are small. **Chancellor's Scholars, however, must complete both the IB core science courses *and* CHP required courses.** James Scholars are only required to take the IB core classes if they are in IB Honors.

"Each year, a new group of only about 15-20 IB Honors students is admitted, and they share the same IB Honors classes for the three semesters. Then there is the camaraderie. IB Honors students all have 24-hour access to the classroom and lab, and use this as a place to study together or just hang out. Of course, it is often the case the IB Honors students find themselves in the same Chemistry, Math or Physics classes, too."

MCB Honors students must have a 3.50 UIUC GPA for the Fall semester of the freshman year and submit a letter of recommendation from a professor or teaching assistant. They should have completed general chemistry **and** organic chemistry, or have concurrent enrollment in organic chemistry for the Spring semester. Credits are compatible with James Scholar required science classes but, again, Chancellor's Honors students will likely have to complete the CHP science requirements in addition to any others.

Students in either IB or MCB honors concentrations "do have to double up on some science and math courses. Since as an IB (or MCB) major you must take biology, chemistry, physics, and math, it is unavoidable that you will have to take at least two of these subjects in the same semester several semesters.

The physics department seems to be very strict, or perhaps structured is a better term, when it comes to requiring extra work for James Scholars (and Chancellor's Scholars who are also James Scholars) to receive honors credit for taking a regular physics class. The Scholars must complete an Honors Credit Learning Agreement (an honors contract).

It should be noted that the CHP offers many more classes in Fall than in Spring.

Average Class Size (4.5): The average CHP honors class size is 16.2 students; the overall average class size for the 50 colleges and programs under review in this edition is 21.2 students.

Adjusted Graduation Rate (4.5): The AGR is not simply the six-year graduation rate of students in the honors college who graduated from the university **(93.3%),** whether or not the students completed the honors program ("honors completers"). The AGR also reflects the extent to which the honors graduation rate from the university is higher than that for the university as a whole. (The **university-wide rate is 84%,** yielding the 4.5 AGR for the college.) **The CHP also provided a** *four-year* **graduation rate--an impressive 84.9%.** The average **honors** six-year **graduation rate for all 50 programs** under review is **89%.**

Ratio of Staff to Honors Students (4.5): Our estimate is that there is 1 staff member for every **111.1** students. (Mean ratio for all 50 programs is 1 staff member for every 159.8 students.)

Honors Residence Halls (3.0): This is the default rating for programs that do not have designated honors residence halls. Programs receive some rating because there are always living/learning opportunities that have special appeal to honors students without being honors-only floors or dorms. "The University of Illinois has been very proactive with initiating and supporting Living and Learning Communities, and many honors students live in the wide variety of communities (from Allen Hall, which was begun in the early 1970's to Global Crossroads and diversity-awareness). Many of these Living and Learning Communities (LLC) integrate academics by combining co-curricular programming with everyday living. While the **'Scholars Community'** in the 'Special Living Options' is relatively new, certainly every LLC has elements of honors programming."

Prestigious Awards (5.0): UIUC students have an **outstanding record of earning prestigious awards as undergraduates and as graduates.** The university ranks 2nd among public universities in the number of Goldwater Scholarships (65), awarded to outstanding undergraduates in the STEM disciplines. On average, 3 out of 4 UIUC students who are nominated are chosen for the award. UIUC undergrads are far above the average in winning both Gilman Scholarships (study abroad for students of limited means) and Boren Scholarships (work or study abroad after graduation).

Illinois graduates rank 1st among all public universities in winning the lucrative and extremely competitive **Churchill Scholarships** that fund graduate study in science, math, and technology at Cambridge University in England (20), and are **6th overall after Princeton, Harvard, Yale, Cornell, and Duke.** The university is 2nd among public universities in the number of Gates Cambridge Scholars (9), and with 23 Marshall Scholars, UIUC is 3rd among public universities. University graduates have also won 9 Rhodes Scholarships and 11 Truman Scholarships.

In addition, graduates do extremely well in winning National Science Foundation Graduate Research Fellowships to fund doctoral studies, ranking 5th among public universities in the number of NSF GRS awards in the last three years; graduates also rank 7th among public institutions in the number of Fulbright Student Scholarships earned in the last three years.

Continuation Requirements: 3.30 GPA

Academic Strengths: It is often the case that universities with an outstanding record of winning prestigious scholarships also have outstanding faculties, and UIUC's 15 major academic departments that we track have an average national ranking among all universities that is better than 20th. These excellent departments include engineering and computer science (both 5th), chemistry (6), psychology (7), physics (9), business (16), history and math (both 22), English (23), and biology (30). No department among the ones we track is ranked worse than 42nd in the nation.

Undergraduate Research: "The University of Illinois does have a new Office of Undergraduate Research which recently began offering a Certificate in Undergraduate Research. The OUR is also working on systematizing all research course numbers to be consistent, though if course credit is not sought, they stand by the position that a student should be paid for their work.

"The Campus Honors Program offers CHP Summer Research grants (up to $2,000), sponsors students to present their work at conferences, and schedules two co-curricular events per year for research."

Study Abroad: UIUC is 17th among all universities in the total number of students who study abroad and 7th in the number of students engaging in longer term studies abroad. "The CHP awards $10,000-$15,000 in CHP Summer Travel grants on an annual basis, up to $1,000 per student.

"The CHP also hosts students on a Summer Intercultural Tour to a variety of locations, including Japan, Ecuador and the Galapagos, and Curacao; the amount required for each student is heavily subsidized by the CHP, so the student must only cover up to half of the cost."

Financial Aid: UIUC is a public elite university that has actually *increased* university sponsorships of National Merit Scholars. In 2013, the university had 85 National Merit Scholars, and 64 of these had university sponsorship.

In addition, "Chancellor's Scholars in the Campus Honors Program are supported by a small stipend ($500) for their first year if they are in-state. Chancellor's Scholars who are domestic out of state and incoming first year students receive a partial tuition waiver that is guaranteed for their first four semesters (as long as they remain in good standing), and which may be renewed at a smaller amount in subsequent semesters if the budget allows.

"All Chancellor's Scholars in good standing may apply for CHP Summer Research and Travel grants, which are up to $2,000 and $1,000, respectively.

"Any Chancellor's Scholar who is selected to a CHP Intercultural Study Tour (ICST examples include Japan, the Galapagos, and Curacao) has their ICST cost subsidized for the program up to $2,000.

"Field trips are fully or partially covered for students for CHP classes, which may range from visits to the Art Institute in Chicago to a research study tour to Yellowstone."

Degree of Difference (Honors students/non-honors students): 3.21 on a scale of 5. Some parents and prospective students might prefer an honors program that in many ways stands apart on campus, while others might prefer a program that is more expansive. The rating here tries to provide an indication of where a given honors program is on the stand apart/expansive spectrum. The rating is based on the difference between (1) the average SAT scores for enrolled honors students and (2) the average test scores for all students in the university as a whole *and* for students with scores at the 75% level or above. A score of 3.5 or higher indicates a high degree of difference. A score of 3.2 to 3.49 indicates a relatively high degree of difference. Finally, a score below 3.2 indicates a modest difference. **Please keep in mind that neither the high nor low selectivity of an honors program determines how effective the program is; this rating is merely "cultural" and *not* qualitative.**

NAME: HUTTON HONORS COLLEGE, INDIANA UNIVERSITY

Date Established: 1965

Location: Bloomington, Indiana

University Full-time Undergraduate Enrollment: 30,949

Honors Enrollment: Approximately 4,000 (mean size of all 50 programs is 1,714)

Review/Admissions Category III: Programs with average SAT scores of 1383--1416 for enrolled students. *Estimated* mean SAT score for enrolled Hutton students is 1385, ACT 31.5.

Fall 2014 basic admissions requirements: 31 ACT or <u>1350-1380</u> SAT and 3.95 or top 5% class rank **OR** 32-33 ACT or 1390-1460 SAT and 3.90 GPA or top 7.5% class rank **OR** 34-36 ACT or 1470+ SAT and 3.85 GPA or top 10% class rank

For **Fall 2015**, students admitted to IU-Bloomington will be automatically invited if they meet one of the following sets of criteria: 31 ACT or <u>1360-1380</u> SAT **and** 3.95 or top 5% class rank; 32-33 ACT or 1390-1460 SAT **and** 3.90 GPA or top 7.5% class rank; 34-36 ACT or 1470+ SAT **and** 3.85 GPA or top 10% class rank

Honors Programs in Admissions Category III (average SAT scores of 1383--1416): Connecticut, Indiana, Kentucky, Miami University, Oklahoma, Penn State, Tennessee, Texas A&M, UC Irvine, and Washington.

Administrative Staff: Hutton Honors College has a staff of 21.

FOR ALL "MORTARBOARD" RATINGS BELOW, A SCORE OF 5 IS THE MAXIMUM AND REPRESENTS A COMPARISON WITH ALL 50 HONORS COLLEGES AND PROGRAMS:

PERCEPTION* OF UNIVERSITY AS A WHOLE, <u>NOT</u> OF HONORS: 🎓🎓🎓🎓

OVERALL HONORS RATING: 🎓🎓🎓🎓

Curriculum Requirements: 🎓🎓🎓

Class Range and Type: 🎓🎓🎓🎓🎓

Class Size: 🎓🎓🎓🎓$^{1/2}$

Adjusted Grad Rate: 🎓🎓🎓🎓

Ratio of Staff to Students: 🎓🎓🎓$^{1/2}$

Priority Registration: No.

Honors Housing: 🎓🎓🎓🎓¹/²

Prestigious Awards: 🎓🎓🎓🎓¹/²

*Perception is based on the university's ranking among public universities in the 2014 U.S. News Best Colleges report. Please bear in mind that the better the U.S. News ranking, the more difficult it is for an honors college or program to have a rating that equals or improves on the magazine ranking.

Curriculum Requirements (3.0): We classify Hutton Honors College as a **blended honors program,** and in the Hutton case, as well as a few other core and blended programs, this means that **the focus on the first two years yields a relatively low completion requirement because the honors curriculum itself does not reach across all four years. For Hutton students, at least, this is not a matter of diminishing opportunities: IU has a very extensive range of honors in the department options and requirements**--but unfortunately, (for the rating, anyway) that departmental honors work is not tied to Hutton completion.

Here are the completion requirements for the General Honors Notation on the diploma:
- "Each student must complete a curriculum consisting of a minimum of **21 graded credit hours** of honors courses, including at least two 3-credit courses offered by the honors college directly.
- "With the exception of honors readings/research courses and honors thesis courses, for honors courses that carry more than 3 credit hours, students may count the entire number of credit hours per course, **up to a maximum of two courses,** toward fulfillment of the general honors requirements. Additional honors courses that carry more than 3 credit hours may be used toward the general honors requirements, as well; however, only 3 credit hours per additional course will be counted. **Please note that 1-credit honors discussion sections that are paired with 3-credit departmental courses (referred to in the previous paragraph) may NOT be counted for 4 credits toward the general honors notation; they may be counted for a total of 3 credits.**
- "For students taking honors readings/research courses and honors thesis courses, only 3 credit hours total may count toward the notation. **Students may not count more than two courses from any one department toward the notation**, except that students who complete a departmental honors thesis course -- i.e., a course that has an honors thesis as a degree or departmental honors requirement -- may count this course toward their notation **and** count a maximum of two additional departmental honors courses from the thesis granting department; however, the two additional departmental honors courses may not include readings/research courses." There is no upper limit on courses offered by Hutton itself.
  Note: Students may take up to 15 hours of approved honors courses in the College of Arts & Sciences and/or in the professional schools (e.g., Kelley School of Business, School of Public & Environmental Affairs), as long as there are **no more than two** courses in any one department. Students are strongly encouraged to take a breadth of Honors courses, across a number of departments, to fulfill the General Honors Notation requirements.
- Hutton students **can** be in the honors colleges **and** enrolled in the Kelley School of Business "Direct Admit" program, as well as other Direct Admit programs. At IU, the term Direct Admit

•

applies to freshman students with credentials so outstanding that they can bypass many preliminary requirements.

AP/IB Credits: It appears that AP calculus scores are used mainly for placement and not for credit.

Range and Type of Honors Courses (5.0): Whatever questions one may have about Hutton's modest honors completion requirements are likely to fade after reviewing the impressive range of Hutton seminars and departmental honors classes. In Spring 2014, we estimate that there were about 30 honors seminars and another 119 department honors sections.

Here is the most important thing to know about Hutton Honors courses: they reflect a conscious (and wise) decision to combine the intellectual and the practical, to integrate the world of ideas with the world of making a living--and they do so with remarkable consistency.

Each semester, Hutton offers a series called **Ideas and Experience I and II, an exploration of the impact great artists and intellectuals have on the world—and of the effect their work has on them in the process.** An excellent example is this class with an explicitly historical emphasis:

"History is full of crises. From big battles that changed the fate of continents to stories of unrequited love that only mattered to one or two sad souls, what we know about the past is often centered on painful experiences. These crises didn't just change the lives of the people who wrote history; they changed the way history writing worked. This class examines how crises changed both people and the literary practices of people who wrote history…. From the Battle of Thermopylae to the Fall of Rome to the Black Death, we'll focus on large-scale crises, the societies they affected and the texts written by people who lived through crises."

Here are additional Hutton seminars and colloquia from Spring 2014: Madness and Melancholy; The Production of Culture; History of Consumer Culture; Encountering the Digital Past; History of Documentary Film; Issues in Bioethics; and **a favorite, Business Lessons from Humanities.**

About **Business Lessons: "Bridging the academic disciplines of both business and humanities is the objective of this course**...Students will study several enduring lessons from a broad range of humanities courses (of their choosing) and apply their perspectives of the practical value of those learnings to the world of business…**even a solid education in humanities alone seems insufficient preparation for meeting today's rigors of making a living after graduation. This course intends to make the bridge of interdependence a part of every students learning regardless of their chosen academic major."**

The list of excellent seminars goes on, including several in each Gen Ed category (humanities, fine arts, science, and social sciences). Two of these are on the Use of Force from World War II until the present. Others focus on literature and writing. More of our favorites include **Great Problems, Great Decisions; Science and Ethics; Scientific Uncertainty and Discovery; and The Intricate Human.**

The departmental honors sections are comprehensive, except for engineering courses (IU does not have an engineering department) and the absence of an economics section. We should note that there is a seminar titled The History of Money, and additional courses related to management and budgeting. There are, however multiple sections in computer science--more than in most programs--and **the number of honors business classes is indeed impressive**: financial accounting, business presentations, business communication, the computer in business, the legal environment of business, managing and behavior in organizations, leadership, negotiation, management, finance budgeting, and human resources. The practical side is also in evidence in the honors sections of health care administration. English, history, political science, are also well represented. **Math sections are plentiful:** calculus IV, two sections of differential equations, and one each in linear algebra, analysis II, and modern algebra. (It appears that some of these meet with larger math sections.) The university's excellent music school leads to more and better sections in that discipline than one can find in other programs. **Discipline-specific classes in the sciences are not numerous, but several of the seminars take an interdisciplinary perspective on the sciences.** Two examples: History and Philosophy of Physics, and the previously mentioned Scientific Uncertainty and Discovery.

Average Class Size (4.5): The average Hutton Honors class has **20 students,** and the average class size is 21.2 students per section for all 50 programs under review.

Adjusted Graduation Rate (4.0): The AGR is not simply the six-year graduation rate of students in the honors college who graduated from the university **(89%),** whether or not the students completed the honors program ("honors completers"). The AGR also reflects the extent to which the honors graduation rate from the university is higher than that for the university as a whole. (The **university-wide rate is 75%.**) The average **honors** six-year **graduation rate for all 50 programs under review is 89%.**

Ratio of Staff to Honors Students (3.5): Our estimate is that there is 1 staff member for every **190.5** students. (Mean ratio for all 50 programs is 1 staff member for every 159.8 students.) **Note: the Hutton emphasis on the first two years has the effect of mitigating what appears statistically to be a staff shortage.**

Honors Residence Halls (4.5): IU is all about the campus "neighborhoods. There are Honors Residential Communities (HRCs) in the Central, Northwest, and Southeast neighborhoods.

The Central HRC is the largest honors community on campus and, as a result, probably has more honors group activities. Recently, one of those was a trip to New York City. The **Central HRC is in the Teter complex,** with honors floors in Boisen. Boisen is air-conditioned with suite-style rooms and connecting baths. It is coed but separated into wings on the honors floors. As its name suggests, the Central HRC has a good location, only about a quarter mile from the Student Center, Health Center, Wells Library, and even **closer to Wright Food Court** and the School of Education. Teter is about half a mile from the Kelley School of Business and the Jacobs School of Music.

According to the most recent information we have, the **Northwest HRC is in Briscoe,** a modern well-designed residence hall that features shared baths in each double room. Briscoe is about a third of a mile from **Gresham Food Court** and about half a mile from the Kelley School of Business. Briscoe is coed, with mixed genders on honors floors, i.e., not separated by floor wings.

In the **Southeast Neighborhood,** the HRC is in **Forest Residence Hall.** The rooms in Forest are traditional corridor double rooms with hall baths. Forest is air-conditioned and coed, with genders separated by wings. Dining is at the Restaurants of the Woodland, which is part of the large Forest Complex. Forest is closest to the Wright School of Education and the Jacobs School of Music, but about three-quarters of a mile from the Kelley School of Business.

After one year at Hutton, students are eligible to live in the Honors Residential Communities in the new Union Street Center, Willkie Residence Hall, or they can choose to return to Briscoe, Teter, or Forest HRCs.

Prestigious Awards (4.5): IU has an impressive record of winning the best-known annual postgraduate awards, such as Rhodes, Marshall, Churchill, and Truman Scholarships. The university is tied for 6th among public universities in the number of Marshall Scholars, 7th in the highly competitive Churchill Scholarships, and tied for 10th in Truman Scholars. IU also has 14 Rhodes Scholars, above the mean for that award. IU undergraduates have earned 39 Goldwater Scholarships for outstanding promise in the STEM disciplines, above the mean of 34. The IU achievement is notable because most institutions that do well in the Goldwater competition have recognized engineering departments, while IU lacks a department in that discipline.

Continuation Requirements: "Students must maintain a minimum grade point average of 3.40 in their notation courses, with no course grade lower than a C. Courses taken satisfactory/fail (S/F) cannot be counted toward the notation. Students must also have a minimum overall grade point average of 3.40 at graduation."

Academic Strengths: IU has an excellent faculty, with an average academic department ranking of better than 30th in the nation among all universities public or private. Leading departments include business (10th), sociology (12), education (22), English (22), history (23), political science (25), psychology (26), and chemistry (26). Math and physics are ranked 30th and 40th, respectively.

Undergraduate Research: IU Bloomington offers two main undergraduate research tracks.

The **Integrated Freshman Learning Experience** (IFLE) is a six-week summer research experience prior to freshman year followed by a year-long research-based honors course integrating biology, biochemistry, and neuroscience.
Eligibility

- Incoming IU freshmen with a strong interest in scientific research.
- Students with identified major in biology, biochemistry, chemistry, microbiology, or neuroscience, although others may be considered on a case-by-case basis and fit within program parameters.

Cost
- Summer housing and meals are provided at no cost.
- Academic year housing and meal expenses will be at the regular IU rate and your responsibility.
- Eligible students will receive a $1,000 scholarship during the academic freshman year if enrolled in both semesters.

The **Science, Technology, and Research Scholars** (STARS) program offers **four years** of faculty-mentored research experience in all science disciplines. Below is an outline of the STARS process:
- Join a research lab beginning freshman year
- Receive mentoring by a leading faculty scientist
- Interview with faculty mentors to discover your best fit

- Acquire lab skills and develop your own project
- Gain exposure to other research areas through faculty research talks
- Participate in annual student research symposium
- Eligible for summer research scholarships
- Eligible for scholarships for conferences
- Earn course credit toward graduation

Study Abroad: IU ranks 13th in the nation among universities with the most students engaged in long-term study-abroad programs. The IU Office of Overseas Study has more than 100 programs to choose from in the following countries:

Argentina (2); Australia (6); Austria (4); Belize (1); Botswana (1); Brazil (3); Cayman Islands (1); Chile (4); China (8); Czech Republic (2); Denmark (3); Dominican Republic (1); Ecuador (2); Egypt (2); England—mostly London—(10); France (8); Germany (5); Ghana (1); Greece (2); Hungary (2); India (3); Ireland (4); Israel (1); Italy (7); Japan (4); Jordan (1); Mexico (1); Morocco (1); The Netherlands (5); New Zealand (1); Portugal (1); Russia (2); Senegal (2); Serbia (1); South Africa (3); South Korea (1); Spain (17); Switzerland (2); Thailand (1); Turkey (1); and Vietnam (1). These do not include study programs that combine different countries.

Degree of Difference (Honors students/non-honors students): 3.49 on a scale of 5. Some parents and prospective students might prefer an honors program that in many ways stands apart on campus, while others might prefer a program that is more expansive. The rating here tries to provide an indication of where a given honors program is on the stand apart/expansive spectrum. The rating is based on the difference between (1) the average SAT scores for enrolled honors students and (2) the average test scores for all students in the university as a whole *and* for students with scores at the 75% level or above. A score of 3.5 or higher indicates a high degree of difference. A score of 3.2 to 3.49 indicates a relatively high degree of difference. Finally, a score below 3.2 indicates a modest difference. **Please keep in mind that neither the high nor low selectivity of an honors program determines how effective the program is; this rating is merely "cultural" and *not* qualitative.**

NAME: UNIVERSITY OF IOWA HONORS PROGRAM

Date Established: 1958

Location: Iowa City, Iowa

University Full-time Undergraduate Enrollment: 19,639

Honors Enrollment: approximately 1,688 (mean enrollment of 50 programs is 1,714).

Review/Admissions Category I: Programs with **average SAT scores of 1235--1342 for enrolled students**. The actual average (mean) SAT score for enrolled students in Iowa Honors is not available, but the actual ACT average is 29.5, which converts to an estimated SAT of 1320. The average (mean) high school GPA for entering honors students is 4.03, and the average high school rank is top 9%.

These are the **minimum** requirements for admission:

SAT 1210 (with 3.8 GPA) or 1330 (with 3.7 GPA)
ACT 27 (with 3.8 GPA) or 30 (with 3.7 GPA)
GPA 3.8 (with 27 ACT) or 3.7 (with 30 ACT)

Honors Programs in Admissions Category I (average SAT scores of 1235-1342): Arizona, Arizona State, Arkansas, Colorado State, Iowa, Maine, Mississippi, Oklahoma State, Oregon, Oregon State, Rhode Island, Texas Tech, University at Albany, and Washington State.

Administrative Staff: The Honors Program has full-time staff of 8.

FOR ALL "MORTARBOARD" RATINGS BELOW, A SCORE OF 5 IS THE MAXIMUM AND REPRESENTS A COMPARISON OF ALL 50 HONORS COLLEGES AND PROGRAMS:

PERCEPTION* OF UNIVERSITY AS A WHOLE, <u>NOT</u> OF HONORS: 🎓🎓🎓🎓

OVERALL HONORS RATING: 🎓🎓🎓

Curriculum Requirements: 🎓🎓🎓^1/2

Class Range and Type: 🎓🎓🎓🎓

Class Size: 🎓🎓🎓

Adjusted Grad Rate: 🎓🎓🎓🎓

Ratio of Staff to Students: 🎓🎓🎓

Priority Registration: No, but "over half of Honors students qualify for the Old Gold scholarship, which allows students to register as seniors beginning in their second semester. The criteria for this scholarship are 30 ACT and 3.8 GPA with no application required."

Honors Housing: 🎓🎓🎓🎓[1/2]

Prestigious Awards: 🎓🎓🎓🎓

*Perception is based on the university's ranking among public universities in the 2014 U.S. News Best Colleges report. Please bear in mind that the higher the U.S. News ranking, the more difficult it is for an honors college or program to have a rating that improves on the magazine ranking.

Curriculum Requirements (3.5): The Iowa Honors Program is in the process of a major transition to a more structured and cohesive program under a recently-hired Director with years of experience in honors administration. The honors education experience at Iowa is now a definite enhancement for current students, but the trajectory of the program is toward a new standard of excellence.

The Director tells us that "we introduced new requirements in Fall 2013 to allow students to graduate with University Honors. [For now] we have implemented a more flexible transitional version of these requirements to allow current students to earn University Honors. These allow for a student to use more experiential learning towards our requirement of 24 total semester hours of Honors experiences and courses. This transitional version will be phased out as students graduate.

"Our Engineering curriculum is more flexible for students in the structured engineering curriculum, allowing more experiences to count, including specific leadership and teaching activities within the Engineering College."

Therefore, the requirements that you see outlined below will become more defined and rigorous as time goes on.

To meet the interim University Honors completion requirements, students must have at least 12 semester hours of honors course credit along with the same number of honors experience credits. Only one course of the honors credit requirement may be through a contract course. Graduate course credit also counts toward course completion.

Honors experiences emphasize "learning while doing," and include the following:

- **Honors in the major** (departmental honors course work, including a thesis) completely satisfies the honors experience requirement. Honors in the major can itself also be an honors completion option.
- Mentored research (12 semester hours or the equivalent).
- Study abroad for a minimum of two semesters (fall and/or spring) or the equivalent. Single semesters of study abroad, including summer and between-semester experiences, may count for up to half of the second level requirement. For honors credit, students must carry out an

•

100

- independent project while abroad and conduct a poster presentation or write a report on the project.
- Internships may count for up to half (6-semester hours) of the second level requirement. In some cases, internships may count for the entire requirement (12 semester hours or the equivalent). Honors credit requires students to carry out an independent project while interning and to conduct a poster presentation or write a report on the project.

AP/IB credit: These do not count as replacements for honors courses.

Range and Type of Honors Courses (4.0): During the transitional period, the program will likely work to develop a wider range of departmental honors classes. Although we classify Iowa Honors as a **blended program,** in its current form it also resembles a **core program** because it offers about as many seminars as departmental courses. The university has strong academic departments in almost every major discipline, so it makes sense that the expansion of the program would be in the direction of more (and probably smaller) departmental honors sections.

Now as for the seminars, we counted almost **forty 1-credit First-Year seminars,** almost every one of them with a course title that would entice almost any student to pick not just one but all of them if possible. We will try to limit our list to six or seven:

Let's begin with a long title: Superheroes Unleashed: 3,000 Years of Heroes, Villains, and a Mad Race for Immortality. If that doesn't work for you, try these: Remarkable Adventures in the Search for Origins of the Species; How I Learned to Stop Worrying and Love Global Suicide; Rocks from the Sky: Volcanic Eruptions; Classical Mythology and the Discovery of the Self; Sex: Why We Do it; and, not even that is our favorite, but this one is: **Physics: The Law or Just a Good Idea?** (Okay, that's eight.)

So here is what they say about **Physics: The Law or Just a Good Idea**?--"This seminar will explore the laws of physics, from the quantum mechanics of tiny atoms to the gravity that rules the entire universe, to see how our conceptions of these laws have changed over time, and where we stand today. Do we make theories to understand the truths of our observations, or do we observe to test the truth in our theories? **Are we approaching a deeper truth of how the world works, or do we simply obtain better predictions of the functioning of a world that is at its heart completely inscrutable?"**

And then there are the 19 sections of **Rhetoric,** each with a topical focus that provides context for the explorations of language and argument. These sections carry 4 credits each. One favorite:

Rhetoric: Networks, Strategies, and Tactics--"We will also look at modes of social control and resistance and the opportunities and problems that tend to be missed when daily life and its design are looked at as a foregone conclusion. **In short, this course will make the everyday uncanny for students and will help train students to best pitch and implement their ideas for social innovation."**

The current picture is somewhat less bright when we consider **departmental honors courses,** although mathematics, biology, chemistry, and economics are present. However, some of these sections in Spring 2014 (not so much in mathematics and biology) are mixed sections in which the honors component is in the lab or the breakout discussion sections. It must be said that some of these discussion sections and labs require two to four hours a week of attendance, so they are likely to be substantial; yet the main sections of several departmental courses are big ones. This is not unusual in programs with a departmental honors structure, nor is it especially rare even in expanded core or blended programs. Mathematics classes include at least two all-honors sections--one an introduction to linear algebra and the other an intro to matrix study. But when it comes to history, the three sections all appear to be discussion sections only, with the main lecture sections being in larger classes. The four political science sections, on the other hand, appear to be three honors courses and only one discussion section that breaks out from a large section. There are additional English lit sections, beyond the English and grammar focus of several Rhetoric sections and other seminars. And we cannot forget the innovative class for **Honors Writing Fellows—Writing Theory and Practice.**

With the preeminent writing program in the nation, it is only right that such a class would be a part of the honors list. Students learn "how gender, class, culture, academic discipline and language background can affect writing and the tutoring of writing. They learn effective commenting and tutoring strategies that address strengths and weaknesses in argumentation, organization, style, and mechanics."

What we did not find in Spring 2014 were honors departmental sections in physics, psychology, and sociology, a surprise when one considers the academic reputation of the last two at Iowa, especially.

Average Class Size (3.0): Because of the current emphasis on mixed sections for departmental honors classes, the average Iowa Honors class size may be as high as 32-36 or so. That said, most of the seminars will be in the 20-student range. (The average class size for all 50 programs under review is 21.2 students.)

Adjusted Graduation Rate (4.0): The AGR is not simply the six-year graduation rate of students in the honors college who graduated from the university **(88%),** whether or not the students completed the honors program ("honors completers"). It also reflects the extent to which the honors graduation rate from the university is higher than that for the university as a whole. The **university-wide rate is 70%,** yielding the 4.0 AGR for the college. The average six-year **honors graduation rate for all 50 programs under review is 89%.**

Ratio of Staff to Honors Students (3.0): Our estimate is that there is 1 staff member for every **211** students. (Median ratio for all 50 programs is 1 staff member for every 159.8 students.)

Honors Residence Halls (4.5): Honors first-year students and upperclassmen both have on-campus residential options at Iowa: Daum Hall houses mostly first-year students, 344 in all; Centerstone, an apartment building near Honors Hall, accommodates 125 honors upperclassmen. Daum Hall features traditional double rooms along with a few singles and triples. It has hall baths, it is air conditioned, and there is on-site laundry. **Students can dine at Burge Hall, which they can reach by a tunnel connecting Daum and Burge. Students also have the convenience of a skywalk that can take them from Daum directly to the Honors Center and offices.**

The Centerstone apartments are all suite-style, air conditioned, and close to dining at Burge Hall.

Prestigious Awards (4.0): Iowa students have an excellent record of winning Goldwater Scholarships for very high-achieving undergraduates in the STEM disciplines—45 of the scholarships to date. Iowa graduates have also earned an impressive 18 Rhodes Scholarships, 13 Truman Scholarships, and 4

Churchill Scholarships. Churchill awards only number about 14 per year, so winning 4 of them is a notable achievement.

Continuation Requirements: 3.33 cumulative GPA

Academic Strengths: The average national ranking of 15 major UI academic departments is better than 50th, evidence of the strong research focus at the university. Psychology ranks 30th; education and English both rank 32nd. Not far behind are business (34), sociology (35), economics (40), and history (42). All 15 of the major academic departments are ranked 69th in the nation or better.

Undergraduate Research: "The Iowa Center for Research by Undergraduates, or ICRU, promotes and provides oversight for undergraduate research at the University of Iowa," the Director tells us. "To promote research ICRU works directly with faculty, research staff, and students to foster mentoring relationships. **The center provides nearly $400,000 annually in funding for undergraduates to work with faculty, and this is principally as stipend support although travel support is also available for students to perform and present their work.**

"ICRU also supports annual opportunities for undergraduates to present their work on campus at events such as the Spring Undergraduate Research Festival and Summer Research Conference and off campus at Research in the Capitol, where a group of undergraduate researchers present their work at the Iowa Statehouse. Students and mentors who have excelled in their efforts are recognized by ICRU on behalf of the University through the Excellence in Undergraduate Research and ICRU Distinguished Mentor awards."

Study Abroad: In 2012-2013, Iowa students studied abroad in 75 countries. It may come as no surprise that Italy led the way with 218 students; but before Spain, the UK, and France the second preferred destination was India, with 164 Iowa students taking the opportunity to study and visit that complex and fascinating country.

Financial Aid: According to the Director, **"95% of the incoming class of Honors students in Fall 2013 received at least one merit scholarship.** The majority of these were the Iowa and National Scholars Awards, awarded to in-state and out-of-state students respectively. On top of these scholarships, many students earn the Old Gold or Presidential Scholarships, which combine with the Iowa/National Scholars Award, to cover a significant portion of tuition. An in-state student earning the Old Gold and Iowa Scholars Award has over half of his/her tuition covered.

"Note that the requirements for admissions to Honors match with those for Level I of the Iowa Scholars award, giving all in-state Honors students (admitted in Fall 2014 and later) $2,000 a year in scholarships automatically. There are also many other scholarships that students can qualify for based on more specific criteria."

Degree of Difference (Honors students/non-honors students): 2.86 on a scale of 5. Some parents and prospective students might prefer an honors program that in many ways stands apart on campus, while others might prefer a program that is more expansive. The rating here tries to provide an indication of where a given honors program is on the stand apart/expansive spectrum. The rating is based on the difference between (1) the average SAT scores for enrolled honors students and (2) the average test scores for all students in the university as a whole *and* for students with scores at the 75% level or above. A

score of 3.5 or higher indicates a high degree of difference. A score of 3.2 to 3.49 indicates a relatively high degree of difference. Finally, a score below 3.2 indicates a modest difference. **Please keep in mind that neither the high nor low selectivity of an honors program determines how effective the program is; this rating is merely "cultural" and *not* qualitative.**

Testimonials:

Tom Keegan, Lecturer, Rhetoric—"I am always impressed by the extent to which my Honors students view their studies as inextricable from their personal and professional lives. They don't so much take classes as absorb and apply their learning. They want to know how what they learn today can be used *today* and tomorrow. They are creative pragmatists who will undertake any assignment – digitally-oriented, community-based, or research-intensive –as a means to honing skills that they can put to use in the broader world."

Waltraud Maierhofer, Professor, German—"I was drawn to teaching in the Honors program by everything it advocates, especially small class sizes, interdisciplinary study, students from very different majors, creative and more in-depth course design, focus on the students and peer activities instead of lectures. Yet the rewards of teaching in Honors have far exceeded my initial expectations, and that is because of the students in the Honors program. They are not only academically gifted and often have an exceptional basic education with great speaking and writing skills; they are curious, hardworking, and highly motivated individuals who challenge each other as well as me and with whom it is a pleasure to learn."

Maya Amjadi-First Year in Biology and Spanish, Pre-Med—"I thought studying at a big university, it would be difficult to find my crowd--but Honors made it easy. I live in Daum Hall, the honors residence hall on campus. I can hardly believe how close I have gotten with the people on my floor. The people that live here are so talented and well rounded, not to mention they all have so many unique experiences. I really like taking honors coursework because in my experience, the classes are smaller, the students are more engaged, and the teachers are able to go more in-depth with the subject material."

Nicholas Rolston (Nick)-Senior in Physics and Math—"My journey in the University of Iowa Honors Program began before classes began when I participated in the Honors Primetime Seminar, a three-day workshop which created my network with faculty and students. In my first day of class, I stayed after class to talk to my Physics professor about receiving Honors credit for the class. After visiting his office to discuss an Honors project, he offered me the opportunity to conduct independent research in his lab. I eagerly accepted and immediately had access to a $1.5 million semiconductor growth facility."

NAME: UNIVERSITY HONORS PROGRAM, UNIVERSITY OF KANSAS (KU)

Date Established: 1929—**the oldest honors program among the 50 being reviewed.**

Location: Lawrence, Kansas

University-wide, Full-time Undergraduate Enrollment: 17,130

Honors Enrollment: approximately 1,294 (mean enrollment of all 50 programs is 1,714).

Review/Admissions Category IV: Programs with **average SAT scores of 1417 or higher for enrolled students**. Actual average (mean) score for enrolled honors students at KU is1420; ACT average is 32.4. Mean adjusted HSGPA for entering honors students is 3.96, unweighted, with a high school rank in the top 5 percent.

"We utilize holistic admissions, examining a student's entire profile in making admissions decisions. We receive over 10,000 inquiries annually for about 380 total spots in the program. We equally weigh all five of the following in making admissions decisions: ACT/SAT composite, unweighted GPA, strength of curriculum, extra-curricular activities, and critical writing skills."

Honors Programs in Admissions Category IV (average SAT of 1417 and higher): Auburn, Clemson, Georgia, Illinois, Kansas, Michigan, Minnesota, North Carolina, Rutgers, South Carolina, UT Austin, Virginia.

Administrative Staff: The Honors Program has 10 full-time staff members, not counting 38 advisers in the academic departments.

FOR ALL "MORTARBOARD" RATINGS BELOW, A SCORE OF 5 IS THE MAXIMUM AND REPRESENTS A COMPARISON OF ALL 50 HONORS COLLEGES AND PROGRAMS:

PERCEPTION* OF UNIVERSITY AS A WHOLE, NOT OF HONORS: 🎓🎓🎓 1/2

OVERALL HONORS RATING: 🎓🎓🎓🎓🎓

Curriculum Requirements: 🎓🎓🎓 1/2

Class Range and Type: 🎓🎓🎓🎓

Class Size: 🎓🎓🎓🎓 1/2

Adjusted Grad Rate: 🎓🎓🎓🎓🎓

Ratio of Staff to Students: 🎓🎓🎓🎓 1/2

Priority Registration: Yes, honors students register for **all** courses, honors and otherwise, with the first group of students during **each** year they are in the program. "We **are** the first group, no one else enrolls when we do, including Athletics."

Honors Housing: 🎓🎓🎓🎓$^{1/2}$

Prestigious Awards: 🎓🎓🎓🎓$^{1/2}$

*Perception is based on the university's ranking among public universities in the 2014 *U.S. News Best Colleges* report. Please bear in mind that the higher the *U.S. News* ranking, the more difficult it is for an honors college or program to have a rating that improves on the magazine ranking.

Curriculum Requirements (3.5): In the first edition of our *Review,* we placed an even greater emphasis on the honors completion requirements for each program, i.e., how many credit hours were required to complete honors at the highest level. During the last two years, our conversations with honors professionals have been instrumental in leading us toward a better overall methodology, one in which curriculum completion requirements still have a prominent place but other factors, such as the depth and range of courses, class size, and honors staff ratios to honors students, now have a collective weight that is about equal to that of the basic completion requirements. KU Honors is an example of how the new methodology does not utilize any one rating category that dominates to such an extent that a program or college cannot do well unless it achieves a high rating in that single category. That a given program requires 36-40 hours for completion, for example, does not necessarily mean that the courses and classes available to honors students will be outstanding.

The KU Honors approach has never been to define honors completion in terms of a lot of credit hours but, rather, in the words of the associate Director, "all Honors sections have been mapped onto the University's Core curriculum requirements. Every general education requirement at the University of Kansas is offered as an Honors course. We aim to provide as broad of an honors curriculum as can possibly be offered. **We also believe that we have an obligation to best serve our students by providing them with a wide variety of curricular, co-curricular, and extra-curricular options, NOT in providing arbitrary requirements that make our job as a program easier.**"

All of that said, we still use total completion requirements as an important metric; in the case of the KU Honors Program, the 24 credit hours required is not a high number but one that, considered in combination with the other factors mentioned above, does not detract from the extremely high quality of the program. At least six of the eight courses or experiences (out of eight total courses) must be in honors classes. The other two courses can come from a combination of an additional honors course along with an honors experience, or from two honors experiences. Honors experiences that carry credit are study abroad, research, internships, or community service projects. Program completion **does not require a thesis, although a thesis can count as one of the honors experiences.**

AP/IB credit does **not** replace honors courses.

Range and Type of Honors Courses (4.0): We classify the KU honors program as a **department-based program**, which means that even though the program has some honors seminars, the strength lies in the departmental honors courses that are available. As for **contract courses,** there is no limit on the number that may be counted toward completion; however, with so many honors sections to choose from, we suspect that contract courses are more of a convenience or an opportunity to take an advanced section that is not specifically designated as honors. "The Honors Course Contract is designed to allow students to pursue individualized work within the framework of a non-honors class. The Honors Course Contract leads students to deepen and/or broaden their understanding of course content. The project must be developed by the student and instructor, and both must endorse the proposal. The project must also be approved by the University Honors Program, at the latest by the first week in October for the Fall semester and the first week in March for the Spring."

There were at least **seven 1-credit freshman honors seminars** listed for Spring 2014. These seminars are meant "to introduce students to an area of studies and appropriate research methods within this field." Two pro-seminars in English were offered—pro-seminars include both undergraduate and graduate students. Another three small class sections are offered in Humanities and Western Civilization.

One of the most impressive features was the presence of at least five sections of honors mathematics in Spring 2014, a large number for a relatively small honors program. Two of the sections were in calculus and one each in differential equations, vector analysis, and linear algebra. Also impressive was that the two honors physics sections were not large, and the same for two management sections, the latter often among the largest classes offered in honors programs. Remarkable, too, were the three sections of honors electrical and computer engineering. Often, such courses are deemed demanding enough as they are. We found only one economics section, in macroeconomics, but KU honors students can also be eligible for business honors, and more economics and finance-related classes were available by that means. Missing was an honors section in political science—but then, maybe that's what honors contracts are for. Otherwise, **the honors departmental offerings are among the most comprehensive in the nation:** there are honors sections in almost all departments, including astronomy, Serbo-Croatian, painting, journalism, classics, religion, sculpture, Spanish, Jewish studies, theater, linguistics, Greek, and printing. Yes, printing.

Average Class Size (4.5): The largest honors sections are likely to be in introductory biology, where a few class lecture segments are *really* large. These, as in the case of many honors programs, are offset to a considerable extent by the much smaller honors breakout (discussion) sections that typically meet for at least one hour per week. The 1-credit freshman seminars have only 11 or 12 students. Humanities and Western Civilization average 24 students per section. Even the chemistry sections are not large, about 35 students each, and the five math sections average 20 students each. All in all, the **average KU honors class has about 15.4 students**, compared to 21.2 students per section in our entire sample of 50 programs.

Adjusted Graduation Rate (5.0): KU has an outstanding AGR, which is not simply the six-year graduation rate of students in the honors program who graduated from the university **(97.0%),** whether or not the students completed the honors program ("honors completers"). It also reflects the extent to which the honors graduation rate from the university is higher than that for the **university as a whole (64%),** yielding the 5.0 AGR for the college. The college also provided a **four-year honors graduation rate, 73.0%.** The average six-year **honors graduation rate for all 50 programs** under review **is 89%.**

Ratio of Staff to Honors Students (4.5): Our estimate is that there is 1 staff member for every **129.4** students. (Median ratio for all 50 programs is 1 staff member for every 159.8 students.)

Honors Residence Halls (4.5): The Associate Director of KU Honors tells us that "Templin Hall is the most popular dorm on campus for its renovated, suite-style rooms and location. Beginning in 2012, the Department of Housing agreed to turn over the entire hall to the University Honors Program for its students, **due to its immediate proximity to Nunemaker Center, the University Honors Program's unique, full-service home.** Students are NOT required to live in the Honors hall, but it is recommended, and it is the most popular option amongst our students. We do offer additional Honors-only floors on the occasion that we have more demand than rooms in Templin Hall."

Templin houses about 300 students in air-conditioned, suite-style rooms with adjoining baths. There is on-site laundry, and a very convenient dining option at Ekdahl Dining Hall. **Also...there are kitchenettes in every room.**

Prestigious Awards (4.5): KU is one of the highest achieving universities in the nation when it comes to winning prestigious undergraduate scholarships, especially the Goldwater Scholarships (57) awarded to outstanding undergraduate students in the STEM fields. The strong Goldwater showing is neither rooted in past achievement nor based on a recent surge; rather, it has been a continuing record of high achievement. KU students have also won 26 Rhodes Scholarships, one of the highest levels of achievement among public universities. The KU record of winning what is probably the second most prestigious postgraduate award--the Marshall Scholarship--is also excellent, along with great success in earning Truman Scholarships.

According to the Associate Director, "every Rhodes Scholar at the University of Kansas has been an Honors student since the inception of the program in 1929. In the last four years that I've been with the program, all Rhodes, Marshall, Truman, Goldwater, Churchill and Udall nominees and winners have been Honors students.

"Research is particularly emphasized for honors students, resulting in the University of Kansas leading the nation in Goldwater winners in the period in which I have been at KU."

KU Honors has a full-time scholarship coordinator for the University Honors Program.

Continuation Requirements: 3.25 GPA

Academic Strengths: The top departments at KU are education, psychology, history, earth sciences, political science, business, architecture, English, sociology, chemistry, and engineering.

Undergraduate Research: "We publish annually a *Journal of Undergraduate Research.* We have also set up the Office of Undergraduate Research at the University. Honors students have the option of utilizing full-time laboratory research as a capstone experience for Honors completion."

Study Abroad: The Associate Dean reports that the **"University of Kansas is a world leader in study abroad. Our honors students study at three times the rate of non-honors students. Programs are available in 139 locations in 74 countries. The University Honors Program, however, sends students to far more destinations than the standard Office of Study Abroad offerings. Honors students have studied in locations as diverse as North Korea and Antarctica.** Essentially, if there is an academic benefit to be gleaned, we will help students coordinate and fund any study abroad destination they might choose. **Typically, 100% of honors students who apply for study abroad funding for such programs receive funding from the University Honors Program to pursue that opportunity."** KU is listed among the top 20 major universities in the nation when it comes to the number of students doing long-term study-abroad work.

Financial Aid: "By dint of the University's scholarship structure," the Associate Director tells us, "virtually all Honors students will receive a 4-year, renewable scholarship. All in-state students will receive packages ranging from $4,000 to approximately $80,000 (full tuition, room and board, fees, etc.). Out of state students virtually all have their tuition reduced to a rate of 1.5 times that of in-state students."

Degree of Difference (Honors students/non-honors students): 4.13 on a scale of 5. Some parents and prospective students might prefer an honors program that in many ways stands apart on campus, while others might prefer a program that is more expansive. The rating here tries to provide an indication of where a given honors program is on the stand apart/expansive spectrum. The rating is based on the difference between (1) the average SAT scores for enrolled honors students and (2) the average test scores for all students in the university as a whole *and* for students with scores at the 75% level or above. A score of 3.5 or higher indicates a high degree of difference. A score of 3.2 to 3.49 indicates a relatively high degree of difference. Finally, a score below 3.2 indicates a modest difference. **Please keep in mind that neither the high nor low selectivity of an honors program determines how effective the program is; this rating is merely "cultural" and *not* qualitative.**

Testimonials:

Honors student--"I came to the University of Kansas (KU) as an international transfer student, not knowing what to expect from my time at KU. I had the intention of doing nothing else but being a student who goes to class, studies hard, and obtains good grades. All of that changed three days before my first semester at KU began when I received an email from my Honors Advisor welcoming me to campus. I felt touched by the simple gesture and it made me look forward to meeting her the next week. Her care and encouragement motivated me to be more involved on campus and I started holding leadership positions in student organizations and pursued research projects my second semester at KU.

"Today, two and a half years from my first day at KU, I have studied abroad twice, published my first research paper, received an Undergraduate Research Award for my second research project, founded two student organizations, participated in international conferences, and have been awarded with a Woman of Distinction honor. I know that all this would not have happened if I did not have the encouragement from my Honors Advisor who took the time to get to know me and always being there to support and empower me to pursue every project I want to initiate at KU."

NAME: UNIVERSITY OF KENTUCKY HONORS PROGRAM

Date Established: 1961

Location: Lexington, Kentucky

University Full-time Undergraduate Enrollment: 37,917

Honors Enrollment: 1,185 (mean size of all 50 programs is 1,714)

Review/Admissions Category--III: Programs with **average SAT scores of 1383--1416 for enrolled students**. Kentucky Honors relies almost entirely on ACT scores, and the average (mean) score of enrolled students is 32. The average high school GPA is 3.92, unweighted.

The **minimum** requirements are ACT 28, SAT 1250, and an unweighted high school GPA of 3.50.

Honors Programs in Admissions Category III (average SAT scores of 1383--1416): Connecticut, Indiana, Kentucky, Miami University, Oklahoma, Penn State, Tennessee, Texas A&M, UC Irvine, and Washington.

Administrative Staff: The Honors Program has a staff of 7.

FOR ALL "MORTARBOARD" RATINGS BELOW, A SCORE OF 5 IS THE MAXIMUM AND REPRESENTS A COMPARISON WITH ALL 50 HONORS COLLEGES AND PROGRAMS:

PERCEPTION* OF UNIVERSITY AS A WHOLE, NOT OF HONORS: 🎓🎓🎓

OVERALL HONORS RATING: 🎓🎓🎓^{1/2}

Curriculum Requirements: 🎓🎓🎓^{1/2}

Class Range and Type: 🎓🎓🎓^{1/2}

Class Size: 🎓🎓🎓🎓

Adjusted Grad Rate: 🎓🎓🎓🎓^{1/2}

Ratio of Staff to Students: 🎓🎓🎓^{1/2}

Priority Registration: **Yes,** honors students register for **all** courses, honors and otherwise, with the first group of students during **each** year they are in the program.

Honors Housing: 🎓🎓🎓🎓🎓

Prestigious Awards: 🎓🎓🎓$^{1/2}$

*Perception is based on the university's ranking among public universities in the 2014 U.S. News Best Colleges report. Please bear in mind that the better the U.S. News ranking, the more difficult it is for an honors college or program to have a rating that equals or improves on the magazine ranking.

Curriculum Requirements (3.5): The Honors Director (at the time of our survey) provided us with an excellent, succinct summary of the requirements:

"Honors students at the University of Kentucky take 6 hours of Honors seminars in their first year (the 6 hours of Honors courses may be departmental honors courses or upper-level Honors seminars, contracted Honors course conversions, or graduate-level courses); 6 hours of Honors experiences (undergraduate research, education abroad, or service learning) in **both** their second and third years; and complete a 3-credit-hour capstone project, typically tied closely to the major. Because of the flexibility in options to complete Honors, it is not just possible but probable that every single Honors student will have a unique Honors curriculum." **The total minimum completion requirement is 21 credits.**

Kentucky also has the Global Scholars Program, centered in the Gatton College of Business but designed by Gatton College in cooperation with the Kentucky Honors Program. Gatton College says that the "The Global Scholars Program is a four-year UK Honors program designed for high-achieving, highly-motivated business students who have a passion for international business and leadership. Every student in the program will graduate with a major from the Gatton College of Business and Economics as well as a minor in international business [including] a semester-length education abroad experience. The program is selective and small by design."

The **minimum requirements** for freshman admission to Global Scholars are an unweighted high school GPA of 3.5 or above **or** an ACT score of 28 or higher (or SAT score of 1240 or higher**). "Typically, students who are admitted into the program have an unweighted GPA well above a 3.5 as well as test scores well above the 28/1240 mark."**

Along with other coursework, first-year Global Scholars must take a 1-credit orientation class and three honors/Gatton courses as follows: Leadership in the Global Marketplace; an Honors Seminar; and Honors Advanced Composition and Communication (total of 10 credits). Second-year students take a 1-credit course in Challenges in Leadership, financial accounting, and microeconomics in the Fall, and Larger World Issues in Business in the Spring (total of 7 credits).

In the junior year, Global Scholars must complete the **International Core:** At least one semester of studying abroad **and a minor in international business,** which in itself requires 6 credits of prerequisites and another 12 credits in international finance, management, marketing, and an intro course in international business (a total of 15 credits for the minor, not counting prerequisites).

Seniors are prepped for an annual Business Career Fair, where they meet and network with potential employers. Seniors also complete on additional course, in Strategic Management (3 credits).

At least 35 credits are required to complete the Global Scholars Program, which requires the minor in international business.

AP/IB credits are **not** counted as replacements for UK Honors Program courses.

Range and Type of Honors Courses (3.5): Many of the courses for Global Scholars are discussed above. The UK Honors Program is very much a **core honors program** with relatively few departmental or upper-division courses. About two-thirds of the 23 honors seminars offered in Spring 2014 are meant to be taken in the first year of study and fulfill the university's Gen Ed requirements in the humanities, natural sciences-physics-math, the social sciences, and the arts and creativity. The variety and substance of the honors seminars at UK are quite impressive.

Here are some examples of honors first-year seminars, including some of our favorites in bold:

The Inquiry in the Humanities series offers a pair of seminars, the first called **The Medieval and Renaissance World** and the second **The Early Modern World.** Not typical survey courses covering many different sub-disciplines of history, they instead focus on intellectual history from the Middle Ages and the Reformation through the growth of industrialization in the 19th Century. A third course in the series brings us into the present day with the truly felicitous title of **How to Be Happy in the 21st Century.**

As almost everyone would like to learn how to be happy, we took a look at the course description and discovered that the class may be more about the *origins* of the *idea* of happiness rather than a prescription for it: "The list of books published on the subject of happiness numbers in the thousands. In 2008 alone, 4,000 books were published ranging from the mystery of happiness to how to sing in the morning. Even Harvard now offers a certificate in Happiness Studies. In HON 151, we will plan to explore this 'happiness frenzy' which may, in fact, date back to Aristotle's *Nicomachaen Ethics.* This course is also intended to lead in to an optional May term education abroad course in Australia." It would be interesting to see how Aristotle and Australia get together.

Other honors Gen Ed seminars include the **Impact of Emerging Technologies on Society--A Convoluted Journey;** Threshold Concepts in Biomedical Sciences; and **Mother of All Ironies: Making a Science of Intelligence.**

As for Mother of All Ironies, here is part of what we found: "The third [assigned] book is an edited collection of eleven serious studies on its otherwise **tantalizing titular topic, Robert J. Sternberg's *Why Smart People Can Be So Stupid.*** The title promises a popular, anecdote-festooned book but in actuality its eleven articles address (behavioral) stupidity as an objective rather than moral phenomenon."

In Spring 2014, some notable upper-division honors seminars were The Founders, the Courts and Religion: the American Experience; Early Christian Women; Intersubjectivity; and **Reason in the Earth.** The last focuses on the big question of whether inherent design and rational purpose are present in our lives and the life of the planet, otherwise known as the study of teleology—an excellent word for prospective and current college students to ponder.

"Since Aristotle, philosophers and scientists have questioned whether nature can (or ought to) be analyzed in terms of purposes," the course description says. "This question is especially pertinent to the biological sciences, and Darwin is often understood as having been singularly instrumental in evacuating teleological notions from biology. Drawing on ancient, modern, and contemporary sources, this course will investigate the history and philosophy of natural teleology."

The offerings of **departmental honors classes** are quite modest but some have the same seminar appeal of the Gen Ed classes. There is a class a CIS course that teaches students how to analyze the unceasing flow of cultural information that comes their way through technical media, a political science class on world politics, and a great 2-credit course in genomics and epigenetics (which studies "cell and tissue function by global analysis of gene expression and gene regulation." And—a section of honors chemistry.

Average Class Size (4.0): The average honors class size is 20.1 students; the overall average class size for the 50 colleges and programs under review in this edition is 21.2 students.

Adjusted Graduation Rate (4.5): The AGR is not simply the six-year graduation rate of students in the honors college who graduated from the university **(87.3%),** whether or not the students completed the honors program ("honors completers"). The AGR also reflects the extent to which the honors graduation rate from the university is higher than that for the university as a whole. The **university-wide rate is 58%,** yielding the 4.5 AGR for the college. The average six-year **honors graduation rate for all 50 programs** under review **is 89%.**

Ratio of Staff to Honors Students (3.5): Our estimate is that there is 1 staff member for every **169.3** students. (Mean ratio for all 50 programs is 1 staff member for every 159.8 students.)

Honors Residence Halls (5.0): "As part of its goal of increasing the size of the Honors Program," the Honors Director said, "UK has dedicated two new residence halls, Central I and Central II, for Honors students. Central Residence Hall houses a total of 16 active learning centers, two recreation rooms, three smart classrooms, and the Honors Program administrative and advising offices, providing students with a truly integrated residential learning experience."

Central now houses 356 first-year and upperclassmen honors students in suite-style, air-conditioned double rooms with shared baths between suites. The complex has two on-site laundries and two kitchens. The nearest dining is Ovid's. As its name suggests, Central is in a good location, especially close to chemistry and physics buildings and the library.

Prestigious Awards (3.5): "The Honors Program at the University of Kentucky has a very deliberate connection to the university's Office of External Scholarships," the Director told us. "We manage invitations to Honors faculty to identify and recommend potential competitive scholarship applicants in their Honors seminars from students' first semesters on campus; those students are then worked with on an individual basis in the Office of External Scholarships to lay the groundwork for successful competitive scholarship applications. Additionally, all first-year Honors students are required to attend a mandatory competitive scholarships information session in their first year at the university."

The efforts have begun to pay off, as UK undergrads won two Goldwater Scholarships in 2014. UK graduates have also won 9 Rhodes Scholarships and 13 Truman Scholarships. In 2014, UK graduates won 15 prestigious National Science Foundation Graduate Research Fellowships to pursue doctoral studies at leading universities.

Continuation Requirements: 3.00 GPA

Academic Strengths: In line with the appeal of Global Honors Program in the Gatton College of Business, the strongest academic departments at UK are business and economics, both ranked 58th in the nation. Other especially well-respected departments are education, math, political science, and psychology.

Undergraduate Research: Among several commendable programs of the Office of Undergraduate Research (OUR) is the **Bucks for Brains Summer Research Program.** According to the OUR, the program "is designed to provide undergraduate students with opportunities to work one-on-one with leading faculty on research projects that are funded by the state's Research Challenge Trust fund (RCTF), commonly known as 'Bucks for Brains.' The goal of the program is to increase diversity of the student population in UK laboratories, thus strengthening the student research pipeline at UK.

"The program requires a minimum of 6 hours per day for a period of 8 weeks, depending on individual faculty requirements. Generally, students should expect to work at the discretion of their faculty mentor, not to exceed 40 hours per week or 10 weeks. Students may take one summer school class concurrent with this experience, but those who elect to take academic courses must accept responsibility for paying all tuition and fees. **Students will receive a $3,500 scholarship for the summer,** and participating RCTF faculty will receive $1,000 for supplies and research needs."

Study Abroad: Undergraduate research and study abroad meet happily through the Undergraduate Research Abroad Scholarship, a collaborate effort of the Office of Undergraduate Research (UGR) and Education Abroad (EA) office. The scholarship "pays up to $5,000 to a full-time undergraduate student to cover the costs of a well-defined, credit-bearing research project abroad during the summer term for approximately 8 weeks. The student applying for the scholarship must be highly recommended by a UK faculty mentor with whom they have already done research."

The UK Honors Director told us that "Honors offers a variety of scholarship opportunities for Education Abroad, including the Student Skills Development Award, the Journal-Journey Scholarship, and the Kate Johnson Scholarship. The Program typically offers 3-5 Honors-sponsored education abroad courses in an academic year, all in the summer or winter intersessions. Honors at UK gives students the option to complete Honors experience requirements by completing education abroad programs identified on their Honors, major, or minor menu of options."

Financial Aid: "While most Honors students receive some kind of merit and need-based financial aid from university-wide and external sources, Honors offered for the first time in Fall 2013 a four-year scholarship for tuition," according to the Director. **"The T.W. Lewis Scholarship Fund will provide up to 10 new scholarships in the amount of $5,000 per year for eligible Honors Program students.** Up to five scholarships will be awarded to applicants from a 10-county region in Eastern Kentucky, including Breathitt, Clay, Floyd, Harlan, Jackson, Knott, Leslie, Letcher, Perry and Wolfe counties. Up to five scholarships will be awarded to applicants from Fayette County. **The Singletary Scholarship (full**

tuition, room, board, and additional travel award) is the most prestigious academic scholarship at the university, and all recipients of that award are members of the Honors Program. Additionally, Patterson Scholars (full tuition) are primarily in the Honors Program."

Degree of Difference (Honors students/non-honors students): 3.93 on a scale of 5. Some parents and prospective students might prefer an honors program that in many ways stands apart on campus, while others might prefer a program that is more expansive. The rating here tries to provide an indication of where a given honors program is on the stand apart/expansive spectrum. The rating is based on the difference between (1) the average SAT scores for enrolled honors students and (2) the average test scores for all students in the university as a whole *and* for students with scores at the 75% level or above. A score of 3.5 or higher indicates a high degree of difference. A score of 3.2 to 3.49 indicates a relatively high degree of difference. Finally, a score below 3.2 indicates a modest difference. **Please keep in mind that neither the high nor low selectivity of an honors program determines how effective the program is; this rating is merely "cultural" and *not* qualitative.**

NAME: LSU HONORS COLLEGE

Date Established: Began as Honors Division of College of Liberal Arts in 1966; became an honors college in 1992.

Location: Baton Rouge, Louisiana

University Full-time Undergraduate Enrollment: 22,681

Honors Enrollment: approximately 1,491 (mean enrollment of 50 programs is 1,714).

Review/Admissions Category II: Programs with **average SAT scores of 1343--1382 for enrolled students**. Actual average (median) SAT score for enrolled students at LSU Honors College is 1380, although most students submit the ACT score. The median ACT is 31. The median High School GPA for entering honors students is 3.85.

These are the **minimum** requirements for admission:

SAT=1330 Critical Reading + Math (combined) with 660 Critical Reading
ACT=30 Composite with 30 English, or 29 Composite with 31 English
ACT or SAT Writing Test also required for admissions
GPA=3.5 (weighted by LSU)

Honors Programs in Admissions Category II (average SAT scores of 1343-1382): Alabama, Delaware, Florida State, LSU, Massachusetts, Missouri, North Carolina State, Ohio University, Temple, Purdue, UCLA, Utah, Vermont, and Wisconsin.

Administrative Staff: The Honors College has full-time staff of 13.

FOR ALL "MORTARBOARD" RATINGS BELOW, A SCORE OF 5 IS THE MAXIMUM AND REPRESENTS A COMPARISON OF ALL 50 HONORS COLLEGES AND PROGRAMS:

PERCEPTION* OF UNIVERSITY AS A WHOLE, <u>NOT</u> OF HONORS: 🎓🎓1/2

OVERALL HONORS RATING: 🎓🎓🎓1/2

Curriculum Requirements: 🎓🎓🎓1/2**

Class Range and Type: 🎓🎓🎓1/2

Class Size: 🎓🎓🎓🎓

Adjusted Grad Rate: 🎓🎓🎓1/2

Ratio of Staff to Students: 🎓🎓🎓🎓¹ᐟ²

Priority Registration: "Honors College students have Priority Registration privileges for ALL class registration for their entire career at LSU as long as they remain in Good Standing with the Honors College (3.0 GPA, enrollment in at least two Honors courses per year)."

Honors Housing: 🎓🎓🎓🎓¹ᐟ²

Prestigious Awards: 🎓🎓🎓¹ᐟ²

*Perception is based on the university's ranking among public universities in the 2014 U.S. News Best Colleges report. Please bear in mind that the higher the U.S. News ranking, the more difficult it is for an honors college or program to have a rating that improves on the magazine ranking.

**Curriculum Requirements (3.5): The honors completion requirement is a very substantial 32 semester hours, but because AP credit (see below) can replace 6 of those hours, the rating for the LSU Honors College is based on 26 hours instead of 32.

Assuming that a first-year student has not received any honors AP credits, the **College Honors completion level** requires 32 semester hours of honors credit, of which at least 6 credits must be from honors college seminars and courses and at least 12 credits must be in upper-division honors. Students must also complete a senior thesis. **Almost all of the upper-division credits come from honors option courses.** These are regular class sections in which an honors student and the instructor have agreed on extra reading, research, writing, presentations, or projects that the student must complete in order to receive honors credit. There is no limit on the number of honors option courses that may be taken. Students must have a 3.50 cumulative GPA to complete College Honors.

Upper Division Honors Distinction requires completion of 12 semester hours in higher level courses and 3-6 credits for the senior thesis. A 3.50 cumulative and upper-division GPA is required.

AP/IB credit: Students can receive up to 6 hours of credit for the introductory chemistry sequence with an AP score of 4 or higher.

Range and Type of Honors Courses (3.5): The honors college is a **blended program** in which a sizable number of lower-division honors seminars combine with relatively few formal departmental sections, especially in upper-division courses. As previously noted, most upper-division honors credits come from honors option courses. The honors seminars fulfill university Gen Ed requirements.

We counted 18 honors seminars in Spring 2014, including the following: Natural Disturbances and Society; **The Constitution and American Civilization;** Romantics and Rebels; **Art of Thinking;** Great Britain in the 20th Century; The Cold War; **Character and Strategy in U.S. Corporations;** Art and Its Markets; The Synoptic Gospels; **Leadership, Ethics, and What It Means to Be Human;** and World Literature: 20th Century Short Stories and Post-colonialism.

Two other seminars are part of a **commendable experiential learning program: Louisiana Service and Leadership (LASAL),** an Honors College program "designed to produce leaders who are ready to use their knowledge and experience to help change Louisiana. No other college or university in the nation has a program like LASAL, which empowers students to solve chronic local problems.

"LASAL Scholars are a select group of Honors students who are passionate about solving Louisiana's problems, from coastal erosion to poverty, education to health care. They are passionate about social justice and serving their community. LASAL Scholars may pursue any major because the program of study complements any major."

The two LASAL seminars in Spring 2014 were The Coastal Louisiana Ecosystem: Place and People; and another called The State of Louisiana.

There were about 30 formal **departmental honors sections** in Spring 2014, with math (calculus with analytical geometry), biology, chemistry (including organic), art, architecture, communications/journalism, music, environmental studies, and sociology all offering 2-3 classes on average. Although we found no specific English sections, many of the honors seminars fulfilled the university's writing requirements. We did not find any formal honors upper-division classes in political science, psychology, anthropology, or physics. History, philosophy, **oceanography,** and geology each had one honors section. Again, many honors upper-division credits from honors option classes and research for the senior thesis or project.

Average Class Size (4.0): The Dean reported that the average honors class has **21.9** students, almost exactly the mean for all 50 colleges and programs under review in this edition--21.2 students. Enrollments of honors students in honors option classes were not counted, but because these are all upper-division, the class sizes may not be that large.

Adjusted Graduation Rate (3.5): The AGR is not simply the six-year graduation rate of students in the honors college who graduated from the university **(84.7%),** whether or not the students completed the honors program ("honors completers"). It also reflects the extent to which the honors graduation rate from the university is higher than that for the university as a whole. (The **university-wide rate is 67%,** yielding the 3.5 AGR for the college.) The average honors six-year **graduation rate for all 50 programs under review is 89%.**

Ratio of Staff to Honors Students (4.5): Our estimate is that there is 1 staff member for every **114.5** students. (Median ratio for all 50 programs is 1 staff member for every 159.8 students.)

Honors Residence Halls (4.5): The College Dean (at the time of our survey) provided us with an excellent, detailed summary of honors housing and facilities at LSU:

"The Honors College facilities include the Laville Honors House (residence hall) and the adjacent French House (classrooms and administrative offices) which together **occupy 10 acres at the center of the LSU campus, comprising a 'campus within the campus.'**

"The **Laville Honors House is the residential home** to the Honors College. **The buildings were originally constructed in the 1930s and therefore sit in the heart of the campus, across the street from the Student Union and adjacent to the home of the Honors College, the French House. One of only two dining halls on campus is connected to the Laville Honors House.**

"Beginning in 2008, the residence hall underwent a $50 million complete renovation including the construction of a new 'in-fill' building that connects two wings of the residence. The in-fill provides both halls with a 24-hour front desk, large common areas and a computer lab. In addition, a Faculty Residence apartment is located on the second floor of the in-fill directly above the front desk. The renovations were completed in fall 2012, and improvements include a new central air and heating system with independent control in the bedrooms. The bedrooms are completely new from floor to ceiling, including new flooring, walls, ceiling tiles, moveable/loftable beds, moveable desks, chests and chair. The hall bathrooms are completely new, and there are study rooms on every floor, along with a new kitchen, laundry facility and huge common space.

"The renovation preserved the classic and historic beauty of the building but replaced everything inside with state-of-the-art furnishings, fixtures and equipment.

"The Honors College has classrooms and offices in the building in addition to our own building, the French House (see below). **One of the Associate Deans of the Honors College serves as Rector for the Residential College and has his offices in the Laville Honors House. All programming is designed jointly by the Honors College and Residential Life.**

"Adjacent to the Laville Honors House, the Honors College also occupies The French House--La Maison Française--a Renaissance-style Normandy château built in 1935 as a center for intense study of French language, culture, and literature. The French House remains the only non-Quadrangle LSU structure on the National Register of Historic Places. In its prime, the facility was host to formal entertainment and distinguished visitors to campus.

"Since 1999, it has housed the daily administrative and student life functions of the LSU Honors College. The 16,000 square foot structure currently houses 4 classrooms, 12 administrative offices, a student lounge, and a large public space--The Grand Salon--which is used for events, receptions, concerts, ceremonies, and performances.

"Beginning spring 2014, the building will undergo a complete $5 million renovation, creating state-of-the-art classrooms, administrative offices, a student lounge, and a public event area. All renovations will retain the historic architectural features of the building (original wood floors, terrazzo tile floors, dormer windows, etc.) while making the space accessible and functional for students and faculty."

Laville Honors House features traditional double rooms for the most part, with shared hall baths. It is home to more than 600 honors students, making it one of the largest all-honors residence halls. All rooms are air conditioned with room controls. Although the building is coed, men and women are assigned to separate floors. Laville has two kitchens and two laundry rooms. "The building has two large lounge/study areas on the first floor and additional study lounges on each floor. In addition, there is a large public lounge area at the entrance to the building, and an outdoor patio/grove that is enclosed on three sides by the building and on the fourth side by the dining hall."

Prestigious Awards (3.5): LSU students have won 29 Goldwater Scholarships to date, awarded to outstanding undergraduates in the STEM fields. LSU grads have won 14 Rhodes Scholarships, 4 Marshall Scholarships, and 9 Truman Scholarships. The best is yet to come, as the Honors Dean reported that "**most of these awards have been secured since the establishment of the LSU Honors College Office of Fellowship Advising in 2005**, with LSU achieving more student successes in national scholarship competitions than in the preceding 30 years collectively. All 3 of the university's Udall recipients, 7 of 8 Truman, 14 of 29 Goldwater have been awarded since the Honors College instituted an office to assist in scholarship preparation."

Continuation Requirements: 3.00 GPA to remain in good standing, but a 3.50 for honors completion.

Academic Strengths: The strongest departments at LSU are earth sciences, business, chemistry, political science, sociology, physics, English, history, and math.

Undergraduate Research: "The Honors College awards special funds towards completing a student's Honors Thesis in order to pay for supplies, travel, and reimbursement for research participants," the Dean said. **"Undergraduate research is promoted throughout the Honors College but formally serves as the theme for the senior year.** The culmination of the Honors curriculum is the Honors Thesis, a two-semester independent study with a professor in the student's major on a topic of the student's choosing. The Honors Thesis is a requirement to graduating with College Honors, the highest distinction the LSU Honors College offers. **The Honors Thesis is expected to reflect graduate-level research and must be defended before a committee towards the end of the second semester of enrollment."**

More than 115 honors college students are current members of the Chancellor's Future Leaders in Research Program, which pairs students with faculty research mentors as early as the freshman year. And more than 50% of honors graduating seniors are currently enrolled in thesis coursework.

Study Abroad: "Honors College students comprise the largest number of LSU students participating in study abroad opportunities including summer trips, one semester, and full year programs," the Dean reported. "The Honors College provides scholarships for students participating in semester and year-long academic programs abroad.

"The Honors College offers special summer programs for Honors students and, from 2006-2010, ran the Gateway to China Program fully funded by the university. This program led to LSU's exchange agreement with Tongji University in Shanghai. In Summer 2011, the Honors College led a service learning trip to South Africa in partnership with the University of California (UCLA, UCSB, UCSD, UC Berkeley). In Summer 2014, the Honors College is planning a study abroad trip to Cuba."

Financial Aid: In this category, the Dean also provided an outstanding summary, ***and also discussed the Career and Internship Placement Services that the college offers to honors students.*** "LSU freshman scholarship programs are purposefully aligned with Honors College admission requirements. While Honors admission is not required for these programs, the design ensures a comprehensive overlap with the Honors entering population.

"Louisiana resident students who meet Honors College criteria receive the state's TOPS scholarship that provides full tuition. These students also receive a $1,500 -$2,500 per year stipend at graduated levels, beginning slightly below standardized test score requirements for Honors admission and rising at tiers above that level. A large majority of students also receive a campus job award of $1,550 per year, which may be used for research employment, a distinct academic advantage.

"Non-resident students receive $7,500-$20,500 per year stipends at levels that mirror the in-state student program outlined above. A large majority of non-resident students also receive the campus job award of $1,550 per year.

"The Honors College also offers several distinct scholarship programs:

- direct support for up to five special projects per year at $5,000 each through our Roger Hadfield Ogden Honors Leaders program,
- support for thesis research at $500-$750,
- support for study abroad activity with $500-$1,000,
- scholarships for underrepresented groups in Engineering and in Business with $4,000 over four years,
- scholarships through the Shell Honors Student Leaders program at $3,500 over four years including interaction with this major energy company."

Career and Internship Advising:

"In December 2006, the LSU Honors College established an Office of Career Development to serve as a resource for both students seeking and obtaining experiential education opportunities-- internships, cooperative education, community service/volunteer experience--and for employers searching for motivated, high-achieving students to fill those positions with their companies. The Director of Career Development assists students through each step of the internship process including providing general information and workshops, assisting with résumé writing and application procedures, and **connecting students with employers and other useful resources.**

"The Office of Career Development in the LSU Honors College provides information sessions, workshops, individual advising appointments internship postings and service opportunities.

"A series of Career Panels is undertaken to offer students the opportunity to interact with professionals in designated career fields, hearing their stories and experience, asking questions, receiving career tips, and building networking resources. This series has expanded from three panels the first year in the areas of Law, Medical and Healthcare, and Arts and Humanities to the current number of seven. In addition to the aforementioned career fields, panels have focused on Allied Health Sciences, Communication in the Professions, **Medical School Admissions**, Social Justice, Nonprofit Management, Business/Entrepreneurial, Internships, and the upcoming 'Going Abroad' panel.

"The number of student contacts has risen each year, and during the 2012-2013 academic year, almost 400 face-to-face, email, and telephone contacts were made with students."

Degree of Difference (Honors students/non-honors students): 2.85 on a scale of 5. Some parents and prospective students might prefer an honors program that in many ways stands apart on campus, while others might prefer a program that is more expansive. The rating here tries to provide an indication of where a given honors program is on the stand apart/expansive spectrum. The rating is based on the difference between (1) the average SAT scores for enrolled honors students and (2) the average test scores for all students in the university as a whole *and* for students with scores at the 75% level or above. A

score of 3.5 or higher indicates a high degree of difference. A score of 3.2 to 3.49 indicates a relatively high degree of difference. Finally, a score below 3.2 indicates a modest difference. **Please keep in mind that neither the high nor low selectivity of an honors program determines how effective the program is; this rating is merely "cultural" and *not* qualitative.**

NAME: THE UNIVERSITY OF MAINE HONORS COLLEGE

Date Established: 1935

Location: Orono, Maine

University Full-time Undergraduate Enrollment: 7,520

Honors Enrollment: 861 (mean size of all 50 programs is 1,714).

Review/Admissions Category I: Programs with **average SAT scores of 1235--1342** for enrolled students. The average (mean) test scores for honors enrollees are SAT 1235, ACT 27.76. The average high school GPA is 3.22.

Minimum admission requirements: "In addition to GPA, class rank, SAT and ACT scores, a number of other factors may be considered when inviting students to join the Honors College."

Honors Programs in Admissions Category I (average SAT scores of 1235-1342): Arizona, Arizona State, Arkansas, Colorado State, Iowa, Maine, Mississippi, Oklahoma State, Oregon, Oregon State, Rhode Island, Texas Tech, University at Albany, and Washington State.

Administrative Staff: The Honors College has 5.5 full-time equivalent employees.

FOR ALL "MORTARBOARD" RATINGS BELOW, A SCORE OF 5 IS THE MAXIMUM AND REPRESENTS A COMPARISON WITH ALL 50 HONORS COLLEGES AND PROGRAMS:

PERCEPTION* OF UNIVERSITY AS A WHOLE, <u>NOT</u> OF HONORS: 🎓🎓

OVERALL HONORS RATING: 🎓🎓🎓

Curriculum Requirements: 🎓🎓🎓1/2

Class Range and Type: 🎓🎓🎓1/2

Class Size: 🎓🎓🎓🎓🎓

Adjusted Grad Rate: 🎓🎓🎓

Ratio of Staff to Students: 🎓🎓🎓🎓

Priority Registration: No.

Honors Housing: 🎓🎓🎓1/2

Prestigious Awards: 🎓🎓🎓

*Perception is based on the university's ranking among public universities in the 2014 U.S. News Best Colleges report. Please bear in mind that the better the U.S. News ranking, the more difficult it is for an honors college or program to have a rating that equals or improves on the magazine ranking.

Curriculum Requirements (3.5): To complete the College curriculum, students must earn at least 27 honors credits, as follows:

- Honors Civilizations: Past, Present, and Future, a sequence of four courses over two years=16 credits
- One honors tutorial=3 credits
- A 1-credit Currents and Contexts course and one more 1-credit course, either A Cultural Odyssey or another optional course
- A senior thesis=6 credits

AP/IB credits are **not** counted as replacements for Honors College courses.

Range and Type of Honors Courses (3.5): The College was an early leader in developing a **core honors** program, characterized by excellent interdisciplinary seminars in the first two years, a thesis requirement in the last year, and very few, if any, departmental honors programs in specific academic disciplines. Core programs are central to providing "a liberal arts education" in the context of a (usually large) public university. The University of Maine perhaps comes closest to this idea because the total number of full-time undergraduates is less than 8,000, making the university the smallest of the 50 universities whose honors programs are being rated. Similar core programs are at the universities of Washington, Washington State, Oregon, UC Irvine, Vermont, and Kentucky.

We should add that the Maine core program is perhaps the purest of the pure public university core programs in the country because the *Civilizations* sequence, with its readings in classical and early modern primary works (Homer, Sappho, Plato, Galileo, Pericles, Laozi, Virgil, Dante, Chaucer, Machiavelli, Shakespeare, Kant, Locke, Rousseau, and others) not only hearkens back to the days of a truly classical education but reminds us of the current curriculum at the St. John's Colleges in Santa Fe and Annapolis.

The College provided an excellent and detailed summary of its courses:

"Civilizations: Past, Present and Future I-IV are four credit courses taken in the first two years and form the foundation of the Honors program. **Class size is limited to 15 students, although the average is 12 students per section.** The *Civilizations* sequence is **a great books curriculum organized chronologically, which includes primary source material from philosophy, history, literature, art and the natural and social sciences.** Over the course of two years, students are given the opportunity to ask and consider fundamental questions on what it means to be human, what is justice, the role of belief and the construction of knowledge, among others. Students develop interpretive and analytical skills and the ability to think and write critically. The *Civilizations* sequence satisfies many of the General Education requirements and completion of the Honors program satisfies almost all of them.

"One special feature of the first year experience in the University of Maine Honors College is the Honors Read. **The summer before entering university, all incoming students are given a copy of a contemporary work that they read together with the faculty teaching HON 111. The book is chosen by upper level students in an Honors Read tutorial** (see explanation below) and recent selections include *Persepolis* (Marjane Satrapi), *An Omnivore's Dilemma* (Michael Pollan), *The Sparrow* (Mary Doria Russell), and *Eaarth* (Bill McKibben).

"Two one-credit courses are also required: Currents and Context and A Cultural Odyssey, which may be taken at any time in the student's enrollment in Honors. Currently, a third one credit course, Citizen Scholar: Introduction to Civic Engagement, is being offered experimentally. Introduction to Thesis Research is another one credit course offered to Honors students, but it is not currently a requirement for graduation with Honors.

"Honors students are required to take a three-credit tutorial, typically in their third year, and each year a variety of special topics courses are offered to students (the current list of offerings is available on the Honors College website along with examples of past tutorials). Most of these courses take place over the course of a semester, but we also offer an intensive two-week research experience at Mount Desert Island Biological Laboratory (MDIBL) and occasionally an intensive May term tutorial.

"As well, the Honors College has a provision for tutorial alternatives, which are academic or experiential learning opportunities such as study abroad, Research Experiences for Undergraduates and other kinds of internships, Semester at Sea, cultural and/or language immersions programs, for example. With the approval of the Dean of the Honors College, these experiences may substitute for the tutorial requirement.

"The Honors College in conjunction with the Maine IDeA Network for Biomedical Research Excellence, (which includes Mount Desert Island laboratory), offers two additional three credit courses for first year students: **Genome Discovery I–From Dirt to DNA** and **Genome Discovery II–From DNA to Genes.** Admission to these courses is limited by capacity of the lab.

"An additional opportunity available to our students is the **Maine Track Early Assurance Program of Tufts University School of Medicine.** Students across the state apply in the second semester of their second year of university and if accepted, are offered placement at Tufts University School of Medicine upon graduation in good standing. Honors College students have been consistently successful in getting accepted to Tufts through the Early Assurance Program since its inception.

"Honors students undertake thesis research and writing typically in their final year, although it is not uncommon for students to begin research that culminates in a thesis earlier than that. The thesis is defended before a five-person thesis committee, which is made up of the student's advisor, members of faculty in and outside the field as well as one from Honors. **In addition to the thesis, students compile a Reading List consisting of books and other works (film, art, music) which have shaped their thinking over the course of their tenure in the Honors College. The Reading List is also discussed at the thesis defense and is often one of the favorite parts of the experience."**

Average Class Size (5.0): The average honors class size at the College is **14.8 students.** (The overall class size for the 50 colleges and programs under review in this edition is 21.2 students.)

Adjusted Graduation Rate (3.0): The relatively low rating in this category is perplexing, and we do not have an explanation. The AGR is not simply the six-year graduation rate of students in the honors college who graduated from the university **(75%),** whether or not the students completed the honors program ("honors completers"). The AGR also reflects the extent to which the honors graduation rate from the university is higher than that for the university as a whole. The **university-wide rate is 59%,** yielding the relatively low 3.0 AGR for the college. The average honors six-year **graduation rate for all 50 programs under review is 89%.**

Ratio of Staff to Honors Students (4.0): Our estimate is that there is 1 staff member for every **156.5** students. (Mean ratio for all 50 programs is 1 staff member for every 159.8 students.)

Honors Residence Halls (3.5): The honors residence halls **(for upperclassmen only)** are Colvin, Balentine, and Penobscot Halls. All feature traditional double rooms and hall baths and on-site laundry facilities; but none is air-conditioned, probably not an issue in a town not far from the coast of Maine. The nearest dining is York Dining Hall.

"Located next to Colvin Hall is the lovely Charlie's Terrace, an outdoor classroom and gathering space, where students, faculty and other members of campus can be found reading or relaxing in one of the signature orange Adirondack chairs. Honors will soon be expanding into adjacent Eastbrooke Hall and together all of these spaces form an Honors community within the larger campus."

Prestigious Awards (3.0): Maine graduates have won 3 Rhodes Scholarships and 4 Truman Scholarships. To date, Maine undergrads have won 9 Goldwater Scholarships.

Continuation Requirements: 3.30 cumulative GPA

Academic Strengths: The strongest departments at Maine are earth sciences, marines sciences, engineering, education, and English. (The novelist Stephen King is an English alum.)

Undergraduate Research: Once again, we defer to the excellent summary provided by the College: "All of the students who graduate from the Honors College have a thesis requirement and thus engage in independent research. As well, many of our students have the opportunity to work closely with professors and mentors on research projects in a variety of disciplines, some very early on in their university experience.

"A variety of scholarships and fellowships are available to support student research. In the Honors College itself undergraduate research support is made available through the study abroad support noted above as well as: INBRE, which supports junior and senior research fellowships; the Charlie Slavin Research Fund; the Bernard Lown Thesis Fellowship; the Carolyn Reed Pre-Medical Thesis Fellowship; and the Rendle A. Jones '65 and Patricia K. Jones '65 Thesis Fellowship.

"University of Maine Honors College students are competitive for the prestigious scholarships named in [the honors survey questionnaire] and others including, for example, the NOAA Ernest F. Hollings Undergraduate Scholarship Program. The University of Maine's Center for Undergraduate Research (CUGR) offers fellowships and Honors students are consistently well-represented among the recipients.

Research by junior and senior Honors students may also be supported by the Maine Policy Scholars Program.

"Finally, the Honors College regularly takes over a dozen students to the National Collegiate Honors College Conference where students showcase their research in poster sessions, roundtable discussions and panel presentations. Participation in the conference generally entails a research component on the part of the honors student."

Study Abroad: According to College staff, "the Honors College has several scholarships available to our students for study abroad including the Charles V. Stanhope '71 Honors College Study Abroad Fellowship and the Rezendes Global Service Scholarship. Our students can also take advantage of the George J. Mitchell Peace Scholarship for study abroad in Ireland along with a host of other scholarships available through our Office of International Programs." **The University of Maine has over 700 study abroad opportunities and over two dozen direct exchange programs with universities around the world."**

The Honors College is a member of the Honors Principia Consortium with the University of Glasgow in Scotland and is developing an exchange program with Tembusu College in Singapore.

While not actually a study-abroad program, the **Semester by the Sea,** requiring 16 weeks of study at the UM Darling Marine Center in Walpole, Maine, is a great option. "SBS courses are unique. They meet one day a week, most for the whole day, with lectures, labs and field trips scheduled around the tides. Ready access to a myriad of marine environments and faculty mentors makes the DMC the perfect venue for capstone and honors projects. The DMC is one of the leading marine research stations on the eastern seaboard of North America. We have research vessels, flowing seawater classrooms/laboratories, electron microscopes, marine library and dormitory/dining facilities."

Financial Aid: The university has several generous merit scholarships available to both in-state and out-of-state students. **Two awards offer $15,000 a year to highly-talented out-of-state students.**

Presidential Scholarships are given to the top student in a class or National Achievement semi-finalist; **all National Merit semi-finalists receive the UM Merit Scholarship.** The renewable amounts are **$8,000 a year for in-state and $15,000 a year for out-of-state students.** (Out-of-state tuition averages about $25,740 a year.)

Students with a GPA of 85/3.0 and a 1400 SAT/32 ACT score receive the **Flagship scholarship, valued at $5,000 annually for in-state students and $15,000 annually for out-of-state students.**

A GPA of 85/3.0 and SAT 1250/28-31 ACT score can earn the All Deans' scholarship with a value of $3,000 a year for in-state students and $10,000 a year for out-of-state students.

Students with a GPA greater than 3.5 or 90 and SAT scores of 1100-1240 and ACT scores of 25-27 may receive the Black Bear Scholarship worth $1,000 a year to in-state students and $4,000 a year to out-of-state students.

"Honors students often are the recipients of the George J. Mitchell Scholarship given annually to one student from each high school in Maine. Native American students in the Honors College are beneficiaries of the Native American Indian Waiver and Education Program, which waives tuition fees and provides support for room and board. Students are also eligible for a State of Maine grant.

"Within the College, students are eligible for the study abroad scholarships and thesis fellowships listed in previous sections along with the Barbara B. Thomson Memorial Honors Award given annually to a junior in political science and in art."

Degree of Difference (Honors students/non-honors students): 2.26 on a scale of 5. Some parents and prospective students might prefer an honors program that in many ways stands apart on campus, while others might prefer a program that is more expansive. The rating here tries to provide an indication of where a given honors program is on the stand apart/expansive spectrum. The rating is based on the difference between (1) the average SAT scores for enrolled honors students and (2) the average test scores for all students in the university as a whole *and* for students with scores at the 75% level or above. A score of 3.5 or higher indicates a high degree of difference. A score of 3.2 to 3.49 indicates a relatively high degree of difference. Finally, a score below 3.2 indicates a modest difference. **Please keep in mind that neither the high nor low selectivity of an honors program determines how effective the program is; this rating is merely "cultural" and *not* qualitative.**

Testimonial:

Eliot Gagné '16, second year Biochemistry--"The Honors College has also allowed me the opportunity to do scientific research as a first year student. My early exposure to research has led to a number of internship opportunities as well as an opportunity to do cutting edge zebra fish research in the Kim lab at UMaine. Aside from research opportunities, one of the aspects of the Honors College I appreciate the most is its ability to create a small community within the larger university. In this Honors community I have formed lifelong friendships and relationships with professors that have enriched my life as an undergraduate. Finally, the Honors College's curriculum fostered both my intellectual and personal development. **The diversity of texts in Honors allowed me to investigate many of the questions that evoke what it means to be human. In the words of one of my Honors College professors, I have had the chance to, 'think hard about things that matter.'"**

NAME: COMMONWEALTH HONORS COLLEGE, UNIVERSITY OF MASSACHUSETTS AMHERST

Date Established: 1999

Location: Amherst, Massachusetts

University Full-time Undergraduate Enrollment: 20,306

Honors Enrollment: 3,000 (mean size of all 50 programs is 1,714)

Review/Admissions Category II: Programs with **average SAT scores of 1343--1382 for enrolled students**. Actual average (mean) SAT score for enrolled honors college students is 1356, and the average ACT is 30. The average high school GPA is 4.21 (weighted) and high school class rank top 4.2%.

Minimum Admission Requirements: SAT 1300, ACT 29; high school GPA, A-; high school class rank, 90th percentile.

Honors Programs in Admissions Category II (average SAT scores of 1343-1382): Alabama, Delaware, Florida State, LSU, Massachusetts, Missouri, North Carolina State, Ohio University, Temple, Purdue, UCLA, Utah, Vermont, and Wisconsin.

Administrative Staff: The Honors College has a staff of 25.

FOR ALL "MORTARBOARD" RATINGS BELOW, A SCORE OF 5 IS THE MAXIMUM AND REPRESENTS A COMPARISON WITH ALL 50 HONORS COLLEGES AND PROGRAMS:

PERCEPTION* OF UNIVERSITY AS A WHOLE, **NOT** OF HONORS: 🎓 🎓🎓[1/2]

OVERALL HONORS RATING: 🎓 🎓 🎓[1/2]

Curriculum Requirements: 🎓 🎓 🎓 🎓

Class Range and Type: 🎓 🎓 🎓 🎓 🎓

Class Size: 🎓 🎓 🎓[1/2]

Adjusted Grad Rate: 🎓 🎓 🎓[1/2]

Ratio of Staff to Students: 🎓 🎓 🎓 🎓[1/2]

Priority Registration: No, but most honors students can register early for most honors classes.

Honors Housing: 🎓 🎓 🎓 🎓

Prestigious Awards: 🎓🎓🎓$^{1/2}$

*Perception is based on the university's ranking among public universities in the 2014 U.S. News Best Colleges report. Please bear in mind that the better the U.S. News ranking, the more difficult it is for an honors college or program to have a rating that equals or improves on the magazine ranking.

Curriculum Requirements (4.0): The first thing we want to say about the CHC is that *it has all the signs of a five-mortarboard honors college that is waiting to happen.* If the honors college simply offered priority registration it would raise the rating of the CHC to at least a 4.0 and possibly to a 4.5.

When it comes to the nuts and bolts of an honors program, the college does very well, with honors completion requirements that are above the mean among all 50 programs and a choice of honors courses and seminars that rank with the best--not to mention excellent honors housing (see below).

Honors completion at the highest level (Commonwealth Honors College Scholar, with Departmental Honors) requires at least 30 hours of honors credit, of which 8 hours must be in departmental honors course work and **6 hours for thesis research and thesis**. The other 16 hours must be in honors college courses.

A similar completion option is Commonwealth Honors College Scholar, with Multidisciplinary Honors. The option requires 30 credit hours as well, but with 24 hours of honors interdisciplinary courses and no departmental honors credits. **There is also a thesis requirement**.

Two less demanding options are Departmental Honors, with completion requiring the same 8 hours of *departmental honors* courses along **with a 6-hour thesis** that is required for the CHC Scholar; and Multidisciplinary Honors, which requires 8 hours of *interdisciplinary* honors courses **plus a 6-hour thesis.**

AP/IB credits are **not** counted as replacements for honors courses. Note: "Students who complete some or all of their General Education coursework through AP scores must take other honors courses in place of their Honors College Writing or other honors General Education courses they would otherwise take. Alternative honors coursework must be negotiated with an Honors Advisor and noted in an addendum to their Honors Contract/Academic Plan."

Range and Type of Honors Courses (5.0): The range and type of honors courses form the backbone of the CHC, which has one of the best selections of honors courses in the nation. Even though a sizable number of departmental sections are mixed, the college awards extra credit for the small breakout sections (discussion sections) that honors students attend in addition to the time they spend in the larger lecture sections. We classify the CHC as a **blended honors program** because students have the opportunity to take excellent honors seminars with a multidisciplinary emphasis along with an extremely broad range of honors courses centered in the academic departments.

We counted 25 sections in Spring 2014 of Honors Seminar I: Ideas That Change the World, a signature series that requires students "to examine texts and works of art that have profoundly shaped the world we live in. The 4-credit hour course is divided into four units: Models of Inquiry; the Impact of

Science and Technology; Social Philosophy and Civic Engagement; and Art in the World. The course is supplemented with several plenary lectures by distinguished honors faculty speakers." (In Fall 2014, far more of these sections are offered.)

Another seminar in Spring 2014 was Violence in American Culture. In addition, there were twenty-four 1-credit hour seminars available for upperclassmen. The topics for these are varied, and the format is discussion-based. Other small, seminar-type sections deal with leadership, peer advising, mentorship, preparation for studying abroad, and many other topics.

On the departmental honors side, there are definitely some large mixed sections (those that enroll honors and non-honors students). As is the case with several other programs, the CHC has opted to make more departmental sections available to honors students even if that means the students will have larger classes than they would in a more restrictive program. The largest classes are in microbiology, statistics, sports management, and animal science--but, again, how many honors programs offer any kind of honors class in sports management? In some ways a typical mixed section is a lot like an honors contract class: in both, a student is in a class with more non-honors students than honors students but usually does some level of extra work. Professors may volunteer to add a 1-credit honors colloquium discussion section to their standard course, allowing professors to have more close contact in a small-group format with honors students and giving students more opportunities to know and become known by additional distinguished professors.

The upside to the CHC approach is that there is much to choose from: lots of history classes, the aforementioned microbiology, marketing, political science, anthropology, a nice range of honors math classes ranging up to differential equations and multivariate analysis. There's more: lots of sections in biology, chemistry, and most remarkably, about half a dozen reasonably-sized sections in economics. For physics, we found just one section, in statistical physics, but in most semesters there are the small 1-credit hour honors physics discussion sections.

The CHC has made a strong commitment to hiring and retaining honors faculty. The likely result will be fewer mixed sections in the future while not losing the broad range of courses available.

"Since 2010 fifteen new tenure-track Honors Faculty have been hired through collaborations between Commonwealth Honors College and [15 academic departments].... Searches are currently in process for four additional new tenure-track Honors Faculty in English; Environmental Health Sciences; Mechanical & Industrial Engineering; and Psychology.

"Memos of Understanding between the CHC Dean, the Provost, the academic departments, and the Deans of the departments' colleges stipulate **the new Honors Faculty will teach two honors courses each year as part of their teaching load;** that the CHC Dean will have input on their annual reports and tenure evaluations; that, when Honors Faculty are on sabbatical or otherwise unavailable to teach, the department is responsible for providing the honors courses to be taught by other tenured or tenure-track faculty; and how each department, as a whole, will strengthen and expand their support of honors instruction and mentoring."

Average Class Size (3.5): In order to make so many departmental courses available for honors credits, the college has resorted to quite a few large mixed classes. Therefore, the overall **average class size is 26.5**, compared to the average class size of 21.2 among all 50 programs under review.

Adjusted Graduation Rate (3.5): The AGR is not simply the six-year graduation rate of students in the honors college who graduated from the university **(84%),** whether or not the students completed the honors program ("honors completers"). The AGR also reflects the extent to which the honors graduation rate from the university is higher than that for the university as a whole. (The **university-wide rate is 70%**, yielding the 3.5 AGR for the college.) **However, the CHC also reports that its *four*-year graduation rate is an impressive 78%.** The average **honors** six-year **graduation rate for all 50 programs under review is 89%.**

Ratio of Staff to Honors Students (4.5): Our estimate is that there is 1 staff member for every **107.1** students. (Mean ratio for all 50 programs is 1 staff member for every 159.8 students.)

Honors Residence Halls (4.5): The college has no less than five residence hall options for honors students--two for freshmen and three for upperclassmen. All are part of the **new Honors Residential Community that opened in 2013.**

Sycamore Hall and Oak Hall, both for freshmen, have traditional double rooms with corridor baths on the floors. This configuration is thought by many to promote more interactions among new students, and thereby enhance their first year experience. Both dorms are air conditioned with on-site laundry.

Sycamore has living/learning communities in Concepts in Philosophy; Creativity; Science and Math; and Biology majors.

Oak has living/learning themes in Leadership; Health Sciences; Management; Nursing; and Engineering.

Designed to accommodate 1,500 of the 3,000 students in the Commonwealth Honors College, the Honors Residential Community opened for the Fall 2013 semester. Designed by award winning architects with a modern style, this community was designed to bring honors students together in a variety of ways.

This residential community features:

Easy Access to Honors faculty and staff:
- Two Faculty in Residence
- Honors Advising Center
- The Dean's Office and all honors administrative offices
- Faculty offices
- Nine classrooms

Additional features:
- Wi-Fi throughout
- **Roots Café - open 24/7--the new café continues the campus' reputation for creating and serving healthy, sustainable food. (Recently, UMass Amherst was ranked the 9th healthiest college in the U.S.--and second healthiest public university--according to Greatlist.com. The *Princeton Review* has ranked UMass Amherst second nationally for best campus food.**
- A uniquely designed events hall offers flexible seating for small, intimate gatherings or large honors programs. The full space seats up to 290 audience style. When the moveable wall is closed, the west

- side with floor to ceiling windows has a barn door that can be opened to the café providing lounge space with upholstered furniture and additional study space with tables and chairs. The east side can be set up audience style for 120 or with tables and chairs for up to 72. Both sides have full A/V capability.
- Gallery space (current exhibit, "The Student Experience: 150 Years of Living and Learning at UMass Amherst," curated by honors students guided by Art History faculty)
- **Located in the campus core, on Commonwealth Avenue**
- near the Recreation Center and the main library
- Short distance to other classrooms and facilities on campus

Prestigious Awards (3.5): The difficulties the university has had in the past in this category can and should be attributed to its being in the immediate neighborhood of some of the most selective private universities in the entire world. Imagine going to your regional interview for, say, a Marshall or Rhodes Scholarship, and having as your competitors the brightest students from Harvard, MIT, Williams, Amherst, and Yale.

The university has been doing better lately in competing for Goldwater Scholarships, awarded to outstanding undergraduates in the STEM majors. Despite a relative lack of success in winning such "name" awards as the Rhodes, Marshall, and Truman Scholarships, university students have done quite well in earning National Science Foundation Graduate Research Fellowships and Fulbright Student Scholarships.

The Office of National Scholarship Advisement, located in Commonwealth Honors College, serves all UMass Amherst undergraduate and graduate students applying for national, prestigious scholarships. In January 2014, a UMass Amherst Commonwealth Honors College student was selected to receive a 2014 Churchill Scholarship to study at Cambridge University.

Continuation Requirements: 3.4 GPA

Academic Strengths: UMass has an outstanding faculty, one that would rank across most disciplines as one of the top 50 in the nation. Especially strong departments are computer science, sociology, earth sciences, psychology, physics, and English. Engineering programs are also solid at UMass.

Undergraduate Research: Some 26% of all honors students participated in research for academic credit in 2012-2013; this included **87% of senior honors students**.

"Commonwealth Honors College (CHC) has a Research Assistant Fellowship program for sophomores and juniors, and students may receive up to $1,000 per semester. Juniors and seniors may apply for Honors Research Grants of up to $1,000 per semester to support their research.

"CHC established its Community Engaged Research Program with a summer REU program in 2012. The program offers a research preparation course on the principles and practices of community engaged research, through which students also complete a human subjects training certificate. The program offers research grants and helps match students and faculty to arrange research experiences.

"The Commonwealth Honors College sponsors the annual Massachusetts statewide Undergraduate Research Conference in which undergraduate students from any of the 28 undergraduate campuses in the Massachusetts Public System of Higher Education may participate. **More than 1,000 students presented their research at the 20th annual conference in April 2014.**

"All students who complete Departmental Honors or Multidisciplinary Honors and all those who graduate as Commonwealth Honors College Scholars must complete honors research and thesis/project. In 2012-2013, that included 87% of honors college graduates."

Study Abroad: UMass Amherst-sponsors over 400 study abroad programs in more than 50 countries around the world. **Honors students make up approximately 18% of the more than 1,000 UMass undergraduates who study abroad each year.**

Commonwealth Honors College (CHC) provides scholarships for honors students participating in the **Oxford Summer Program and the Alternative Theaters summer honors program in Edinburgh.**

"The honors college also offers a special 3-year academic program, the International Scholars Program (ISP) which combines academic learning with a period of study abroad in order to provide students with the global competencies they will need to become informed and effective citizens of our ever-expanding world. The program invites all honors students, regardless of major, to develop a concentration in international studies and cross-cultural communication as a supplement to their regular disciplinary work. Students complete two preparatory classes in their sophomore year and a re-entry seminar in their senior year. ISP students receive a scholarship from CHC in support of their study abroad. ISP students may also complete the International Scholars Program Certificate. This undergraduate certificate builds on ISP, adding a three-course supplemental curriculum that students design to meet their personal, academic and professional goals."

Financial Aid: The University offers merit scholarships to all entering first-year students accepted to Commonwealth Honors College (CHC); $2,000 for Massachusetts residents and approximately $5,000 for out of state students.

"In 2012-2013, CHC awarded donor-funded scholarships to 73 entering or continuing students and 54 seniors. Honors research fellowships and grants were awarded to 131 students. The honors college also awards a limited number of tuition waivers to Massachusetts residents who are continuing students or entering transfer students."

Degree of Difference (Honors students/non-honors students): 2.87 on a scale of 5. Some parents and prospective students might prefer an honors program that in many ways stands apart on campus, while others might prefer a program that is more expansive. The rating here tries to provide an indication of where a given honors program is on the stand apart/expansive spectrum. The rating is based on the difference between (1) the average SAT scores for enrolled honors students and (2) the average test scores for all students in the university as a whole *and* for students with scores at the 75% level or above. A score of 3.5 or higher indicates a high degree of difference. A score of 3.2 to 3.49 indicates a relatively high degree of difference. Finally, a score below 3.2 indicates a modest difference. **Please keep in mind that neither the high nor low selectivity of an honors program determines how effective the program is; this rating is merely "cultural" and *not* qualitative.**

Testimonials:

Melicia Morris '11. Major: Political Science; Minor: History; Certificate: Public Policy & Administration--"Completing my honors thesis was one of the most meaningful experiences I had as an Honors student because it gave me the opportunity to hone my research and writing techniques. Now, as **a student at Cornell Law School**, I am building upon the skills that I developed at UMass. I am thankful that this unique program gave me the tools to succeed in the legal profession."

Rebecca Spencer, Associate Professor of Psychology--"I've seen real value from students' completing an Honors Thesis. The relationship that a student develops with me presents an opportunity for me to understand his or her learning process and work ethic. As a professor, my comments on these qualities can be crucial for the recommendations students may seek for graduate school or employment."

Dianne Pfundstein, Assistant Professor and Commonwealth Honors Professor in Political Science "…I assign some very challenging graduate-level texts in my thesis seminar, and I know that I can count on the honors students to give it their best, even when the work is difficult."

NAME: MIAMI UNIVERSITY HONORS PROGRAM

Date Established: 1964

Location: Oxford, Ohio

University Full-time Undergraduate Enrollment: 14,657

Honors Enrollment: Approximately 1,551 (mean size of all 50 programs is 1,714)

Review/Admissions Category III: Programs with average SAT scores of 1383--1416 for enrolled students. Note: *The following test scores and class rank are **estimates only**. This profile of Miami Honors is based on an "external review" of information regarding the program.*

-

The estimated average SAT score is 1409, and the estimated average ACT score is 31-32; the average high school graduation percentile is 96-97%.

Minimum Admission Requirements: "Due to the high caliber students applying to Miami University, admission to the University Honors Program is highly competitive. Miami University's application review process is holistic; as part of this process, admission to the University Honors Program is based on a variety of factors. Students invited into the Honors Program have exceptional academic records and impressive extra- and co-curricular accomplishments."

Honors Programs in Admissions Category III (average SAT scores of 1383--1416): Connecticut, Indiana, Kentucky, Miami University, Oklahoma, Penn State, Tennessee, Texas A&M, UC Irvine, and Washington.

Administrative Staff: The Honors Program has a staff of 9.

FOR ALL "MORTARBOARD" RATINGS BELOW, A SCORE OF 5 IS THE MAXIMUM AND REPRESENTS A COMPARISON WITH ALL 50 HONORS COLLEGES AND PROGRAMS:

PERCEPTION* OF UNIVERSITY AS A WHOLE, NOT OF HONORS: 🎓🎓🎓🎓

OVERALL HONORS RATING: 🎓🎓🎓🎓

Curriculum Requirements: 🎓🎓🎓 1/2

Class Range and Type: 🎓🎓🎓🎓

Class Size: 🎓🎓🎓🎓🎓

Adjusted Grad Rate: 🎓🎓🎓🎓

Ratio of Staff to Students: 🎓 🎓 🎓¹ᐟ²

Priority Registration: Yes, after the first semester, honors students have priority registration for **all** classes.

Honors Housing: 🎓 🎓 🎓 🎓

Prestigious Awards: 🎓 🎓 🎓¹ᐟ²

*Perception is based on the university's ranking among public universities in the 2014 U.S. News Best Colleges report. Please bear in mind that the better the U.S. News ranking, the more difficult it is for an honors college or program to have a rating that equals or improves on the magazine ranking.

Curriculum Requirements (3.5): The program describes its curriculum as "cutting edge" and "unique," in its combination of honors courses in the academic disciplines and experiential learning in the form of hands-on leadership instruction and volunteer activities in area social services organizations. (The rating in this category is related to the quantity of total credit hours required than to the quality of the courses. That is assessed in Range and Type of Honors Courses, below.)

"We are more than a prestigious title, additional requirements, harder classes, and a quiet dorm. Honors at Miami is a cutting-edge educational program. Increasingly, success after college requires students to possess skills that cannot be obtained in the traditional classroom, so we have cast aside the traditional expectations and developed a program that will take students beyond the classroom to acquire the experience and abilities identified by major employers and educational leaders as crucial for success." Taking lessons from the business, scholarly, and professional worlds, the honors program emphasizes the following areas as being crucial for success.

- Knowledge of Science & Technology, Global Issues, Culture & Society, Math & Stats
- Intercultural Knowledge

- Integrity & Ethics
- Communication
- Problem-solving
- Critical Thinking
- Collaboration

- The program backs up its ambitious goals with statistics to show that its graduates do indeed find a high degree of success after graduation. Using data provided by 84% of the program's 2013 graduates, the program reports the following achievements by the grads **by the time of their graduation:**

- Law school placement=100% (9 of 9 grads)
- Graduate school placements=**89%** (56 of 63 grads)
- Job placement=75% (114 of 153)
- Graduation in **four** years=71% (299 of 420)
- Graduates of the three classes during the 2010-2012 period, **medical school placement rate=86%**, versus the national average of 45%

The program has simplified the honors completion requirements beginning in Fall 2014 after several years of reworking and transitioning to such an extent that it was somewhat difficult to keep up with the changes. Here is what the requirements are now:

University Honors--Completion of two Honors Cluster courses (see below) and two "honors experiences" the second year, which can be courses or actual experiential classes in leadership or volunteer work. We could not determine how many credit hours are necessary for completion.

Honors cluster courses, actually a related set of two courses, are designed for approximately 24 first-year Honors students. The two courses are paired together to help students integrate their learning across the curriculum. Prior to Summer Orientation, accepted students receive an email notifying them of the Honors cluster that has been assigned to them based on their stated preferences.

Advanced University Honors—In the last two years, students add two interdisciplinary workshops, one of which appears to require a thesis or senior project. Students must also complete two more honors experiences. Again, we have not been able to determine the number of credit hours that are required for completion.

However, our *rough estimate* is that completion at the Advanced University Honors level requires between 24 and 29 semester hours of credit.

Students must also create and maintain an **honors portfolio.** In this they organize material from classes and reflect on what they have learned and the impact their classes have had on them. Peer and faculty advisers are involved in the process. The e-portfolio requirement at one time was much more complicated and time-consuming but seems to have been streamlined in the last year or so.

Range and Type of Honors Courses (4.0): It is difficult to classify the Miami Honors Program by generic type, but based on the presence of a representative number of sections in the academic disciplines, we are calling it a **department-based program.**

Most of the seminars and very small sections appear to be in the leadership and volunteer 1-2 credit hour classes, of which there are about 20 each term. Examples include Engaging in Outdoor Leadership, Facilitating Dialogues, and multiple sections of Opening Minds through Art **Volunteering** Experience. These last involve volunteer activities at area nursing centers among other locations. The 2-credit sections called Opening Minds through Art **Leadership** Experiences feature similar locations but emphasize the leadership roles. Other 2-credit sections include Introduction to Leadership and Leadership Theory, Scholarly Personal Narrative, and **Leadership in Argentina**.

Here we should add that of the 85 or so honors sections in Spring 2014, about 34 were honors-only classes and the remainder are called "contract" classes. A better term would probably be honors add-on classes, for they appear similar to many of the classes offered by the Delaware Honors Program in that they are formally lined up and scheduled for honors participation rather than being subject to ad hoc honors petitions presented to instructors.

Departmental honors classes at Miami that are in the honors-only category include Art History: People of the World; Environmental Biology and Principles of Human Physiology; **Fundamentals of Ecology;**

College **Chemistry,** along with labs; at least three Communications sections; Principles of Macroeconomics; **Culture and Literature in the American South; Remembering Slavery in Art and Letters;** two honors journalism sections; **Epidemiology;** two sections of honors **marketing;** one section of **Calculus III;** and additional honors-only classes in philosophy, political science, and psychology. The psychology sections are particularly interesting.

Most of the add-on sections are in history, European studies, environmental engineering, organic chemistry for majors, and lower-level math.

Our favorite among several in the Special Topics category: **Buddhist Biology: Ancient Eastern Wisdom Meets Modern Western Science.**

The departmental honors classes included at least three sections of honors math--calculus with analytical geometry, accelerated calculus, and advanced calculus, all carrying 5 units of credit and a physics class on wave theory.

Average Class Size (5.0): We *estimate* that the average UHP honors class has **12-15 students,** partly the result of the leadership and volunteer sections being small and partly because the honors cluster seminars are limited to 24 students. The average class size for all 50 programs under review is 21.2 students.

Adjusted Graduation Rate (4.0): The AGR is not simply the six-year graduation rate of students in the CHP who graduated from the university *(estimated at* **90%),** whether or not the students completed the honors program ("honors completers"). The AGR also reflects the extent to which the honors graduation rate from the university is higher than that for the university as a whole. (The **university-wide rate is 80%,** yielding an AGR of 4.0.) The average **honors** six-year **graduation rate for all 50 programs under review is 89%.**

Ratio of Staff to Honors Students (3.5): Our estimate is that there is 1 staff member for every **172.3** students. (Mean ratio for all 50 programs is 1 staff member for every 159.8 students.)

Honors Residence Halls (4.0): It is surprisingly difficult to learn which residence halls, or floors therein, make up the Honors Living/Learning Community (LLC). Anecdotal information from college websites and general information from the university point to sections of **two residence halls, Tappan and Emerson**, as being designated Honors LLC, and it also appears that **Bishop Hall** has honors rooms as well. In addition, there is a **Scholar Leader LLC**, which would seem to be an ideal location for students in a leadership-centered program. Students in Scholar Leader LLC commit to a one-year residency in the renovated Stoddard or Elliot Halls, two of the most historic residence halls on campus with a central location on the academic quad adjacent to the Bell Tower. According to a student reporter, "every room at Scholar Leader LLC is assigned an average endowment of $1,700." We do not profess to know what this means exactly, but it could hardly be a bad thing.

As for Tappan and Emerson, both house first and second year honors students (we think). They are traditional corridor-type dorms with hall baths; they are air conditioned.

Prestigious Awards (3.5): Miami undergraduate students have a very good record of winning the prestigious Goldwater Scholarships for work in the STEM disciplines, so far taking 32 of those awards.

In the area of postgraduate awards, Miami students have won an impressive 13 Truman Scholarships.

Undergraduate Research: "Miami is nationally recognized by U.S. News & World report for its 'unusually strong commitment to undergraduate teaching,'" according to the university. "Getting involved in research allows students to build meaningful relationships with our dedicated Miami faculty outside of the traditional classroom setting. Our model of engaged inquiry encourages critical thinking and peer-assisted learning to provide students with personal, educational, and professional growth. By participating in undergraduate research, students gain experience and skills valued by employers, graduate schools and medical schools."

Miami has a **First Year Research Experience** program (FYRE) that pairs first-year students with faculty for the purpose of completing a research project in time for poster presentation at the university's **Undergraduate Research Forum held each April.** Students need to devote 4-6 hours a week to the program. Honors students have the option of choosing the FYRE living/learning community rather than the Honors LLC.

The **Undergraduate Summer Scholarship** program is a highly appealing option for students who have completed at least 60 credit hours of work. Tenured or tenure-track faculty mentor students, each of whom must commit to spending at least one semester at Miami following the summer scholarship.

"Each student receives: a $2,600 fellowship award, a $400 project expense, and a tuition only waiver for 6 credit hours of independent study credit to conduct a 9-week mentored summer research project between May 20 and end of summer term in 2014."

Study Abroad: The university ranks 23rd among all universities in the total number of students who study abroad each year—usually around 1,500 a year from Miami.

The centerpiece of the university's study-abroad program is the Miami University John C. Dolibois Center (MUDEC) in Luxembourg. Truly an academic center, the MUDEC offers an exciting range of classes including multiple courses in business, humanities, social sciences, independent study, and foreign language study. Because of Luxembourg's prime location among European countries (bordering Belgium to the west, Germany to the east, France to the south) it is perfectly placed for rapid rail travel throughout most of Europe, and both French and German are primary languages.

Financial Aid: Excellent merit scholarships are available to freshman entrants. The awards are based on a combination of SAT/ACT scores, high school GPA, and a record of "rigorous coursework" in high school.

SAT 1400+, ACT 32+, and GPA 3.50+ can bring total awards over four years to in-state students of $24,000-$48,000 (half to full tuition).

SAT 1330-1390, ACT 30-31, and GPA 3.50+ can bring total awards over four years to in-state students of $20,000-$40,000 ($5,000-$10,000 a year).

SAT 1250-1320, ACT 28-29, and GPA 3.50+ can bring total awards over four years to in-state students of $12,000-$28,000 ($3,000-$7,000 a year).

SAT 1170-1240, ACT 26-27, and GPA 3.50+ can bring total awards over four years to in-state students of up to $8,000 (up to $2,000 a year).

Degree of Difference (Honors students/non-honors students): 3.30 on a scale of 5. Some parents and prospective students might prefer an honors program that in many ways stands apart on campus, while others might prefer a program that is more expansive. The rating here tries to provide an indication of where a given honors program is on the stand apart/expansive spectrum. The rating is based on the difference between (1) the average SAT scores for enrolled honors students and (2) the average test scores for all students in the university as a whole *and* for students with scores at the 75% level or above. A score of 3.5 or higher indicates a high degree of difference. A score of 3.2 to 3.49 indicates a relatively high degree of difference. Finally, a score below 3.2 indicates a modest difference. **Please keep in mind that neither the high nor low selectivity of an honors program determines how effective the program is; this rating is merely "cultural" and *not* qualitative.**

NAME: LSA HONORS PROGRAM, THE UNIVERSITY OF MICHIGAN

Date Established: 1957

Location: Ann Arbor, Michigan

University-wide, Full-time Undergraduate Enrollment: 27,046

Honors Enrollment: approximately 1,800 (mean enrollment of all 50 programs is 1,714).

Review/Admissions Category--IV: Programs with **average SAT scores of 1417 or higher for enrolled students**. *Estimated* mean SAT score for enrolled LSA students is 1450; *estimated* ACT average is 33. High school rank GPA 3.80-4.0 unweighted.

Honors Programs in Admissions Category IV (average SAT of 1417 and higher): Auburn, Clemson, Georgia, Illinois, Kansas, Michigan, Minnesota, North Carolina, Rutgers, South Carolina, UT Austin, Virginia.

Administrative Staff: LSA Honors has a staff of 9, not counting faculty advisers.

FOR ALL "MORTARBOARD" RATINGS BELOW, A SCORE OF 5 IS THE MAXIMUM AND REPRESENTS A COMPARISON OF ALL 50 HONORS COLLEGES AND PROGRAMS:

PERCEPTION* OF UNIVERSITY AS A WHOLE, <u>NOT</u> OF HONORS: 🎓🎓🎓🎓🎓

OVERALL HONORS RATING: 🎓🎓🎓🎓🎓

Curriculum Requirements: 🎓🎓🎓🎓🎓

Class Range and Type: 🎓🎓🎓🎓🎓

Class Size: 🎓🎓🎓^{1/2}

Adjusted Grad Rate: 🎓🎓🎓🎓^{1/2}

Ratio of Staff to Students: 🎓🎓🎓^{1/2}

Priority Registration: **No,** but LSA Honors students have little difficulty registering for honors courses.

Honors Housing: 🎓🎓🎓🎓

Prestigious Awards: 🎓🎓🎓🎓🎓

*Perception is based on the university's ranking among public universities in the 2014 U.S. News Best Colleges report. Please bear in mind that the higher the U.S. News ranking, the more difficult it is for an honors college or program to have a rating that improves on the magazine ranking.

Curriculum Requirements (5.0): After more than fifty years, the honors curriculum remains focused on developing "a sound base for the undergraduate experience and [allowing] students to acquire knowledge, develop analytic skills, and exercise creative abilities and critical faculties of mind."

There are three ways to achieve honors completion:

College Honors--College Honors requires successful completion of eight honors courses, ranging from 3 to 5 credits apiece; these courses are taken in the first two years. There is **no requirement for an honors thesis.** The total number of credits earned ranges from 25-34 hours.

Departmental Honors (Honors Major)--This option includes the two-year course requirements listed above (eight courses), and then tracks what the departments would normally require, usually one or two honors classes, including a research tutorial or seminar, **along with the departmental honors thesis.** (**Exceptions**: Honors in math, statistics, and computer science typically are based on a combination of coursework and GPA only). The Department Honors option (former "Honors Concentration") requires 34-43 credit hours.

Honors in the Liberal Arts—The HLA also includes the two-year course requirements, **but requires five more honors courses approved for the HLA curriculum. (See below.)**

For HLA, students find a topic or issue that they want to pursue. Then they work with an honors advisor, usually at the end of the second year or the beginning of the third, and develop a plan for courses that are aligned with the topic.

Students submit a proposal that describes the issue they want to address and list the courses that they would like to take. Students have to explain how the courses address the question or topic of their HLA plan. One course may overlap with their major(s) and/or academic minor. And then…students must meet this requirement: **All HLA courses must carry graduate credit in their home department.**

In the spring of senior year, HLA students must write an essay that summarizes what they have learned about their chosen topic in the courses they have taken, especially the ways that the courses provided "an integrated look" at the topic. Students then submit the essay, along with a portfolio that consolidates and organizes what they have learned in more detail, to the Honors Academic Board by April 1st of their senior year (December 1st for students graduating in December). After reading and evaluating the essay and portfolio, the Honors Faculty Advisory Board decides whether to grant the Honors in the Liberal Arts. If so, the notation "Honors in the Liberal Arts" will be noted on the transcript.

Our estimate is that the minimum credit hours for HLA completion is about **43 credit hours. But if it is accomplished in addition to an Honors Major, the total credits could exceed 50 credit hours, and a thesis would be involved as part of the Honors Major.**

Range and Type of Honors Courses (5.0): Although we classify LSA Honors as a **department-based** honors program based on the breadth and quality of honors courses in the academic disciplines, this is not to say that seminars and discussion sections in core areas are lacking. (In fact, many of the departmental honors courses *are* seminars.) For more than 50 years, LSA Honors freshmen took the renowned Great Books classes, centered on readings and discussions of ancient and classical texts (Homer, Aeschylus, Sophocles, Herodotus, Thucydides, Plato, Seneca, the Bible, and readings from the Renaissance). The Great Books classes satisfied the "Text and Ideas" component of the honors core. But for Fall 2014, the core offerings have changed:

"Designed specifically for Honors students by innovative faculty the Honors Core Curriculum provides rigorous, wide-reaching introductory courses across the three academic divisions in LSA: the Natural Sciences, the Social Sciences, and the Humanities. **The Honors Core builds on the fine tradition of our historic Great Books course, which remains a Core Humanities course. The Core extends to other areas the many strengths of Great Books: foundational content, critical analysis, excellent instruction in writing, and social bonding.**"

These are new core courses slated for Fall 2014: The West Since 1492; Deep Time: the Science of Origins; and Great Performances. The last carries this description:

"Designed for the new Honors Core Curriculum, this course is an introduction to performance studies in music, theater, dance and related arts. Students will attend a series of live performances presented by the University Musical Society; the UM School of Music, Theater, and Dance; and other performing arts organizations in the university community.

"In a combination of lecture and discussion, the course will focus on specific works to be performed, while also exploring the relation between tradition and innovation in performing 'great' works, and asking what makes a 'great' performance.

"Throughout the academic term, students will consider the concept of performance from different historical, critical and creative perspectives, and develop their skills in writing about performance."

Students may also choose from several other courses with an international flavor or, in two instances, courses that cover areas reminiscent of the Great Books series: Ancient Philosophy, and Art & Philosophy in the Renaissance Tradition. For honors credit, however, if the course is not already an honors course, students must do an **honors conversion,** essentially the same thing as an honors contract with the instructor, which requires additional reading, writing, or research for the honors credit.

On the seminar side, LSA Honors has the Ideas in Honors series of "minicourses" that provide 1 credit each. Examples for Fall 2014 include: Perspectives on Consciousness; The Higgs Boson and Other Discoveries: A Survey of Modern Particle Physics; Reading Outside the Lines: Texts on the Edge; and our favorite in this category: **Is the Personal Political?--Women's Issues and Public Policy.**

In addition to the core classes listed above, there are these engaging seminars: Transforming America: Immigrants Then and Now; The Symphonic Century: Music and Revolution in the 19th Century; Creativity in the Sciences and Arts; another favorite of ours—**Cyberscience: Computational Science**

and the Rise of the Fourth Paradigm; and another one simply called "Imagination." Is it simple? Not so much:

"The Romantics made major claims for imagination: that it was both an artistic and cognitive faculty. Thus the seminar will begin by considering both the structure of the Romantic literary imagination and the romantic theory of knowledge in works by Wordsworth, Blake, Coleridge, Kant, and Fichte. Attention will then shift to more general questions: Does artistic imagination tell us anything about reality? Can imagination become a rigorous mode of cognition? What is its relationship to rationality?"

And you may be wondering **what that Fourth Paradigm mentioned above could be**. Well, it's a "new, data-intensive paradigm of scientific discovery that will dramatically enhance the scope and scale of data analysis from experiments, observations and simulations. This new **4ᵗʰ paradigm of science** is empowered by the union of computational science, statistical methods and domain science (*e.g.,* astronomy, bioengineering, public policy)."

The **departmental honors courses** are plentiful and rigorous. The math sections are among the best anywhere: Eleven honors sections, including five in calculus II or III, two in differential equations, and one each in honors math II, analysis II, and advanced algebra. There are honors physics sections on three levels. History, psychology, political science, biology, anthropology, English—all are well represented. In Winter 2014, the honors chemistry sections included two in physical chemistry and another in "structure and reactivity." In economics, there was only one seminar—global macroeconomics. But in art history, there are seven, including **Nazi²s and Art: Promoting, Demeaning, Plundering.**

We can go on and on…so we will: senior seminars in Romance languages, psychology as a natural science, political economy, philosophy, French, Russian, communications…and more.

Average Class Size (3.5): Yes, there are some large sections, including a few that are very large. The core sections can be big enough to have four discussion sections, each with 18 or so students. All of the intro science classes will have break-out discussion sections for honors students. But most honors seminars are in the 22-student range. The many math sections are capped at 25 students each. Since we do not count tutorial and independent study sections in most cases, the true average class size is probably lower than **our estimate of 26.67**. And there is this: it's Michigan, so if you are in a section that's a little bit large or has a mix of honors and non-honors students, it's very likely that you're still in one of the best college classes (whatever the subject may be) in the world. For all 50 programs in this review, the average honors class size is 21.2.

Adjusted Graduation Rate (4.5): The AGR is not simply the six-year graduation rate of students in the honors program who graduated from the university **(estimated at 95.6%)**, whether or not the students completed the honors program ("honors completers"). It also reflects the extent to which the honors graduation rate from the university is higher than that for the university as a whole. The university-wide rate is 90%, yielding the 4.5 AGR for the college. The average six-year **honors graduation rate for all 50 programs** under review **is 89%.**

Ratio of Staff to Honors Students (3.5): Our estimate is that there is 1 staff member for every **200.0** students. (Median ratio for all 50 programs is 1 staff member for every 159.8 students.) However, if faculty advisers were to be counted, the ratio would be better.

Honors Residence Halls (4.0): Honors Housing has returned to its traditional home in the **newly renovated South Quad.** Honors has reserved spaces in the following South Quad Houses: Frederick, Taylor, Hunt, and Bush. "Single-gender and substance-free housing options are available in Frederick House. We plan to make Bush House (5th and 6th floors) our reserved space for returning Honors students (i.e. sophomores, juniors, and seniors), although we have also made selected singles in other houses available to returners."

South Quad, like the former honors housing in West Quad, has traditional corridor dorms with hall baths. The dorm rooms are not air-conditioned. But renovations have brought notable improvements:

- Created a new central campus dining center in South Quad with a capacity for 950 diners.
- Improved student bathrooms with the addition of new plumbing, fixtures and shower privacy stalls.
- Refurbished and created **new community lounges, with air conditioning.**
- Redesigned the building's entrance to allow better access from West Quadrangle and the Michigan Union.
- Created and improved group study rooms, music practice rooms and two central laundry rooms.

"Honors students serve as Resident Advisors (HRAs) in Honors halls; they are responsible both to Housing and to Honors for their work with students, and for programming events. For their Honors events, HRAs seek to provide higher levels of intellectual and cultural engagement, and to probe issues more deeply than in other student programming. Last year the HRAs were awarded 'Program of the Year' by University of Michigan's Hillel for a complex program centered on the Broadway musical, *The Book of Mormon.*"

Prestigious Awards (5.0): Michigan is the leader among all public universities in the total number of prestigious undergraduate and postgraduate awards its students and graduates have earned, according to the figures we have *for the awards that we track.* The university is tied for third among public universities in the Goldwater Scholarship competition, and Michigan students also earn a high number of Boren Scholarships for international study. Michigan is third among public universities in the National Science Foundation Graduate Research Fellowships its graduates have received in the last three years and first in the number of Fulbright Student Scholarships won during the same period. In the entire history of the Rhodes, Marshall, Gates Cambridge, Churchill, and Truman Scholarships, all awarded annually, the university ranks third among all public universities and can boast a strong record of winning *each* of these annual awards, a rare achievement.

Continuation Requirements: 3.40 overall GPA; 3.50 for Honors in the Liberal Arts

Academic Strengths: Next to UC Berkeley, the University of Michigan has the highest-rated faculty in the nation among public universities and the 7th highest-rated faculty among all universities public or private. Of the 15 academic departments that we track, **the average ranking for all 15 disciplines at Michigan is in the top ten in the nation.** The list: business (2); political science, psychology, and sociology (4); engineering and history (7); math (8) earth sciences (9); education and physics (11); English, computer science, and economics (13); chemistry (16) and biology (20).

Undergraduate Research: The Undergraduate Research Opportunity Program (UROP) creates research partnerships between undergraduate students and University of Michigan researchers. All schools and colleges are active participants in UROP, which provides a wealth of interesting research topics for program participants. UROP started with 14 student/faculty partnerships in 1988, and has expanded to include more than 1300 students and 800 faculty researchers.

"UROP is now recognized as a model program for engaging undergraduate students in research. In 2002 **U.S. News and World Report ranked UROP Number 1 in the category, Undergraduate Research/Creative Projects. UROP has consistently ranked at the top of this category in the ensuing years.**"

Note: If students are accepted to a work-study gig in UROP, they receive $8.50 per hour.

Study Abroad: The university ranks 10ᵗʰ among all universities in the number of students studying abroad. The university's Center for Global and Intercultural Study administers most of the programs. Students must attend a Ready, Set, Go Global (RSGG) session before making application. The application process requires a meeting with a UROP adviser, followed by an electronic application; it must include letters of recommendation from UM faculty who have taught and graded the student. UM has 60 programs for international study, not including foreign language study. Third and fourth year language study programs are available in China, France, Italy, Argentina, Spain, and Costa Rica.

Financial Aid: "We have donor funds to provide grants for research expenses and travel, travel to present papers and posters at conferences, and to support study abroad travel. We have no scholarships or financial aid of our own for tuition or fees. We do participate in the College merit scholarship committee but that program is very small (fewer than 20 awards in a year) and not restricted to Honors students."

Michigan, like UC Berkeley, Virginia, Wisconsin, UCLA, UT Austin, and, more recently, UNC Chapel Hill and Ohio State, have sharply reduced or ceased university sponsorship of National Merit Scholars. This does not mean, however, that NMS awardees at these schools are not eligible for corporate-sponsored National Merit Scholarships.

Degree of Difference (Honors students/non-honors students): 2.75 on a scale of 5. Some parents and prospective students might prefer an honors program that in many ways stands apart on campus, while others might prefer a program that is more expansive. The rating here tries to provide an indication of where a given honors program is on the stand apart/expansive spectrum. The rating is based on the difference between (1) the average SAT scores for enrolled honors students and (2) the average test scores for all students in the university as a whole *and* for students with scores at the 75% level or above. A score of 3.5 or higher indicates a high degree of difference. A score of 3.2 to 3.49 indicates a relatively high degree of difference. Finally, a score below 3.2 indicates a modest difference. **Please keep in mind that neither the high nor low selectivity of an honors program determines how effective the program is; this rating is merely "cultural" and *not* qualitative.**

NAME: UNIVERSITY HONORS PROGRAM, UNIVERSITY OF MINNESOTA-TWIN CITIES

Date Established: 2007

Location: Minneapolis, Minnesota

University-wide, Full-time Undergraduate Enrollment: 29,125

Honors Enrollment: approximately 2,320 (mean enrollment of all 50 programs is 1,714).

Review/Admissions Category IV: Programs with **average SAT scores of 1417 or higher for enrolled students**. Mean SAT score for enrolled UMTC students across all programs is 1436; ACT average is 32.1. Average high school rank is the top 3%.

Honors Programs in Admissions Category IV (average SAT of 1417 and higher): Auburn, Clemson, Georgia, Illinois, Kansas, Michigan, Minnesota, North Carolina, Rutgers, South Carolina, UT Austin, Virginia.

Administrative Staff: UHP Honors has a staff of 18. The Director emphasizes that "11 of the 18 staff members of the University Honors Program are professional Honors Advisors who provide students not only with guidance within the major curriculum (both regular and Honors) but also with broader mentorship that complements faculty advising. Indeed, an Honors advisor will see students from more than one college and develop a wide knowledge of opportunities from across the University, which is especially helpful to students with multiple majors. Having such a large number of staff dedicated to one-on-one, personalized advising from the first day of the freshman year on is, I believe, a distinctive feature of our program."

FOR ALL "MORTARBOARD" RATINGS BELOW, A SCORE OF 5 IS THE MAXIMUM AND REPRESENTS A COMPARISON OF ALL 50 HONORS COLLEGES AND PROGRAMS:

PERCEPTION* OF UNIVERSITY AS A WHOLE, NOT OF HONORS: 🎓🎓🎓🎓 1/2

OVERALL HONORS RATING: 🎓🎓🎓🎓 1/2

Curriculum Requirements: 🎓🎓🎓🎓🎓

Class Range and Type: 🎓🎓🎓🎓 1/2

Class Size: 🎓🎓🎓 1/2

Adjusted Grad Rate: 🎓🎓🎓🎓 1/2

Ratio of Staff to Students: 🎓🎓🎓🎓^{1/2}

Priority Registration: "Students in the University Honors Program have priority access to register for Honors Global Challenge Courses, Honors Seminars, and all departmental Honors courses. There is currently no other form of 'priority registration' for our students."

Honors Housing: 🎓🎓🎓🎓^{1/2}

Prestigious Awards: 🎓🎓🎓🎓🎓

*Perception is based on the university's ranking among public universities in the 2014 *U.S. News Best Colleges* report. Please bear in mind that the higher the *U.S. News* ranking, the more difficult it is for an honors college or program to have a rating that improves on the magazine ranking.

Curriculum Requirements (5.0): "The UMTC University Honors Program maintains one set of requirements for all students in any major across the University," according to the UHP Director. "This set of requirements is, by design, flexible enough to accommodate all majors. Students work with their honors advisor to determine how they can fulfill the requirements through the lens of their particular major or discipline. Please keep in mind that these are minimum requirements…."

The UMTC honors curriculum is an excellent mix of coursework and experiential learning:

The requirements are based on the accumulation of a minimum number of "honors experiences" during each academic year. **The honors experiences can be honors course work, learning abroad (maximum of two experiences for honors credit), research, significant internship or service experience, national conference presentations, or a creative project.**

In the **freshman year**, four honors experiences are required, including two from one of the following: honors seminars, departmental honors courses, or freshman seminars, totaling at least 6 credit hours. The other two experiences in the freshman year most often are in honors coursework, but they can be one of the other types listed above.

Sophomores must also meet the four-experience requirement and the same credit hour total, though of course with different courses and seminars.

In the **junior year,** students must take at least one honors course with a minimum of 3 credits. Two non-course experiences are also required: "Students engage in research, scholarship, or creative activity with a faculty mentor—an important step toward the development of a project for the **honors thesis**—while deepening and broadening their knowledge and skill base. They are also encouraged to consider research abroad, service in concert with their research where appropriate, and internships."

Seniors must take at least one 3-credit course, complete a thesis, and complete one more honors experience, either a course or one of the other experiences listed above. "Research/scholarship is done prior to and many times during the final writing. Creative projects are presented in the final term with a written document supporting their works."

Although it is somewhat difficult to quantify the **minimum** total hours (coursework and non-coursework **hours) needed for completion, we have estimated that minimum completion requires approximately 36 credit hours.**

AP/IB credits do **not** replace required honors courses.

Range and Type of Honors Courses (4.5): As the UHP is the only entity on campus that works with and coordinates honors curricula and degrees in all majors and departments, it has a significantly stronger presence than many honors programs that we classify as being departmental-centered. Having recognized this more central role for the UHP, it remains that there is an extremely wide range of honors classes in the academic disciplines.

Yet even though the number of honors seminars is relatively modest--12-18 per semester, usually a few more in the Fall--the topics are compelling. Here are some examples for this coming Fall (note the environmental themes):

Avoiding the Apocalypse: Humans, the Environment, and Our Future; Experiencing Local Environmental Solutions; Six Degrees of Interdisciplinary Connection; Writing Makes a Difference: Writing and Social Change in America; Tropical Forests: Conservation, Carbon, and Conflict; Chasing the American Dream: Economic Opportunity and Inequality in the United States; and two of our favorites, **NANO: Small Science, Big Deal,** and **The Future.**

Here is the course description for **The Future**: "What will the future bring? Will the years, decades, or even centuries to come bring prosperity or despair? A technological utopia or an apocalypse? Unbounded freedom or enslavement? For numerous writers, filmmakers, and thinkers, questions about the future of humanity have inspired works of speculation that touch on every imaginable aspect of the human condition. In this course, we will use the exploration of the future in science fiction novels and films as a way to understand the past--especially the culture, concerns, and preoccupations of the places and times where these futures were imagined."

Each term, the UHP also features at least one **Global Challenge Course**. For Fall, the title is Can We Feed the World Without Destroying It? "In this challenge-based course students will study the issue of global food security, seeking to answer the question of 'Can we feed the world without destroying it?' **Students will learn the complexity of the problem and the issues and actors involved. While there isn't a 'right' answer, progress can still be made through collaboration and innovation.** Students will feel empowered to impact the global food system, from personal to career choices."

The **departmental honors classes** include all of the major disciplines and then some: how about retail merchandising and sports management? Regardless of the semester, expect to see math and science classes up front. For this coming Fall, there are about nine honors math sections, including honors calculus I, II, and III; topology, and analysis. The science sections include 3-5 physics sections each term, about the same in biology, and two or more chemistry classes. The humanities and social sciences are far from neglected, with about 20 sections of history scheduled for Fall, classics courses each semester, and three or four English or Comp Lit classes. Economics classes are likewise well represented in each semester; in Spring 2014, Mathematical Economics and International Trade were two of the course offerings in that discipline. The political science classes that term had a similar quantitative emphasis: one 4-hour section was titled Quantitative Analysis. Like several other programs, the UHP encourages honors students to take speech/communications classes, a worthy addition to the list. The program also provides honors sections of psychology, two or so, and an excellent selection in sociology, a somewhat neglected discipline by many honors programs. Criminology was one such course set for this Fall.

Note: The UHP also facilitates honors study groups: "Study Groups are available in the areas of **chemistry, computer science, math, and physics**. Honors students in both honors and non-honors versions of these courses are encouraged to participate in these groups!"

Average Class Size (3.5): As we have noted in profiles of other prominent honors programs with a lot of departmental honors courses, the upside is course variety in the disciplines, the downside is that some departmental honors courses are large, mixed sections with both honors and non-honors students, the former almost always meeting separately for 1-2 hours a week in all-honors break-out sections. The UHP does have its share of these sections, with some of the largest (again, like most other honors programs) being in the sciences, geography, and in a couple of calculus sections. The **average class size is 26.7** students, versus the average for all 50 programs of 21.2.

Adjusted Graduation Rate (4.5): The AGR is not simply the six-year graduation rate of students in the honors program who graduated from the university **(estimated at 91.6%)**, whether or not the students completed the honors program ("honors completers"). It also reflects the extent to which the honors graduation rate from the university is higher than that for the university as a whole. **The university-wide rate is 73%**, yielding the 4.5 AGR for the program. The average six-year **honors graduation rate for all 50 programs** under review **is 89%**.

Ratio of Staff to Honors Students (4.5): Our estimate is that there is 1 staff member for every **128.9**. (Median ratio for all 50 programs is 1 staff member for every 159.8 students.)

Honors Residence Halls (4.5): Honors students may choose to live in Middlebrook Hall, where five or six floors are assigned to freshman honors students along with students in the Honors Second-Year Experience program. Honors students have about 450 of the 900 rooms in the large hall.

The residence hall features mostly traditional corridor double rooms with hall baths, but just under 20% of the honors rooms are suite-style. The residence hall is air conditioned with a kitchen, on-site laundry, and a lounge on each floor. Dining is convenient indeed--Middlebrook has its own dining hall.

"[Middlebrook] is located adjacent to the west bank of the Mississippi River, Ted Mann Concert Hall, Wilson Library, and is near downtown Minneapolis. The west bank Riverside area offers a variety of music clubs, coffee shops, co-ops, historical buildings, and ethnic and vegetarian restaurants. Middlebrook is easily accessible by foot, bike, free campus connector and shuttle system, and soon to be completed - light rail. Most west bank classroom buildings are connected by underground tunnels. Middlebrook Tower was built in 1969 and the east wing expansion added in 2001."

Prestigious Awards (5.0): UMTC has long been prominent among public universities in the number of prestigious scholarships awarded to its students and graduates. **Ranking 8th among all public universities in the number of undergraduate Goldwater Scholarships (53)** is evidence of the strong undergraduate research programs the university offers in the STEM disciplines. UMTC students also receive a high number of Gilman Scholarships, awarded to students of limited means so they can pursue academic studies or internships abroad. UMTC students are perhaps even more successful at winning prestigious postgraduate scholarships, **ranking 8th among all public universities in the total number major annual awards.** These include 24 Rhodes Scholars; 9 Churchill Scholars (STEM disciplines); and 20 Truman Scholars. UMTC also ranks 7th in National Science Foundation Graduate Research Fellowships (mostly STEM studies) and performs far above the mean in earning Fulbright Student Scholarships.

Continuation Requirements: 3.50 GPA

Academic Strengths: UMTC is one of the leading research institutions in the world, as evidenced by an **outstanding national departmental ranking of 23rd, across 15 disciplines**. These include psychology (9th in the nation), economics (11), business and math (both 18), political science (19), sociology (20), chemistry (21), engineering (23), history (24), education and physics (both 26), and earth sciences (28). *All* **of the major academic disciplines at UMTC are ranked 36th or higher nationally.**

Undergraduate Research: "The University of Minnesota's Undergraduate Research Opportunities Program (UROP) provides funding to U of MN undergraduates who work on a research project with a faculty mentor. UROP provides a stipend (up to $1,400 for approximately 120 hours of research) and expense money (up to $300 for project related expenses) to students. UROP is open to freshmen through seniors who are in an undergraduate degree program in good academic standing.

"URS students are given a scholarship for a research project done in conjunction with a faculty mentor. Scholarships must be used in the first two years of college study (projects must be completed by the end of the summer following the sophomore year). The scholarship includes two payments of $700 each directly into the student's account, and up to $300 in expense money. Students must submit an application (application form, proposal and mentor recommendation) prior to beginning the research. At the end of the project, students must submit a final report, an evaluation and do a presentation before receiving the final $700."

Study Abroad: The university has received national recognition for the quality of its study-abroad programs and **ranks third among all U.S. universities in the number of students studying abroad.** According to the UHP Director, UMTC has "one of the largest learning abroad offices in the country with 300 program offerings in over 80 countries.

"These programs have been developed to address the diverse needs of students. Programs vary in length, level, academic focus, teaching format, language requirements, cost, and degree of independence demanded of the participant.

"Because of the support of the University Honors Program, we are now able to fund some research abroad experiences in collaboration with the Undergraduate Research Program."

The Learning Abroad Center features an excellent website that easily gives students information about programs according to region, country, semester, academic major, academic discipline, and student year (freshman, sophomore, junior, senior).

Just as easily, students can research programs to see if they are exchange or affiliated programs with foreign universities and to determine which languages are used in course instruction. Yet another state-of-the art web page provides quick access to scholarship funding options and benefits. Dollar amounts range from $300 to $3,000, not counting national Gilman Scholarships ($5,000) and Boren Scholarships ($8,000-$20,000).

Financial Aid: "By virtue of their academic qualifications," the UHP Director tell us, "students invited into the University Honors Program typically receive a proportionate amount of merit-based scholarships." Despite a national trend among public universities of declining sponsorship of National Merit Scholars, UMTC sponsored almost exactly the same number of scholars in 2013 as in 2012—107 and 114, respectively.

Merit scholarships at UMTC that focus on National Merit Finalists include the Gold Scholar Award of up to $10,000 per year for four years, and the Cyrus Northrop Scholarship, valued at $5,000 a year for four years. **To qualify for either of these, applicants must list UMTC as their first-choice college by the National Merit Scholarship Corporation deadline.**

The Bentson/Niblick Scholarship likewise gives preference to National Merit Finalists, and awards up to $2,500 a year for four years. (There is no requirement that applicants list UMTC as their first-choice college.)

Several other merit awards are available to Minnesota residents.

Degree of Difference (Honors students/non-honors students): 3.25 on a scale of 5. Some parents and prospective students might prefer an honors program that in many ways stands apart on campus, while others might prefer a program that is more expansive. The rating here tries to provide an indication of where a given honors program is on the stand apart/expansive spectrum. The rating is based on the difference between (1) the average SAT scores for enrolled honors students and (2) the average test scores for all students in the university as a whole *and* for students with scores at the 75% level or above. A score of 3.5 or higher indicates a high degree of difference. A score of 3.2 to 3.49 indicates a relatively high degree of difference. Finally, a score below 3.2 indicates a modest difference. **Please keep in mind that neither the high nor low selectivity of an honors program determines how effective the program is; this rating is merely "cultural" and *not* qualitative.**

NAME: SALLY McDONNELL BARKSDALE HONORS COLLEGE, UNIVERSIY OF MISSISSIPPI

Date Established: 1997 (an honors program began in 1952)

Location: Oxford, Mississippi

University Full-time Undergraduate Enrollment: 14,933

Honors Enrollment: 1,123 (mean size of all 50 programs is 1,714)

Review/Admissions Category I: Programs with **average SAT scores of 1235--1342 for enrolled students**. The **actual average** test scores for enrollees at SMBHC are SAT 1340, ACT 30.3. The average high school GPA is 3.96.

Minimum admission requirements are SAT, 1250; ACT 28; and high school GPA, 3.50.

Honors Programs in Admissions Category I (average SAT scores of 1235-1342): Arizona, Arizona State, Arkansas, Colorado State, Iowa, Maine, Mississippi, Oklahoma State, Oregon, Oregon State, Rhode Island, Texas Tech, University at Albany, and Washington State.

Administrative Staff: The Honors College has a staff of 9.

FOR ALL "MORTARBOARD" RATINGS BELOW, A SCORE OF 5 IS THE MAXIMUM AND REPRESENTS A COMPARISON WITH ALL 50 HONORS COLLEGES AND PROGRAMS:

PERCEPTION* OF UNIVERSITY AS A WHOLE, NOT OF HONORS: 🎓🎓

OVERALL HONORS RATING: 🎓🎓🎓🎓$^{1/2}$

Curriculum Requirements: 🎓🎓🎓🎓

Class Range and Type: 🎓🎓🎓🎓🎓

Class Size: 🎓🎓🎓🎓🎓

Adjusted Grad Rate: 🎓🎓🎓🎓

Ratio of Staff to Students: 🎓🎓🎓🎓$^{1/2}$

Priority Registration: Yes, honors students register for **all** courses, honors and otherwise, with the first group of students during **each** year they are in the program.

Honors Housing: 🎓🎓🎓🎓🎓

Prestigious Awards: 🎓🎓🎓¹/²

*****Perception is based on the university's ranking among public universities in the 2014 U.S. News Best Colleges report. Please bear in mind that the better the U.S. News ranking, the more difficult it is for an honors college or program to have a rating that equals or improves on the magazine ranking.**

Curriculum Requirements (4.0): The honors completion requirement at SMBHC is 29 credit hours, **including a thesis of 3-6 hours of credit.** All honors students must take the Honors 101-Honors 102 Freshman Honors seminars, both of which meet the composition requirement for the university (please see descriptions of these courses below).

The honors courses in the academic disciplines are spread over 20 departments, including 6 open to honors students through a partnership with the UM School of Law.

AP/IB credits are **not** counted as replacements for honors courses.

Range and Type of Honors Courses (5.0): We classify the college as a **blended program**, in which interesting seminar sections are a significant part of the course schedule along with a strong range of classes in the academic disciplines.

The freshman honors seminars are a wonderful introduction to the big questions and our attempts to understand them. Honors 101, offered in the Fall, "introduces students to influential core texts that address fundamental aspects of the human condition. Topics under consideration deal with concepts of the self and of the individual and society. To this end, questions such as the following can be considered: Who am I? What makes me who I am? Do I have free will? Am I essentially a product of my genetic code or of my social environment? Is my essence determined mainly by gender, race, class, or some other factor? Other typical questions include: How are societies organized? What is the proper relationship between the society and the individual? What is the nature of a just society? What is the ideal state?"

In the Spring, students continue their examination of the human experience in Honors 102. In Spring 2014, the college offered 26 sections of Honors 102. "Core texts are selected around the themes of self and cosmos, and experience and the natural world. The former theme treats the nature and importance of religious experience and focuses on vital concerns such as *what is ultimate reality?* How do we as individuals fit into the universe as a whole? The latter theme examines various ways we perceive the physical universe and deals with questions such as *what is science?* What are its methods? How does it develop?"

Selected readings for Honors 101 may include *Man's Search for Meaning,* by Victor Frankl; *Light in August,* by William Faulkner; *In the Lake of the Woods,* by Tim O'Brien; *Things Fall Apart,* by Chinua Achebe; and *The Second Sex,* by Simone de Beauvoir.

Honors 102 readings may include *The Fall,* by Albert Camus; *The Selfish Gene,* by Richard Dawkins; *The Autobiography of Charles Darwin; The Screwtape Letters,* by C.S. Lewis; *Religion and Science,* by Bertrand Russell; and *Year of Wonders,* by Geraldine Brooks.

The honors courses in the disciplines are spread over 20 departments, including six to eight courses open to honors students through a partnership with the UM School of Law. Among the departmental classes, the math sections are notable for the number of sections available in Unified Calculus and Analytical Geometry. There are multiple sections in physics, chemistry, and biology, and classes in the last could be some of the larger ones for honors students. Unlike many programs, the SMBHC features honors sections in foreign languages, including four in Chinese as well as classes in French, Spanish, and Portuguese. We also like the "Introduction to Southern Studies" course. Given the prevalence of economics majors nowadays, the multiple sections of macro- and microeconomics should be reassuring. Another great addition is the honors course in astronomy and a colloquium in Integrated Science. The only disciplines that did not appear to be represented were anthropology and sociology.

And then there are the **six courses in the law school that are open to SMBHC students**: Introduction to Law and Reasoning; Criminal Procedure; Sports Law; Entertainment Law; International Rights Law; and Gender and the Law.

Average Class Size (5.0): The average honors class size at SMBHC is 14.8 students, an impressively low number even for a blended honors program. (The overall class size for the 50 colleges and programs under review in this edition is 21.2 students.)

Adjusted Graduation Rate (4.0): The AGR is not simply the six-year graduation rate of students in the honors college who graduated from the university (**83%**), whether or not the students completed the honors program ("honors completers"). The AGR also reflects the extent to which the honors graduation rate from the university is higher than that for the university as a whole. The **university-wide rate is 58%**, yielding the 4.0 AGR for the college. **The Dean reports that the four-year grad rate is an impressive 76%.** The average six-year **honors graduation rate for all 50 programs** under review **is 89%.**

Ratio of Staff to Honors Students (4.5): Our estimate is that there is 1 staff member for every **124.8** students. (Mean ratio for all 50 programs is 1 staff member for every 159.8 students.)

Honors Residence Halls (5.0): The honors living/learning community is centered in Ridge South, a modern air-conditioned facility with suite-style rooms and connecting baths. The nearest dining hall is JC East. "No residence halls are co-ed, although the floors in the Ridge have women at one end and men at the other. All rooms in the Ridge are double suites. Only honors freshmen are allowed on the honors floors of Ridge South; some honors freshmen will choose to live in other accommodations on campus." Ridge South is somewhat closer to humanities, social sciences, and business classroom buildings than to science and math buildings; however, the academic buildings on the University campus are relatively close together.

Prestigious Awards (3.5): UM students have a solid record of winning Rhodes Scholarships, although relatively few have been recorded in recent years. Many UM students have been awarded Truman Scholarships, among the most prestigious. In the case of undergraduate awards, the university does best when some facet of international study is involved. UM students receive significant numbers of Gilman Scholarships, which go to students of limited means and pay for academic studies abroad or for career-oriented, credit-bearing internships. The university's students also earn a relatively high number of Boren Scholarships, and these can be valued at $20,000. Boren Scholars study in countries where U.S. interests are high but American student involvement is low. Western European countries and Canada are not included. Most students study in Africa, Latin America, Central and Eastern Europe, Eurasia, and Middle East.

Continuation Requirements: "Students must have **a minimum of a 3.50 grade point average in order to graduate as a Sally McDonnell Barksdale Honors Scholar**. In the service of accomplishing this goal, Honors students **must attain a minimum GPA of 3.20 at the end of the freshman year, a 3.40 at the end of the sophomore year, and a 3.50 by the end of the junior year. During the senior year, students must have at least a 3.50 cumulative GPA.** The Honors College does not use a probationary period; however, students dismissed because of a poor GPA can re-enter the SMBHC if they bring their GPA up to the minimum for their year.

Academic Strengths: The leading academic departments at Ole Miss are English, history, accounting, and modern foreign languages.

Undergraduate Research: Honors students, both SMBHC Scholars and Junior-Entry students, must complete a research project and senior thesis in order to graduate from the Honors College. Typically, the work done in the research project feeds into the thesis. Unless the student successfully petitions to do something else, the work is performed in the student's major. The length and content of the thesis is based on the type of work each discipline expects.

Study Abroad: "Honors students comprised 7% of the undergraduate student body in 2012-2013, but made up 39% of those who studied abroad a full summer, semester or a year. **The Honors College has Fellowships that can be awarded to support study abroad; we prioritize year-long or semester-long experiences and give lower priority (and funding) to summer experiences.**"

There are four primary types of **Short-Term Programs:**

Faculty-led programs are programs led and taught by a UM faculty member and are typically attended by a group of UM students. These programs are offered for a specific, pre-determined UM course credit. Recent destinations were Denmark, Tanzania, Belize, Venice, Costa Rica, and Sydney.

Partner University programs involve **86 UM partner universities in 37 countries** around the world that host Summer Schools (or short terms in January). UM students may attend these summer schools abroad and take courses taught by the partner university's faculty members. The countries with the most partner universities are Germany, the United Kingdom, Japan, South Korea, and France.

Internships are available in places such as London, Dublin, and Sydney during the summer. Students from any major on campus are eligible to participate and students can work in a variety of jobs and earn academic credit for their participation.

Language Programs in Spanish, French, Italian, German, Chinese, Japanese, and Russian are available; some of these programs are taught by UM faculty members, or by faculty members at UM partners abroad.

There are two primary types of **Long-Term Study-Abroad Programs**:

Exchange Programs--The University of Mississippi currently has exchange agreements with approximately 86 universities around the world. Through these agreements UM students can spend a semester or year abroad and students from international universities can come to Ole Miss in their places. *UM students who study abroad through Exchange Programs remain enrolled as University of Mississippi students while abroad and receive UM credit. Students who study abroad on an exchange pay University of Mississippi tuition and fees for the semester they are abroad.*

Affiliate programs--These allow students to study at sites that may not be available through exchanges. Some also offer unique programs that are tailored to particular academic or career interests. *UM students who study abroad through Affiliate Programs remain enrolled as University of Mississippi students while abroad and receive UM credit. They are billed through their UM Bursar accounts, though the program price is not set at the cost of UM tuition and typically costs more than an exchange program.*

Financial Aid: Many extremely generous awards are specifically related to the SMBHC:

McDonnell Barksdale Scholarship--with an award of $32,000 ($8,000 per year), is **for Mississippi residents only**. The deadline to apply is January 5.

Doris Raymond Honors Scholarship--provides the same award, has the same deadline as the previous scholarships, but is *not* **limited to Mississippi residents.**

Harold Parker Memorial Scholarship, SMBHC Honors College--award amount, deadline, and conditions are the same as for the Doris Raymond Honors Scholarship--*not* **limited to Mississippi residents.**

"Because of the qualifications necessary to be admitted to the Honors College, most students are eligible for academic excellence awards from the University. Mississippi residents with at least a 29 on the ACT are also eligible for Mississippi Eminent Scholar Grants. Various schools and departments, as well as the University, award executive-level scholarships for which honors prospects are competitive, and the Honors College awards ten-eleven executive-level scholarships per year."

Ole Miss increased its sponsorship of National Merit Scholars from 28 in 2012 to 36 in 2013, despite a national trend of declining university sponsorships.

Degree of Difference (Honors students/non-honors students): 3.72 on a scale of 5. Some parents and prospective students might prefer an honors program that in many ways stands apart on campus, while others might prefer a program that is more expansive. The rating here tries to provide an indication of where a given honors program is on the stand apart/expansive spectrum. The rating is based on the difference between (1) the average SAT scores for enrolled honors students and (2) the average test scores for all students in the university as a whole *and* for students with scores at the 75% level or above. A score of 3.5 or higher indicates a high degree of difference. A score of 3.2 to 3.49 indicates a relatively high degree of difference. Finally, a score below 3.2 indicates a modest difference. **Please keep in mind that neither the high nor low selectivity of an honors program determines how effective the program is; this rating is merely "cultural" and *not* qualitative.**

NAME: UNIVERSITY OF MISSOURI HONORS COLLEGE

Date Established: 1958

Location: Columbia, Missouri

University Full-time Undergraduate Enrollment: 25,178

Honors Enrollment: *Estimated enrollment,* 2,050 (mean size of all 50 programs is 1,714).

Review/Admissions Category--II: Programs with **average SAT scores of 1343--1382 for enrolled students.** *Estimated* average (mean) SAT score for enrolled honors students is 1358-1378, and the *estimated* ACT is 31. We do not know the average high school GPA.

Minimum Admission Requirements:

An ACT score of 31 (SAT 1360) AND either a top 15% class rank OR a high school core GPA of 3.58
An ACT score of 30 (SAT 1330) AND either a top 10% class rank OR a high school core GPA of 3.74
An ACT score of 29 (SAT 1290) AND either a top 5% class rank OR a high school core GPA of 3.91

"Core GPA is calculated by MU using your grades from all English, science, social studies, and foreign language courses, all math courses Algebra I and higher, and your highest fine art grade."

Honors Programs in Admissions Category II (average SAT scores of 1343-1382): Alabama, Delaware, Florida State, LSU, Massachusetts, Missouri, North Carolina State, Ohio University, Temple, Purdue, UCLA, Utah, Vermont, and Wisconsin.

Administrative Staff: Honors College has a staff of 11.

FOR ALL "MORTARBOARD" RATINGS BELOW, A SCORE OF 5 IS THE MAXIMUM AND REPRESENTS A COMPARISON WITH ALL 50 HONORS COLLEGES AND PROGRAMS:

PERCEPTION* OF UNIVERSITY AS A WHOLE, **NOT** OF HONORS: 🎓🎓🎓1/2

OVERALL HONORS RATING: 🎓🎓🎓1/2**

Curriculum Requirements: 🎓🎓🎓

Class Range and Type: 🎓🎓🎓🎓🎓

Class Size: 🎓🎓🎓🎓

Adjusted Grad Rate: 🎓🎓🎓🎓

Ratio of Staff to Students: 🎓 🎓🎓^{1/2}

Priority Registration: **No.** *This is the main reason MU Honors does not have 4 mortarboards.*

Honors Housing: 🎓🎓🎓🎓

Prestigious Awards: 🎓🎓🎓🎓

*Perception is based on the university's ranking among public universities in the 2014 U.S. News Best Colleges report. Please bear in mind that the better the U.S. News ranking, the more difficult it is for an honors college or program to have a rating that equals or improves on the magazine ranking.

**Editor's Note: *MU Honors College has many exemplary features, and the 3.5 Overall rating is the result of two factors: (1) a relatively low honors completion requirement and (2) the lack of priority registration for honors students. A low honors completion requirement, though not rewarded by our rating system, can be considered a positive factor because honors students are generally more likely to complete modest requirements rather than drop out of honors (often because of a thesis requirement). As we have noted elsewhere, 13 of the 50 honors colleges and programs reviewed in this book do not provide the "perk" of priority registration for honors students. In many cases, this is because the universities or honors programs do not want to add to the perception that honors students are considered "elite" or receive too much preferential treatment.*

Curriculum Requirements (3.0): To receive the Honors Certificate, which signifies completion of all MU Honors College requirements, students must have at least 20 credit hours of honors courses.

"The 20 hours may include any number of General Honors and Departmental Honors course credits but no more than 6 hours of honors transfer credit, 8 hours of Learning-by-Contract credit, and 8 hours of *approved* graduate credit. Students must achieve a minimum letter grade for each course: a C or better for regular honors or graduate courses or a B or better for Learning-by-Contract courses."

AP/IB credits are **not** counted as replacements for Honors College courses.

Range and Type of Honors Courses (5.0): The principal strengths of the MU Honors College are (1) an interesting series of topical seminars; (2) a solid range of departmental honors classes; and (3) an **exemplary program of "service learning,"** including extensive for-credit opportunities for community service, special training, and research projects. Of all the 50 honors programs under review, **the MU Honors College is unsurpassed in the integration of honors seminars, departmental classes, and service learning.**

The following quote from the Honors College site is a succinct summary of the Honors College philosophy: "By offering honors courses and programs that emphasize the importance of public scholarship, **we are creating a new generation of scholars who will transform the academy from an 'ivory tower' into a place where knowledge is produced for the public and with the public.**"

Beginning with the honors seminars and colloquia offered in Spring 2014, there are five 1-credit sections, four of which are wide-ranging and mostly informal discussion groups in which students explore the excitement and occasional humility that comes from spirited give and take. An elective 2-credit colloquium in Decoding Science: Getting the Message, aims at "the problem of getting science messages across to a non-science audience from multiple disciplinary angles."

Among our favorites are the five sections of **The Middle Ages and the Renaissance** that offer students "the challenging opportunity to read and discuss literature, art, architecture, music, and philosophy from the dawn of the Middle Ages with Augustine and Beowulf to the Renaissance with Montaigne and Shakespeare." Among the topics included in these seminars are the Crusades and the Arab Experience of the Middle Ages; the History of the Book; Luther and the Rise of Protestantism; **and Machiavelli's Fundamental Question: "Is it Better to be Feared than Loved?"**

A humanities colloquium on **Modern Israeli Film** is especially topical with its promise to explore "universal themes, such as democracy and righteousness, as seen in the context of a society which is subject to constant challenges in most areas of its national life. We will conclude with the younger generation of writers and directors, who reject much of the centrality of the Israeli experience and reflect a more universalistic trend, often of an alienated, surreal and idiosyncratic nature."

We also like **Energy: From Particles to Civilizations** for its focus on "the big ideas of thermodynamics, laws of motion, atomic and molecular structure, electricity, and magnetism. The crux of the course…is derived from the intersections and connections between these concepts. We will therefore also begin to understand how energy is generated and used by living systems, from individual organisms to entire civilizations, and we will investigate some of the environmental impacts and ethical questions resulting from energy production and consumption."

Before we leave the "seminar discussion," here is another one that "focuses on 13 different ways to think about color. Color is everywhere in our world; it informs our sense of everything from interior decoration to fashion; sex to race." In **Thinking about Color,** students will "embrace color's paradoxical combination of ubiquity and mystery as we explore subjects like Impressionism, perception, whiteness, film noir, color wheels, Technicolor, advertising, Goethe, and blushing. Sound eclectic? That's precisely the point. Taught by three professors with different areas of expertise and interests, this course seeks to explore the many dimensions of color through the lenses of science, art, and popular culture.

"Thinking about Color will be the first course offered under the new Humanities Series in the Honors College, whose general topics are Narratives and Histories, Aesthetics and Performance, Big Ideas, Big Questions, and The Digital Humanities."

While participating in **community service (service learning),** "students attend class and labs in which they work on research projects, investigate social problems and propose solutions. By offering a variety of community service projects, spanning all ages and walks of life, **we hope that students will become involved and express themselves through service."**

A good course to start off the summary of the service learning component is **Theory and Practice of Tutoring Writing,** which "qualifies students for a part-time job working as Writing Lab/Online Writing tutors in future semesters." In addition, as part of the Honors MU Community Engagement Project, there are sections and assignments that are "designed to assist members of the community and offer honors students problem-solving and leadership experiences. Service projects include mentoring at-risk adolescents, working with low-income pre-school children, and doing investigations and providing service for local public health agencies."

In Spring 2014, there were two discussion sections in community engagement, one for youth programs (37 honors students) and the other for public health (22 honors students). The sections train students for their 3-5 hours/week of community service.

The **Civic Leaders Internship** is both a 3-6 credit course (about 65 students) and a means of placing honors students as interns in many state government offices and agencies.

As for **departmental honors classes,** the selection is good--except that we found no honors sections in political science, a popular subject that, as we have noted elsewhere, is sometimes hard to find in honors programs. Since it is the University of Missouri, it makes sense that there **are two honors courses in journalism,** one in Career Explorations and the other in the fundamentals of News Writing. **We commend the Honors College for making available multiple sections of French, German, and Spanish, and really going the extra mile by offering one course each in Greek in Latin.** The offerings in psychology are also outstanding.

We found two honors classes each for biology, chemistry, and math (calculus), along with a section in honors physics. Philosophy, English, history, classics, geology, speech, accounting, economics (1), art, education, and even aerospace engineering were offered in Spring 2014.

Average Class Size (4.0): The average honors class size is 23.8 students; the overall average class size for the 50 colleges and programs under review in this edition is 21.2 students. **The smaller class sizes available in the Honors College are important at MU, where only 15% of classes have fewer than 20 students.**

Adjusted Graduation Rate (4.0): The AGR is not simply the six-year graduation rate of students in the honors college who graduated from the university (*estimated at* **87.5%),** whether or not the students completed the honors program ("honors completers"). The AGR also reflects the extent to which the honors graduation rate from the university is higher than that for the university as a whole. The **university-wide rate is 71%,** yielding the 4.0 AGR for the college. The average honors six-year **graduation rate for all 50 programs under review is 89%.** MU Honors is likely to have a relatively high honors completion rate because of the modest credit requirement and the lack of a thesis requirement.

Ratio of Staff to Honors Students (3.5): Our estimate is that there is 1 staff member for every **186.4** students. (Mean ratio for all 50 programs is 1 staff member for every 159.8 students.)

Honors Residence Halls (4.0): The Honors Learning Community (HLC) is located on the east side of campus in **Schurz Hall.** The large residence hall is also home to other living/learning programs, including **honors pre- med and honors journalism.**

"Schurz Hall draws students from the entire campus and has the highest GPA of all residential halls on campus. Renovated in 2008, it offers coed floors that house men and women on different wings of the building in traditional-style rooms." The residence hall is air conditioned and has an on-site laundry in the basement. Rooms are coed by dorm wing.

According to one student, "**One perk of living in Schurz is that it's close to Plaza 900, which is arguably the best dining hall** on campus. Also, if you're not in the mood to leave the hall, Baja Grill is in Bingham Hall, between Hatch and Schurz. For those who believe variety is the spice of life, Mizzou Market in Pershing Commons and Eva J's dining hall are also a short walk away."

What is not always a *short* walk away are some classes, but the dining options are far above average.

Prestigious Awards (4.0): MU students have won an impressive 18 Rhodes Scholarships, 3 Gates Cambridge Scholarships, 4 Marshall Scholarships, and 13 Truman Scholarships. MU graduates have won more prestigious National Science Foundation Graduate Research Fellowships than most of the 50 universities under review. MU undergraduates in the STEM disciplines have won 26 Goldwater Scholarships and also do very well in winning Gilman Scholarships, awarded to students of limited means for studying abroad.

Continuation Requirements: 3.50 cumulative GPA

Academic Strengths: Aside from its world-renowned journalism department, MU has seven academic departments that are ranked 65th in the nation or better. These include education (51), psychology (52), business (58), political science (61), English and math (both 63), and history (64).

Undergraduate Research: MU Honors offers **The Discovery Fellows Program** as a way to learn about the process of conducting research. "Discovery Fellows work on new and up-and-coming projects in their academic discipline, meet other students and faculty who share similar interests, and use these experiences to help pave the way for future research projects. Fellows will gain insight into the professional world, enhance their knowledge base and critical thinking skills, and better prepare themselves for graduate school."

Eligibility:

First-semester freshmen and sophomores with an ACT composite score of 33 or better are eligible for the Honors College Discovery Fellows Program. "Students are identified from application data and are contacted by January of their senior year of high school to complete the application for the first-year program and by February of their freshman year of college for the second-year program.

Selection: Deans of the respective colleges or schools make their decisions in the spring.

Stipend: Fellows work 8-10 hours per week during the academic year and receive a stipend of $1,700 for the year. (This stipend should not affect a student's financial aid package.) Fellows also receive automatic acceptance to the Honors College.

Study Abroad: MU ranks 37th in the nation in the total number of students who study abroad. MU students can study in 60 countries around the globe, and there are 29 programs that offer honors credit. Below are a few of the faculty-led programs for honors students:

Rome: From Fascism to Liberation (summer); Engineering: Electrical Circuit Theory (Dublin, summer); From the Bronze Age to the Byzantine Empire (Greece, summer); French Language and Culture (Paris and Lyon, summer); Sustainability in Europe (Copenhagen, semester or full academic year); Spanish Language, Literature, and Culture (Oviedo, summer); Renewable Energy (Bonn, Germany, summer).

Some study-abroad scholarships are available through the MU International Center.

Financial Aid: The Honors College has some endowed scholarships for high-achieving students, and several additional scholarships affiliated with Arts and Sciences or with outstanding accomplishments in honors sequences (arts and humanities, sciences, social sciences) or special programs (Discovery Fellows). There is also an award given to the outstanding senior honors student each year.

MU sponsorship for National Merit Scholars has declined in the past year. But many **in-state** honors students should be eligible for the **Curators Scholarship--$4,500 per year**. Minimum eligibility requires a 1250 SAT or 28 ACT, and a high school rank in the top 5%. Even better is the **Chancellor's Award, valued at $6,500 per year.** Minimum eligibility requires at least a 1360 SAT or 31 ACT and a high school rank in the top 10%.

The **Mizzou Heritage Scholarship for out-of state students** waives the non-resident portion of tuition (approximately $14,000 per year), leaving the in-state amount to be paid (approximately $10,300). To be eligible an out-of-state student must have at least a 1210 SAT or 27 ACT along with a high school rank in the top 25%.

Another scholarship for out-of-state students is the **Mark Twain Non-Resident Scholarship.** Minimum requirements are an SAT of at least 1330 or ACT of at least 30 (very likely higher to earn the award). The value is $10,000 for students in the top 25% of the high school class or $8,500 for students in the top 50% of the high school class. Lesser awards are also available for lower test scores.

Degree of Difference (Honors students/non-honors students): 3.35 on a scale of 5. Some parents and prospective students might prefer an honors program that in many ways stands apart on campus, while others might prefer a program that is more expansive. The rating here tries to provide an indication of where a given honors program is on the stand apart/expansive spectrum. The rating is based on the difference between (1) the average SAT scores for enrolled honors students and (2) the average test scores for all students in the university as a whole *and* for students with scores at the 75% level or above. A score of 3.5 or higher indicates a high degree of difference. A score of 3.2 to 3.49 indicates a relatively high degree of difference. Finally, a score below 3.2 indicates a modest difference. **Please keep in mind that neither the high nor low selectivity of an honors program determines how effective the program is; this rating is merely "cultural" and *not* qualitative.**

NAME: HONORS CAROLINA, UNIVERSITY OF NORTH CAROLINA-CHAPEL HILL

Date Established: 1954

Location: Chapel Hill, North Carolina

University-wide, Full-time Undergraduate Enrollment: 17,562

Honors Enrollment: approximately 1,478 (mean enrollment of all 50 programs is 1,714).

Review/Admissions Category IV: Programs with **average SAT scores of 1417 or higher for enrolled students**. Mean SAT score for enrolled UNC-CH students across all programs is 1443 (median is 1460); ACT average is 32 (median is 33). Average high school rank is the top 3%.

Honors Programs in Admissions Category IV (average SAT of 1417 and higher): Auburn, Clemson, Georgia, Illinois, Kansas, Michigan, Minnesota, North Carolina, Rutgers, South Carolina, UT Austin, Virginia.

Administrative Staff: Honors Carolina has a staff of 10.

FOR ALL "MORTARBOARD" RATINGS BELOW, A SCORE OF 5 IS THE MAXIMUM AND REPRESENTS A COMPARISON OF ALL 50 HONORS COLLEGES AND PROGRAMS:

PERCEPTION* OF UNIVERSITY AS A WHOLE, NOT OF HONORS: 🎓🎓🎓🎓🎓

OVERALL HONORS RATING: 🎓🎓🎓🎓 1/2

Curriculum Requirements: 🎓🎓🎓 1/2**

Class Range and Type: 🎓🎓🎓🎓 1/2

Class Size: 🎓🎓🎓🎓

Adjusted Grad Rate: 🎓🎓🎓🎓🎓

Ratio of Staff to Students: 🎓🎓🎓🎓 1/2

Priority Registration: Yes, to the extent that members of Honors Carolina register for honors courses before other eligible students each semester. (Many honors courses are open to UNC students who are not in honors.)

Honors Housing: 🎓🎓🎓🎓

Prestigious Awards: 🎓🎓🎓🎓🎓

*Perception is based on the university's ranking among public universities in the 2014 U.S. News Best Colleges report. Please bear in mind that the higher the U.S. News ranking, the more difficult it is for an honors college or program to have a rating that improves on the magazine ranking.

**Curriculum Requirements (3.5): *Editor's Note: The modest completion requirement--24 credit hours--and the lack of priority registration for non-honors classes are the only reasons that Honors Carolina is not listed with five "mortarboards" overall.*

Here's what Honors Carolina has to say about the basic requirements:

"For members of Honors Carolina to remain in good standing each academic year, they must complete two honors courses (typically two 3.0 credit-hour courses) or course equivalents. Course equivalents may include an independent project supplementing work in a regular course within a student's major (honors contract), a study abroad experience, faculty-mentored research, graduate-level coursework, or participation in a honors student-led service project.

"For undergraduate students at UNC Chapel Hill **to graduate with honors or highest honors, they must successfully complete a senior honors thesis** project in their major that culminates in an original academic product or artistic piece or performance…To be eligible to begin a senior honors thesis, students must have a cumulative grade point average of 3.30 or higher. Individual departments may require a higher GPA within a student's major field(s) of study."

The **minimum** hours required for completion are 24, since the eight-course requirement could be met with 3-hour courses only. The Honors Carolina total number of hours required is a bit below average for all 50 programs in this review.

Below are some additional details about the course requirements:

The Honors Contract option counts as one honors course. **One honors contract may be completed each semester. Note: Contracts are limited to honors students with 60 or more credit hours, and the contract courses must be upper-division courses in the major.**

Honors research in biology or chemistry counts as one honors course. Honors thesis counts as one honors course.

Note: Graduate courses provide honors credit, but only if they are strictly graduate courses, and not set up as combined courses for advanced undergrads and graduate students.

Range and Type of Honors Courses (4.5): By any reasonable standard, the University of North Carolina at Chapel Hill is one of the top five public universities in the nation as well as a premier university among all institutions public or private. One example: **Honors Carolina has a spectacular graduation rate,** even when the four-year standard is applied. (Please see **Adjusted Graduation Rates,** below).

Differentiating UNC Chapel Hill from UC Berkeley, UCLA, Michigan, or the University of Virginia is not a matter of determining excellence, which is manifest in all five universities, but of deciding on a particular form of excellence. As selective as the University of Virginia, UNC Chapel Hill, like that nearby institution, has quality students and classes in and out of honors. That is one reason why students who are not formally a part of Honors Carolina can take honors courses, provided they have a strong academic record (overall GPA of 3.0). Given that the quality of classes and teaching is outstanding, in this category we address only the quantity and variety of classes for Honors Carolina students.

Honors Carolina is a **blended program,** offering a near-perfect balance of seminars and more specialized course in the academic disciplines. Yet many of the departmental courses are themselves seminar-type classes, much like many of the departmental honors classes at the University of Michigan.

From Spring 2014, our favorites among the honors seminars are **American Intellectual History**; Ghettos and Shtetls? Urban Life in East European Jewish History; Self Knowledge; Translational Skills: From Academy to Market; Artisans and Global Culture; and **Borders and Walls in the Arab World.**

About **American Intellectual History:** "This course explores the evolution of intellectual culture in late 19th and 20th-century America…how trends in philosophy, art, theology, economics, science, and literature have shaped the wider culture and, in turn, how popular culture has transformed these ideas. Themes include national identity; the clash between faith and reason; solutions to social injustice; and conceptions of human nature."

The description of **Borders and Walls**: "Especially in the past decade there has been an explosion of artists, writers, and filmmakers from the Arab world responding to border practices and their attendant violence. They have attested to the consequences of that violence, resisted their applications, and creatively circumvented their effects…."

As noted before, the **departmental honors classes** are often seminars themselves or at least have class titles that strike a seminar tone: The Dismal Science--Economic and Intellectual Origins of Classical Economic Thought (history); The Elements of Politics: Moderns (political science); **Doctors and Patients** (English!).

On Doctors and Patients: "When the medical anthropologist Arthur Kleinman writes that 'illness has meaning,' he reminds us that the human experience of being sick involves more than just an ailing body. In this course we will analyze a diverse collection of writers who have taken as their topic the human struggle to make sense of suffering and debility. The course…will allow us to explore not just the medical, but the personal, ethical, cultural, spiritual, and political facets of illness."

One computer science course is titled The Business of Games; a music section is called Music and Politics; a philosophy course--Ethics of Sports.

Of all the disciplines, history probably has the best representation, as befits a university with an outstanding history department. Economics is also a strong presence, though it is not always so in many honors programs. Philosophy, political science, English, and even the now-neglected classics are very much in evidence. Some of the honors biology and chemistry honors classes are actually honors labs, but each discipline has one excellent full-course offering in Spring 2014. We found only one honors math section--differential equations--and no honors physics sections. (There were some science sections that took a "mathematical approach," such as Ecology and Population Evolution.)

167

(The comparative lack of math and physics honors courses explains the 4.5 rating, but few would doubt the quality of math and physics classes at Carolina, whether they are called honors or not. **Note: in Fall 2014, there will be a class titled, Introduction to Astronomy: Stars, Galaxies, and Cosmology as well as some math-heavy biology and chemistry courses.)**

Average Class Size (4.0): The average size of Honors Carolina classes is **20.1** students, compared to the average size among all programs of 21.2 students.

Adjusted Graduation Rate (5.0): The AGR is not simply the six-year graduation rate of students in the honors program who graduated from the university **(97%),** whether or not the students completed the honors program ("honors completers"). It also reflects the extent to which the honors graduation rate from the university is higher than that for the university as a whole. (The **university-wide rate is 89%,** yielding the 5.0 AGR for the program.) The average **honors** six-year **graduation rate for all 50 programs under review is 89%**.

Honors Carolina reports that the <u>four-year graduation rate</u> for freshmen entering Honors Carolina in 2008 <u>was 95%</u>. To put this in perspective, consider that Williams, Carleton, and Bowdoin all have a four-year grad rate of 91%. The four-year rate at Yale is 89%, at Princeton and Dartmouth 88%, at Duke 87%, and at Harvard 86%. (The university-wide, four-year grad rate at UNC Chapel Hill is 77%.)

Ratio of Staff to Honors Students (4.5): Our estimate is that there is 1 staff member for every **147.8**. (Median ratio for all 50 programs is 1 staff member for every 159.8 students.)

Honors Residence Halls (4.0): Honors Carolina freshmen may live in Koury Hall, a suite-style coed residence with connecting baths, air conditioning, and on-site laundry. There is a kitchen in the residence, and the nearest dining is at Rams Head Dining Hall. Upperclassmen can choose Cobb Residence Hall. In many honors programs, the freshman hall is corridor-style with hall baths, a configuration that is often thought to be better at promoting more socialization; but the Honors Carolina approach reverses that pattern by giving upperclassmen the traditional corridor-style dorm. Cobb is air conditioned, with on-site laundry and a kitchen. The nearest dining is at Lenoir Dining Hall.

Prestigious Awards (5.0): The University of North Carolina at Chapel Hill is the preeminent public institution when it comes to its overall record of winning these five major prestigious scholarships awarded annually: the Rhodes, Marshall, Gates Cambridge, Churchill, and Truman Scholarships. UNC Chapel Hill is second in total Rhodes Scholars among public universities; second in Truman Scholarships; second in Churchill Scholarships; and tied for seventh in Marshall Scholarships. The university's students and graduates also perform far above the mean in winning National Science Foundation Graduate Research Fellowships and Fulbright Student Scholarships.

The university is tied for third in the number of undergraduates who have won Udall Scholarships for work in Native American or environmental studies, and has a record well above the mean in earning Goldwater Scholarships (40) for students in the STEM fields.

Continuation Requirements: 3.0 cumulative GPA

Academic Strengths: The average departmental rank across 15 major academic disciplines at UNC-CH is 26, and 9 of the 15 departments are ranked in the top 25 nationwide among all universities public and private. Those are sociology (6), business (7), history (11), psychology (12), political science and chemistry (both13th), English (15), and biology (24). Earth sciences (52) and engineering (79) are the only academic departments not ranked in the top 50 nationally.

Undergraduate Research: From the Honors Director: "Cutting-edge research is an integral part of the culture at Carolina. Honors Carolina students enjoy countless opportunities to work with faculty members conducting breakthrough research in almost any field. Honors Carolina students get involved in research projects, and **many begin that work as early as their first year**. Research may take the form of a senior honors thesis project, an advanced course in the major, a faculty-mentored independent research project, or through participation in one of our competitive summer research fellowships.

"The Burch Fellowships are competitive research awards that allow students to design their own unique educational experiences and travel the globe to pursue their passions. Designed for students who possess extraordinary ability, promise, and imagination, the Burch Fellows Program **provides up to $6,000 to support self-designed, off-campus learning experiences** like these: **Working with NASA astrobiologists** to answer questions about the possibility of life on other planets; **jamming with jazz musicians in Cuba**; traveling to the Philippines to study how bamboo can mitigate the effects of climate change.

"The Taylor Mentored Research Fellowships provide $4,000 grants for students working on a faculty-mentored research project during the summer. The fellowships provide opportunities for students to continue work they may already have begun with a faculty member, to get a head start on a senior honors thesis, or to travel to distant libraries, labs, or archives that might otherwise be beyond reach. Applications are encouraged from all disciplines.

"Research grants are available to help offset the cost of conducting a Senior Honors Thesis. The grants, up to $500, can cover the cost of equipment, supplies, software, publications, transportation, and other expenses."

Study Abroad: If we assigned a rating for study abroad in this edition, Honors Carolina would receive the highest rating possible.

"With Chapel Hill as a launching pad, Honors Carolina students pursue opportunities to live and study in some of the world's greatest cities," the Director tells us. **"A notable curricular feature of Honors Carolina programs in Cape Town, London, Washington, DC, and China is an internship component, with placements available in such fields as global finance, public health, public policy, legal advocacy and human rights, journalism, and the arts.** In addition, a rotating roster of Burch Field Research Seminars combine faculty scholarship and undergraduate teaching to produce unique hands-on learning experiences in changing locations stateside and around the globe.

"Students on any of our **London programs** are based at **Winston House, UNC Chapel Hill's European Study Center located in the heart of Bloomsbury** in Bedford Square. A Georgian townhouse **built in 1790,** Winston House has been fully updated and offers three classrooms, two large seminar rooms, two spacious faculty/project offices, a library/administrative office, a comfortable student reading room with computer lab, a small kitchen, a patio garden, and a faculty residential suite consisting of two bedrooms, a living/dining room, a kitchen, and a bath. Fully outfitted for video teleconferencing and wireless computer access throughout, the building also offers an eight-person lift and is disability accessible.

"While abroad, students remain enrolled at UNC-CH…**All programs are led by permanent UNC Chapel Hill faculty who teach on location as part of the program**. Honors Carolina also employs local instructional staff.

"Financial aid can be applied to the program costs and Honors Carolina offers additional need- and merit-based scholarships. **During the 2012-2013 academic year, Honors Carolina awarded thirty-six study abroad scholarships totaling, $66,400. In addition, three Weir Fellows received support totaling $62,716.**

The Director reports that 53% of Honors Carolina students study abroad prior to graduation.

Financial Aid: "UNC's Office of Scholarships and Student Aid, along with the Morehead-Cain Foundation and the Robertson Scholars program, award merit- and need-based scholarships to **members of Honors Carolina.**

"Of the 438 incoming **first-year members of Honors Carolina** last fall (Fall 2013)," the Director says, "210 **(48%) were awarded some form of merit scholarship.**" However, the university as a whole appears to have stopped sponsoring National Merit Finalists, though some of these will still receive corporate sponsorships.

Degree of Difference (Honors students/non-honors students): 2.45 on a scale of 5. Some parents and prospective students might prefer an honors program that in many ways stands apart on campus, while others might prefer a program that is more expansive. The rating here tries to provide an indication of where a given honors program is on the stand apart/expansive spectrum. The rating is based on the difference between (1) the average SAT scores for enrolled honors students and (2) the average test scores for all students in the university as a whole *and* for students with scores at the 75% level or above. A score of 3.5 or higher indicates a high degree of difference. A score of 3.2 to 3.49 indicates a relatively high degree of difference. Finally, a score below 3.2 indicates a modest difference. **Please keep in mind that neither the high nor low selectivity of an honors program determines how effective the program is; this rating is merely "cultural" and *not* qualitative.**

Testimonials:

Natalie Deuitch, Honors Carolina Class of 2015--"In a typical day I go to biology classes taught by world-renowned professors. Then I'm off to Peifer lab to do some tissue cultures or take pictures on a multimillion-dollar microscope to research biological signaling. Over lunch I Skype with international friends [who are] studying abroad in Spain. Afterwards, I'm at a round table discussion with a food systems researcher in my Eats 101 class or visiting a local farm to see NC agriculture at its finest. Later I have dinner with my classmates, professors and visiting speakers. If I'm not attending a club meeting I catch a show like Iron & Wine, or even President Obama and Jimmy Fallon with my friends at Memorial. The best part is I know I'm going to do it all again tomorrow. **Last summer I conducted original research in India with a Burch Fellowship and this summer I'll be continuing my work at Peifer lab, which will be published in the near future.**

Dr. Randall Styers, Chair, Department of Religious Studies—"Honors Carolina students are the students faculty members dream of. **They arrive in the classroom with creativity, motivation, and passion about their studies,** and it's an inspiration for me as a scholar to see their eagerness to explore new ideas, to solve problems, and to envision new possibilities for the world—**these are students willing to take intellectual risks.** An Honors classroom at UNC is a place all of us learn from one another, and as that happens we form connections that last long into the future. When these students graduate, they represent the best that this university has to offer the world."

NAME: NC STATE UNIVERSITY HONORS PROGRAM

Date Established: 2002

Location: Raleigh, North Carolina

University Full-time Undergraduate Enrollment: 21,821

Honors Enrollment: 700 students; (the mean size of all 50 programs is 1,714.)

Review/Admissions Category II: Programs with **average SAT scores of 1343--1382 for enrolled students**. Actual average (mean) SAT score for enrolled honors students is 1367, and the *estimated* ACT is 31. The average high school GPA is 3.87 (unweighted).

Minimum Admission Requirements: 1300 SAT or 30 ACT; high school GPA 4.5 weighted, 3.75 unweighted.

Honors Programs in Admissions Category II (average SAT scores of 1343-1382): Alabama, Delaware, Florida State, LSU, Massachusetts, Missouri, North Carolina State, Ohio University, Temple, Purdue, UCLA, Utah, Vermont, and Wisconsin.

Administrative Staff: The Honors Program has a staff of 7.

FOR ALL "MORTARBOARD" RATINGS BELOW, A SCORE OF 5 IS THE MAXIMUM AND REPRESENTS A COMPARISON WITH ALL 50 HONORS COLLEGES AND PROGRAMS:

PERCEPTION * OF UNIVERSITY AS A WHOLE, **NOT** OF HONORS: 🎓🎓🎓 1/2

OVERALL HONORS RATING: 🎓🎓🎓 1/2

Curriculum Requirements: 🎓🎓🎓

Class Range and Type: 🎓🎓🎓🎓

Class Size: 🎓🎓🎓🎓

Adjusted Grad Rate: 🎓🎓🎓 1/2

Ratio of Staff to Students: 🎓🎓🎓🎓 1/2

Priority Registration: Yes, honors students register for **all** courses, honors and otherwise, with the first group of students during **each** year they are in the program.

Honors Housing: 🎓🎓🎓🎓

Prestigious Awards: 🎓 🎓 🎓 🎓¹ᐟ²

*Perception is based on the university's ranking among public universities in the 2014 U.S. News Best Colleges report. Please bear in mind that the better the U.S. News ranking, the more difficult it is for an honors college or program to have a rating that equals or improves on the magazine ranking.

Curriculum Requirements (3.0): "Students entering the UHP as freshmen must enroll in and complete at least one 3-credit hour HON seminar in their first semester, preferably one of the seminars restricted to incoming freshmen. Students must also complete an additional three 3-credit honors seminars (ideally within the first four semesters). Alternatively, it is possible to accumulate 1-and 2-credit hour honors courses to substitute for one (or more) 3-credit hour honors seminars. **Please note that Honors sections of [departmental] courses and Honors contracts in regular courses do not satisfy the [above] honors course requirement.**" Students must complete at least 12 credits in honors courses.

In addition, students must complete a **two-semester 6-credit capstone project**, "typically done in the junior and/or senior year. **For many students the capstone requirement will be satisfied in whole or in part by the research/thesis** project of their disciplinary honors program. It MAY also be satisfied by **modified** senior design projects in the College of Engineering and the College of Design, subject to approval in advance by the UHP Director."

The total required for completion is a modest 18 credit hours. One likely reason for this is that, with so many STEM (especially engineering) majors, a high completion requirement would be unrealistic.

AP/IB credits are **not** counted as replacements for honors courses.

Range and Type of Honors Courses (4.0): The honors program is a **core type program** that emphasizes interdisciplinary honors seminars (that count for Gen Ed credit) supplemented by a thesis or capstone project. In Spring 2014, there were 15 excellent honors seminars, and 20-25 or so departmental honors sections not counting thesis research. (In Fall, there are 2-3 more seminars overall, but about eight of them are part of the honors freshman seminar series called Inquiry, Discovery, and Literature.) The total number of sections may seem small, but remember that the program is relatively small with only 700 students. The NC State UHP resembles the Purdue Honors College in that both are centered in universities with very high engineering enrollments, and both seek to offer opportunities for their technically-oriented students to develop communication and critical thinking skills in small, seminar-type classes that require more personal engagement.

The honors program is not designed to provide a wide selection of honors engineering classes, although some of the seminars and departmental classes are certainly related to other STEM disciplines. The breadth that the honors seminars offer is especially valuable at NC State, which is second only to Georgia Tech among public universities in the percentage of engineering graduates (Purdue is third).

But this is not to say that the main purpose of the UHP is to give engineering and other STEM students a broader perspective; indeed, NC State's 25-year-old Franklin Scholars Program is specifically designed to allow a small number of students pursue majors in the humanities and engineering simultaneously. The UHP, on the other hand, is a great addition for hundreds of NC State students who, while attending a university known for its STEM programs, still want to have outstanding seminars that are relevant to all disciplines.

"The UHP seeks to cultivate students as public intellectuals interested in and capable of making a meaningful contribution to their discipline, NC state, and society-at-large. The UHP is designed to be a transformative experience which is catalyzed through a process of creativity, inquiry, and discovery. Undergraduates can pursue research and scholarship in any discipline. In fact, there are students from every undergraduate college at NC State in the UHP."

(NC State has several honors programs, including the University Scholars Program (USP), which is more focused on enrichment activities (75%) than on honors coursework (about 25%). The UHP is described as 75% coursework and 25% enrichment. However, UHP and USP students can take many of the same departmental honors courses. See below.)

The Spring UHP-only seminars include **Frauds and Mysteries in History;** Code Breakers: Unveiling the Mysteries of One Human Language; Interpreting American Cultures; **Pollination: Biology and Economics;** A Global History of American Food; and **The Creative Process in Science—Realities, Comparisons, and Cultural Perceptions.**

Frauds and Mysteries in History introduces students "to myths, mysteries, and misconceptions that surround history, archaeology, and our understandings of the past, such as alien visitations, pyramid mania, archaeo-astronomy, and Atlantis. We will examine reasons why people are fascinated by the past, how common logical fallacies are invoked in historical myths, and how the past has been appropriated and manipulated throughout time."

In **Pollination,** students learn that the honey bee is "our premier pollinator... We then go on to compare the other pollinators with the honeybee, which is unfortunately seriously declining in numbers throughout the world. We also look at the economics of pollination and the impact of such factors as succession and global warming on our pollinators. We finish the semester by examining **a world without honey bees: what it would be like and what we could do about it."**

As noted above, there are 20-25 departmental honors-level sections, many of them open to UHP and USP students alike. Foremost among these would be the math sections, at least seven in Spring 2014, covering the ground from three levels of calculus to differential equations to modern algebra and analysis. At least five sections are on business-related topics, including financial and operations management and marketing. Two more are in economics, another two in history, and two in English. It was good to see two sections of honors physics and three in biology/microbiology. What we did not find was an honors section in chemistry. Political science and psychology each offered one honors section.

Average Class Size (4.0): The *estimated* overall **average class size is 22.5 students**, versus the average for all 50 programs under review—21.2 students.

.

Adjusted Graduation Rate (3.5): The AGR is not simply the six-year graduation rate of students in the **honors program** who graduated from the university **(84%),** whether or not the students completed the honors program ("honors completers"). The AGR also reflects the extent to which the honors graduation rate from the university is higher than that for the university as a whole. (The **university-wide rate is**

71%, yielding the 3.5 AGR for the college.) The average **honors** six-year **graduation rate for all 50 programs under review is 89%.**

Ratio of Staff to Honors Students (4.5): Our estimate is that there is 1 staff member for every **100** students. (Mean ratio for all 50 programs is 1 staff member for every 159.8 students.)

Honors Residence Halls (4.0): "The University Honors Village is housed in Bagwell and Becton Residence Halls in the east area of campus. These two halls, along with Berry Residence Hall, combine to form what is affectionately known as 'The Quad.' The Honors Village has the highest return rate on campus between the freshmen and sophomore years."

"In the Village, first-year residents are assigned upper-class UHP students to serve as mentors (Honors Village Fellows) who will assist in the transition to both university life at NC State and the University Honors Program. In addition to mentoring first year students, HVFs will play an active role in sustaining the Village community by co-chairing one Village committee."

Becton Hall houses the most honors students, 209, first-year and upperclassmen. Becton is air conditioned, has on-site laundry, and features traditional double rooms and hall baths. The nearest dining is Clark Dining Hall. Becton is about 65% coed.

Another 162 honor students live in **Bagwell Hall,** which has similar room features and amenities. Bagwell is about 84% coed. The most convenient dining is also at Clark, which serves The Quad.

Only about 60 honors students live in **Berry Hall.** Berry has features similar to those of the other two honors halls.

Prestigious Awards (4.5): It comes as no surprise that NC State undergraduates do best in winning Goldwater Scholarships for outstanding undergrads in the STEM disciplines, 44 to date. But it may be something of a surprise to learn that NC State is tied for 8th place among all public universities when it comes to winning Udall Scholarships (14) for Native American and environmental studies. (This actually is less a surprise when one realizes that NC State is very close to the Research Triangle, which is home to many companies but also to the research arm of the Environmental Protection Agency.) **In recent years, NC State students have been doing exceptionally well in winning undergraduate awards.**

Again, it is no surprise that NC State graduates would have a strong record of winning the very prestigious and generous Gates Cambridge Scholarships (5) for graduate study (often in STEM disciplines) at Cambridge University in England, and in earning National Science Foundation Graduate Research Fellowships to pursue doctorates.

Continuation Requirements: 3.25 cumulative GPA

Academic Strengths: At NC State, the strongest departments are engineering, ranked 32nd in the nation among all universities public or private, and computer science, with a national ranking of 47. Close behind are economics (48), math (51), physics (52), and sociology (52). Chemistry is ranked 60th in the nation.

Undergraduate Research: About 60% of UHP students complete a capstone research thesis or project. The Office of Undergraduate Research provides $1,000 research grants and $500 travel grants for students to attend national research conferences to make a presentation. **NC State is located near the renowned Research Triangle**, so students have outstanding opportunities for research and internships.

One example is the Undergraduate Research Internship Program hosted by the NC State chemistry department. The program is open to students from across the nation. Students can receive up to $4,000 in stipends plus additional travel funding and free dorm accommodations. "Projects are interdisciplinary and can include organic, chemical biology, inorganic, theoretical and physical chemistry." The program includes visits to local government agencies and industrial partners and provides training "with state-of-the-art equipment (NMR, Mass Spec, Laser Facilities, Biological Instrumental Facilities etc.)."

Study Abroad: NC State students can study abroad in Central and South America, Europe, Africa, China, Russia, Australia, India, Turkey, and New Zealand. Favorite country designations are Spain, the UK, Italy, France, Costa Rica, and Germany. As is the case with some other universities, many NC State academic departments maintain a list of courses and locations that are major-specific. For example, the Electrical and Computer Engineering Department offers semester-long courses in multiple subjects that can be taken at universities in Adelaide and Melbourne, Australia; Hong Kong; Ireland, Wales, and England; Sweden; Spain; China; and the Czech Republic (Prague).

The study-abroad office distributed $220,000 in scholarship funds during the most recent academic year, with an average award of $1,000.

Financial Aid: The most prestigious--and competitive--scholarship at NC State is the Park Scholarship; only 40-45 scholars are selected each year out of more than 1,700 applications for "full-ride" awards currently **valued at $98,000 for in-state students and $166,000 for out-of-state students**. Park Scholars automatically become members of the University Scholars Program, and would certainly qualify as well for the University Honors Program. Selection is not based solely on test scores and GPA, as character and leadership play a very significant role as well.

"Park Scholars are some of the most distinguished students on campus. They hold leadership positions in student government, honorary societies and service organizations; they receive competitive Goldwater Scholarships, Soros Fellowships and Fulbright Grants; they go on to graduate school at prestigious universities including Harvard, Princeton and Oxford; and they find careers at successful companies including Apple, Deloitte, Google and Lockheed Martin.

"Park Scholars are also noted for their devotion to service. Service Raleigh, the largest student-run service endeavor in the Triangle area of North Carolina, is an annual day of service led jointly by Park Scholars and NC State Student Government." In 2013, the Park Foundation gave NC State $50 million to ensure that the scholarship can be funded "in perpetuity."

Other scholarships are available through colleges and departments. We found no scholarships that were directly related to the UHP.

Degree of Difference (Honors students/non-honors students): 2.76 on a scale of 5. Some parents and prospective students might prefer an honors program that in many ways stands apart on campus, while others might prefer a program that is more expansive. The rating here tries to provide an indication of where a given honors program is on the stand apart/expansive spectrum. The rating is based on the difference between (1) the average SAT scores for enrolled honors students and (2) the average test scores for all students in the university as a whole *and* for students with scores at the 75% level or above. A score of 3.5 or higher indicates a high degree of difference. A score of 3.2 to 3.49 indicates a relatively high degree of difference. Finally, a score below 3.2 indicates a modest difference. **Please keep in mind that neither the high nor low selectivity of an honors program determines how effective the program is; this rating is merely "cultural" and *not* qualitative.**

NAME: OHIO UNIVERSITY HONORS TUTORIAL COLLEGE

Date Established: 1972

Location: Athens, Ohio

University Full-time Undergraduate Enrollment: 20,306

Honors Enrollment: 230 (mean size of all 50 programs under review is 1,714)

Review/Admissions Category-- II: Programs with **average SAT scores of 1343--1382 for enrolled students**. Actual average (mean) SAT score for enrolled honors college students is 1356, and the average ACT is 30. The average high school GPA is 4.21 and high school class rank top 4.2%.

Minimum Admission Requirements: SAT 1300, ACT 29; high school GPA, A-; high school class rank, 90th percentile.

Honors Programs in Admissions Category II (average SAT scores of 1343-1382): Alabama, Delaware, Florida State, LSU, Massachusetts, Missouri, North Carolina State, Ohio University, Temple, Purdue, UCLA, Utah, Vermont, and Wisconsin.

Administrative Staff: The HTC has a staff of 7.5 full-time equivalent employees.

FOR ALL "MORTARBOARD" RATINGS BELOW, A SCORE OF 5 IS THE MAXIMUM AND REPRESENTS A COMPARISON WITH ALL 50 HONORS COLLEGES AND PROGRAMS:

PERCEPTION* OF UNIVERSITY AS A WHOLE, NOT OF HONORS: 🎓🎓[1/2]

OVERALL HONORS RATING: 🎓🎓🎓🎓[1/2]

Curriculum Requirements: 🎓🎓🎓[1/2]

Class Range and Type: 🎓🎓🎓🎓

Class Size: 🎓🎓🎓🎓🎓

Adjusted Grad Rate: 🎓🎓🎓🎓🎓

Ratio of Staff to Students: 🎓🎓🎓🎓🎓

Priority Registration: Yes, every term "except before the first semester of their freshman year. They register before all other incoming freshman but not before upperclassmen. **Our students register before any other Ohio University students, including doctoral students. HTCers get first crack at all classes—undergraduate and graduate."**

Honors Housing: 🎓🎓🎓🎓

Prestigious Awards: 🎓🎓🎓 1/2

*Perception is based on the university's ranking among public universities in the 2014 U.S. News Best Colleges report. Please bear in mind that the better the U.S. News ranking, the more difficult it is for an honors college or program to have a rating that equals or improves on the magazine ranking.

Curriculum Requirements (3.5): From the Dean of the HTC: **"In pursuing [the tutorial] method of instruction, the College draws upon the rich educational traditions of British universities, such as Cambridge and Oxford.** Although other colleges and universities have adopted some aspects of the tutorial model, Ohio University remains the only institution in the United States with a degree-granting college incorporating all the essential features of a tutorial-based education."

If we had not applied a very strict rule in this category, a strong argument could be made that the curriculum requirements rating could be 5.0. The reason: the unique, **and we do mean unique**, nature of the Honors Tutorial College is **that all honors tutorial students study one-on-one with professors** and engage in individual research, so that when it comes to the number of hours "required" for a thesis and honors completion, we could have counted up to a dozen or more.

In the end, we took the minimum requirement for honors completion to be about 27 credit hours, including the thesis. The actual average completion total for HTC students is certainly much higher.

"Our curriculum is different from that of other honors colleges throughout the country," the Assistant Dean reports. "In each **of our 34 [now 35] programs of study (majors), students take at least 1 one-on-one or small group tutorial with a faculty member every semester**. Each tutorial ranges in credit hours from 3 to 12 per semester, depending on the content and goals. **During their final year in our program, students must complete a thesis or professional project that makes an original contribution to their discipline. The two senior thesis tutorials often are taken for 10 to 12 credits each.**

"Double majors in our college take at least two tutorials per semester. Single majors are welcome to take up to two tutorials per term if they elect to do so. Tutorials may be taught be faculty in any field. Faculty members from the Heritage College of Osteopathic Medicine, for example, teach biomedical tutorials for students in our biological sciences, neuroscience, and chemistry programs.

"Tutorials do not have to match the content of existing Ohio University courses, so they are highly flexible and customizable. Faculty members spend a minimum of 60 minutes per week meeting with students in **tutorials, which are spirited conversations not lectures.** In the natural sciences and mathematics, a student is often given a problem to solve at the board. The professor asks questions about each step of the solution. Upper-level tutorials may also take place in labs or in the field if the professor deems it most conducive to the learning process.

"Each semester, we offer one to two interdisciplinary special topics seminars that our students may choose to take. The Dean and Assistant Dean teach a mandatory 3-hour freshman seminar that introduces students to academic inquiry across disciplines and explores knowledge and its creation. We offer a 3-

hour academic and research writing seminar to juniors who want extra help in preparing their senior thesis prospectus."

AP credits are **not** counted as replacements for honors courses.

Range and Type of Honors Courses (4.0): Again, this is another rating that could have been a 4.5 or a 5.0. Because we generally do not count tutorials as class sections, the HTC rating derives mainly from the honors classes that have multiple students enrolled. The HTC is classified as a department-based program because the hundreds of honors tutorials are offered by the academic departments. With 35 departments now coordinating honors tutorials with the HTC, the breadth is certain present, if difficult to measure. That we did not find a full honors section in biology/zoology, for example, does *not* mean that there are not multiple and rewarding tutorial opportunities in those important disciplines, one of the 35 departments that do, indeed, offer tutorials and research for HTC students.

As for main sections that we could identify, the following departments were well-represented: business administration, English, journalism, chemistry, philosophy, sociology, economics, social work, communications science and disorders, art, theater arts, and music. At least two sections were available in math, neuroscience, environmental and plant biology, geography, and dance. For a list of the 35 departments affiliated with the HTC, please go to http://www.ohio.edu/honors/future-students/programs/index.cfm#_ .

Of special interest, in addition to those listed above, are tutorial options in astrophysics, computer science, engineering physics, physics, film, neuroscience, Spanish, and women's, gender, and sexuality studies. Another department that works with the HTC is called "Translational Health," which offers "an opportunity to study health and wellness in one-on-one interactions with Exercise Physiology and Nutrition faculty members."

Average Class Size (5.0): Although HTC students will certainly have some large non-honors sections, the extremely small class size that goes along with the tutorial approach to teaching yields the lowest average class size of any program under review, estimated at **10 students per section**. The average class size among all 50 programs we are reviewing is 21.2 students.

Adjusted Graduation Rate (5.0): The AGR is not simply the six-year graduation rate of students in the honors college who graduated from the university **(92%),** whether or not the students completed the honors program ("honors completers"). The AGR also reflects the extent to which the honors graduation rate from the university is higher than that for the university as a whole. The **university-wide rate is 64%,** yielding the 5.0 AGR for the college. The average six-year **honors graduation rate for all 50 programs** under review **is 89%.**

Ratio of Staff to Honors Students (5.0): Our estimate is that there is 1 staff member for every **30.7** students, one of the distinct advantages of a small program. (Mean ratio for all 50 programs is 1 staff member for every 159.8 students.)

Honors Residence Halls (4.0): The honors residence hall is the Reed-Johnson Scholars Complex, a coed facility that features traditional double rooms and hall baths. It is home to all HTC freshmen and sophomores. The complex is air conditioned and has on-site laundry facilities. The closest dining halls are Shively or Nelson Commons.

The complex is in East "Green," Ohio University's most convenient green for business, math, and computer science majors due to its convenient location near Morton and College Green. It is, however, not convenient to the chemistry building.

Prestigious Awards (3.5): The HTC has its own office of prestigious fellowships, including two full-time advisers. The university is developing a solid record of achievement in winning undergraduate awards, especially Udall and Goldwater Scholarships. The university's best performance in postgraduate awards centers on the Marshall, Truman, and Fulbright Student Scholarships, especially the Fulbright Scholarships: University students have won more than 100 since 2002.

Continuation Requirements: 3.50 GPA for continuation and graduation from the HTC. "If students fall below a 3.4 prior to their senior year, they must meet with their faculty adviser and either [the Dean or Assistant Dean] to put an improvement plan in place."

Academic Strengths: Journalism and communications are both very strong at Ohio University. English, physics, business, and engineering are other solid programs at the university, as are many of the fine arts majors.

Undergraduate Research: The Assistant Dean reports that "all of our students conduct original research or creative activity as part of their tutorial curriculum. Many attend academic conferences, and a few publish in peer-reviewed journals each year.

"A senior thesis or professional project that makes an original contribution to the student's academic discipline is a graduation requirement for our students.

"We offer paid research apprenticeships during the summer. At least 20 students are paid to conduct research or creative activity with a faculty mentor **for a minimum of 300 hours (usually 20 hours a week for 15 weeks)."**

Study Abroad: An estimated 20% of HTC students studied abroad during the last academic year. "We invest more than $65,000 in student research and travel expenses," says the Assistant Dean. "Often, we pay for students' study-abroad travel costs. Students may participate in official Ohio University study-abroad programs or those sponsored by other institutions. Many of students conduct thesis research abroad.

The university's Education Abroad office offers programs according to destination preference, academic major, or term preference. The office also has information about work, volunteer, and internship possibilities abroad.

Financial Aid: "*All* students admitted to the Honors Tutorial College as incoming freshman receive a four-year renewable scholarship valued at full, in-state tuition. [Emphasis added.] Out-of-state students receive an additional four-year renewable scholarship to help offset much of the out-of-state differential. Several HTC students receive full tuition and room/board scholarships through the Templeton and Cutler Scholars Programs at Ohio University."

Degree of Difference (Honors students/non-honors students): 5.0 on a scale of 5. Some parents and prospective students might prefer an honors program that in many ways stands apart on campus, while others might prefer a program that is more expansive. The rating here tries to provide an indication of where a given honors program is on the stand apart/expansive spectrum. The rating is based on the difference between (1) the average SAT scores for enrolled honors students and (2) the average test scores for all students in the university as a whole *and* for students with scores at the 75% level or above. A score of 3.5 or higher indicates a high degree of difference. A score of 3.2 to 3.49 indicates a relatively high degree of difference. Finally, a score below 3.2 indicates a modest difference. **Please keep in mind that neither the high nor low selectivity of an honors program determines how effective the program is; this rating is merely "cultural" and** *not* **qualitative.**

Testimonials: *The following mini-profiles were each a part of post that appeared on Public University Honors website.*

Testimonials:

"…**Nyssa Adams**, a recent graduate of the HTC, is now completing the extremely demanding and prestigious combined MD/Ph.D. program at the Baylor University School of Medicine, one of the nation's top medical schools. While at the HTC, Nyssa began working on research to improve cancer drugs used to fight ovarian cancer.

"In writing papers and discussing them in tutorials, Nyssa developed an increased 'respect for research,' not only the difficulties involved, but the exciting challenges it offered to her. Having begun college with an interest in a different field, she made the change to research, giving credit to Jan Hodson, [retired now] of the honors staff, who helped Nyssa to realize that 'there's no reason for me not to succeed.'

"Working so closely with professors gives students interested in science multiple opportunities 'to find your lab' and 'dig into research,' Nyssa says. Her own digging made her one of the outstanding undergrad researchers at HTC, and a student/scholar with the confidence and ability to earn the two doctorates she is well on her way to completing."

"You may know the name **Allie LaForce**, especially if you're a sports fan. Current a co-host of 'Lead Off,' the nightly talk show on the CBS Sports Network, LaForce, only 25, was only a very few years ago a point guard on the Ohio University basketball team.

"But her basketball days at Ohio U came after she was Miss Teen USA…after she was the valedictorian of her high school class in Vermilion, Ohio… after she was a model in New York… and after she was a guest star on a soap opera.

"And another big thing came along after all those accomplishments: LaForce studied broadcast journalism as a member of the highly selective Honors Tutorial College at Ohio University, an elite group of students with an *average* SAT score of 1380. Just another pretty face, hardly."

"LaForce graduated in 2011 from the Honors Tutorial College with a Bachelor of Science in Journalism.

NAME: JOE C. AND CAROLE KERR MCCLENDON HONORS COLLEGE, UNIVERSITY OF OKLAHOMA

Date Established: 1963 as an honors program, 1997 as an honors college.

Location: Norman, Oklahoma

University Full-time Undergraduate Enrollment: 18,931

Honors Enrollment: Approximately 2,600

Review/Admissions Category III: Programs with average SAT scores of 1383--1416 for enrolled students. The *estimated* average (mean) SAT is 1420, and the *actual* average ACT score is 32; the minimum high school GPA is 3.75; no average high school GPA for enrolled students available.

Minimum Admission Requirements: SAT 1330, ACT 30, and high school GPA 3.75.

Honors Programs in Admissions Category III (average SAT scores of 1383--1416): Connecticut, Indiana, Kentucky, Miami University, Oklahoma, Penn State, Tennessee, Texas A&M, UC Irvine, and Washington.

Administrative Staff: The Honors College has a staff of 16, including support staff.

FOR ALL "MORTARBOARD" RATINGS BELOW, A SCORE OF 5 IS THE MAXIMUM AND REPRESENTS A COMPARISON WITH ALL 50 HONORS COLLEGES AND PROGRAMS:

PERCEPTION* OF UNIVERSITY AS A WHOLE, <u>NOT</u> OF HONORS: 🎓🎓🎓¹ᐟ²

OVERALL HONORS RATING: 🎓🎓🎓🎓¹ᐟ²

Curriculum Requirements: 🎓🎓🎓

Class Range and Type: 🎓🎓🎓🎓

Class Size: 🎓🎓🎓🎓🎓

Adjusted Grad Rate: 🎓🎓🎓🎓¹ᐟ²

Ratio of Staff to Students: 🎓🎓🎓¹ᐟ²

Priority Registration: Yes for freshmen year, and all years for National Merit Scholars.

Honors Housing: 🎓🎓🎓🎓

Prestigious Awards: 🎓🎓🎓🎓

*Perception is based on the university's ranking among public universities in the 2014 U.S. News Best Colleges report. Please bear in mind that the better the U.S. News ranking, the more difficult it is for an honors college or program to have a rating that equals or improves on the magazine ranking.

Curriculum Requirements (3.0): The honors college has a basic set of requirements but three levels of distinction upon completion of the basic requirements, based on the student's overall GPA. Below are the basic requirements.

At least 12 hours of honors credit that must include Honors Perspectives (3 credit hours) **or** specific non-western civilization classes (3 credit hours);

At least one Honors Colloquium (3 credit hours) in the junior or senior year;

Complete the Honors Reading and Research requirement (typically in the junior and senior years). If the senior capstone is research-oriented, it may waive the reading requirement. (Zoology majors must complete seven hours of Reading and Research).

The reading and research requirement generates the most questions from students. "Capstone" can mean (1) two to three hours of honors advanced reading plus three hours of thesis work, or (2) two to three hours of a departmental research project or seminar preliminary to a 3-credit thesis. In any case, **a thesis is required.**

Completion requires a minimum of 20-22 honors credits, depending on departmental reading or research requirements preliminary to a thesis. Honors students who complete the requirements with a 3.40-3.59 GPA are eligible to graduate *cum laude;* students with a GPA of 3.60-3.79 are eligible to graduate *magna cum laude*; and students with a GPA of 3.80 or higher are eligible to graduate *summa cum laude.*

The Honors Dean tells us that almost all classes for honors credit are limited in size. Honors format "means the course is strictly limited in size (capped at 19 for Lower Division and capped at 22 for Upper Division), all students must be Honors students, and **the instructor is either a member of the Honors faculty or (in other Colleges and departments) an instructor chosen for their record as an outstanding teacher."**

AP/IB Credits: These cannot be used to replace required honors courses.

Range and Type of Honors Courses (4.0): Even though the completion requirement is modest at 20-22 credit hours, the range and type of courses available to honors students are strong. We classify the college as a **blended honors program,** but the relatively low number of credit hours required for completion is similar to that of many core programs with an emphasis mostly on the first two years.

Of the 23 seminars and colloquia offered in Spring 2014, most are 3-credit classes. Among our favorites in this group are **Politics of U.S. Economic Policy,** *two* **sections taught by the Dean of the Honors College;** Banned Books; **American Social Thought**; American Religions on the Margins; **History,**

Memory, Conflict; Great Books II; and the **American Dream Reconsidered. Note:** The Dean also teaches two 1-credit seminars on Presentation and Interview Skills.

In **American Social Thought,** an introductory seminar for honors students, the class "will touch upon a wide variety of big questions that Americans have grappled with throughout our history: What is the good life? What is the good society? How do we know what we know? Underneath all of these concerns is a more local question: **What should America be?** We will delve into these questions by exploring the ways in which American writers and thinkers have addressed them over the last four centuries."

History, Memory, Conflict is a colloquium that takes on the different and conflicting interpretations of World War II and its aftermath. Students "explore many of the debates and controversies over the meaning of World War II through both primary documents -- including novels, films, journalism, and works of history -- and secondary works. By studying these controversies **we will gain a better understanding not only of the particular legacy of this war, but also more generally of the way in which the memory of major events in the past continues to shape the present."**

The departmental honors courses and electives, both lower and upper division, provide a notable range of course options in almost all of the disciplines considered to be most in demand or of the greatest overall value. In Spring 2014, there was one upper-division honors elective in microbiology. (There is one honors intro to Zoology class offered in Fall 2014.) In Spring 2014, there was only one honors chemistry section, organic chemistry. There were two honors physics sections, however—physics for engineers and intro to physics II for majors. Math was well represented with three advanced calculus/analytical sections. Economics honors sections were especially in evidence in Spring 2014, with two sections of lower-division econ and two more upper-division courses. Political science, a very popular subject, was offered in three honors sections, but psychology, also popular with students, in only one. Anthropology was offered in two sections, accounting, classics, and philosophy in one each. The fine arts, especially music and theater classes, were well represented.

Although not courses in the formal sense, the informal reading groups sponsored by the honors college each semester are an excellent addition. "The groups meet just one hour per week, with 10-15 students and one faculty member from the Honors College, to discuss about 50 pages of reading from specific books. The books cover a very wide range of topics, and most have been recommended by Honors students. To participate, the only commitment is that each student makes a good-faith effort to do the reading and come to the group meeting as often as possible, with the understanding there may be one or two weeks when students need to do other things." In Spring 2014, the reading groups had more than 50 wonderful books to choose from, and about 500 honors students participated. And…they get to keep the books.

We believe these reading groups are worthy of special commendation because, at their best, they instill a love of great books and broad inquiry in an atmosphere that sets aside grading in favor of free, open discussion. In the end, bright students have another creative avenue to follow, one that leads toward a future as ever-inquiring adults even as it enhances their social and critical thinking skills while in college. Here is what engineering major and honors alum Jordan Rogers had to say about his experience in a reading group:

"I remember anticipating the reading group featuring *Other Colors* and commenting to a friend that I did not expect to enjoy myself. This was because of nothing more than the fact that I had, 'no interest in Turkey, and no interest in literature'. As I engaged in the book as well as dialogue with a professor and with other students, especially the ones who had visited Turkey, I found myself thrilled and excited to learn more about Orhan Pamuk, Istanbul, the Ottoman Empire, and Turkey. And then I understood what might be the most important lesson I've ever received: I AM interested in both Turkey and literature.

"Since my epiphany, if it can so be called, I have required myself to read 50 pages of any book every day. At first, this seemed like a chore, for my days were full already with school and clubs. But I pushed myself, and every day it seems less and less like a chore. I'm feeling now the daily desire to read, the feeling that I WANT to read, something I have never felt before. You'll be amazed to hear that I wake up about 90 minutes earlier now just so I can start the day right --with a book. By the time you read this I will have finished three books in as many weeks --all fiction classics."

(This honors engineering student, practical, logical, and focused on his discipline, has also discovered and described the transformative potential of honors education at its best.)

The college prides itself on listening to students and responding with other programs of interest. The Dean says the college sponsors MOOC-based discussion and an organization called the **Oklahoma Teaching Alliance, which is "a student-initiated organization that creates structured study groups for students in specific majors and courses and that are entirely student moderated and student-run.** In the Organic Chemistry OTA study group, about 115 students came to a study session the night before the midterm exam, where the content was all student-generated and student-presented.

"For two years we had a student-run intellectual but highly alternative newsletter, 'The Don Quixote Honors College,' which the student editors converted into a website."

Average Class Size (5.0): The average honors class has **15 students,** partly the result of the enrollment caps on honors seminars and colloquia. The average class size for all 50 programs under review is 21.2 students.

Adjusted Graduation Rate (4.5): The AGR is not simply the six-year graduation rate of students in the CHP who graduated from the university **(91%),** whether or not the students completed the honors program ("honors completers"). The AGR also reflects the extent to which the honors graduation rate from the university is higher than that for the university as a whole. (The **university-wide rate is 66%,** yielding a high AGR of 4.5.) The average **honors** six-year **graduation rate for all 50 programs under review is 89%.**

Ratio of Staff to Honors Students (3.5): Our estimate is that there is 1 staff member for every **162.5** students. (Mean ratio for all 50 programs is 1 staff member for every 159.8 students.)

Honors Residence Halls (4.0): Many first-year honors students live in David L. Boren Hall, named after the former U.S. Senator and current OU president. Boren Hall is in Cate Center close by the Honors College offices and in a good campus location generally...but Boren Hall is not air-conditioned. About 154 honors students reside in the facility, which only houses honors students. Rooms are traditional doubles with hall baths. Students may choose to eat in the Cate dining hall or the Couch Cafeteria. Laundry is not located in Boren Hall but in an adjacent Cate facility.

National Merit Scholars are much appreciated at OU, and those who are in the honors college (most scholars are) can live on their own floor (the 10th) in Walker Hall. About 160 do so. Walker *is* air-conditioned and also features suite-style rooms with shared baths between suites. The floor is coed but gender-separated by wing. The closest dining option is Couch Cafeteria. There is on-site laundry.

Prestigious Awards (4.0): OU undergraduates do very well at winning the prestigious Goldwater Scholarships for outstanding work as a STEM student--so far, 44 Goldwater Scholars have come from OU, well above the mean for the 50 universities under review. Perhaps it is not altogether surprising that OU is among the leaders in the number of Boren Scholars, selected to work and study in foreign countries where the U.S. presence is under-represented. Only Arizona State among the programs under review has more Boren Scholars, although a few others equal the OU total of 8 in the last three years. **OU students have won an extremely impressive 28 Rhodes Scholarships, trailing only North Carolina, Virginia, Washington, and Wisconsin in this category among all public universities.** OU students have also won 11 Truman Scholarships and 6 Marshall Scholarships.

Continuation Requirements: 3.40 cumulative and honors GPA.

Academic Strengths: The best academic departments at OU are business (47 overall, but 18 in entrepreneurship and 23 in international business), earth sciences, education, history, engineering (38 in industrial/materials engineering and 47 in aerospace engineering), and healthcare management (46).

Undergraduate Research: The Dean reports that there are at least five undergrad research options:

"Undergraduate Research Opportunity Program (UROP)--Funds a student's proposed research design, based on a competitive selection process.

"Honors Research Assistant Program--Funds undergraduates as **paid research assistants to faculty** on the faculty's research project, selected on a competitive basis.

"First-Year Research Experience (FYRE)--In conjunction with the Chemistry Department and the College of Engineering, outstanding freshmen are selected by faculty to serve as research assistants in the lab during the second semester of their freshmen year, working on the professor's actual cutting-edge research projects.

"Undergraduate Research Day--An annual academic conference where students in UROP and other programs present their research in discipline-based panels with faculty moderators.

"The Honors College publishes annual volumes of *THURJ (the Honors Undergraduate Research Journal)* which publishes student papers selected on a highly competitive basis by student editors working under the supervision of two Honors faculty advisers."

Study Abroad: "We have an in-house Honors-at-Oxford summer program (one month in Norman, and one month at Oxford, with Oxford tutors, and accompanied by the Honors faculty from the Norman month," the Dean says. "The Honors College sponsored a summer program in Tanzania in 2013, and hopes to continue the program annually. Our university has its own campus in Arezzo, Italy. The university is pushing Study Abroad very aggressively, and we participate in many dozens of programs in Asia, Europe, Latin America, and Africa. There are Presidential Travel Scholarships for the Honors-at-

Oxford program, and **in the overall package for every National Merit Scholar, there is a stipend for study abroad.** Our reported percentage (above) is smaller than the actual number of Honors students who study abroad, since a considerable number of others go for programs during a three-week intersession term, or a one-month summer program."

Financial Aid: We said OU appreciated National Merit Scholars, and here is what the university says about them: "OU is #1 in the nation among all public universities in the number of National Merit Scholars enrolled. Join the over 700 National Merit Scholars currently enrolled at OU!"

The University of Alabama actually surpassed OU in 2012 in the number of school-sponsored National Merit Scholarships awarded that year, but OU came back in 2013 to take the lead among all public universities with 173 total merit scholars, 151 with school funding. Finalists have to choose OU by April 30 in order to qualify. **OU even offers a National Merit tuition waiver for an additional year, five in all, because "Many students will study abroad, double major or will use their scholarship toward graduate school at OU. The five-year tuition waiver will allow you to take advantage of such opportunities."**

Non-Resident National Merit Scholars can receive scholarships valued at $116,200 (2014 level) over five years, which include the following:

Tuition--$81,000; $22,000 to offset books, room, and board; cash stipend of $5,000; housing scholarship, $4,200; technology allowance, $2,000; travel stipend, $2,000.

Degree of Difference (Honors students/non-honors students): 3.51 on a scale of 5. Some parents and prospective students might prefer an honors program that in many ways stands apart on campus, while others might prefer a program that is more expansive. The rating here tries to provide an indication of where a given honors program is on the stand apart/expansive spectrum. The rating is based on the difference between (1) the average SAT scores for enrolled honors students and (2) the average test scores for all students in the university as a whole *and* for students with scores at the 75% level or above. A score of 3.5 or higher indicates a high degree of difference. A score of 3.2 to 3.49 indicates a relatively high degree of difference. Finally, a score below 3.2 indicates a modest difference. **Please keep in mind that neither the high nor low selectivity of an honors program determines how effective the program is; this rating is merely "cultural" and *not* qualitative.**

Testimonial:

Mubeen Shakir, B.S Biochemistry, *summa cum laude, 2013,* **Rhodes Scholar—"Having come to the University of Oxford** and interacted with students and professors from the best institutions in the world, **I firmly believe that both the Honors faculty and students at OU are still among the best I have had the privilege of interacting with.** Now graduated, I know that the Honors College was the one part of my undergraduate education that I could not live without. **Through weekly reading groups and different lecture events, my friends and I had reason to treat the Honors College as more than a place where we just had class.** I am indebted to the Honors College and its faculty for providing a space in which I could learn and grow both inside the classroom and out."

NAME: THE HONORS COLLEGE, OKLAHOMA STATE UNIVERSITY

Date Established: First degrees awarded in 1969

Location: Stillwater, Oklahoma

University Full-time Undergraduate Enrollment: 17,749

Honors Enrollment: approximately 1,299 (mean enrollment of 50 programs is 1,714).

Review/Admissions Category I: Programs with **average SAT scores of 1235--1342 for enrolled students**. Actual average (mean) SAT score for enrolled students at Oklahoma State Honors College is not available because very few students take it. The ACT average is 29.8, which converts to an SAT of approximately 1320. The mean High School GPA for entering honors students is not available.

The minimum requirements for admission are SAT, 1220 and ACT, 27; high school GPA, 3.75.

Honors Programs in Admissions Category I (average SAT scores of 1235-1342): Arizona, Arizona State, Arkansas, Colorado State, Iowa, Maine, Mississippi, Oklahoma State, Oregon, Oregon State, Rhode Island, Texas Tech, University at Albany, and Washington State.

Administrative Staff: The Honors College has full-time staff of 5.

FOR ALL "MORTARBOARD" RATINGS BELOW, A SCORE OF 5 IS THE MAXIMUM AND REPRESENTS A COMPARISON OF ALL 50 HONORS COLLEGES AND PROGRAMS:

PERCEPTION* OF UNIVERSITY AS A WHOLE, <u>NOT</u> OF HONORS: 🎓🎓 1/2

OVERALL HONORS RATING: 🎓🎓🎓🎓

Curriculum Requirements: 🎓🎓🎓🎓 1/2

Class Range and Type: 🎓🎓🎓🎓 1/2

Class Size: 🎓 🎓🎓🎓

Adjusted Grad Rate: 🎓🎓🎓 1/2

Ratio of Staff to Students: 🎓🎓🎓

Priority Registration: Yes, honors students register for **all** courses, honors and otherwise, with the first group of students during **each** year they are in the program.

Honors Housing: 🎓🎓🎓🎓

Prestigious Awards: 🎓🎓🎓^{1/2}

*Perception is based on the university's ranking among public universities in the 2014 U.S. News Best Colleges report. Please bear in mind that the higher the U.S. News ranking, the more difficult it is for an honors college or program to have a rating that improves on the magazine ranking.

Curriculum Requirements (4.5): The College has four completion options:

The General Honors Award requires 21 hours of honors courses, no more than 9 of which can be by honors contract.

The Departmental/Honors College Award requires 12 credit hours, with no limit on the number of contract hours. Also required is a 3-hour thesis.

The Honors College Degree requires 39 total credit hours, including all the requirements for both the General Honors and Departmental/Honors College awards and six additional credit hours. The maximum number of contract hours is 21. Students must have a cumulative honors and university GPA of at least 3.50.

The Honors College Degree with International Study has the same requirements as the Honors College Degree, **including "a traditional study-abroad experience at a college or university outside the United States along with an appropriate academic major/minor or a specially approved plan of study."**

AP/IB credit: "For every three credit hours earned by AP exam with a score of 4 or 5, or IB exam with a score of 6 or 7, we waive one of the 39 credit hours required for the Honors College degree—up to a maximum of six honors credits hours waived."

Range and Type of Honors Courses (4.5): One of the best blended honors programs around, the College has an excellent range of seminars to go along with a solid list of departmental honors classes.

We counted at least 16 seminars offered in Spring 2014, and they all sound extremely interesting: Contemporary Cultures of the Western World; Biology, Race, and Gender; Magic Ring Allegories; Autobiographies of Women; Works of Jane Austen; Perceptions of Reality; Negotiation Essentials; Contemporary Geopolitics in the Heart of Asia; and our favorites, **Literature in Business** and **Constitutional Dimensions of Diversity.**

Students had better be well-prepared for the Constitutional Dimensions seminar: "As is the case in most law school courses, **the Socratic method of instruction will be employed as you learn how to read and brief judicial decisions and then apply principles of law to new fact situations**. You also will learn how to use some of the major legal reference sets in the Edmon Low Library as part of a law library project...."

Also of interest to aspiring attorneys is the seminar in **Negotiation Essentials**: "...although people negotiate all the time, most know very little about the strategy and psychology of effective negotiations. The purpose of this seminar is to understand the theory and processes of negotiation as it is practiced in a variety of settings. This course is designed to foster learning through doing, to explore your own talents, skills, and shortcomings as a negotiator. The negotiation exercises will provide you with an opportunity to attempt strategies and tactics in a low-risk environment, to learn about yourself and how you respond in specific negotiation situations. You will be in a setting in which feedback is plentiful, personal reflection is encouraged, and careful analysis is required."

And we must not forget the **Windows on the World seminar, "designed for top students to evaluate their opportunities for success in a variety of prestigious scholarship competitions and participation in other activities. Students benefit through preparation for graduate school and employment applications and interviews**. Students will be responsible for a class discussion of important topics in the news, including a Q&A interview session with fellow students. At the end of the course, students will submit a short essay (personal statement or research/policy proposal) based on the format of a major scholarship competition. Guest speakers on special topics to be announced." Participants must have prior approval of the Honors Director.

The **departmental honors classes** cover all the important bases, but the English sections seem especially strong--four in composition and three and literature. History is also prominent with five honors sections. All four math sections are in honors calculus, and there is also an honors stats section. The four political science sections are an excellent response to the student demand for courses in that discipline. The sciences are generally well represented with three sections of biology, two of chemistry, and one section in physics. What we did not find in Spring 2014 was an honors section in psychology, although there was substantial honors thesis research activity in that discipline along with a substantial psychological component in the seminar on Negotiation Essentials.

Average Class Size (4.0): The Director reports that the average honors class has **21.5** students, almost exactly the mean for all 50 colleges and programs under review in this edition--21.2 students. Many OSU honors sections have only 15 students, or fewer.

Adjusted Graduation Rate (3.5): The AGR is not simply the six-year graduation rate of students in the honors college who graduated from the university **(83%),** whether or not the students completed the honors program ("honors completers"). It also reflects the extent to which the honors graduation rate from the university is higher than that for the university as a whole. (The **university-wide rate is 62%,** yielding the 3.5 AGR for the college.) The average six-year **honors graduation rate for all 50 programs** under review **is 89%.**

Ratio of Staff to Honors Students (3.0): Our estimate is that there is 1 staff member for every **259.8** students. (Median ratio for all 50 programs is 1 staff member for every 159.8 students.)

Honors Residence Halls (4.0): Stout Hall is home to 225-250 honors students. The residence hall is **alcohol-free,** coed, and features mostly traditional double rooms with hall baths. Renovated in 2002, the dorm is air conditioned, has on-site laundry, and a kitchen for student use. It has retained its original look after renovation and still has a piano parlor and living room, as well as lounge areas on each floor. The fourth floor is for upperclassmen and has some single rooms. A very nice amenity is the **sink in every dorm room in Stout.**

For quick snacks, there is a coffee shop in the basement. For more substantial dining, the **Adams Market** complex is nearby. There, half a dozen eateries are present: sandwiches, Italian fare, Southern-fried, Asian, desserts, and a convenience store.

Prestigious Awards (3.5): "The OSU Henry Bellmon Office of Scholar Development and Undergraduate Research handles prestigious scholarship applications and certain aspects of undergraduate research," the Honors Director tells us. "[The Director and honors college staff] have worked successfully in close collaboration for more than 20 years."

The university has an extremely high record of achievement in winning the undergraduate Udall Scholarships, awarded to students studying Native American issues or environmental sciences. In the postgraduate category, OSU has an excellent record of winning the prestigious Truman Scholarships, 16 to date.

Continuation Requirements: 3.40 GPA, higher for some levels of completion (see above).

Academic Strengths: The strongest departments at OSU are education, business, math, engineering, and physics.

Undergraduate Research: "Forty to fifty undergraduate competitive Went Research Project awards ($4,500 stipends) are offered through the Office of Scholar Development and Undergraduate Research. Honors College students regularly win more than half of these awards each year (although honors students make up only about 6% of the undergraduate student body).

"Similarly, entering honors freshman win a large percentage of the Freshman Research Scholars Award each year."

Study Abroad: OSU has **reciprocal exchange study-abroad arrangements** with 70 academic institutions in 32 countries. These exchanges are important because "the student remains enrolled at Oklahoma State while studying at a partner institution abroad." Students pay their regular OSU tuition, but do have to pay for housing and meals in the host country.

Another option allows the student to study abroad without being enrolled at OSU or paying OSU tuition, so whatever credit they earn while studying abroad is official transfer credit for OSU purposes.

Other short-term options include faculty-led trips abroad; these will require regular OSU tuition plus additional travel-related costs, and the credit will be OSU credit.

Among the many countries where OSU students may study are Austria, Belgium, the Czech Republic (three universities), Denmark, England (three), Estonia, Finland, France (five universities), Germany (four), Ireland, Italy, Greece, the Netherlands, Spain (four), Sweden, and Switzerland.

The university offers the Humphreys' Study Abroad Scholarship, which is based on financial need and requires at least eight weeks of foreign study.

Financial Aid: Oklahoma State University welcomes all Merit Finalists and Merit Scholars. OSU offers very attractive financial assistance opportunities for National Merit Scholars who name OSU as their first choice with the National Merit Scholarship Corporation, and apply for admission/scholarships at OSU. **Oklahoma Resident National Merit Finalists in the 2014 National Merit Program receive annual cash and tuition scholarships totaling approximately $12,900 per year.**

Nonresident National Merit Finalists in the 2014 National Merit Program receive annual cash and tuition scholarships totaling approximately $25,500 per year.

The university has many other merit scholarships, including these based on test scores and high school GPA. Many honors students should be eligible.

Among these awards are Academic Excellence Scholarships of $2,000 per year, with a matrix requirement of test score and high school GPA (the higher the test score, the lower the GPA has to be).

Example: 28-29 ACT or 1250-1320 SAT requires an unweighted high school GPA of 3.25; but with a 24 ACT or a 1090 SAT, a recipient would need a 3.80 unweighted high school GPA.

Non-residents can reap major benefits if they meet the matrix requirements. In this case, the dollar amount of the awards declines as the test scores and high school GPA's go down. **At the high end, an out-of-state applicant with a 30 ACT or 1330 SAT and an unweighted high school GPA of 3.0 may receive an award of up to $12,500 a year.**

On the low end, **an out-of-state applicant with a 24 ACT or a 1090 ACT must have an unweighted high school GPA of 3.0 and may receive up to $7,000 per year.**

Degree of Difference (Honors students/non-honors students): 2.86 on a scale of 5. Some parents and prospective students might prefer an honors program that in many ways stands apart on campus, while others might prefer a program that is more expansive. The rating here tries to provide an indication of where a given honors program is on the stand apart/expansive spectrum. The rating is based on the difference between (1) the average SAT scores for enrolled honors students and (2) the average test scores for all students in the university as a whole *and* for students with scores at the 75% level or above. A score of 3.5 or higher indicates a high degree of difference. A score of 3.2 to 3.49 indicates a relatively high degree of difference. Finally, a score below 3.2 indicates a modest difference. **Please keep in mind that neither the high nor low selectivity of an honors program determines how effective the program is; this rating is merely "cultural" and *not* qualitative.**

Testimonials:

Jamie Vickery, Political Science, 2012 "My honors courses provided an intimate and community-like setting that made it more comfortable for students to become actively involved. This helped me when I took upper-division courses and made me more confident about participating in class."

John Leos, Theatre, 2013 "By contracting my major classes, I was able to gain in-depth knowledge that has made my résumé more appealing in a competitive field."

Chelsie Clement, Animal Science, 2013"Working toward and completing my Honors College Degree helped me find my passion for research."

Michael Veronneau, Biochemistry and Molecular Biology, 2012"The thesis project has been very rewarding. It definitely reinforced the concepts I learned in class and helped me develop more skills in research."

Robert Spurrier, Honors College and Political Science--"Teaching and advising Honors College students has been the highlight of my academic career. Whether it is advising a new freshman, teaching an honors seminar, or supervising a senior honors thesis, I come away enthused about these students' potential, work ethic, and success here at OSU and then in their chosen paths in life following graduation."

Editor's Note: *Bob Spurrier is retiring from his post as the eminent and long-term Director of the Honors College. The honors community (and the editor) look forward, however, to his continued involvement in honors education on the national level.*

NAME: ROBERT D. CLARK HONORS COLLEGE, UNIVERSITY OF OREGON

Date Established: 1960

Location: Eugene, Oregon

University Full-time Undergraduate Enrollment: 18,847

Honors Enrollment: 794 (mean enrollment of 50 programs=1,714).

Review/Admissions Category I: Programs with **average SAT scores of 1235--1342 for enrolled students**. The actual average (mean) score for enrolled DHC students is SAT 1310, ACT 29.

The mean High School GPA for entering honors students is 3.89 (unweighted).

There are no minimum admission statistics because the College uses a holistic admissions process:

"Applications for admission to the Robert D. Clark Honors College are welcomed and encouraged without a minimum GPA or test score requirement. Incoming students typically possess a mean GPA of 3.80 or higher and score in the 90+ percentile of test takers.

"The holistic review incorporates the required application and materials consisting of a self-introduction, essay, and description of accomplishments, transcripts, test scores, and letters of recommendation from two teachers in differing disciplines.

"The Robert D. Clark Honors College seeks bright, thoughtful, and academically motivated students to bring diversity to our community of scholars. All interested students who would enjoy the rigor and challenge of interdisciplinary critical thinking, reading, and writing are encouraged to apply. We seek an incoming class of 240-250 every fall."

Honors Programs in Admissions Category I (average SAT scores of 1235-1342): Arizona, Arizona State, Arkansas, Colorado State, Iowa, Maine, Mississippi, Oklahoma State, Oregon, Oregon State, Rhode Island, Texas Tech, University at Albany, and Washington State.

Administrative Staff: The Honors College has a staff of 14.

FOR ALL "MORTARBOARD" RATINGS BELOW, A SCORE OF 5 IS THE MAXIMUM AND REPRESENTS A COMPARISON OF ALL 50 HONORS COLLEGES AND PROGRAMS:

PERCEPTION* OF UNIVERSITY AS A WHOLE, <u>NOT</u> OF HONORS: 🎓🎓🎓

OVERALL HONORS RATING: 🎓🎓🎓🎓 1/2

Curriculum Requirements: 🎓🎓🎓🎓

Class Range and Type: 🎓 🎓 🎓 ¹/²**

Class Size: 🎓 🎓 🎓 🎓 🎓

Adjusted Grad Rate: 🎓 🎓 🎓 🎓

Ratio of Staff to Students: 🎓 🎓 🎓 🎓 🎓

Priority Registration: Yes, although this is called **Early Registration** at OU. Honors students register for **all** courses, honors and otherwise, with the first group of students during **each** year they are in the program.

Honors Housing: 🎓 🎓 🎓 🎓 ¹/²

Prestigious Awards: 🎓 🎓 🎓 🎓

*Perception is based on the university's ranking among public universities in the 2014 U.S. News Best Colleges report. Please bear in mind that the higher the U.S. News ranking, the more difficult it is for an honors college or program to have a rating that improves on the magazine ranking.

Curriculum Requirements (4.0): The CHC completion requirements are flexible but also somewhat complicated because some courses may count in more than one area of the requirements, others can be taken in approved non-honors sections, and still others can be replaced by AP or IB subject tests.

"Depending on test scores, AP or IB credits count toward math, science, multicultural, and second language requirements, applicable major requirements, or university electives. Courses taken at local community colleges can also fulfill such requirements."

But the Gen Ed honors **"core" requirements in honors are sacrosanct**: Honors College Literature, Honors College History, and Honors College Research in Literature or History. Two 4-credit hours courses are required in each of these, for a total of 24 **quarter credits.** (For readers unfamiliar with quarter credits, graduation from a university on the quarter system typically requires about 180 quarter hours, versus graduation from a school on the semester system, where the typical requirement is about 120 hours. Accordingly, the 24 quarter credits required in the Honors College core series mentioned above would be equivalent to 16 semester hours.)

Another four courses are required in science and math, *but* two of these may be in approved non-honors sections **or** may be replaced by AP/IB tests.

Seven honors colloquia are required, each carrying 4 credits, *but* of these, two can meet both the honors colloquia requirement and the multicultural requirement of the university (not an honors requirement). There are honors colloquia in all three multicultural areas (Identities, International, and American), and CHC students who take these meet the university multicultural requirement and apply them toward honors completion as well. **But** remember that AP and IB credits can replace some university multicultural requirements.

There are three colloquia that are part of the CHC core, and, like the required courses listed under the Gen Ed honors core requirements above, **they must be taken**. They are the Honors College Arts & Letters, Honors College Social Science, and Honors College Science colloquia. Elective colloquia may also be taken to complete the seven colloquia, as needed.

CHC students must also take a 1-credit thesis orientation course and a 2-credit thesis prospectus course, *but* no credit is actually awarded for the required thesis itself. Look at it this way: some of the honors gifts bestowed by AP/IB credits are returned when it comes to producing a thesis as a graduation requirement.

Range and Type of Honors Courses (3.5): CHC is a **core honors program, and true to its original design, the **CHC continues to offer an honors education aimed more at broadening the perspectives of its students in the classic liberal arts fashion** than focusing on a more specialized approach. Most of the CHC completion requirements are fulfilled through core courses in the curriculum categories listed above. Therefore, there are very few honors-designated classes in the departments, although a lot of departmental classes are honors-approved (see below).

CHC students in the Spring 2014 quarter could choose from 13 CHC seminars to meet the requirements for Honors Literature, Honors History, and Research in Literature or History. Some excellent examples are **Endgame, Wasteland, and Apocalypse: Literature at the End of History**; Contemporary British Literature; 21st Century American Poetry; "Build My Gallows High": Written and Cinematic Noir; Currents in History: Research in the History of Humans and Water; and Comparative History: An Approach to Historical Research.

About **Endgame, Wasteland, and Apocalypse:** "Literature has always been obsessed with the end of the world, but this 'sense of ending' is also assumed to offer some imaginary and critical purchase on the world as it is….Our course will examine a range of end-times literary and cinematic texts from across the twentieth century--a period particularly full of apocalyptic thinking…. Along the way we will address some theoretical currents in philosophy, ecology and risk, as well as the histories of modernization and globalization."

To meet the core Arts and Letters, Social Science, and Science colloquia requirements, students had at least seven options in the Spring 2014 quarter, not counting overlapping multicultural courses. Examples: John Muir's Backpack; Digital Humanities; Scoundrels in Literature; Quantum Mechanics for Everyone; Origin of Life; Normal People Behaving Badly; Bread 101; and one of our favorites, **The Animal-Human Bond in Science, Art, and History.**

About **The Animal-Human Bond:** "Do animals make us human? How has this relationship changed over time and varied by social setting? Is separation from 'the animal world' a general trend in human evolution? What can spindle cell research tell us about the capacity for empathy in whales and humans? The human-animal bond is a complex relationship, often a mix of emotional attachment and dissociation surrounded by philosophical, religious, and practical considerations."

The following multicultural courses could satisfy both the university requirement in this area *and* the CHC colloquia requirement: Autobiography as Political Agency; Contemporary Jewish Writers; The Role of Natural Disasters in the Dispersal of Cultures; or Freedom Summer—Civil Rights 1964: Students Join the Movement in Mississippi.

The CHC does not itself offer honors math classes; rather, in cooperation with math and other departments, lists about 100 pre-approved rigorous course sections that CHC students can take to meet the math and science requirements. Of these departmental classes and labs, three in biology and four in chemistry do carry an "honors" designation. There are 13 honors-approved sections in anthropology, two in architecture, three in astronomy, 20 in biology, 16 in chemistry, 16 in geology, and about the same number if physics. Honors-approved math sections include Math 105 and higher. Math 105 covers logic, sets, probability and statistics, with applications to finance and biology. Remember, however, that CHC students can place out of the 8-credit math and science requirement.

Average Class Size (5.0): The CHC reports that the overall <u>CHC</u> honors class size is a very impressive 16.9 students, but honors-approved departmental sections can be much larger. (The overall class size for the 50 colleges and programs under review in this edition is 21.2 students.)

Adjusted Graduation Rate (4.0): The AGR is not simply the six-year graduation rate of students in the honors college who graduated from the university **(88%),** whether or not the students completed the honors program ("honors completers"). It also reflects the extent to which the honors graduation rate from the university is higher than that for the university as a whole. (The **university-wide rate is 68%,** yielding the 4.0 AGR for the college.) The average six-year **honors graduation rate for all 50 programs** under review **is 89%.**

Ratio of Staff to Honors Students (5.0): Our estimate is that there is 1 staff member for every **56.7** students. (Median ratio for all 50 programs is 1 staff member for every 159.8 students.)

Honors Residence Halls (4.5): "The Global Scholars Hall is home to students in the Robert D. Clark Honors College who can attend lectures, discussions, film screenings, and academic advising offered right where they live. Students in the five language immersive communities in Spanish, German, Mandarin Chinese, Japanese, and French share a section of rooms with other people studying the same language so that they can become more fluent through everyday communication. Whether chatting in German while eating lunch in the Fresh Market cafe or learning to make sushi in the demonstration kitchen, students in these programs will create and participate in a global academic experience."

Opened in Fall 2012, the air-conditioned GSH houses both first-year CHC honors students and upperclassmen, along with other students participating in the language-immersive communities. About 60% of the rooms are traditional doubles with hall baths; the rest are singles or suite-style, providing an unusual range of choices. Dining is on-site, along with laundry facilities and a communal kitchen.

Prestigious Awards (4.0): Perhaps because of the university's (and CHC's) emphasis on foreign language competence, UO students have done extremely well in earning high-value Boren Scholarships for extended study and work abroad as well as Gilman Scholarships that allow students of limited means to study abroad. UO students have also won a very impressive 19 Rhodes Scholarships and four Marshall Scholarships.

Continuation Requirements: Cumulative 3.0 GPA for continuation and graduation.

Academic Strengths: UO has an excellent faculty, with an overall ranking across 14 academic departments averaging better than 50th among all universities public or private. Leading departments include education (8), psychology (30), earth sciences (34), business (47), English and history (both 52), and chemistry (53).

Undergraduate Research: "The University of Oregon holds a campus-wide celebration of undergraduate research and creative and performance works at the Undergraduate Symposium each May. While Clark Honors College student body represents just under 4% of the UO's undergraduate population, each year Clark Honors College students represent 30% or more of the participants in the Undergraduate Symposium. Many of the posters and oral presentations result from the direct experience Clark Honors College students have in research laboratories and projects across the University of Oregon.

"Every student who graduates from Clark Honors College must research, write and orally defend an undergraduate thesis. This process often takes more than a year, and the experience of defining a unique research question, conducting research, writing and defending the thesis in front of a committee of faculty members gives Clark Honors College students excellent preparation for graduate school. Many theses have become published articles in refereed journals."

Study Abroad: "The Clark Honors College frequently awards international thesis research grants to students conducting research for their senior thesis while abroad. The University of Oregon's Office of International Affairs coordinates study abroad programs, offering over 190 programs in more than 90 countries. Faculty from the Clark Honors College regularly lead study abroad programs. Examples:

- Clark Honors College@ Oxford brings approximately 17 Clark Honors College students to live in the center of the city of Oxford, England. The quarter-long program, in parallel with Oxford's Trinity term, provides students with two honors college colloquia, taught by Oregon and Oxford faculty, and an Oxford tutorial in the student's major, taught by Oxford faculty at the oldest university in the English-speaking world.
- In March 2013, the University of Oregon and [the University of] Sciences Polytechnique entered into a strategic partnership that will enable students to study at the most prestigious university for social sciences in France. UO and Clark Honors College students who participate in the exchange program will experience a French university that is internationally oriented in terms of its academic program, student body, and faculty.
- **During the Summer of 2014 the Clark Honors College launched an inaugural research and field school project on Rapa Nui (Easter Island) led by the Clark Honors College Dean, renowned archaeologist and Pacific researcher, Terry Hunt.** Research will include students and focus on the island's prehistoric settlement, subsistence, monumentality, and environmental change.
- In fall 2014 the Clark Honors College will also offer courses taught in Siena, Italy, by one of our distinguished tenured faculty members for Honors College elective colloquium credit.
- Preparations for fall 2015 courses in Venice and Istanbul for Clark Honors College students are currently underway.
- National University of Singapore exchange program, designed for five to ten Clark Honors College students, and two to four UO students, to study at one of the best institutions in the Asia Pacific region.

Financial Aid: "Incoming Clark Honors College students for fall 2013 received in excess of $1.9 million in scholarship awards."

- Incoming CHC first-year students may receive: Stamps Scholarship (covers tuition, room, and board for four years as well as enrichment funds to pursue study abroad, unpaid internships, etc.; total four-year award up to $110,000
- Presidential Scholarship (value of $36,000 over four years of undergraduate study)
- Diversity Excellence Scholarship (annual award amount of $6,500 for undergraduates in 2013-2014)
- Summit Scholarship for Oregon top scholars (value of $20,000 over four years for residents, $32,000 for non-residents)
- Apex Scholarship for top scholars ($12,000 over four years for Oregon residents, $16,000 for non-residents)
- Staton Scholarship for incoming Oregon freshmen with extraordinary financial need (value of $23,000 over four years)
- National Merit Scholarship to academically talented high school seniors ($8,000 over four years)

"Oregon students who are Federal Pell Grant-eligible may attend the University of Oregon and Clark Honors College as part of the Pathway Oregon program. The program covers UO tuition and fees for up to four years."

Degree of Difference (Honors students/non-honors students): 3.48 on a scale of 5. Some parents and prospective students might prefer an honors program that in many ways stands apart on campus, while others might prefer a program that is more expansive. The rating here tries to provide an indication of where a given honors program is on the stand apart/expansive spectrum. The rating is based on the difference between (1) the average SAT scores for enrolled honors students and (2) the average test scores for all students in the university as a whole *and* for students with scores at the 75% level or above. A score of 3.5 or higher indicates a high degree of difference. A score of 3.2 to 3.49 indicates a relatively high degree of difference. Finally, a score below 3.2 indicates a modest difference. **Please keep in mind that neither the high nor low selectivity of an honors program determines how effective the program is; this rating is merely "cultural" and *not* qualitative.**

NAME: UNIVERSITY HONORS COLLEGE, OREGON STATE UNIVERSITY

Date Established: 1995

Location: Corvallis, Oregon

University Full-time Undergraduate Enrollment: 17,795

Honors Enrollment: approximately 916 (mean enrollment of 50 programs=1,714).

Review/Admissions Category I: Programs with **average SAT scores of 1235--1342 for enrolled students**. Actual average (mean) score for enrolled honors college students is SAT (3-part), 1980, and ACT 30.1. The mean High School GPA for entering honors students is 3.92 (unweighted).

The **minimum requirements** for admission are SAT 1820, ACT 27, 1240, and high school GPA 3.75.

Honors Programs in Admissions Category I (average SAT scores of 1235-1342): Arizona, Arizona State, Arkansas, Colorado State, Iowa, Maine, Mississippi, Oklahoma State, Oregon, Oregon State, Rhode Island, Texas Tech, University at Albany, and Washington State.

Administrative Staff: The Honors College has 9.5 full-time equivalent employees.

FOR ALL "MORTARBOARD" RATINGS BELOW, A SCORE OF 5 IS THE MAXIMUM AND REPRESENTS A COMPARISON OF ALL 50 HONORS COLLEGES AND PROGRAMS:

PERCEPTION* OF UNIVERSITY AS A WHOLE, **NOT** OF HONORS: 🎓🎓 1/2

OVERALL HONORS RATING: 🎓🎓🎓🎓 1/2

Curriculum Requirements: 🎓🎓🎓

Class Range and Type: 🎓🎓🎓🎓

Class Size: 🎓🎓🎓🎓🎓

Adjusted Grad Rate: 🎓🎓🎓🎓

Ratio of Staff to Students: 🎓🎓🎓🎓🎓

Priority Registration: Yes. All students at Oregon State register according to their class standing. "Honors students register for all courses in advance of the registration date established for all other students with the same class standing."

Honors Housing: 👕👕👕👕

Prestigious Awards: 👕👕👕^{1/2}

*Perception is based on the university's ranking among public universities in the 2014 U.S. News Best Colleges report. Please bear in mind that the higher the U.S. News ranking, the more difficult it is for an honors college or program to have a rating that improves on the magazine ranking.

Curriculum Requirements (3.0): The college, like several honors programs that are a part of a university with large numbers of engineering and science majors, has a lower than average credit requirement for honors completion. **OSU is on the quarter system**, and converted to semester hours, we estimate the honors completion total to be about 20 semester hours (30 quarter hours).

Of the 30 **quarter** hours that are required, 6 credits must be in honors baccalaureate core classes; 6 credits in honors colloquia; 12 credits in honors electives; and 6 credits for the **honors thesis or research project.**

There is a lesser requirement, called the Honors Associate track, which is for students transferring into OSU, mostly for the last two or three years of work. This track requires **15 quarter credits minimum, including 6 credits in honors colloquia, 6 credits in honors electives, and 3 credits for the honors thesis or research project.**

AP/IB credit does **not** replace required honors classes.

Range and Type of Honors Courses (4.0): The honors college is a **blended** honors program, in this case one that has extremely interesting honors seminars along with a decent range of departmental honors courses.

Here is a partial list of the engaging seminars offered by the college, although each is for only 2 quarter hours of credit: Historical Fictions and Fictional Histories; The Social Impact of Obsessive Sports; Robots and Romance: Science Fiction and the Erotic Imagination; Principles of Comparative Planetology; Science, Aesthetics, and the Invention of Altered States; Sing a Song of Science; God, Pain, and the Problem of Evil: An Introduction to C.S. Lewis. **Our favorite: Making Robust Decisions for Technology, Business, and Life.** The class sizes of all these seminars are kept very small.

As for the departmental classes, the range is satisfactory but not extensive, with two sections of history (4 quarter hours of credit); two of anthropology; two in biology; two in chemistry; three in English composition; and one each in French, geology, and music. There are two physics discussion (recitation) sections, which are small all-honors sections of typically much larger, usually mixed (honors and non-honors students) classes. Although we did not see any math sections, we do know that in the Fall quarter at least six honors math sections are offered, including classes in vector calculus, differential equations, and matrix/power series.

Average Class Size (5.0): The College reports that the overall honors class size is a very impressive 14.5 students, but as noted above a few sections may be quite a bit larger. (The overall class size for the 50 colleges and programs under review in this edition is 21.2 students.)

"Lower division honors versions of general courses are capped at 20-24 students," the Dean tells us, "and faculty take advantage of the format to teach in more interactive, engaged ways. Upper division honors courses and classes unique to the Honors College, such as our honors colloquia, are capped at 12-25 students. The curriculum also includes courses and colloquia on special topics, as proposed by faculty members. A call for honors coursework proposals goes out to all faculty on an annual basis, allowing for a rich, diverse, and dynamic set of honors course options each year."

Adjusted Graduation Rate (4.0): The AGR is not simply the six-year graduation rate of students in the honors college who graduated from the university **(86%),** whether or not the students completed the honors program ("honors completers"). It also reflects the extent to which the honors graduation rate from the university is higher than that for the university as a whole. (The **university-wide rate is 60%,** yielding the 4.0 AGR for the college.) The average **honors** six-year **graduation rate for all 50 programs under review is 89%.**

Ratio of Staff to Honors Students (5.0): Our estimate is that there is 1 staff member for every **96.4** students. (Median ratio for all 50 programs is 1 staff member for every 159.8 students.)

Honors Residence Halls (4.0): About 185 freshmen and upperclassmen live in West Hall, which has traditional double rooms, not air-conditioned, and hall baths. There is on-site laundry. The nearest dining hall is Marketplace West, in the same quad. A small number of honors upperclassmen may also live in Cauthorn and Halsell Halls, both with the same room configurations and amenities as West Hall. Cauthorn residents are also served by Marketplace West dining. The most convenient dining hall for Halsell residents is Southside Station, at Arnold.

"The University Honors College has several student lounge and study spaces in the college's teaching, advising, and administrative facilities open to all Honors College students," the Dean reports. "These include two computer labs with free printing, a lounge area, two private study rooms, and one group study and meeting room. In addition, there is a main lounge and floor lounges, with computers and a central printer, in West Hall for honors students and college activities. All residence halls, including Halsell and Cauthorn, have on-site hall lounge areas."

Prestigious Awards (3.5): The most consistent performance, especially in recent years, has been in earning Goldwater Scholarships for outstanding undergraduate students in the STEM fields. From 2008 through 2013, OSU students won 14 Goldwater Scholarships, including at least one each year. OSU students have also done well recently in winning Udall Scholarships. OSU students have also earned a sizable number of National Science Foundation Graduate Research Fellowships.

Continuation Requirements: 3.25 GPA

Academic Strengths: Leading departments are earth sciences, computer science, education, engineering, chemistry, and physics. The university is also known for its excellent forestry department.

Undergraduate Research: "Honors students must complete a thesis involving original research in a recognized scholarly field. This research can be conducted in any area the student chooses and is not necessarily in the student's major field(s) of study. Research is conducted under the mentorship of a tenure/tenure-track faculty member or senior instructor and is supported and assessed by this mentor and

203

two other committee members, one of whom must also be a tenure/tenure-track faculty member or senior instructor at Oregon State University."

Study Abroad: The University Honors College has funding resources available to support study abroad experiences. In the 2012-2013 academic year, **the college provided 42 students with $63,000 in funding support for study, research, and internships abroad.**

For the past two years, the college has offered an honors international service learning class that involves coursework during the year, focusing on international service issues, and culminates in an international service trip through Habitat for Humanity during the summer.

Financial Aid: The University Honors College awards between 50 and 60 tuition scholarships from college funds each year. Scholarship awards are typically in the amount of $1,000 for one year, although a small number of merit-based awards entail additional funds and/or years. The college also supports experiential learning with scholarship and grant awards. In 2012-2013, approximately forty $1,000 awards were made in support of research and conference travel expenses from college administered funds.

"In recent years, the Honors College has been granted additional tuition and experiential scholarship awards from central university funds, greatly expanding support for students. From these funds, an additional $140,000 in support of out-of-class experiences and $166,000 in tuition and merit awards was awarded to students in 2012-2013."

Degree of Difference (Honors students/non-honors students): 3.62 on a scale of 5. Some parents and prospective students might prefer an honors program that in many ways stands apart on campus, while others might prefer a program that is more expansive. The rating here tries to provide an indication of where a given honors program is on the stand apart/expansive spectrum. The rating is based on the difference between (1) the average SAT scores for enrolled honors students and (2) the average test scores for all students in the university as a whole *and* for students with scores at the 75% level or above. A score of 3.5 or higher indicates a high degree of difference. A score of 3.2 to 3.49 indicates a relatively high degree of difference. Finally, a score below 3.2 indicates a modest difference. **Please keep in mind that neither the high nor low selectivity of an honors program determines how effective the program is; this rating is merely "cultural" and *not* qualitative.**

Testimonials:

Dr. Jeremy Cutsforth-Gregory, Class of 2005 – HBA Spanish & International Studies/HBS Biochemistry & Biophysics--"One of my most memorable early college experiences was Honors Writing in the basement classroom of McNary Hall [a previous honors residence hall], the professor of which later led a group of UHC students on a three-week, history- and literature-laden trek through the British Isles and France. The UHC fosters learning well beyond the classroom in many ways. Later I spent a full year as an exchange student in Ecuador. I returned fluent in Spanish, and the policy of converting a generous percentage of foreign course credits to honors credits ensured that I remained on track for graduation.

"The capstone thesis project for me meant several months of exciting basic science research in the NIH-funded laboratory of Distinguished Professor of Zoology Dr. Frank Moore (an interdisciplinary relationship fostered by another honors faculty member, Dr. Kevin Ahern, who was my advisor in Biochemistry/Biophysics). **My undergraduate thesis was just the first step toward a career in academic medicine and certainly gave me a leg up when applying to the country's most competitive medical schools.**

"Now I am Chief Resident in Neurology at the Mayo Clinic in Rochester, Minnesota, and I credit the UHC for critical thinking and leadership skills that I use every day to treat patients and lead a cohort of extremely talented colleagues."

Dr. Erin Haynes, Class of 2004 – HBA Anthropology--"I began my undergraduate degree at a small elite liberal arts college on the East Coast. After two years, my financial aid dried up, and I decided to transfer to Oregon State University's Honors College in my home state. It turned out to be the best decision I have ever made. At the UHC, I had the same type of small, interesting courses taught by talented professors that I had come to appreciate at my liberal arts college. Moreover, though I was essentially attending a small college, I had all of the options and resources of a large research university at my disposal. I majored in anthropology, but I took honors courses in philosophy, business administration, botany, women's studies, and engineering; traveled to a Shakespeare festival; and studied the history of the Columbia Gorge. The UHC was truly the best of all worlds, and it cost fully 85 percent less than my private school had.

"After I graduated, I went on to earn my PhD in linguistics from the University of California, Berkeley. I attribute my ability to get into the graduate school of my choice to my experiences in the UHC."

Dr. Gary Ferngren, Professor – School of History, Philosophy, & Religion--"For many years I've taught an honors seminar every quarter. One that has enjoyed some popularity is "God, Evil, and the Problem of Pain: An Introduction to C. S. Lewis." The format is discussion-based and allows students from a variety of perspectives to engage with Lewis's ideas. **I encourage the open and free discussion of controversial ideas, provided that mutual respect is given to all points of view, and treat my students as intellectual equals.** The class is one of the most personally rewarding that I've offered, and its continuing attraction attests to Lewis's ability to raise questions of perennial interest to successive generations of students."

Dr. Brady Gibbons, Associate Professor – School of Mechanical, Industrial, & Manufacturing Engineering--"My most recent mentee's thesis resulted in a United States patent application submitted in collaboration with Hewlett-Packard, as well as two presentations at the annual Semiconductor Research Corporation's TECHCON national meeting. **I've also sent students off to graduate schools such as the University of Wisconsin and North Carolina State University based on the work they completed during their honors thesis."**

NAME: SCHREYER HONORS COLLEGE AT PENN STATE UNIVERSITY

Date Established: 1997 (University Scholars Program in existence at Penn State since 1980)

Location: University Park, Pennsylvania

University Full-time Undergraduate Enrollment: 37,917

Honors Enrollment: 1,900 (mean size of all 50 programs is 1,714)

Review/Admissions Category-- III: Programs with **average SAT scores of 1383--1416 for enrolled students**. "The Schreyer Honors College does not set minimum academic requirements for grades or standardized tests. Candidates will be assessed based on the academic and extracurricular documents submitted with the application, as well as responses to essay questions and letters of recommendation. An interview is also an optional component of the application process."

However, we *estimate* that the average test scores are SAT, 1410, and ACT, 32. The high school GPA will also be very competitive.

Honors Programs in Admissions Category III (average SAT scores of 1383--1416): Connecticut, Indiana, Kentucky, Miami University, Oklahoma, Penn State, Tennessee, Texas A&M, UC Irvine, and Washington.

Administrative Staff: The Honors College has a staff of 24.

FOR ALL "MORTARBOARD" RATINGS BELOW, A SCORE OF 5 IS THE MAXIMUM AND REPRESENTS A COMPARISON WITH ALL 50 HONORS COLLEGES AND PROGRAMS:

PERCEPTION* OF UNIVERSITY AS A WHOLE, NOT OF HONORS: 🎓🎓🎓🎓🎓

OVERALL HONORS RATING: 🎓🎓🎓🎓🎓

Curriculum Requirements: 🎓🎓🎓🎓🎓

Class Range and Type: 🎓🎓🎓🎓🎓

Class Size: 🎓🎓🎓🎓 1/2

Adjusted Grad Rate: 🎓🎓🎓🎓 1/2

Ratio of Staff to Students: 🎓🎓🎓🎓🎓

Priority Registration: Yes, honors students register for **all** courses, honors and otherwise, with the first group of students during **each** year they are in the program.

Honors Housing: 🎓🎓🎓🎓

Prestigious Awards: 🎓🎓🎓🎓[1/2]

*Perception is based on the university's ranking among public universities in the 2014 U.S. News Best Colleges report. Please bear in mind that the better the U.S. News ranking, the more difficult it is for an honors college or program to have a rating that equals or improves on the magazine ranking.

Curriculum Requirements (5.0): We estimate that honors completion requires about 35 credit hours of honors course credit, **including an honors thesis.** The college provided this detailed description of its requirements:

First-Year Academic Requirements

--Enroll in and pass ENGL 137H or CAS 137H during their first semester and ENGL 138T or CAS 138T in their second semester at Penn State. (Please see "Class Range and Type" below for course descriptions.)
--Students admitted to the SHC Fall 2009 or after must maintain a semester GPA of at least 3.40 and cumulative GPA of at least 3.40. (Students admitted to the SHC prior to Fall 2009 must maintain semester and cumulative GPAs of at least 3.33.)
--Submit, on time, an adviser-approved **Academic Plan**. The first-year academic plan is due one day prior to priority registration in the fall semester. The sophomore-year academic plan is due in the spring semester.
--Complete 21 honor credits in the first two years at Penn State. **"While we do not mandate credit distribution between freshman and sophomore years, it is preferable to complete 12 honor credits in the first year and 9 honor credits during the second year at Penn State."**

Sophomore Academic Requirements

--Students admitted to the SHC Fall 2009 or after must maintain a semester GPA of at least 3.40 and a cumulative GPA of at least 3.40. (Students admitted to the SHC prior to Fall 2009 must maintain semester and cumulative GPAs of at least 3.33.)
--The adviser-approved **Academic Plan** for all sophomores in their junior year is due in the spring semester of the sophomore year. *For sophomore Gateway entrants: Sophomore entrants to the SHC must file an Academic Plan by midnight the day before Priority Registration during the fall semester.*
--Complete a four-semester total of 18 honors credits (counting honors courses taken in the first year). Start planning for the **honors thesis**. The **thesis proposal** must be submitted one year prior to your intended semester of graduation.

Junior Academic Requirements

--Students admitted to the SHC Fall 2009 or after must maintain a semester GPA of at least 3.40 and a cumulative GPA of at least 3.40. (Students admitted to the SHC prior to Fall 2009 must maintain semester and cumulative GPAs of at least 3.33.)
--The adviser-approved **Academic Plan** for senior year is due in the spring of the junior year.

207

--Begin the completion of at least fourteen (14) **honors credits** required during the junior/senior block.
--Continue implementing the **honors thesis** plans. Submit a **thesis proposal** one year prior to intended semester of graduation.

Senior Academic Requirements

--Students admitted to the SHC Fall 2009 or after must maintain a semester GPA of at least 3.40 and a cumulative GPA of at least 3.40. (Students admitted to the SHC prior to Fall 2009 must maintain semester and cumulative GPAs of at least 3.33.)
--Have on file with the Honors College a current, adviser-approved **Academic Plan**. File a new one, for your fifth year, if graduation is extended beyond eight semesters.
--Have on file with the Honors College an up-to-date **thesis proposal** approved by the thesis supervisor and the appropriate honors adviser.
--Complete at least fourteen (14) **honors credits** during the junior/senior block.

--**Submit *completed honors thesis*, with original signatures of all readers by the deadline.**

AP/IB credits are **not** counted as replacements for honors courses.

Range and Type of Honors Courses (5.0): Although we classify Schreyer as a **department-based** honors program that offers mostly departmental subject classes, the Honors College itself also has a series of exceptional small classes in its "Rhetoric and Civil Life" series. (These are the English and Communications 137 and 138 classes listed above as parts of the freshman year requirement.) These classes number about 13 sections per semester and enroll 22 students per section. The Rhetoric and Civil Life courses are laudable for their combination of practical, analytical, and advocacy skills and their emphasis on ethics. It is reassuring to know that smart, engaged students are involved in courses of this type, valuable not only to themselves but to the "Civil Life" of which they are a part.

The courses require honors students "to use rhetorical skills and principles to develop strategies for persuasion and advocacy in the context of civic issues. The course continues the multimodal emphasis-- the focus on oral, written, visual, and digital communication...Students will develop a repertoire of communication skills through hands-on practice at composing and delivering speeches and essays, and they will work with digital media to create multimedia texts, podcasts, and websites... **The course's civic and ethical components take center stage as students learn how to deliberate important public issues thoughtfully and with civility and respect. They will learn the difference between persuasion and advocacy and develop strategies for both in the context of pertinent local, national, and global issues**...The forum will be organized to allow small deliberative action groups as well as large forum-style meetings. The course focuses on ethics in many contexts--e.g., community action and public deliberation; ethics of persuasion; ethical controversies in the disciplines."

As for the **departmental honors sections,** they are present in abundance, including multiple sections in the engineering specialty fields, a rarity among honors programs. The same goes for geology and earth sciences, geography, and environmental sciences, all of which deserve more emphasis than they receive in the class listings of many programs. Math, physics, chemistry, biology, are all well represented, mostly in sections that are significantly smaller than average. Economics and psychology, two major fields whose popularity often leads to large class sizes even in honors sections, are available in reasonable class sizes as well. The humanities are well represented, including honors courses in classics. We did not find any sections in anthropology.

Average Class Size (4.5): The average honors class size at Schreyer Honors College is 16.9 students, an impressively low number for a **department-based honors program**. (In general, the smaller class sizes are more evident in core honors programs that feature a preponderance of freshman and sophomore seminars.) The overall average class size for the 50 colleges and programs under review in this edition is 21.2 students.

Adjusted Graduation Rate (4.5): The AGR is not simply the six-year graduation rate of students in the honors college who graduated from the university **(94%),** whether or not the students completed the honors program ("honors completers"). The AGR also reflects the extent to which the honors graduation rate from the university is higher than that for the university as a whole. The **university-wide rate is 86%,** yielding the 4.5 AGR for the college. **Note:** It is difficult to improve dramatically on a university-wide rate that is as high as that for Penn State, with its very loyal and happy student body. The average six-year **honors graduation rate for all 50 programs** under review **is 89%.**

Ratio of Staff to Honors Students (5.0): Our estimate is that there is 1 staff member for every **79.2** students. (Mean ratio for all 50 programs is 1 staff member for every 159.8 students.)

Honors Residence Halls (4.0): Schreyer Scholars also talk about the Honors College being a small community within the larger university. "We call it the living-learning community with Atherton and Simmons halls, part of the South Halls residence complex, being what anchors the Schreyer Honors College on campus."

The two halls are located on South Campus, right by College Avenue, a great location for social activities and the closest residence halls to downtown. On College Avenue, students can find bookstores, theaters, pharmacies, pizza and hamburger joints, restaurants, and pubs.

The halls are traditional, meaning that residents share rooms, mostly doubles, and also share corridor bathrooms. Atherton has a 24/7 computer room that has a printer and 29 computer terminals for student use. The Schreyer Honors College administration offices are also in Atherton. The mailroom for both halls is in Simmons. Some students consider Simmons to be the best dorm on the entire Penn State campus. Both halls also have a grand piano.

Simmons is also home to the international theme floor. Although neither Atherton nor Simmons has air conditioning, both are extremely popular with students. The nearest university dining hall is Redifer Commons.

Prestigious Awards (4.5): Penn State is a national leader in the number of its students who have won Goldwater Scholarships (63), awarded to outstanding undergraduates in the STEM disciplines. The university is also a national leader in Udall Scholars (20) for environmental research, and in the generous postgraduate Gates Cambridge Scholarships (8) for study at Cambridge University. Penn State graduates also do well in winning National Science Foundation Graduate Research Fellowships and Fulbright Student awards for teaching or study overseas.

Continuation Requirements: 3.4 GPA.

Academic Strengths: Among Penn State's many highly-ranked academic departments, the earth sciences department is renowned, ranking number 5 in the nation. The **average national ranking** for 15 academic departments at Penn State is an extremely impressive 25.9, much higher than many well-known private colleges and universities. Other prominent departments include sociology, chemistry, business, engineering, and physics--all ranked better than 25th in the nation among all universities public or private.

Undergraduate Research: "All Schreyer Scholars are required to complete an undergraduate honors thesis. This work represents the culmination of a student's honors experience. Through the thesis, the student demonstrates a command of relevant scholastic work and a personal contribution to that scholarship.

"The thesis project can take many forms - from laboratory experiments all the way to artistic creations. The thesis document captures the relevant background, methods and techniques, as well as describing the details of the completion of the individual project.

"In addition to writing the thesis, most Scholars conduct other kinds of undergraduate research during their years at Schreyer Honors College."

Study Abroad: "Penn State offers nearly 300 programs each year to many different countries spread across six continents. Schreyer Scholars take advantage of these programs to enhance their academic experience and are eligible to receive **Schreyer Ambassador Travel Grants to help meet their travel expenses. Over $200,000 in travel grant funds are awarded each year to scholars studying overseas.**

Schreyer Honors College Programs Include:

INDIA: (Launched in 2013) "In the spring, students take a three-credit honors interdisciplinary course that introduces them to contemporary India. This course follows the specific disciplinary interests of the instructors, but includes a wide range of topics and issues to prepare students for the in-country experience. While enrollment in the course does not require participation on the trip, it is highly encouraged and in the first year 13 of 15 students traveled to India for the five-week program hosted by the Shri Ram College of Commerce of the University of Delhi in Delhi, by Wipro Technologies (courtesy of SHC External Advisory Board member Steve Snyder) in Bangalore, and by The IIS University in Jaipur. The fall two-credit 'integration course' gives students an opportunity to revisit the topics of the spring course through the lens of their India experience, and prepares students to write a thesis proposal on an India-related topic."

SOUTH AMERICA: (2014) "We are applying the model of the (continuing) India program to South America, specifically to Brazil and Colombia. Brazil is, of course, the largest country in South America by a wide margin in both area and population, while Colombia is the largest Spanish-speaking country in South America by population. In some regards these two countries exemplify wider South American trends, while in others they provide a useful comparison and counterpoint. In spring 2014, we will offer a three-credit honors interdisciplinary course on contemporary South America, and we expect most or all of the enrolled students to participate in the five-week travel component in the summer (two weeks in Colombia, three weeks in Brazil)."

LONDON STUDY TOUR: "For thirty-one years the SHC has offered a short-term theatre and cultural studies program in London over spring or winter break. Our goal is to provide Scholars who otherwise would not have an opportunity for arts and humanities study abroad with an honors-quality experience that will make a lasting impact on them, and we know from our alums that the LST has done that.

"Students receive pre-departure orientations both in class and by attending theatrical events at Penn State, and upon their return they complete a research paper; during the 10-day trip they see 8 to 10 shows from a wide variety of genres, and they visit significant cultural and historical sites in London and the surrounding area."

RADBOUD 'THINK TANKS': "This collaboration with Radboud University in the Netherlands creates groups of students from both institutions for a year-long collaboration on a significant issue of public interest."

FREIBURG HONORS EXCHANGE: "Within the overall Penn State-University of Freiburg exchange framework, the SHC and University College Freiburg (UCF) will start an honors-to-honors exchange in 2014-15. UCF is a new liberal arts unit within UF, which shares important elements of the SHC's mission and teaching/enrichment philosophy. During the fall, second-year UCF students will spend a semester at Penn State taking courses appropriate to their overall plan of studies, while in the spring second-year Schreyer Scholars will study in UCF's interdisciplinary program."

Financial Aid: The Schreyer Honors College offers a $4,000 Academic Excellence Scholarship to all scholars entering the college their freshmen year. This award is renewable for each of the four years they are enrolled in the honors college.

Additional need and merit-based scholarships are available to Schreyer Scholars. Each academic year, the honors college awards over $1 million to scholars to support their academic studies, research and internship experiences.

"Full-time students who list Penn State as a first-choice school on the National Merit application by February are considered. Award amounts vary with the maximum amount of $2,000 per year with up to four years of eligibility."

Degree of Difference (Honors students/non-honors students): 3.45 on a scale of 5. Some parents and prospective students might prefer an honors program that in many ways stands apart on campus, while others might prefer a program that is more expansive. The rating here tries to provide an indication of where a given honors program is on the stand apart/expansive spectrum. The rating is based on the difference between (1) the average SAT scores for enrolled honors students and (2) the average test scores for all students in the university as a whole *and* for students with scores at the 75% level or above. A score of 3.5 or higher indicates a high degree of difference. A score of 3.2 to 3.49 indicates a relatively high degree of difference. Finally, a score below 3.2 indicates a modest difference. **Please keep in mind that neither the high nor low selectivity of an honors program determines how effective the program is; this rating is merely "cultural" and *not* qualitative.**

NAME: PURDUE HONORS COLLEGE, PURDUE UNIVERSITY

Date Established: 2013 – Honors College, 2005 – University Honors Program (transitioned to Honors College)

Location: West Lafayette, Indiana

University Full-time Undergraduate Enrollment: 28,738

Honors Enrollment: 1,057 total in 2013-2014, of which 727 are in the Honors College and 330 are finishing the Honors Program. In Fall 2014, the total enrollment will rise to 1,555. (The mean size of all 50 programs is 1,714.)

The Dean reports that **"our goal is to reach 2,000 students and maintain at that level (which is about 7-8% of undergraduate enrollment here). We take in a freshman class of 500 students each fall semester.** We still serve our University Honors Program students (330) until they graduate and no more admissions are accepted into this program."

Review/Admissions Category II: Programs with **average SAT scores of 1343--1382 for enrolled students**. Actual average (mean) SAT score for enrolled honors students at Purdue is 2034 (3-part), and the average ACT is 31. The average high school GPA is 3.83.

Minimum Admission Requirements: The College uses a holistic admissions process, and there are no set minimum requirements.

Honors Programs in Admissions Category II (average SAT scores of 1343-1382): Alabama, Delaware, Florida State, LSU, Massachusetts, Missouri, North Carolina State, Ohio University, Temple, Purdue, UCLA, Utah, Vermont, and Wisconsin.

Administrative Staff: The Honors College has a staff of 17.

FOR ALL "MORTARBOARD" RATINGS BELOW, A SCORE OF 5 IS THE MAXIMUM AND REPRESENTS A COMPARISON WITH ALL 50 HONORS COLLEGES AND PROGRAMS:

PERCEPTION* OF UNIVERSITY AS A WHOLE, NOT OF HONORS: 🎓🎓🎓🎓

OVERALL HONORS RATING: 🎓🎓🎓🎓$^{1/2}$

Curriculum Requirements: 🎓🎓🎓🎓$^{1/2}$

Class Range and Type: 🎓🎓🎓🎓

Class Size: 🎓🎓🎓🎓

Adjusted Grad Rate: 🎓🎓🎓🎓🎓

Ratio of Staff to Students: 🎓🎓🎓🎓🎓

Priority Registration: Yes, honors students register for **all** courses, honors and otherwise, with the first group of students during **each** year they are in the program.

Honors Housing: 🎓🎓🎓🎓

Prestigious Awards: 🎓🎓🎓🎓

*Perception is based on the university's ranking among public universities in the 2014 U.S. News Best Colleges report. Please bear in mind that the better the U.S. News ranking, the more difficult it is for an honors college or program to have a rating that equals or improves on the magazine ranking.

Curriculum Requirements (4.5): For honors completion, students must take 24 credit hours of honors coursework and "complete research or other scholarly activity that leads to **a culminating thesis or comparable scholarly project,** the requirements for which are set by the student's college or department. The thesis or scholarly project should demonstrate deep engagement with a student's chosen field and should be presented in a public forum (e.g. publication, presentation, display, or performance)." The research/thesis component provides at least another six hours of credit.

Of the required credit hours of coursework, at least nine hours must be taken after the first year. In that first year, all freshman entrants must take the HONR 19901-19902 series. In 2013-2014, the series focus was on Sustainability; in the Fall, students developed an understanding of the issues, and in the Spring they completed a practicum in which they worked on solutions under the supervision of undergraduate mentors and faculty. The series provides two hours of credit.

Students must also complete at least one 3-hour HONR seminar. In the Spring, they could choose from several, including Animals in Global Culture; Brain Disorders; and **one of our favorites, Economics in Literature, Drama, and Art.**

The remaining 19 hours of honors credit may come from additional HONR seminars; honors classes in the departments; honors contract courses; graduate courses; or undergraduate research.

AP/IB credits are **not** counted as replacements for honors courses.

Range and Type of Honors Courses (4.0): "Honors College students take small classes with top teachers," the Dean tells us. "Our professors include award winners, in the 'Book of Great Teachers' at our university. The focus of the Honors courses is to be interdisciplinary in nature, as well as coordinating with departments to offer discipline specific honors courses."

Indeed, one of the key purposes of the Honors College appears to be to provide academic breadth and balance to a talented group of Purdue undergraduates whose major fields tend to be not only demanding but highly technical and specialized. We applaud this effort as a wise approach in the context of an institution that is revered for producing some of the world's best researchers and engineers, whose contributions can only be enhanced by the wider vision that the honors curriculum provides. We have classified the Honors College as a **blended program** as a result of its integration of excellent interdisciplinary seminars with rigorous courses in the disciplines.

At least five engineering **departmental honors sections are available**, including one in electrical and computer engineering. There is a 2-hour lab in advanced organic chemistry, at least nine sections of math through multivariate analysis, and four sections of physics. As part of the goal to give honors students the full range of non-technical skills, the College offers no less than seven communications/speech sections. Another strength of the departmental offerings are three sections in psychology with a behavioral and cognitive neuroscience focus. What we did not find was a biology section.

The range of honors seminars certainly provides balance, as evidenced not only by the examples we listed in the Curriculum Requirements section above, but also by the following seminar titles: Science and Pseudoscience; **Making the Human;** Photography and Cultural Value; The Rise and Fall of the American Empire; Science Theater: Science and Technology; and Introduction to Visual Studies.

Average Class Size (4.0): There are a few large sections—animal science and chemistry, each with about 100 students. These break out into honors discussion sections of 16-18 students. The Sustainability practicums are limited to 18 students. The engineering sections average about 62 students each; communications/speech only 17-20, philosophy 12, physics about 22 per section. The overall **average class size is 22.3 students**, versus the average for all 50 programs under review--21.2 students.

Adjusted Graduation Rate (5.0): The AGR is not simply the six-year graduation rate of students in the **honors program** who graduated from the university **(94%),** whether or not the students completed the honors program ("honors completers"). The AGR also reflects the extent to which the honors graduation rate from the university is higher than that for the university as a whole. (The **university-wide rate is 70%.**) The average **honors** six-year **graduation rate for all 50 programs under review is 89%.**

Ratio of Staff to Honors Students (5.0): Our estimate is that there is 1 staff member for every **58.3** students. (Mean ratio for all 50 programs is 1 staff member for every 159.8 students.)

Honors Residence Halls (4.0): Honors students, whether freshmen or upperclassmen, can live in Shreve Hall, a large residence that houses 600 total students. The rooms are traditional corridor-style with hall baths; they are air-conditioned. There is a laundry on-site, and Earhart Dining Hall is very convenient at adjacent Earhart Hall.

Many dorm rooms at Purdue are smallish, but many students consider it a big plus to have air conditioning, especially in the early Fall when it can be hot in West Lafayette. Shreve is one of a few residence halls that do have A/C, and Shreve also has a relatively good location; many Purdue residence halls do not.

Prestigious Awards: (4.0) "Purdue's National and International Scholarship Office is housed in the Honors College, and works with students across campus to pursue campus nominated scholarships. The university participates in the Astronaut Scholars program, as well as twelve other scholarships, including Goldwater." Purdue is now tied for 15th among public universities in the number of prestigious Goldwater Scholarships (44) awarded to outstanding students in the STEM subjects. Purdue also ranks

214

4th in Churchill awards among all public universities, an award well worth the effort since it provides $50,000 for graduate study at Cambridge University, usually in a STEM field. Additionally, Purdue students have won Fulbright awards and now have a first ever two-time Udall winner. Purdue students have also won seven of the very prestigious Marshall Scholarships, which fund two years of study at any British university.

Continuation Requirements: 3.60 cumulative GPA, one of the highest.

Academic Strengths: Okay, it's Purdue so, yes, the best department is engineering, ranked 10th in the nation among all universities. Other especially strong departments include computer science (20), chemistry (21), **business (22),** math (27), education (32), earth sciences (39), and physics (40).

Undergraduate Research: "Each student must complete a thesis or creative project by working directly with a faculty member," the Dean says. "This is a requirement, and also dictates that each student will identify, design, and conduct a research project. The Honors College also provides a research support fund that students can apply to for support."

Of interest to us is the Discovery Park Undergraduate Research Internship (DURI) program, "designed to involve Purdue undergraduates in the interdisciplinary research environment of Discovery Park. The program provides opportunities for students to work with faculty affiliated with Discovery Park on cutting edge research projects that involve combining two or more disciplinary strengths. Working closely with faculty, students experience the excitement, challenge, and power of truly interdisciplinary research in the fast-paced, entrepreneurial environment that is Purdue's Discovery Park."

DURI has 50 part-time (6-10 hours/week) student internship slots per academic semester.

DURI Program Highlights

- Earn 1 credit for the internship core seminar series
- Potentially earn research credits through a project's sponsoring department
- **Receive a $500 scholarship per semester in DURI**
- Take part in year-end Undergraduate Research Forum and Poster Session

Study Abroad: The Dean says that the Honors College "has **two new Honors-only study abroad programs (one European and one South American).** Additionally, Purdue University has a new program, effective in 2014, for each student to apply and **receive up to $3,000 to support study abroad** goals. This level of support enables the majority of our students to participate in study abroad programs, if they choose to do so. Our advisors work with each student to identify applicable opportunities and incorporate into scholarly goals."

Purdue is also among the top 40 major universities nationwide in the total number of students studying abroad.

Financial Aid: The Dean reports that "80% [of honors students] receive some sort of **merit-based** aid from the central Division of Financial Aid (DFA) office."

Awards include the following:

The Beering Scholarship: up to full cost of attendance and provisions for undergraduate, graduate or medical school, restrictions apply.

Stamps scholarships: up to full cost of attendance and enrichment fund stipend of $5,000 to $10,000. Trustees and Presidential scholarships: amounts vary from $4,000 to $16,000.

"Further, Emerging Leaders scholars are invited to enroll in the Honors College. This is a scholarship for varying costs of attendance."

Degree of Difference (Honors students/non-honors students): 3.47 on a scale of 5. Some parents and prospective students might prefer an honors program that in many ways stands apart on campus, while others might prefer a program that is more expansive. The rating here tries to provide an indication of where a given honors program is on the stand apart/expansive spectrum. The rating is based on the difference between (1) the average SAT scores for enrolled honors students and (2) the average test scores for all students in the university as a whole *and* for students with scores at the 75% level or above. A score of 3.5 or higher indicates a high degree of difference. A score of 3.2 to 3.49 indicates a relatively high degree of difference. Finally, a score below 3.2 indicates a modest difference. **Please keep in mind that neither the high nor low selectivity of an honors program determines how effective the program is; this rating is merely "cultural" and *not* qualitative.**

Testimonials from Honors Students:

Michael Wadas, Mechanical Engineering--"The Honors College combines diversity and sameness in such an awesome way. We are diverse not only in race and heritage, but also in our academic interests, viewpoints and ambitions. But, **we have one important thing in common: We are all driven to use our skills and our passions to make an impact.**"

Eli Hugghis, Plant Sciences--"Being a part of a residential honors community is awesome. Not only do we have study buddies right next door, but we also do tons of fun things as a community, like floor vs. floor soccer matches, **community dinners with our Faculty Fellows and activities to work off the stress of exams.**"

Allison Turner, Political Science, Natural Resources and Environmental Sciences--"I think some of the best experiences have been getting outside of my academic bubble and interacting with people from various disciplines. Also, the Honors College connects me with some magnificent faculty who challenge me to pursue opportunities that I might not otherwise consider."

Alice Grasso, Interdisciplinary Science--"I have enjoyed everything about the Honors College. Being part of the Honors College has allowed me to take terrific classes with wonderful faculty, but **I've also had the opportunity to study abroad and interact with classmates from so many different disciplines.**"

Andrew O'Connor, First-year Engineering-- "The residential aspect of the Honors College is great because of all the interaction. **I can talk about our engineering homework with someone else on the same floor from a totally different discipline. It is an amazing way to get a much bigger picture.**"

216

NAME: UNIVERSITY HONORS PROGRAM, THE UNIVERSITY OF RHODE ISLAND

Date Established: No information available.

Location: Kingston, Rhode Island

University Full-time Undergraduate Enrollment: 11,945

Honors Enrollment: Approximately 580, but more may be taking honors classes (see note below). The mean size of all 50 programs is 1,714.

Review/Admissions Category I: Programs with **average SAT scores of 1235--1342** for enrolled students. The *estimated* average (mean) test scores for honors enrollees are SAT 1300, ACT 29. The *estimated* average high school GPA is 3.80.

Minimum admission requirements: A 3.8 or above high school GPA, **regardless of test scores**, *or* a minimum high school GPA of 3.5 and a combined Critical Reading and Math SAT score of at least 1200, or 27 ACT.

Note: Other students who "have graduated with a grade point average of 3.4 or higher from their high school and have a combined SAT score of at least 1100 in Critical Reading and Mathematics (or a minimum ACT composite score of 24) will be eligible to enroll in honors courses during their first semester. Eligible students may take as many or as few honors courses as they wish. They have the option to **explore the Honors Program** and take only those honors courses that strongly interest them. **Students who have completed six credits of honors courses or have completed at least three credits in honors and are in their second semester of honors courses work can join the Honors Program."**

Honors Programs in Admissions Category I (average SAT scores of 1235-1342): Arizona, Arizona State, Arkansas, Colorado State, Iowa, Maine, Mississippi, Oklahoma State, Oregon, Oregon State, Rhode Island, Texas Tech, University at Albany, and Washington State.

Administrative Staff: The Honors Program has a staff of 7.

FOR ALL "MORTARBOARD" RATINGS BELOW, A SCORE OF 5 IS THE MAXIMUM AND REPRESENTS A COMPARISON WITH ALL 50 HONORS COLLEGES AND PROGRAMS:

PERCEPTION* OF UNIVERSITY AS A WHOLE, NOT OF HONORS: 🎓🎓

OVERALL HONORS RATING: 🎓🎓🎓

Curriculum Requirements: 🎓🎓🎓

Class Range and Type: 🎓🎓🎓 1/2

Class Size: 🎓🎓🎓🎓🎓

Adjusted Grad Rate: 🎓🎓🎓🎓

Ratio of Staff to Students: 🎓 🎓🎓🎓🎓

Priority Registration: **Yes,** honors students register for **all** courses, honors and otherwise, with the first group of students during **each** year they are in the program.

Honors Housing: 🎓🎓🎓¹ᐟ²

Prestigious Awards: 🎓🎓🎓

*Perception is based on the university's ranking among public universities in the 2014 U.S. News Best Colleges report. Please bear in mind that the better the U.S. News ranking, the more difficult it is for an honors college or program to have a rating that equals or improves on the magazine ranking.

Curriculum Requirements (3.0): URI Honors has a low completion requirement of 18 credits. At least 15 credits must include one honors course from each of the following types: honors seminar; colloquium; tutorial; senior project; and a senior seminar **or** a second senior project. The other 3 credits may be from any of the above types of honors courses. **There is no thesis requirement.**

AP/IB credits are **not** counted as replacements for URI Honors Program courses.

Range and Type of Honors Courses (3.5): The URI Honors Program as a small **blended program** with a mixture of honors seminars (see above) along with a selection of departmental honors classes. **(At first glance, one fact seems surprising: among the departmental honors sections is a series of Chinese language courses. Please see below.)** Allowing qualified students who are not enrolled honors students to explore honors courses in the Fall semester means that there are more honors sections in Fall (about 55) than in Spring (35). Another notable difference in the semester offerings is that Fall listings include two sections each of math and physics and an additional section of economics.   In addition, there are about twice as many seminars in Fall than in Spring.

Looking at the honors courses according to the types listed above, examples of lower-division seminars offered in Fall 2014 include five sections of honors communications. Three of these sections "integrate theory and experience in various contexts such as public speaking, small groups, and interpersonal communication. Students examine human differences to develop more effective communication skills." The other two sections "examine fundamental skills and concepts of communication through the lens of rhetoric, and the ways language and symbols have shaped and continue to shape attitudes, values, and the understanding of poverty in the US."

 A unique and interesting class is a math seminar in **Computer Forensics,** in which honors students study "the science behind obtaining and analyzing computer evidence in crimes and civil cases: the basics of computer hardware, software, and networking; computer security; personal property; tracking offenders and legal issues."

Other lower-division seminars include American Indian/Indigenous Representation in Literature; **Race, Gender, and Sexual Identity;** Introduction to Islam; **The Psychology of Violence and Non Violence;** The Irish in Ireland, America, and Rhode Island; Introduction to Academic and Professional Writing; and **Jane Austen, Good Judgment, and You.**

The **Jane Austen seminar** looks at Jane Austen's novels and their recent screen adaptations as fascinating early-19th Century drawing rooms filled with clever, calculating, and ultimately prudent judgments, at least on the part of the heroines. "In Austen we have something for everyone: witty women resisting ridiculous marriages; social-climbing sons of the landed gentry; sociopathic charmers out for a fortune alongside good times."

Of the tutorials, students could take **Tibetan Buddhism: Journey to Nirvana** or **Mass Death in American Culture, 1978-Present,** or **Images of Masculinity in Film,** among others.

Mass Death "explores death events, responses, and their aftermath in American culture over recent decades through historical and psychosocial critical lenses. Topics include cult suicides, terrorist acts, gang-related shootings, and murder in workplace and school settings." Serious, even grim, but did you know that **URI has a minor in Thanatology?**

The **honors colloquia theme** in Fall 2014 is Cybersecurity, and students can take a 1-credit course describing the threats to national security and personal privacy posed by modern technology.

An interesting **senior seminar** is **Writers Writing Their Lives,** a workshop course in which students "read distinguished and prize-winning memoirs by prominent writers worldwide and will use these texts to develop advanced creative nonfiction craft to write their own essays." Yet another unique seminar is **Humor Communication,** which asks students to "examine humor in all of its dynamic contexts including humor in relationships, families, organizations, medicine, education, intercultural relations, and mediated communication."

As for the honors **departmental** sections, as noted above there are many more in the Fall than in the Spring. Two calculus/analytical geometry classes (in addition to the forensic math seminar) and two physics classes appear in Fall. We found no biology or chemistry honors courses in either semester. The **Chinese language sequence** is not for the faint-hearted, as all four sections of intensive language immersion and composition meet five days a week.

It turns out that the Chinese language emphasis is quite logical given the fact that the University of Rhode Island has an **International Engineering Program (IEP).** "IEP graduates earn two degrees simultaneously: **a B.S. in an engineering discipline and a B.A. in Chinese, French, German, Italian or Spanish.** By combining the power of a strong engineering program, immersion in a foreign language and culture, and a year abroad, the five-year program graduates students prepared for rewarding careers in a diverse array of fields around the world."

Another extremely interesting, interdisciplinary course of study at URI is **Environmental Natural Resource Economics.** The ENRE department offers courses in both the natural sciences and economics.

"Through our integrative curriculum you can prepare for careers protecting and responsibly utilizing our tropical rain forests, drinking water, clean air, biodiversity, sustainable fisheries, endangered species, and other natural assets." **Majors in the department include** Green Markets and Sustainability; Environmental Economics and Management; **and a double major in Business and Environmental Economics.** (Now it becomes clear why URI students do so well in winning Udall Scholarships.)

Average Class Size (5.0): The average honors class size is only 15 students; the overall average class size for the 50 colleges and programs under review in this edition is 21.2 students.

Adjusted Graduation Rate (4.0): The AGR is not simply the six-year graduation rate of students in the honors college who graduated from the university *(estimated at 85.8%),* whether or not the students completed the honors program ("honors completers"). The AGR also reflects the extent to which the honors graduation rate from the university is higher than that for the university as a whole. The **university-wide rate is 63%,** yielding the 4.0 AGR for the college. The average **honors** six-year **graduation rate for all 50 programs under review is 89%.**

Ratio of Staff to Honors Students (5.0): Our estimate is that there is 1 staff member for every **96.7** students. (Mean ratio for all 50 programs is 1 staff member for every 159.8 students.)

Honors Residence Halls (3.5): URI honors students who have **at least sophomore standing** may choose to live in the honors living/learning community at **Garrahy Hall,** an apartment-style residence hall. "The Honors floor is co-ed and includes eight 5-bedroom apartments, one 4-bedroom apartment, and one 10-bedroom suite. All units include living rooms and bathrooms, and all the apartments also include a kitchen. (The 10-bedroom suite does not have a kitchen and therefore requires its residents to have a Resident Meal Plan.)

Garrahy Hall is air-conditioned and has on-site laundry facilities. The nearest dining is at Butterfield Hall. The rating in this category would be higher if there were honors housing for first-year students.

Prestigious Awards (3.0): URI undergraduates have done extraordinarily well in winning Udall Scholarships (8), awarded to outstanding undergraduates for study and research in Native American and environmental disciplines. Undergraduates have also earned three Boren Scholarships in the last three years, enabling outstanding students to work and study in foreign countries where the U.S. presence is under-represented. URI graduates have so far won 13 Truman Scholarships, **and "URI is the only public university in New England to be designated as a Truman Scholarship Honor Institution."**

Continuation Requirements: 3.30 cumulative GPA

Academic Strengths: In addition to the International Engineering Program, the **department of Environmental Natural Resource Economics,** also mentioned above, is ranked nationally with other similar departments at Cornell, UC Berkeley, and Wisconsin. As both a land grant and a sea grant university, URI also has strong departments in marine biology and oceanography.

Undergraduate Research: The Undergraduate Research Initiative at URI provides students with grant support for undergraduate research and for creative or artistic projects.

"Proposals for these grants will be evaluated by the Undergraduate Research Initiative Committee, which is composed of faculty and students from various disciplines. Students chosen for support will receive a grant of up to $1,000 to help support his or her project. All undergraduate students in good standing are eligible.

"The program provides funds to undergraduates to participate in original research or creative or artistic projects of their own design. These projects require supervision by a faculty sponsor."

Students may be eligible to receive up to $1,000 for project funding, and an additional $200 for each additional student involved (maximum of three.)

Study Abroad: URI offers faculty-led programs during Spring, Summer, and Winter breaks. Marine science students can study during Winter break in Bonaire, an island in the Caribbean in the same group as Aruba. During the same break, nursing students (a very popular major at URI) can receive credit for providing community service and public health education in the Dominican Republic. Students interested in political and social change can study in Cuba during Winter Break.

Students studying international engineering with a French language concentration can study in Compiegne, France, and spend part or the time in Paris. For international engineering students studying German, there are "visits to VW, Lufthansa Technology, Deutsche Bahn, and Bayer. Students will also attend city tours of Hamburg, Braunschweig, Berlin and Cologne. Students will visit research institutes at the Technische Universitat Braunschwig and URI's partner University in Germany. Additionally students will visit the Phaeno Science Museum, Chocolate Museum, and the Miniatur Wunderland and Maritime Museum. The Chocolate Museum!

The Office of International Education offers scholarships ranging from $100-$500 to students participating in URI Faculty-Led Programs.

Financial Aid: It appears that virtually all honors students should at least be *eligible* for some form of merit scholarship. "The University of Rhode Island offers a wide range of merit scholarships to students who have demonstrated academic success in a challenging college preparatory curriculum. You may be eligible for these awards if you have earned a GPA of 3.2/4.0, as well as SATs of 1050+ (critical reading and math) or ACT of 23+, and have demonstrated leadership and involvement in your school and/or community. All applicants are considered for these scholarships by submitting a complete application by February (December 1 recommended)." There is no information about the amount of the awards.

Degree of Difference (Honors students/non-honors students): 3.59 on a scale of 5. Some parents and prospective students might prefer an honors program that in many ways stands apart on campus, while others might prefer a program that is more expansive. The rating here tries to provide an indication of where a given honors program is on the stand apart/expansive spectrum. The rating is based on the difference between (1) the average SAT scores for enrolled honors students and (2) the average test scores for all students in the university as a whole *and* for students with scores at the 75% level or above. A score of 3.5 or higher indicates a high degree of difference. A score of 3.2 to 3.49 indicates a relatively high degree of difference. Finally, a score below 3.2 indicates a modest difference. **Please keep in mind that neither the high nor low selectivity of an honors program determines how effective the program is; this rating is merely "cultural" and *not* qualitative.**

NAME: RUTGERS UNIVERSITY SCHOOL OF ARTS AND SCIENCES (SAS) HONORS PROGRAM

Date Established: 2007. The School of Arts and Sciences Honors Program was established in 2007 through a merging of the four existing Honors Programs at the undergraduate colleges of Rutgers University's New Brunswick/Piscataway Campus: Douglass College, Livingston College, Rutgers College, and University College; those programs had been established between the 1970s-1990s. **In 2015, a new cross-school Honors College, Rutgers, New Brunswick will open.** Incoming Honors students will be housed in a state-of-the-art residential complex on College Avenue Campus.

Location: New Brunswick, New Jersey

University-wide, Full-time Undergraduate Enrollment: 30,038

Honors Enrollment: approximately 1,397 (mean enrollment of all 50 programs is 1,714).

Review/Admissions Category IV: Programs with **average SAT scores of 1417 or higher for enrolled students**. Mean SAT score (3-part) for enrolled Rutgers students 2190 **(verbal and math 1470), one of the highest among 50 programs under review; ACT average is 33**. Average high school GPA is 4.49, and average high school rank is the 96th percentile.

Honors Programs in Admissions Category IV (average SAT of 1417 and higher): Auburn, Clemson, Georgia, Illinois, Kansas, Michigan, Minnesota, North Carolina, Rutgers, South Carolina, UT Austin, Virginia.

Administrative Staff: SAS Honors has a staff of 14.

FOR ALL "MORTARBOARD" RATINGS BELOW, A SCORE OF 5 IS THE MAXIMUM AND REPRESENTS A COMPARISON OF ALL 50 HONORS COLLEGES AND PROGRAMS:

PERCEPTION* OF UNIVERSITY AS A WHOLE, <u>NOT</u> OF HONORS: 🎓🎓🎓🎓

OVERALL HONORS RATING: 🎓🎓🎓🎓

Curriculum Requirements: 🎓🎓🎓[1/2]

Class Range and Type: 🎓🎓🎓🎓[1/2]

Class Size: 🎓🎓🎓[1/2]

Adjusted Grad Rate: 🎓🎓🎓🎓🎓

Ratio of Staff to Students: 🎓🎓🎓🎓🎓

Priority Registration: No, although honors students have exclusive access to all honors courses.

Honors Housing: 🎓🎓🎓🎓

Prestigious Awards: 🎓🎓🎓🎓^1/2^

*Perception is based on the university's ranking among public universities in the 2014 U.S. News Best Colleges report. Please bear in mind that the higher the U.S. News ranking, the more difficult it is for an honors college or program to have a rating that improves on the magazine ranking.

Curriculum Requirements (3.5): "To be designated a 'School of Arts and Sciences Honors Scholar' at the time of graduation, an SAS Honors Program student must complete the following requirements:

"Honors Courses: A minimum of four 3- or 4-credit courses totaling 12 or more credits that are designated as honors courses, with a grade of C or better; these could include interdisciplinary honors seminars and departmental honors offerings. Please note: this requirement cannot be satisfied with honors research credits (courses taken for departmental honors/senior honors theses).

"Students must take a minimum of one [1-credit hour] Honors Colloquium, preferably in the student's first year as a member of the SAS Honors Program.

"Proficiency in a foreign language through the intermediate level, (3-16 credits, depending on option).

"Capstone--Work completed to satisfy the Capstone Requirement must total a minimum of 6 credits (3 credits per semester), and must involve a substantial, sustained, and original writing/research component; in all cases, an approved faculty advisor is required. **Students are encouraged to complete a research or special academic project prior to, and as preparation for, the Capstone. Students can complete their capstones by writing an Honor Thesis with their major department or writing an Interdisciplinary Honors Thesis.**

"The School of Arts and Sciences offers an optional 1-credit Introduction to the Thesis course for students in the junior year."

We estimate that a **minimum** of 25 credit hours would be required for honors completion.

Range and Type of Honors Courses (4.5): SAS Honors is a **blended honors program** with a high percentage--about 30%--of honors classes offered in a seminar format and the remainder in departmental honors.

SAS Honors has to be in the running for best seminar course titles in Spring 2014: Materializing the Sacred: Medieval Art Between Visible and Invisible; Jung for the 21st Century; Wonderful Life Genes and Evolution; The Aesthetics of Rap; Language, Categories, and Cognition; **Catastrophe, Collective Memory, and Everyday Life; Theories of Life: Creation Myths Through the Ages**; and Heaven and Hell in the Western Tradition.

Taking a close-up view of **Catastrophe, Collective Memory, and Everyday Life,** we read that the "scholarship on genocide, natural disasters, war, narratives of survivors and perpetrators, the politics of commemoration, and programs of reconciliation and forgiveness all suggest a growing interest in disaster and recovery as well as our collective memory of a traumatic past...**Our work in this seminar is guided by the literature on collective memory--i.e., how people remember the past, in the present, for the future.**"

Going right at the heavy stuff is the task of **Theories of Life.** "Every culture in the history of humankind has explored ideas concerning the 'big questions': How did we get here? How did the Universe start? What is the ultimate meaning of existence? In this course, we will take a historical approach to these queries, from the Babylonian and Judeo-Christian religious perspective, down to our current 'scientific' understanding of the Big Bang and the expanding Universe. What do all these ideas share in common? How do they differ? Why do they differ? Can any conclusive statements actually be made with respect to these issues?"

While the **department-based honors courses** are perhaps not as numerous as in some other programs, that is characteristic of many blended programs--and, anyway, the SAS departmental courses cover all of the essential territory: Two or more honors sections in biology, chemistry, physics, mathematics (4), psychology, anthropology, and American Studies in Spring 2014; one section in economics, genetics, geology, comparative literature, art history--even in French and Spanish, part of the usually forgotten group of language classes in most honors programs. Four honors Political Science and Law courses were offered in the fall term.

Some of the **honors seminars** touch on subjects in the humanities. In a university known for its outstanding English and history departments, perhaps three of the 18 honors seminars in the Spring semester are historically grounded, and one is definitely English: **Reading Shakespeare Across Texts and Cultures**. In the Fall there were two more in English, and one in History. We found no departmental honors courses in those disciplines.

It is notable that there are five sections of business-related courses: accounting, intro to business, intro to management, intro to marketing, and operations management, the last with a *very* quantitative emphasis.

Equally of note, Rutgers recently acquired the University of Medicine and Dentistry of New Jersey. The SAS Honors Program offers an extensive array of departmental courses in the sciences, and interdisciplinary seminars that deal with medical and ethical issues.

Average Class Size (3.5): The average size of SAS classes is **25.2** students, compared to the average size among all programs of 21.2 students. Honors seminars are capped at 15 students, however, and the great majority of honors sections will have fewer than 25 students. The average honors class size for all 50 programs is **21.2** students.

Adjusted Graduation Rate (5.0): The AGR is not simply the six-year graduation rate of students in the honors program who graduated from the university **(96%),** whether or not the students completed the honors program ("honors completers"). It also reflects the extent to which the honors graduation rate from the university is higher than that for the university as a whole. (The **university-wide rate is 79%,** yielding the 5.0 AGR for the program.) The average six-year **honors graduation rate for all 50 programs** under review **is 89%.**

The SAS Dean also reports that the honors **freshman retention rate is 96%.**

Ratio of Staff to Honors Students (5.0): Our estimate is that there is 1 staff member for every **99.8.** (Median ratio for all 50 programs is 1 staff member for every 159.8 students.)

Honors Residence Halls (4.0): "School of Arts and Sciences honors housing is available on Busch, College Avenue, Douglass, and Livingston Campuses," the Dean tells us. **"All students in the SAS Honors Program are eligible to live in honors housing, and the honors program highly recommends that all first year students live in honors housing.** Honors residence halls are vibrant communities where students live and learn together. Students living in honors housing have access to many special programs and events run by the honors program and Residence Life Office: drop-in academic advising, honors colloquium films, and guest speakers."

As the Dean states, Rutgers does indeed have five mini-campuses, including the Cook Campus, not mentioned above. According to *U.S. News,* "each campus has a unique setting and identity, from the hip student feel of the College Avenue campus to the farmland and science buildings at Cook Campus. **Each mini-campus has its own student center and dining options."** Below are the honors housing options, by campus, not counting Cook Campus:

Busch Campus: McCormick High Rise is the honors residence hall on this campus, and **it is for upperclassmen only.** McCormick has about 167 honors residents, all living in suite-style, air-conditioned rooms with connecting baths. Busch has on-site laundry and its own dining hall. Busch sits entirely within the township of Piscataway, NJ, and still retains the golf course that was part of a country club before the campus was built. **Busch is home to the STEM disciplines: math, statistics, biology, chemistry, engineering, geology, and physics, as well as pharmacy and psychology.**

College Avenue Campus: sBrett Hall is the honors residence hall on this campus, and houses about 167 freshmen and upperclassmen in mostly double rooms with hall baths (but 18% of the rooms are singles, for upperclassmen). Brett is not air conditioned, but it does have on-site laundry and convenient dining at Brower Commons. **This campus is in the heart of the original university and close to shops and restaurants in New Brunswick--and to convenient transportation to NYC.**

Douglass Campus: Jameson H is the honors dorm, with the same configuration, room mix, and amenities as Brett Hall. Dining is at Neilson Dining Hall. **Douglass Campus shares many of the open fields with adjacent Cook Campus; Douglass is also home to the Douglass Residential College for women.**

Livingston Campus: The honors residence is North Tower, top floor, where about 47 freshmen and upperclassmen live. Freshmen live in doubles, and upperclassmen in singles. North Tower is not air-conditioned but does have on-site laundry and dining. **Livingston Campus is the location of many social science departments and the business school.**

Prestigious Awards (4.5): University students have earned several Gilman Scholarships in the last three years, awarded to students of limited means for study abroad. Rutgers students have won 23 Goldwater Scholarships, and the university is very likely to improve on that performance given the strength of its STEM departments. It could be that the university has been focused primarily on postgraduate awards:

Rutgers is tied for **third among all public universities in the number of Gates Cambridge Scholarships (8),** often awarded for STEM research at Cambridge University. **Rutgers is also third among all public universities in the number of Fulbright Student Scholarships won in the last three years.**

Continuation Requirements: 3.25 first year; 3.50 each year thereafter.

Academic Strengths: Rutgers has mostly top-50 national departments in the major disciplines, including six in the top 30 among all U.S. universities public or private: English (17), history (20), math (20), physics (26), computer science (28), and sociology (28).

Undergraduate Research: From the Honors Dean: "SAS Honors Program students pursue undergraduate research in two ways. One is provided as an opportunity, the other is mandatory.

"1. Honors students of all class years are encouraged--by their Honors Program Deans, by their Faculty Mentors, by the faculty teaching Honors Seminars--to get involved in research. Honors students may apply for **research opportunities and funding** through the University's Aresty Undergraduate Research Center--not a component of the SAS Honors Program, but the two programs work very closely together...

"Of 53 Aresty-Summer Science Scholars in Summer 2013, 15 were members of the SAS Honors Program, or 28%. Of 256 Aresty undergraduate Research Assistants at the university in 2013-2014, 59 are members of the SAS Honors Program, or approximately 23%." **Honors students served as Research Assistants on faculty research projects in 30 academic departments.** Of 75 Aresty-Chemistry Scholars in 2012-2013, 19 were members of the SAS Honors Program.

"Each spring, the Aresty Research Center hosts a university-wide Undergraduate Research Symposium. Rutgers students not yet involved in research will find that attending the symposium is a great way to learn about the broad range of research opportunities for undergraduates. The presentations range from the life sciences, chemistry, and engineering to medical ethics, literature, and politics. At last year's symposium, a total of 459 students presented; of that group, 196 were members of the SAS Honors Program.

"2. Within the SAS Honors Program itself, completion of a senior honors thesis is one of the requirements for a student to graduate with Honors Scholar standing. The thesis must be original research, at least 6 credits over two semesters, undertaken by a student under the supervision of a faculty advisor.

"Each year, about half of the students complete all requirements, including the research, or on average 175 per year in an Honors class of approximately 350."

Study Abroad: According to the Dean, the SAS honors program **"provides scholarships to cover up to fifty percent of the student cost of participating" in study abroad.** The SAS Honors Program in conjunction with the Rutgers University Center for Global Education provides honors students with a range of global educational opportunities:

Yucatan: during Spring Break--Students explore ancient ruins and underground lakes, hiking a rainforest, and meeting with local villagers. They study history, archaeology, anthropology, and ecological science with local guides.

Spain, May/June 2014—Study is in southern Spain, where Christian, Muslims, and Jews shared culture and history; this trip is connected to an Honors Seminar offered in Spring 2014, "Muslims, Christians, and Jews: Conflict and Co-existence."

"The SAS Honors Program is a member of Principia Consortium, a group of 26 honors programs at liberal arts colleges and universities from across the United States that provide opportunities for Honors students to take honors courses in the humanities and sciences offered by and at University of Glasgow, Scotland.

"The SAS Honors Program also directly supports, financially and logistically, allied faculty-run international programs and Study Abroad experiences in:

- Indonesia: Borneo/Orangutan/Rain Forest field school
- Greece: Service Learning and community development
- Iceland: GREEN -- The Global Renewable Energy and Education Network, engaging students with international renewable energy sources and university coursework in wind, geothermal, and sustainable fuel sources."

Financial Aid: "Many SAS Honors Program students are offered University Merit Scholarships as incoming students," the Dean reports. Examples and requirements:

Presidential Scholarship--Up to $25,000 per year *and* a living stipend, renewable all four years if the student maintains at least a 3.25 GPA. Eligibility requires an SAT of 2250, or ACT of 35, and "an A grade point average."

James Dickson Carr Scholarship--Provides $10,000 a year; renewable with a 3.0 GPA.

Scarlet Scholarship--Provides $3,500 a year, renewable with 3.0 GPA. Eligibility requires an SAT of at least 1950 or an ACT of at least 30.

In 2012-2013, the university sponsored 16 of 23 National Merit Scholars, maintaining its support in spite of a national trend of declining university sponsorships.

Degree of Difference (Honors students/non-honors students): 3.80 on a scale of 5. Some parents and prospective students might prefer an honors program that in many ways stands apart on campus, while others might prefer a program that is more expansive. The rating here tries to provide an indication of where a given honors program is on the stand apart/expansive spectrum. The rating is based on the difference between (1) the average SAT scores for enrolled honors students and (2) the average test scores for all students in the university as a whole *and* for students with scores at the 75% level or above. A score of 3.5 or higher indicates a high degree of difference. A score of 3.2 to 3.49 indicates a relatively high degree of difference. Finally, a score below 3.2 indicates a modest difference. **Please keep in mind that neither the high nor low selectivity of an honors program determines how effective the program is; this rating is merely "cultural" and *not* qualitative.**

Testimonials:

Andrew Smith, Class of 2013--"Rutgers is not a small school and it is easy to get overwhelmed by all that it has to offer, both socially and academically. The SASHP served to build a community that approached the countless social and academic opportunities that you have in a school as big as ours in a way that made it feel more manageable, and a tremendous amount of the way this was accomplished was through the honors housing. I met some of my best friends in Brett hall, and the sense of togetherness we all had as members of the same program helped foster that sense of camaraderie."

Madiha Aziz, Class of 2012--"I cannot imagine my college experience without my honors Dean; she helped me grow professorially as well as personally…I remember hitting a wall while applying to med schools…but the Dean helped me work through my road block. She pulled out a piece of paper and wrote down my thoughts while we had a free-wheeling discussion. A few days later, I sent her a draft of my essay… It is thanks to her help that I will be attending GW School of Medicine this fall. Aside from that, she has become a close friend."

Chuck Keeton, Professor of Physics--"The universe is not what it used to be. That is what students learn in my Honors Seminar 'The Preposterous Universe.' We spend the semester reviewing recent discoveries that the universe is dominated not by the familiar matter that makes up stars, planets, and people, but by an exotic 'dark matter' that pulls on everything but is utterly invisible, and an even more bizarre 'dark energy' that acts as a cosmic anti-gravity."

Thomas Figueira, Professor of Classics--"Students at Ivy League schools receive significant intellectual advantage through opportunities to research, report, and write under close mentoring. How great a gift is directed revision and learning through reformulation/rewriting! My seminar emphasizes supervised research, presentations with visuals, circulated material, and commentary from seminar members. A final paper responds to collegial commentary, my critique, and, not least, to the other presentations."

NAME: SOUTH CAROLINA HONORS COLLEGE, UNIVERSITY OF SOUTH CAROLINA

Date Established: 1968 (program), 1978 (honors college)

Location: Columbia, South Carolina

University-wide, Full-time Undergraduate Enrollment: 24,180

Honors Enrollment: approximately 1,400 (mean enrollment of all 50 programs is 1,714).

Review/Admissions Category--IV: Programs with **average SAT scores of 1417 or higher for enrolled students**. Actual average (mean) score for enrolled honors college students at South Carolina is 1431; ACT average is 32.1. Mean adjusted high school GPA for entering honors students is 4.65, with a high school rank in the top 4 percent. The college does not list minimum admission requirements.

Honors Programs in Admissions Category IV (average SAT of 1417 and higher): Auburn, Clemson, Georgia, Illinois, Kansas, Michigan, Minnesota, North Carolina, Rutgers, South Carolina, UT Austin, Virginia.

Administrative Staff: The Honors College has 26 full-time employees, plus 13 student workers.

FOR ALL "MORTARBOARD" RATINGS BELOW, A SCORE OF 5 IS THE MAXIMUM AND REPRESENTS A COMPARISON OF ALL 50 HONORS COLLEGES AND PROGRAMS:

PERCEPTION* OF UNIVERSITY AS A WHOLE, <u>NOT</u> OF HONORS: 🎓🎓🎓

OVERALL HONORS RATING: 🎓🎓🎓🎓🎓

Curriculum Requirements: 🎓🎓🎓🎓🎓

Class Range and Type: 🎓🎓🎓🎓🎓

Class Size: 🎓🎓🎓🎓$^{1/2}$

Adjusted Grad Rate: 🎓🎓🎓🎓$^{1/2}$

Ratio of Staff to Students: 🎓🎓🎓🎓🎓

Priority Registration: Yes, honors students are advised and register for **all** courses, honors and otherwise, prior to non-honors students during **each** year they are in the program.

Honors Housing: 🎓🎓🎓🎓🎓

Prestigious Awards: 🎓🎓🎓🎓

*Perception is based on the university's ranking among public universities in the 2014 *U.S. News Best Colleges* **report. Please bear in mind that the higher the** *U.S. News* **ranking, the more difficult it is for an honors college or program to have a rating that improves on the magazine ranking.**

Curriculum Requirements (5.0): Honors college students must complete at least 37.5% of their college work in honors, an extremely high percentage. The College also has special tracks for pre-law, pre-med, pre-dental, pre-vet, and pharmacy majors.

"Graduation with a degree with Honors from the South Carolina Honors College **requires 45 honors credits** including courses across the liberal arts curriculum, **and a culminating senior thesis or project.**"

"The Honors College is open to all majors. In addition, the Honors College gives students the opportunity to design their own major through the Baccalaureus Artium et Scientiae degree." (This option adds flexibility to the extensive requirements.) "Students interested in law may want to pursue **the 6-year joint BA/BS/law degree.** Your personal advisor will help guide you through fulfilling Honors College curriculum requirements."

The college offered at least 242 honors sections in the Spring semester of 2014. Although there is a contract course option, almost no students use it to fulfill course requirements. Honors contract classes permit an honors student in a non-honors section to do extra work under a "contract" with the instructor in order to receive honors course credit.

AP credit may count as honors credits through a process of "honorization." In order to "honorize" advanced placement biology credits, for example, "a student must earn a 'B+' or better in an Honors College course in the same or related discipline. These Honors course credits 'honorize' the advanced placement credits."

Yet students seldom pursue this option. "Our students very rarely end up using any 'honorized' credits," the college Dean reports. "Our advisors guide students into honors classes rather than rely upon honorization (it's a prime directive), but the students also quickly realize that they want to take honors classes rather than non-honors."

Range and Type of Honors Courses (5.0): The honors college is a **blended program**, meaning that it offers interdisciplinary seminars along with a sizable number of discipline-specific classes centered in the academic departments. Of the more than 200 honors sections in the Spring of 2014, thirty were honors seminars. Representative seminar titles include: Descriptive Astronomy, Representations of the Holocaust, Introduction to Neuroscience, Knitting and Philosophy, The Nature of Religious Experience, Curmudgeons, and Religion in the Age of Science. **Our favorite: Authenticity: How to Live the Good Life and Be True to Yourself.**

Here is a partial course description for **Authenticity**--"'This above all: to thine own self be true, /And it must follow, as the night the day, /Thou canst not then be false to any man.' ---William Shakespeare, *Hamlet*

"From Shakespeare to today we are deeply concerned with being true to ourselves. But what can this mean? How is it that we are creatures that cannot be true to ourselves? Does this require us to be a mystery to ourselves, to discover ourselves? How does the desire to be true to us affect our art? Our politics? To be true to ourselves, at least in Polonius' speech quoted above, is an ethical precept, but how is it that we have an ethical obligation toward ourselves? And what does all of this have to do with living well?" This made us want to read on—and so we did:

"Authenticity and its connected concepts have played a significant role in the development of social and political thought since at least the early Enlightenment. **In this course we will examine the importance of authenticity and the related ideas of sincerity, self-expression, autonomy, and creativity in contemporary social thought.**"

The departmental offerings are among the most comprehensive in the nation, but like all programs that make a wide range of departmental courses available, some class sections will combine honors and non-honors students.

Departmental offerings include multiple sections of computer science and engineering classes. Humanities are strongly represented with 19 English sections, 10 in philosophy, and seven in history, not counting the historical emphasis in several seminars. There were five econ sections (high for this subject), and nine math sections, including classes in analysis, differential equations, and linear algebra. **Foreign language sections were also represented**, including Russian, Chinese, and Japanese. (Many programs do not include honors foreign language sections.) Popular disciplines such as political science and psychology have multiple sections, along with sections in sociology. Honors political science classes, in general, are not as available across all 50 programs under review as one might expect. Other well-represented disciplines include international business, the sciences, nursing and nutrition. The college also offers internship opportunities in the state capital of Columbia and in Washington, DC.

Average Class Size (4.5): As noted above, some departmental sections have a mix of honors and non-honors students, but unlike most programs that have mixed sections, those at the college are seldom large. One anthropology section had 154 students, out of which about 23 were honors students who also met in their own, smaller discussion sections. But otherwise, the mixed sections run small, especially in the excellent honors business classes. **The overall honors class size is 18.29 students, but in most honors seminars and honors-only classes the average is in the 13-15 student range.** (The overall class size for the 50 colleges and programs under review in this edition is 21.2 students. The college deserves a great deal of credit for combining high completion requirements with an extremely large section of courses, offered in generally small classes. It takes a lot of resources to accomplish all three at once.

Adjusted Graduation Rate (4.5): The AGR is not simply the six-year graduation rate of students in the honors college who graduated from the university **(91.7%),** whether or not the students completed the honors program ("honors completers"). It also reflects the extent to which the honors graduation rate from the university is higher than that for the university as a whole. The **university-wide rate is 72%,** yielding a high AGR for the college. The college also provided a four-year honors graduation rate, 84.2%. The average six-year **honors graduation rate for all 50 programs** under review **is 89%.**

Ratio of Staff to Honors Students (5.0): Our estimate is that there is 1 staff member for every **59.6** students, one of the best ratios around. (Median ratio for all 50 programs is 1 staff member for every 159.8 students.)

Honors Residence Halls (5.0): The two residence halls, one for both freshmen and upperclassmen and the other for upperclassmen only, are both coed, air-conditioned, and have on-site laundry. They are conveniently located for access to many classroom buildings, and one, the 537-person **Honors Residence Hall** (freshmen and upperclassmen) has suite-style rooms and the Honeycomb Café on site. **The Horseshoe** is on the main quad and oldest section of the university and includes five buildings for 237 honors upperclassmen. The rooms there are apartment style—kitchen, living room, bathroom, and individual bedrooms.

Prestigious Awards (4.0): The Office of Fellowships and Scholar Programs (OFSP), has a staff of six and is closely affiliated with and partially funded by the Honors College, although it serves students throughout the university. **South Carolina students have an impressive 22 straight years of winning Goldwater Scholarships for outstanding undergraduates in the STEM disciplines.** Honors college students have been notably successful in winning other undergraduate awards, including Udall, Gilman, and Boren scholarships. The university has eight Rhodes and two Marshall Scholars. In 2012, the university was named a Fulbright top-producing school with 13 Fulbright Student Scholars.

Continuation Requirements: B+ average (approximately 3.30)

Academic Strengths: The highest-ranked departments at USC are business, political science, sociology, English, chemistry, and earth sciences. **The international business program is especially strong, ranked 1st in the nation by *U.S. News* for 17 years in a row.**

Undergraduate Research: As many as 50% of honors students participate in undergraduate research funded by the College. The Science Undergraduate Research Fellowship Program (SURF) for STEM students, and the Exploration Scholars Program for arts, humanities, and journalism, provide about $250,000 in research funding annually. The Director of Undergraduate Research for the honors college coordinates these efforts. Senior Thesis Grants provide additional funding of about $40,000 annually. Funded students must complete the research ethics course required of NSF and NIH researchers. In addition, honors students are eligible for research and travel funds through the University's Magellan programs, which in 2013-14 amounted to over $170,000.

Study Abroad: "As part of our effort to encourage study abroad, the Honors College credits students who spend a summer studying abroad with 3 elective honors credits; students who spend a semester abroad receive 6 elective honors credits, and students who spend an academic year abroad receive 12 elective honors credits."

"A total of 256 honors students participated in study-abroad programs in 2012-2013, or almost 19% of all honors students enrolled. Honors students accounted for 20.4% of all USC students studying abroad during that period. The Honors College sponsors a variety of faculty-led spring and summer study abroad programs each year."

The majors most represented when it comes to studying abroad are business (including specialty fields, such as the school's renowned international business program); political science; biological sciences; public relations; exercise science; psychology; retailing; and Spanish. About 62% of students chose at least one country in Europe as the destination for study, with Latin America and the Caribbean next in popularity. Spain, Italy, Germany, France, and England were the most popular European destinations.

The university provides an average of $1,743 in financial assistance to eligible students for study abroad, and the most recent total annual expenditures for that purpose was $456,331. Most USC students travel abroad in the "Maymester" and Summer terms, but the Spring semester is also a favorite time, especially in the junior year when more than half of all annual study-abroad experiences occur. An even larger source of travel funds come from grants--more than $600,000 in each of the last two years. Grant sources include the U.S. Passport Travel Grant, the USC Beyond Boundaries Award and Magellan Grant, the USC Global Study Scholarship, the Deborah Edwards Endowment, and the Benjamin A. Gilman Award for outstanding students with limited means.

Financial Aid: *100% of entering honors freshmen receive a University of South Carolina merit scholarship.* McNair, Carolina, and Carolina-Stamps scholars, of which there are 45 a year, receive at least $10,000 to $15,000. Carolina-Stamps scholars receive an additional $8,000 to be used for educational enhancement. There are multiple other merit scholarships, which are worth between $1,500 and $10,000. All out-of-state honors students receive reduced tuition in addition to their scholarships. All in-state students are eligible for the South Carolina Lottery Scholarships, up to $10,000 a year.

The college has about a dozen different endowed scholarships for honors students, ranging from $1,000 to full tuition. Most of the scholarships are renewable for four years. The university has actually increased its sponsorships of National Merit Scholarships in spite of a national decline, using school resources to sponsor 44 of 54 scholarships, mostly in the form of partial tuition waivers.

Degree of Difference (Honors students/non-honors students): 3.78 on a scale of 5. Some parents and prospective students might prefer an honors program that in many ways stands apart on campus, while others might prefer a program that is more expansive. The rating here tries to provide an indication of where a given honors program is on the stand apart/expansive spectrum. The rating is based on the difference between (1) the average SAT scores for enrolled honors students and (2) the average test scores for all students in the university as a whole *and* for students with scores at the 75% level or above. A score of 3.5 or higher indicates a high degree of difference. A score of 3.2 to 3.49 indicates a relatively high degree of difference. Finally, a score below 3.2 indicates a modest difference. **Please keep in mind that neither the high nor low selectivity of an honors program determines how effective the program is; this rating is merely "cultural" and *not* qualitative.**

Testimonials:

From David Lee Miller, Carolina Distinguished Professor of English and Comparative Literature-- "The flexibility of the curriculum is wonderful. I can offer intensive, custom-designed seminars limited to fifteen bright and motivated students. Teaching doesn't get any better than that, and the students know how lucky they are. I teach a class that stages a mock trial of Othello for the murder of Desdemona, complete with social media coverage, actors playing the characters, and trial lawyers from Columbia advising the prosecution and defense. It's an amazing experience."

From Professor Scott Goode, Chemistry Department--"We offer five different Chemistry courses specifically for members of South Carolina Honors College: General Chemistry I and II (Fall/Spring) Quantitative Analysis (both semesters) Organic I and II (each offered Fall and Spring). These small classes further subdivide in recitation/discussion and laboratory sections of 12-15 students for discussions

233

of principles and applications of chemistry… All faculty in Chemistry are research-active; the NSF ranks the Department 14th in the country in R&D spending. About 25 students earn a Ph.D. each year. The faculty are all skilled in mentoring research at all levels and many Honors College students begin research in their sophomore year. We encourage students to consider three semesters of undergraduate research; one recent graduate had 12 papers in print or in press in synthetic organic chemistry when he graduated. This level of productivity has earned our students fellowships to graduate schools such as Cal Tech, Berkeley, MIT, Harvard, and Stanford and national honors such as Goldwater and NSF Fellowships."

From Joseph Studemeyer, SCHC Class of 2014--"Two months ago, I found myself deciding between attending graduate programs at the University of Oxford or Harvard. I found the decision-making process to be both bizarre and humbling, not to mention surreal, but I found encouragement in knowing that within the South Carolina Honors College, I was merely the latest in a string of students faced with such a 'dream decision.'…I am certain that I could not have gained admission to such prestigious graduate schools without the research I have conducted, research that has been supported and directed by the Honors College. My Honors College advisor, Susan Alexander, was a huge asset, encouraging me in my (admittedly eclectic) interests and constantly alerting me to funding opportunities for research."

NAME: TEMPLE UNIVERSITY HONORS PROGRAM

Date Established: 1987

Location: Philadelphia, Pennsylvania

University Full-time Undergraduate Enrollment: 24,710

Honors Enrollment: 1,575 (mean size of all 50 programs is 1,714)

Review/Admissions Category II: Programs with **average SAT scores of 1343--1382 for enrolled students**. Actual average (mean) SAT score for enrolled honors students is 1371, and the average ACT is 31. The average high school GPA is 3.85, top 9% of high school class. **Late update: the average SAT for the incoming class of 2014-2015 was 1388.**

Previous Minimum Admission Requirements: SAT 1300, ACT 29; high school GPA, 3.75; high school class rank, top 10%.

"New: **Effective for the class entering fall 2015,** Temple University is offering a new admissions path, the Temple Option, for talented students whose potential for academic success is not accurately captured by standardized test scores. This change enables applicants to decide how best to present their academic strengths and potential. If submitted, standardized test results will be considered holistically along with the high school transcript and other applications materials. Those applicants not submitting test scores will complete short-answer questions in substitution for standardized tests. All candidates will be considered for merit scholarships and our Honors Program."

Honors Programs in Admissions Category II (average SAT scores of 1343-1382): Alabama, Delaware, Florida State, LSU, Massachusetts, Missouri, North Carolina State, Ohio University, Temple, Purdue, UCLA, Utah, Vermont, and Wisconsin.

Administrative Staff: The Honors Program has a staff of 8.5 full-time equivalent employees, with an additional employee coming on board in Fall 2014.

FOR ALL "MORTARBOARD" RATINGS BELOW, A SCORE OF 5 IS THE MAXIMUM AND REPRESENTS A COMPARISON WITH ALL 50 HONORS COLLEGES AND PROGRAMS:

PERCEPTION* OF UNIVERSITY AS A WHOLE, NOT OF HONORS: 🎓🎓🎓

OVERALL HONORS RATING: 🎓🎓🎓🎓 1/2

Curriculum Requirements: 🎓🎓🎓🎓

Class Range and Type: 🎓🎓🎓🎓🎓

Class Size: 🎓🎓🎓🎓[1/2]

Adjusted Grad Rate: 🎓🎓🎓

Ratio of Staff to Students: 🎓🎓🎓[1/2]

Priority Registration: Yes, honors students "can register for any course (Honors, non-Honors) on the first day that registration opens for the upcoming semester. Honors students in good standing, along with veterans and athletes, can register ahead of the rest of the undergraduate population regardless of their credit totals."

Honors Housing: 🎓🎓🎓🎓🎓

Prestigious Awards: 🎓🎓🎓

*Perception is based on the university's ranking among public universities in the 2014 U.S. News Best Colleges report. Please bear in mind that the better the U.S. News ranking, the more difficult it is for an honors college or program to have a rating that equals or improves on the magazine ranking.

Curriculum Requirements (4.0): Here is what the Honors Director has to say: "Honors courses include Honors versions of General Education courses, upper level major-specific courses, upper level interdisciplinary electives, and independent study. Completing the Honors Program does not require taking additional courses toward graduation; rather, Honors courses dovetail with school/college requirements.

"Students have a minimum number of courses they are required to take in the Honors Program (either 10, 8, or 6 depending on when they started in Honors), but they can choose to take as many as they would like. [There are] Honors versions of Temple's General Education requirements; in addition, the honors program offers upper level courses across the curriculum. **When appropriate, students are allowed to contract two non-honors upper level courses for honors credit;** they may also petition to take graduate level courses for Honors credit. Many choose to take many more than the required minimum of required courses. Students are expected to maintain satisfactory academic progress while in the program: **three Honors courses by the end of their freshman year, six by the end of their sophomore year, eight by the end of their junior year, and 10 by the time of graduation.**

"There are also several departmental and college honors tracks, notably the College of Liberal Arts and the Fox School of Business; Honors works closely with honors students in their specific school or college."

AP and IB credits are **not** counted as replacements for honors courses.

Range and Type of Honors Courses (5.0): The Temple Honors Program is an outstanding example of what we call a **blended honors** program, offering a wonderfully balanced selection of interesting seminars along with a broad and deep range of honors courses in the academic disciplines.

Beginning with the 26 seminars that honors program students can take to meet their Gen Ed requirements in seven broad areas, we find, in fulfillment of the "Arts" requirement: Greek Theater and Society; Shall We Dance?; and Shakespeare in the Movies. To meet their "Human Behavior" Gen Ed requirement, honors students can choose from Workings of Mind, and Sexual Orientation, Gender Identity, and Law, among others. For "Quantitative Literacy," they can opt for **Mathematical Patterns**. On behalf of those of us forever in search of such patterns, we choose this as our favorite.

To meet the "Race and Diversity" requirement, students have the History and Significance of Race in America, a title as ambitious as it is essential to understand. Students may also choose Race and Judaism, and Race, Identity, and Experience in American Art.

The requirement for "Science and Technology" has some wonderful options: Cyberspace and Society, Bionic Human, and two sections of The Environment (environmental engineering and technology). The other two Gen Ed requirements are "U.S. Society" and "World Society." Here the course choices include Law and American Society or Dissent in America; Fate Hope, and Action: Globalization Today; and World Society in Literature and Film. Students are strongly encouraged to fulfill their Global requirement through education abroad.

As for **departmental honors courses,** they are plentiful and almost entirely escape the usual burden of having to be offered in larger sections. Even the biology sections, almost universally large in honors programs, average about 52 students each. There are at least six sections of honors calculus, including calc I, II, and III, and they average about 22 students. Seminars in English (e.g., Award Culture: Hollywood Stardom, Image Management, and the American Film Industry) only have about 15 students. It is reassuring to see at least three honors chemistry sections and even more so to see business classes that include a strong ethics component. As befits a university that has a strong psychology department, there are eight honors sections in that discipline, all of small class size. Small history seminars include Cold War Culture and Game of Thrones: How Did the Popes Win? And every year Temple Honors has all-honors or mixed sections in Spanish, lower and upper division.

Average Class Size (4.5): Given the number of honors courses in the departments, the Temple **average honors class size of 17 students** is remarkable. The average class size is 21.2 among all 50 programs under review.

Adjusted Graduation Rate (3.0): The AGR is not simply the six-year graduation rate of students in the honors program who graduated from the university **(81%),** whether or not the students completed the honors program ("honors completers"). The AGR also reflects the extent to which the honors graduation rate from the university is higher than that for the university as a whole. (The **university-wide rate is 66%,** yielding the 3.0 AGR for the program.) The average six-year **honors graduation rate for all 50 programs** under review **is 89%.**

Ratio of Staff to Honors Students (3.5): Our estimate is that there is 1 staff member for every **197.7** students. (Mean ratio for all 50 programs is 1 staff member for every 159.8 students.)

Honors Residence Halls (5.0): The "Honors Program Living-Learning Community is situated in the 2nd, 3rd, and 4th floors of the **1300 Residence Hall** on Temple University's Main Campus. Located one block from the Honors Program advising office, the Honors LLC is a residential community of students in the program. The support of Honors Program staff, Honors Peer Mentors, and the Honors Activities

Board helps foster relationships among upper and lowerclassmen through tailored programming and learning opportunities."

"1300 features Honors advising offices and a dedicated Honors classroom on the 3rd floor, where many Honors courses, including first-year seminars, are offered during the academic year. In addition, 1300 affords numerous recreation and dedicated study spaces."

The Honors spaces in 1300 are two-thirds suite-style and one-third apartment-style. They are air-conditioned and house 450 students. The Director tells us that 78% of Honors first-year students living on campus reside in 1300. Honors floors are coed with one gender per suite. The second and third floors are for first-year students, and the fourth floor is for upperclassmen. **All apartments on the fourth floor have kitchenettes.** Honors students may opt to **live in the Honors LLC for all four years at Temple.**

Prestigious Awards (3.0): Like many other public universities in the orbit of elite upper-Atlantic and New England private institutions, Temple has a difficult time when it comes to winning these awards. However, in the case of Udall Scholarships, awarded to undergraduates pursuing Native American or environmental studies, Temple is far above the median in achievement. The same holds true for the number of Temple students who have received Benjamin Gilman awards for undergraduate studies abroad. In the category of prestigious postgraduate awards, Temple students have won four of the extremely prestigious Marshall Scholarships, a strong record of performance, and six other Temple students made it to the finalist round for Marshall Scholarships. Temple has also had five Truman Scholars and five finalists for that award. Temple students are also on an upward trend in winning National Science Foundation Graduate Research Fellowships. The university created the Office of Scholarship Development and Fellowship Advising in 2013.

Continuation Requirements: 3.25 cumulative GPA

Academic Strengths: The top academic departments at Temple are psychology, education, business, English, history, sociology, political science, and math. **And new and exciting at Temple: The Institute of Genomics and Evolutionary Medicine (iGEM.**

Undergraduate Research: "We oversee our own thesis-level research track called the Honors Scholar Project, which is interdisciplinary. This is an alternative track for our students because there are ample programs for them to undertake undergraduate research within their college and/or department (e.g., students in the College of Science and Technology can undertake research through the Undergraduate Research Program; students in the psychology department can pursue the Psychology Honors Research track, etc.)…last year we had 13 Honors Scholars, which made up 4% of our graduating seniors.

"Temple now offers a summer research stipend available for every Honors student admitted as an incoming first-year student as of 2013. Going forward, students designated at the highest tier of scholarship (Presidential Scholars) are awarded two such summer stipends.

"Another relatively new research opportunity is available to Honors students in the College of Science and Technology: The Science Scholars Program. This program supports exceptional incoming College of Science and Technology students from the Honors Program with research opportunities, as well as academic and professional development. **Fox School of Business supports Alter Scholars, a research program for a very select number of Honors students in Fox."**

Financial Aid: As of Fall 2015:

PRESIDENT'S SCHOLARS
Pennsylvania and **Non-**Pennsylvania residents
- Full Tuition
- plus two $4,000 summer educational enhancement stipends*

Qualifications:
- High School GPA ≥ 3.80
- SAT Critical Reading + Math ≥ 1420
- ACT Composite Score ≥ 32

PROVOST'S SCHOLARS
- Pennsylvania residents - $10,000
- Non-Pennsylvania residents - $18,000
- plus one $4,000 summer educational enhancement stipend*

Qualifications
- High School GPA ≥ 3.60
- SAT Critical Reading+ Math ≥ 1360
- ACT Composite Score ≥ 31

"President's and Provost's Scholars are automatically admitted to the Honors Program. If, upon further review, any other recipients with lower levels of merit scholarships are admitted to the Honors Program, they will also receive a summer $4,000 educational enhancement stipend."

Summer Educational Enhancement Stipend (new as of 2013-14):

"Summer Educational Enhancement Stipends can be used to offset the costs of pursuing experiential learning opportunities, and **they may be used for approved study abroad, faculty-mentored research or unpaid internships. President's Scholars receive two stipends, and all other accepted Honors students receive one."**

Degree of Difference (Honors students/non-honors students): 4.21 on a scale of 5. Some parents and prospective students might prefer an honors program that in many ways stands apart on campus, while others might prefer a program that is more expansive. The rating here tries to provide an indication of where a given honors program is on the stand apart/expansive spectrum. The rating is based on the difference between (1) the average SAT scores for enrolled honors students and (2) the average test scores for all students in the university as a whole *and* for students with scores at the 75% level or above. A score of 3.5 or higher indicates a high degree of difference. A score of 3.2 to 3.49 indicates a relatively high degree of difference. Finally, a score below 3.2 indicates a modest difference. **Please keep in mind that neither the high nor low selectivity of an honors program determines how effective the program is; this rating is merely "cultural" and *not* qualitative.**

Testimonials:

Dr. Jeffrey Boles, Honors Professor--"Participating in Temple's Honors Program as a faculty member is a professional joy. Together with my peers, I have the ability to foster top talent by developing Honors students' critical thinking skills and by encouraging students to explore their intellectual passions. From this engagement, students leave our program motivated with an appreciation of the ways in which they can substantively contribute to society."

Tyler Horst '15--"Honors' sense of community has really helped to make my experience at Temple feel like more than just an education of textbooks and lecture halls. Living in the LLC in 1300, I was surrounded by people who shared my motivation and passion for ideas, even though we weren't necessarily interested in and motivated by the same things. Even though I live off-campus now (with five friends I met in the LLC), the Honors lounge is like a microcosm of that same community; if you have thirty minutes to decompress between classes, you can stop by the lounge and be drawn into a discussion about particle physics, contemporary philosophy, or what Kanye West did this week. The Honors Appalachian Experience has also become a staple of my summers, spending a week working with communities in Kentucky and Honors students who want to connect with people with a different perspective on life."

Monique Jenkins '15--"Honors courses are made to encourage discussion and the professors engage you in scholarly ways. My Honors classes are continuously my favorite classes. They are small so you get to know both the other students and the faculty. This allows for you to develop a relationship which could help in the future with letters of recommendation and networking. Also, the professors connect what we are learning in class to the real world and modern society so it is easy to see how lessons are extended outside the classroom."

Connor Page '14--"Entering my freshman year of college, I had a bunch of seemingly disparate interests that I had no idea how to reconcile with each other. I was a Psychology major with a concentration in clinical psychology who was interested in sports, writing, and foreign languages and cultures, specifically the Middle East and North Africa. Due to the availability of the staff, I was able to sit down with the Director of the program and engage in a lengthy discussion about what to do and how to synthesize my interests. Two years later, I am the president of Cherry Crusade (the student section and diehard Temple fans), one of the directors/editors of the Honors Program's official blog, HonorsLounge.com, which is maintained entirely by Honors students, the senior research assistant at Temple's Adult Anxiety Clinic, and an Arabic minor who spent the last summer living and studying in Rabat, Morocco, on a Critical Language Scholarship.* Connecting with Honors advisors helped me figure out how I could maximize my college experience to encompass all of my interests. Their availability allows not just me, but all of the students in the Honors Program, to flourish and succeed."

*Connor was in Oman in the Summer of 2014, studying Arabic on his second Critical Language Scholarship.

Jelli Vezzosi '17--"Being an Honors student is a dream when it comes to connecting with research facilities, internships, and other such opportunities. Our professors are some of the top minds in their fields. Because of our small class sizes, we can build lasting relationships with these professors, many of whom will be our references and sometimes even hire us directly. The advisors are also great with helping us network. If we have an interest, the honors advisors find a place where we can explore it. They know everyone, and encourage us to just send them an email. When I finally chose a few summer internships for which I wanted to apply, I went to an advisor and she showed me how to streamline my résumé and what to highlight in my cover letter. Temple Honors has someone for us every step of the way."

NAME: CHANCELLOR'S HONORS PROGRAM, UNIVERSITY OF TENNESSEE

Date Established: 1985

Location: Knoxville, Tennessee

University Full-time Undergraduate Enrollment: 19,588

Honors Enrollment: Approximately 1,585 (mean size of all 50 programs is 1,714)

Review/Admissions Category III: Programs with average SAT scores of 1383--1416 for enrolled students. Mean average ACT for **Chancellors Honors** enrollees is 32; the average high school GPA is 4.3. Submitted SAT scores are converted to an ACT score.

Haslam Scholars (15 per year) must have earned "a truly superior GPA in a rigorous high school curriculum and scored in the top 1 percent of the national distribution of standardized test scores (e.g., 33+ ACT composite, 1460+ SAT, or 2300+ new SAT)."

Minimum Admission Requirements for Chancellor's Honors: "We do not have technical minimums for consideration in Honors; rather, we accept the top 7% of incoming students."

Honors Programs in Admissions Category III (average SAT scores of 1383--1416): Connecticut, Indiana, Kentucky, Miami University, Oklahoma, Penn State, Tennessee, Texas A&M, UC Irvine, and Washington.

Administrative Staff: The Honors Program has a staff of 5.

FOR ALL "MORTARBOARD" RATINGS BELOW, A SCORE OF 5 IS THE MAXIMUM AND REPRESENTS A COMPARISON WITH ALL 50 HONORS COLLEGES AND PROGRAMS:

PERCEPTION* OF UNIVERSITY AS A WHOLE, <u>NOT</u> OF HONORS: 🎓🎓🎓¹ᐟ²

OVERALL HONORS RATING: 🎓🎓🎓🎓

Curriculum Requirements: 🎓🎓🎓

Class Range and Type: 🎓🎓🎓🎓

Class Size: 🎓🎓🎓🎓¹ᐟ²

Adjusted Grad Rate: 🎓🎓🎓🎓🎓

Ratio of Staff to Students: 🎓🎓🎓

Priority Registration: **Yes,** honors students register for **all** courses, honors and otherwise, with the first group of students during **each** year they are in the program.

Honors Housing: 🎓🎓🎓🎓$^{1/2}$

Prestigious Awards: 🎓🎓🎓$^{1/2}$

*Perception is based on the university's ranking among public universities in the 2014 U.S. News Best Colleges report. Please bear in mind that the better the U.S. News ranking, the more difficult it is for an honors college or program to have a rating that equals or improves on the magazine ranking.

Curriculum Requirements (3.0): The rating would be somewhat higher if the CHP did not allow 6 credit hours of the 25 required for completion to be replaced by math AP test scores. The program reports that a "5 on calculus AB receives one honors course credit, 5 on calculus BC receives two honors course credits."

According to the College Board, "Calculus AB includes techniques and applications of the derivative, the definite integral, and the Fundamental Theorem of Calculus. It is equivalent to at least one semester of calculus at most colleges and universities. Calculus BC includes all topics in AB and additional topics in differential and integral calculus (including parametric, polar, and vector functions) and series. It is equivalent to at least one year of calculus at most colleges and universities. Calculus BC is an extension of AB, and each course is challenging and demanding and requires a similar depth of understanding of common topics."

Below are the specific Chancellor's Honors requirements that total 25 credit hours:

All credits but a 1-credit honors topics or enrichment course must be earned in honors courses of at least 3-credits. These can be any combination of lower-level Gen Ed honors courses, departmental honors courses, foreign study courses, other approved off-campus courses, independent study courses, honors contract courses, or graduate courses.

The Haslam Scholars option: "The Haslam Scholars Program is to foster intellectual curiosity and engage the moral sensibilities of scholars through curricular and co-curricular experiences. Haslam Scholars will demonstrate a strong commitment to scholarly pursuits and use their abilities to influence public discourse on questions that shape society."

The university admits only 15 Haslam Scholars each year. Each must complete 21 credit hours in honors course work **including** co-curricular leadership seminars and executive internships. All Haslam Scholars complete a study-abroad experience together, **one that is funded by the university.** Scholars must also complete six hours of research and thesis and make a final presentation.

Range and Type of Honors Courses (4.0): The 1-credit honors **topic** courses are limited to first-year Chancellor's Honors students in the Fall semester, when 10-20 sections are offered subjects "within an academic discipline." The courses give honors students a chance to sample a discipline early on and in an interesting seminar-type setting.

The 1-credit honors **enrichment** seminars are offered to Chancellor's Honors students in the Spring semester. These focus "on a co-curricular area," which usually means a form of experiential learning. The CHP also offers higher level seminars each term. For Spring 2014, there were three with the special UNHO (University Honors) designation, including our favorite, **Avenues to the Self:**

"By reading and discussing fictional (novels, plays, poetry) and non-fictional (psychological, philosophical, sociological) works as well as examining visual art, we will try to come closer to understanding the concept of the Self. Exactly what is the Self: how does it differ, if at all, from one's identity or one's personality, or one's ego? What can the arts offer by way of explanation? To what extent is the concept of Self universal: can one survive without belief in one's Self?"

Other seminar-type classes are offered in the disciplines, including two or three in English, history, and up to 10 in philosophy, one of the strongest subject areas. This makes for an interesting range of Chancellor's courses, combining excellent instruction in the humanities along with generous offerings in departmental math, engineering, and science courses. The overall number of seminars (at least the 3-credit courses) is probably not enough to classify the CHP as a blended honors program, so let's just say that it leans strongly in the direction of being a **department-based program.**

It is in the range of departmental honors sections that the CHP stands out. The three honors chemistry sections appear to be all-honors with an average size of about 25 students; the biology section is, we believe, a mixed section with breakout discussion sections, but even the main lecture class is small by most standards, about 60 students. Now for math--we counted **nine** honors math sections, including statistical reasoning, calculus II and III, matrix algebra, abstract mathematics, advanced calculus II, abstract algebra II, topology, and an advanced math seminar. There are also two additional sections of honors intro to statistics. **If it is math that you love, you will have a hard time improving on the honors math courses offered by the Chancellors Honors Program.**

When it comes to engineering and physics, the CHP does an outstanding job of integrating the two, in the interest of giving engineering majors a more applied version of physics. We counted nine sections of Physics for Engineers II, averaging about 12 students per section. (There is also a section of honors physics for physics majors and another in honors mechanical engineering.)

Honors psychology is another strong area, with half a dozen sections and seminars. Another popular discipline, political science, has two honors sections.

In summary, the departmental classes are excellent, and many of them are seminars, although the CHP-sponsored seminars in the Spring term are fewer than in the Fall.

Average Class Size (4.5): Counting what appear to be a few large sections in anthropology (which have much smaller honors breakout discussion sections), **we estimate that the average CHP class has 16.0 students.** The average class size for all 50 programs under review is 21.2 students.

Adjusted Graduation Rate (5.0): The AGR is not simply the six-year graduation rate of students in the CHP who graduated from the university **(92%),** whether or not the students completed the honors program ("honors completers"). The AGR also reflects the extent to which the honors graduation rate from the university is higher than that for the university as a whole. (The **university-wide rate is 66%,**

yielding a very high AGR of 5.0.) The average **honors** six-year **graduation rate for all 50 programs under review is 89%.**

Ratio of Staff to Honors Students (3.0): Our estimate is that there is 1 staff member for every **300** students. (Mean ratio for all 50 programs is 1 staff member for every 159.8 students.)

Honors Residence Halls (4.5): The new Honors Living/Learning Community is located in Fred D. Brown Hall, a 250,000 square foot facility that features, in truth, state of the art designs and amenities. Foremost among those would be the two types of suite-style rooms. The "standard" room has two **double** beds and a full bath; the "deluxe" room has two bedrooms (for four total students), bunk beds, a private bath, a full-sized refrigerator, and a living room. Of course the entire facility is air conditioned.

Here's what we mean by state of the art:

- 3,000 square foot living room areas on each floor
- An auditorium plus multiple meeting/classroom areas
- Study areas on each wing
- TV monitors that display upcoming meetings, **safety alerts if necessary,** and social functions
- **An electronic mailbox for each student that sends a message each time mail is deposited**
- Two on-site "eateries"
- An outdoor deck with a view of a landscaped pedestrian mall
- A game room with sofa, chairs, and a big-screen TV for video games
- An on-site exercise facility

Prestigious Awards (3.5): UTK undergraduates have won 29 Goldwater Scholarships (for outstanding students in the STEM disciplines); many have also won Gilman Scholarships, awarded to students of modest means for foreign study. Postgraduate awards won by UTK students include seven Rhodes Scholarships, four Truman Scholarships, and two Marshall Scholarships.

Continuation Requirements: For students entering in Fall 2014 and later, a 3.50 cumulative GPA is required.

Academic Strengths: The highest ranked academic departments at UTK are nuclear engineering (6), biological/agricultural` engineering (23), business (47), education (64), engineering overall (65), physics (65), and computer science (70).

Undergraduate Research: Although the UTK Office of Undergraduate Research is not directly affiliated with the CHP, it does coordinate and highlight the research activities offered by the academic colleges with the university.

"Because the college is so diverse, the best way to begin to find the ideal research experience is to go online to the departmental website and find a list of faculty members," the research office advises. "Then, start to explore their various research interests to find someone who is interested in the same things you are. Step two is to contact the faculty member(s) via email, requesting an appointment to further explore your options."

The university also publishes *Pursuit,* a journal dedicated to publishing the research work of UTK undergraduates.

One of the most appealing aspects of undergraduate research at UTK is the Summer Research Internship program that awards $2,000 to about 30 undergraduates each year.

Study Abroad: "The chancellor's honors program offers competitive grants to students for study abroad," the Associate Provost tells us. "The university (through the programs abroad office and paid by students in a $5 semester fee) offers scholarships for study abroad. Honors sponsors a special summer program at the University of Cambridge in the U.K. 'UT Honors in Cambridge' is a humanities program during second summer session that includes housing in a residential college (Emmanuel). The chancellor's honors program has a 'ready for the world' requirement – all honors students are expected to have some type of significant intercultural experience, and most of our students choose study abroad or international research or service to fulfill this requirement."

Degree of Difference (Honors students/non-honors students): 3.4 on a scale of 5. Some parents and prospective students might prefer an honors program that in many ways stands apart on campus, while others might prefer a program that is more expansive. The rating here tries to provide an indication of where a given honors program is on the stand apart/expansive spectrum. The rating is based on the difference between (1) the average SAT scores for enrolled honors students and (2) the average test scores for all students in the university as a whole *and* for students with scores at the 75% level or above. A score of 3.5 or higher indicates a high degree of difference. A score of 3.2 to 3.49 indicates a relatively high degree of difference. Finally, a score below 3.2 indicates a modest difference. **Please keep in mind that neither the high nor low selectivity of an honors program determines how effective the program is; this rating is merely "cultural" and *not* qualitative.**

Testimonials from CHP Students:

Alex Lohmann--"Living on a floor with other Honors program girls instantly gave me a group of people to bond with. We had similar interests and motivations and we all got along from the beginning. The living and learning community gives you an instant niche within this huge campus, and that is a very comforting feeling. **The class size is always smaller and gives a better opportunity for a one-on-one relationship with the professors. Class discussions are very engaging and worthwhile and I always enjoy taking an Honors course here at the University of Tennessee.** I participated in a 3-week study abroad to Cambridge, England and I loved this experience. The faculty I went with were so knowledgeable and engaging and made the experience all of what it was."

Sarah Hall, Class of 2013--"The program's Ready for the World requirement provided the resources and motivation I needed to travel, and **I was able to spend a month in Romania studying osteology. My honors thesis compelled me to engage in research, and, building on interests sparked in Romania, I have worked with my advisor and the McClung Museum on a project I hope to translate into a master's thesis.**"

Evan K. Ford, Class of 2015--"Peer and faculty mentoring helped me orient myself to the requirements and expectations of a university education. **Finally, encouragement to take an honors course my freshman year helped me find one of my greatest passions--philosophy.** At a time when it was hard just to stay on my feet, the Chancellor's Honors Program was an invaluable community of friends and advisors."

Gracie McGuire--"In fact, **the courses that have most impacted me as a student have been honors courses (courses that were not part of my major, I might add). Additionally, the faculty member for whom I gained the most respect as a student and with whom I had a wonderful rapport was an honors faculty member.** I have worked for almost two years as an honors peer adviser and can thus confidently say that the CHP makes a conscious and consistent effort to make students aware of their responsibilities and works with them to fulfill those responsibilities."

NAME: UNIVERSITY HONORS PROGRAM, TEXAS A&M UNIVERSITY

Date Established: 1968

Location: College Station, Texas

University Full-time Undergraduate Enrollment: 36,219

Honors Enrollment: 1,385 (mean size of all 50 programs is 1,714)

Review/Admissions Category III: Programs with **average SAT scores of 1383--1416 for enrolled students**. The average test score at TAMU is SAT, 1400 (ACT converted to SAT would be 32). The average high school class rank is top 7%.

Honors Programs in Admissions Category III (average SAT scores of 1383--1416): Connecticut, Indiana, Kentucky, Miami University, Oklahoma, Penn State, Tennessee, Texas A&M, UC Irvine, and Washington.

Administrative Staff: The Honors Program has a staff of 10.

FOR ALL "MORTARBOARD" RATINGS BELOW, A SCORE OF 5 IS THE MAXIMUM AND REPRESENTS A COMPARISON WITH ALL 50 HONORS COLLEGES AND PROGRAMS:

PERCEPTION* OF UNIVERSITY AS A WHOLE, <u>NOT</u> OF HONORS: 🎓🎓🎓🎓

OVERALL HONORS RATING: 🎓🎓🎓🎓

Curriculum Requirements: 🎓🎓🎓🎓🎓

Class Range and Type: 🎓🎓🎓🎓

Class Size: 🎓🎓🎓

Adjusted Grad Rate: 🎓🎓🎓1/2

Ratio of Staff to Students: 🎓🎓🎓🎓

Priority Registration: **Yes,** honors students register for **all** courses, honors and otherwise, with the first group of students during **each** year they are in the program.

Honors Housing: 🎓🎓🎓🎓🎓

Prestigious Awards: 🎓🎓🎓🎓

*Perception is based on the university's ranking among public universities in the 2014 U.S. News Best Colleges report. Please bear in mind that the better the U.S. News ranking, the more difficult it is for an honors college or program to have a rating that equals or improves on the magazine ranking.

Curriculum Requirements (5.0): Graduation with the Honors Fellows distinction requires 30 semester hours of honors course credit along with a capstone or thesis, which averages another six hours of credit. (Please see information about **another option, Building Your Own Major, after the Honor Fellows description.)**

The 30 hours of course credit can be earned in the following ways:

- 9 hours must meet Core Curriculum requirements as specified in the student's catalog
- 12 hours must be in upper-division (300/400-level) courses
- Additional honors courses to bring the total to 30 hours
- Meet 3.25 GPA in Honors course work

Students can meet the honors requirement by taking any combination of departmental honors classes, graduate classes, honors contract classes, or independent-study classes. There is no limit on contract hours, but their principal function is to provide honors-level credit in a regular class section that the student wants or needs for enrichment or graduation.

The honors capstone requirement may be met by any one of the ways outlined below:

Honors Undergraduate Research Scholars must complete a total of six hours of research and thesis, typically in their major department. In some cases, the thesis or other research work appears in *Explorations: the Texas A&M Undergraduate Journal.*

Honors Undergraduate Teacher Scholars identify a faculty mentor who agrees to work with the student to prepare educational material the first semester and will be the instructor of record the second semester. ***This is one of our favorite options anywhere.***

The current options include:
- Develop a new 1 credit seminar (small, interactive) course.
- Develop educational material to enhance an already existing course.

The **Honors student-instructors lead class discussion**, proctor and grade exams, **and even hold office hours.** Imagine the experience this must be--and the value it has for networking with professors and being prepared for graduate or professional school. It is one thing for an honors student to participate in a seminar, but it is another thing to be the person who is expected to be the most knowledgeable *and* will be judged according to that expectation.

Honors Undergraduate Service Scholars engage in a year-long project that combines their career interests with the development of a community service project in collaboration with an agency and a faculty adviser. Students must write three interim reports and make a public presentation discussing issues and solutions.

And here is another innovative honors completion option: **Building Your Own Major.** Officially known as the University Studies Honors Degree (USHN), it allows students to propose a selected "range of work that defines an 'area of concentration,' in combination [with] two established minor fields of study.

"The combination of courses that comprises the Area of Concentration will be selected by the student and must be conceptually linked. The total must also include at least 18 Honors credit hours. The Honors credit hours will include one to six credit hours of Honors Independent Study, completed as part of the Honors Research Fellows program [see above, requires a thesis]."

At least one of the two minors must be offered from outside the college offering the honors area of concentration.

Within the 120 credits in this degree, the student must have at least 33 credit hours of Honors course work and 36 credits hours of upper-division coursework. The student must graduate with a cumulative GPA of at least 3.50, an Honors GPA of at least 3.25, and no honors class grade lower than a C.

In most cases, AP/IB credits are **not** counted as replacements for honors courses for students entering after 2012.

Range and Type of Honors Courses (4.0): The honors courses offered at TAMU seem to us to reflect the can-do, no-nonsense culture that remains strong on the A&M campus. In the initial notes on the program, we wrote that it was "a serious, department-based program built around the most important courses in the STEM disciplines, with relatively few interdisciplinary courses." So, while the curriculum completion options outlined in the previous section are creative and flexible, the courses are most often straight from the shoulder. There is much to admire in this combination.

Yes, in Spring 2014 we found half a dozen English classes, including two American and British lit survey courses, but two of the classes were in…technical writing. (The others were in the American Novel and Sci-Fi literature.) In history, there was a western civ survey, a class on the Renaissance and Reformation, and another on German history. And there were two more sections on art history and two in philosophy (logic, of course). Okay, well, let's get to the heavy stuff…

There are lots of math sections, about a dozen, one of the most extensive of any program under review. They cover pretty much everything from calculus to differential equations to linear algebra. Also plentiful are the bio sections, 10 or so, although some of these are bound to be large in size. There are also sections in genetics, forestry, and five in ecosystems. Engineering and technical disciplines are much better represented than in most programs--four sections in computer science, six in electrical and computer engineering, and seven in engineering design. Five more are in aeronautical engineering. In chemistry, we found only two--and, the biggest surprise, in physics there was only one honors lab although it's a great one: the Big Bang and Black Hole Lab.

We really like the three additional sections in engineering that cover ethics, professionalism, and the foundations of the discipline. And who else would offer five honors classes in entomology? There is one class in ag economics and astronomy, three in anthropology, three in political science, five in psychology, six in management, and, important for honors students, **five in communications (speech).**

As great as these departmental class offerings are, **what we do not know is how many of the classes are all-honors and how many are mixed. We were also unable to determine from the external data that we reviewed what the exact class sizes were, either.**

Average Class Size (3.0): So…we did an estimate based on university-wide data. Our best guess is that the **average honors-credit class has about 32** or so total students, honors and non-honors, although this could be low. The overall class size for the 50 colleges and programs under review in this edition is 21.2 students. **Conclusion: lots of departmental classes to choose from, but, as is the case with many department-based honors programs, the classes might be somewhat larger than in most honors programs.**

Adjusted Graduation Rate (3.5): The AGR is not simply the six-year graduation rate of students in the honors college who graduated from the university **(88%),** whether or not the students completed the honors program ("honors completers"). The AGR also reflects the extent to which the honors graduation rate from the university is higher than that for the university as a whole. The **university-wide rate is 80%,** yielding the 3.5 AGR for the college. **TAMU honors also provided its four-year grad rate, 73%,** very strong for a university that has so many engineering students. The average **honors** six-year **graduation rate for all 50 programs under review is 89%.**

Ratio of Staff to Honors Students (4.0): Our estimate is that there is 1 staff member for every **138.5** students. (Mean ratio for all 50 programs is 1 staff member for every 159.8 students.)

Honors Residence Halls (5.0): "With few exceptions, **freshmen admitted to the University Honors Program are required to live in Honors freshman housing and do not have the option to choose a roommate.** Continuing students who want to remain in an Honors residence environment may elect to live in Clements Honors Hall."

"A freshman learning community seminar (1 hour, non-credit-bearing) has been developed to complement the Honors residential experience. The Learning Community Seminar (LCS) is designed to challenge Honors Students with activities, provide opportunities to meet students in other majors, and foster critical thinking about oneself and their educational decisions.

"One goal of the LCS is to help create smaller, academically supportive groups within the larger A&M community. It is also the hope of the LCS that students will discover the value of seeking opportunities to advance their own knowledge and skills outside of the classroom so students will continue to engage in co-curricular activities beyond their first year. **The LCS is meant to push students to think and develop beyond their academic curriculum.**"

The two freshmen honors residence halls are **McFadden and Lechner,** with a combined capacity of about 400 students. Both are suite-style with connecting baths, air-conditioned (a necessity in Texas), with an interdisciplinary and critical-thinking living/learning themes. Both residence halls have on-site laundry and convenient dining is available at Sbisa Dining Hall, "one of the largest dining halls in the country."

Honors upperclassmen can choose to living in Clements Hall, which has amenities similar to those listed for the freshmen halls.

Prestigious Awards (4.0): TAMU students are well above the mean when it comes to winning the prestigious Goldwater Scholarships, (41), awarded to outstanding undergraduates in STEM fields. Students also do very well in winning the undergrad Udall Scholarships for study in Native American and environmental fields. Aggies have also done extremely well in earning undergraduate Gilman awards that provide travel funding for students with limited means. When it comes to prestigious postgraduate awards, TAMU students have excelled in earning National Science Foundation Graduate Research Fellowships.

Continuation Requirements: 3.25 honors GPA; 3.50 cumulative GPA

Academic Strengths: Texas A&M has an excellent faculty overall, but, not surprisingly, is strongest in engineering (15th nationally among all universities), followed by chemistry (19), political science (25), and business (27). Other highly respected academic departments include earth sciences (32), math and physics (40 each), and economics (42).

Undergraduate Research: "All students pursuing the university-level Honors distinction are required to complete a capstone project. The most established option, Undergraduate Research Scholars [see above], engages students in a two-semester research project (fall/spring academic year), conducted under the supervision of a Texas A&M faculty mentor. that culminates in a written thesis or other scholarly project. The objective of the program is to involve any qualified undergraduate student in a research project that emulates the 'graduate student' experience and to introduce the student to the academic publication process and the scholarly community."

Study Abroad: TAMU ranks 13th among all major national universities in the total number of students studying abroad. The university offers faculty-led programs, exchange programs, transfer credit, and overseas experiential programs including internships and volunteer assignments.

The exchange programs allow the student to attend an overseas institution for one, two, or three semesters. "You enroll as a full-time, non-degree student at a host university, yet remain in full-time status at Texas A&M University and **pay only Texas A&M tuition and fees."**

"Approximately 30% of students studying abroad in the summer receive a federal and/or private loan. All undergraduate and graduate students are required to have at least half-time status at Texas A&M to be eligible to apply for and receive federal and state loans and grants.

"The MSC L.T. Jordan Institute offers Texas A&M students the MSC Overseas Loan to use toward their study abroad. **This loan is worth up to $1,000 and is a supplemental,** *interest-free* **loan that must be repaid before a student graduates." [Emphasis added.]**

 Financial Aid: Texas A&M, unlike an increasing number of public universities, **did not reduce its number of university-sponsored National Merit Scholars but actually increased their support—** from 113 sponsorships in 2012 to 126 in 2013.

"Students named Finalists in the National Merit Scholarship competition who designate Texas A&M as their first choice college to the National Merit Scholarship Corporation under guidelines established by the Corporation are assured a four-year National Merit Sponsorship with a total value of at least $2,500. **National Merit Finalists who name Texas A&M as their first choice college may also earn a**

Director's Excellence Award and a NM Recognition Award valued at $10,000 and $24,000 respectively over four years.

"National Merit **Semifinalists** enrolling at Texas A&M for their freshman year of study will be granted a one-year $2,000 Merit Plus Award. Designation as a National Merit Finalist, of course, will qualify the recipient for an additional National Merit Sponsorship as described above.

"National Merit Scholars needing a fifth year of undergraduate study may receive a Director's Excellence Supplement Scholarship in the amount of $2,000. Recipients of National Merit, Merit Plus Scholarships, and Director's Excellence Awards may combine them with other scholarships, including Texas A&M awards. Holders of these awards are assured on-campus housing in residence halls as long as they request it for their freshman year of study and maintain continuous on-campus residence. They also are eligible for a $1,000 stipend applicable for participation in Texas A&M's Study Abroad Program."

Degree of Difference (Honors students/non-honors students): 2.83 on a scale of 5. Some parents and prospective students might prefer an honors program that in many ways stands apart on campus, while others might prefer a program that is more expansive. The rating here tries to provide an indication of where a given honors program is on the stand apart/expansive spectrum. The rating is based on the difference between (1) the average SAT scores for enrolled honors students and (2) the average test scores for all students in the university as a whole *and* for students with scores at the 75% level or above. A score of 3.5 or higher indicates a high degree of difference. A score of 3.2 to 3.49 indicates a relatively high degree of difference. Finally, a score below 3.2 indicates a modest difference. **Please keep in mind that neither the high nor low selectivity of an honors program determines how effective the program is; this rating is merely "cultural" and *not* qualitative.**

NAME: TEXAS TECH UNIVERSITY HONORS COLLEGE

Date Established: 1994

Location: Lubbock, Texas

University Full-time Undergraduate Enrollment: 23,588

Honors Enrollment: 1,045 (mean size of all 50 programs is 1,714)

Review/Admissions Category I: Programs with **average SAT scores of 1235--1342 for enrolled students**. The **actual average** test scores for enrollees at the honors college are SAT 1258, ACT 27.5. The average high school GPA is 3.66.

Minimum admission requirements are SAT, 1200; ACT 26; and a high school graduation rank in the top 10%.

Honors Programs in Admissions Category I (average SAT scores of 1235-1342): Arizona, Arizona State, Arkansas, Colorado State, Iowa, Maine, Mississippi, Oklahoma State, Oregon, Oregon State, Rhode Island, Texas Tech, University at Albany, and Washington State.

Administrative Staff: The Honors College has a staff of 14.

FOR ALL "MORTARBOARD" RATINGS BELOW, A SCORE OF 5 IS THE MAXIMUM AND REPRESENTS A COMPARISON WITH ALL 50 HONORS COLLEGES AND PROGRAMS:

PERCEPTION* **OF UNIVERSITY AS A WHOLE, <u>NOT</u> OF HONORS:** 🎓🎓

OVERALL HONORS RATING: 🎓🎓🎓🎓 1/2

Curriculum Requirements: 🎓🎓🎓🎓

Class Range and Type: 🎓🎓🎓🎓 1/2

Class Size: 🎓🎓🎓🎓 1/2

Adjusted Grad Rate: 🎓🎓🎓🎓 1/2

Ratio of Staff to Students: 🎓🎓🎓🎓🎓

Priority Registration: Yes. "Honors College students receive priority registration as long as they are members of the Honors College. Honors College Seniors receive first day registration and all other Honors students receive day 2 registration privileges."

Honors Housing: 🎓🎓🎓🎓🎓

Prestigious Awards: 🎓🎓🎓

*Perception is based on the university's ranking among public universities in the 2014 U.S. News Best Colleges report. Please bear in mind that the better the U.S. News ranking, the more difficult it is for an honors college or program to have a rating that equals or improves on the magazine ranking.

Curriculum Requirements (4.0): The honors college has two completion options, outlined below, but also has programs that lead to **early acceptance to TTU medical and law schools:**

Honors College with Honors--Students complete a total of 24 hours of honors credits, which must include at least 3 hours of upper-level honors seminar work and a 3-credit capstone requirement. A maximum of 6 credits of upper-level work in honors contract courses** can be counted. **All freshmen honors entrants must also complete an honors First Year Experience course,** included in the total of 24 credits.

The Honors First-Year Experience (FYE) Program helps first-year students to transition into university life. Honors students take one of the core courses, each taught by an outstanding professor in a small group. First-year students have a built-in community through a designated Learning Community Group (LCG). These are taught by two upperclassmen "who function as Peer Mentors to guide freshmen though the adjustment phase and integrate them into the Honors and Tech communities."

Honors College with Highest Honors--Completion requires the same 24 honors credits along with an additional 6 credits of research, culminating in a senior honors thesis, for a total of 30 credits.

A minimum grade of B- is required for honors credit in any honors college course or approved contract or graduate course.

The Honors College is a **leader nationwide in crafting policies and requirements for honors contract classes. The College limits the number and level of honors contract courses that can count for honors credit and has well-defined procedures in place that are designed to ensure the highest levels of academic quality and integrity.

Early Acceptance to TTU Medical and Law Schools:

Medical School--"The joint TTU-TTUHSC Early Acceptance Program offers an exciting opportunity to select Honors College students by allowing them to **waive the MCAT (Medical College Admissions Test) and to apply early to the TTUHSC's School of Medicine (SOM), typically in the junior year**. Successful Early Acceptance applicants are notified of their acceptance to the School of Medicine in February and complete their baccalaureate degrees prior to admission."

"The primary goal of this special program is to encourage Honors students to *broaden their educational experiences* before they enroll in their professional studies. The waiver of the MCAT allows students to become actively involved in the Honors College and to include coursework or other experiences in areas such as languages, the humanities, mathematics, and business, enabling them to become more well-rounded professionals. This is not an accelerated program. Therefore, the School of Medicine reserves the right to deny acceptance through this program to students who may contemplate early graduation."

A related opportunity is the **Health and Humanities track within the Honors Arts and Letters major,** designed to allow a flexible course of study for honors students that is firmly rooted in the Humanities in order to "enable them to become more competitive applicants to medical schools and other professional healthcare programs which are increasingly seeking well-rounded applicants with a diverse and comprehensive undergraduate background. Students preparing for entrance to healthcare professional programs must complete all prerequisite courses for their desired program in addition to satisfying course requirements for the HAL major."

Law School--"The Honors College and the Law School cooperate in an Early Decision Plan, which allows exceptional Law School applicants who are **Honors College students in good standing to receive notification of their acceptance to the Law School during their third year at Texas Tech**. Enrollment in the Law School would not occur until after the student receives a baccalaureate degree."

To be eligible to apply for Law School Early Decision, applicants must have a minimum undergraduate GPA of at least 3.50; an LSAT score that places them in the top half nationwide (>152, approximately); an SAT of at least 1300 or an ACT of at least 29; and be enrolled in the Texas Tech University Honors College and making satisfactory progress toward a baccalaureate degree with a diploma designation in Honors studies.

"Students will apply during the fall semester of their third year (or during the fall semester of a year in which they are classified as juniors) and must have taken the LSAT by December of that year. **Students who receive and accept an Early Decision must commit to enroll at the Texas Tech University School of Law and may not apply to other law schools."**

AP/IB credits are **not** counted as replacements for honors courses.

Range and Type of Honors Courses (4.5): A blended honors program, the TTU Honors College offers both an excellent range of core honors seminars, many with an interdisciplinary focus, along with a representative range of more specialized courses in the academic departments.

In Spring 2014, there were 27 honors seminars that encompassed subjects in the humanities, sciences, social sciences and fine arts. These included **Ethics in Research**; Science in American Society; Latin American Cinema; **History of Math;** Constitutional Law (also Property Law, Criminal Law); **Heroic Lives;** Narratives of Mental Disorders; and **Philosophical Issues and Problems in Human Caring.**

In **Heroic Lives,** students learn "how exceptional men and women have significantly influenced the lives of millions of people, in their own and later generations, for the benefit of society. We shall study the character, behavior, and development of these figures to assess whether there are unifying or repetitive patterns among them. Further, why did these figures rise above others of their time to merit attention and study in the 20th and 21st centuries? **Most important, however, is to ask ourselves: What can we learn from these heroic figures that we, as private individuals and as public citizens, can absorb or emulate in order to lead richer, fuller lives and contribute positively to our own and future**

generations?" (This excellent course is taught by former U.S. Senator and U.S. Representative from Texas Bob Krueger.)

Especially prominent among the Spring 2014 **departmental honors sections** are the seven math sections not counting the History of Math seminar mentioned above, one of the best selections of math courses among the 50 honors programs under review. These include a section of calculus I (more in Fall term), two in calculus II, and one each in linear algebra, calculus III, math stats for engineers and scientists, and higher math for engineers and scientists. There is only one honors biology section, but three in physics counting an astronomy section. On the business side, accounting, marketing, and management are represented--and remarkably the classes do not appear to be large.

The social sciences and humanities are solid with multiple sections (and seminars) of English, history, economics, political science, and a **series with the course code of Environmental Humanities.** This interesting series includes classes in Introductory and Advanced Fieldcraft; in the latter, honors students do a comparative study of the semi-arid part of Texas where they are and the rainforests of Southeast Asia. The third class in the series is Current Readings in Natural History. We found one section each in psychology and sociology, but none in anthropology.

Average Class Size (4.5): The average honors class size at the honors college is 19.8 students. The overall class size for the 50 colleges and programs under review in this edition is 21.2 students.

Adjusted Graduation Rate (4.5): The AGR is not simply the six-year graduation rate of students in the honors college who graduated from the university **(88%),** whether or not the students completed the honors program ("honors completers"). The AGR also reflects the extent to which the honors graduation rate from the university is higher than that for the university as a whole. (**The university-wide rate is 62%,** yielding the 4.5 AGR for the college.) The average six-year **honors graduation rate for all 50 programs** under review **is 89%.**

Ratio of Staff to Honors Students (5.0): Our estimate is that there is 1 staff member for every **74.6** students, not surprising given the Early Entrance Programs to the Medical and Law schools at TTU. (Mean ratio for all 50 programs is 1 staff member for every 159.8 students.)

Honors Residence Halls (5.0): Honors first-year students and upperclassmen have two honors residence halls, Gordon and Murray.

Gordon houses 252 total students in air-conditioned, suite-style rooms, with onsite laundry. The rooms are coed by suite, which typically means that the shared double rooms on either side of a shared bath are single sex, but both sexes share the bath. Gordon Hall has onsite dining at the Fresh Plate Dining Hall. Residents may also use a community kitchen, a main study lounge, and smaller study spaces on each floor.

Murray Hall houses 156 honors students, who are all part of the Honors Living/Learning Community on the 3rd floor. Murray has the same room styles and amenities as Gordon Hall, including onsite dining at Sam's Place.

Prestigious Awards (3.0): Tech students have had significant success in recent years when it comes winning the prestigious Goldwater Scholarships for outstanding undergraduates in the STEM fields.

Tech now has 32 Goldwater winners. Tech graduates have also won 1 Rhodes Scholarship, 3 Gates Cambridge Scholarships, and 1 Truman Scholarship.

Continuation Requirements: 3.25 cumulative GPA, and a minimum grade in each honors course of B-.

Academic Strengths: The leading departments at Tech are health care management; engineering (especially industrial, civil and chemical engineering); business; and earth sciences.

Undergraduate Research: The year-long Undergraduate Research Scholars (URS) program "culminates in the student's participation in the TTU Undergraduate Research Conference. Scholars receive a stipend, through an endowment, to participate in research with a faculty mentor. Scholars may participate in URS for two years."

At the annual conference, students make a presentation and meet with other student scholars and faculty. TTU faculty and URS peers review poster and paper presentations.

The Center for Active Learning and Undergraduate Engagement assists undergraduates with finding paid and unpaid research and work opportunities, including some offered in the summer.

Study Abroad: The honors college reports that it has "a $110,000 yearly scholarship fund to assist students wishing to study abroad. Awards vary depending on program length. Generally, a typical full semester award is $3,500." The university has exchange programs with 65 foreign universities, most of them in Europe, but there are programs in Australia, Brazil (several), Turkey, China, and Korea as well.

Perhaps the centerpiece of the university's study-abroad programs is the **Texas Tech University Center in Sevilla, located on the Guadalquivir River in southern Spain, in the heart of the region known as Andalusia.**

"A city of roughly 700,000 inhabitants, Sevilla offers all of the advantages of a big city while still maintaining a small-town feel. In Sevilla, students can still appreciate the splendor of Golden Age Spain as they meander through the nooks and crannies of the medieval city center, whose cathedral holds the tomb of Christopher Columbus, and at the same time take advantage of the modern cultural and leisure activities that this vibrant city has to offer.

"The Center allows students to take catalog TTU classes taught by Texas Tech faculty. The Center has a permanent staff as well as faculty that travel from Lubbock to Sevilla every semester (fall, spring and summer). The Center is located in a building that originally dates back to the 1890s, and today has all of the modern conveniences a university facility needs. It is conveniently situated in a bustling neighborhood, literally steps away from all sorts of eateries and shops."

Financial Aid: "The Honors College awards $300,000 of scholarship funding per year," according to honors staff. "Scholarship decisions are based on exceptional performance as a TTU Honors College student. Scholarship criteria include: honors experiences, overcoming adversity and challenges, work responsibilities, family circumstances, and volunteer experience with the Honors College or in some other setting. Scholarship awards vary from $1,000 to $2,000 per year."

For entering freshmen with "exceptional academic ability," the university has Presidential Scholarships for students who meet these test score and high school GPA standards (for Fall 2014):

At least a 1400 SAT or 32 ACT, and top 10% of high school class= $6,000 a year for four years, plus a one-time award of $4,000; recipients must maintain a 3.50 GPA and earn at least 15 hours of credit each term.

At least a 1300 SAT or 29 ACT, and top 10% of high school class= $4,000 a year for four years; recipients must maintain a 3.25 GPA and earn at least 15 hours of credit each term.

At least a 1250 SAT or 28 ACT, and top 10% of high school class= $3,500 a year for four years; recipients must maintain a 3.00 GPA and earn at least 15 hours of credit each term.

At least a 1200 SAT or 27 ACT, and top 10% of high school class= $3,000 a year for four years; recipients must maintain a 3.00 GPA and earn at least 15 hours of credit each term.

There are many other options for students with even higher test scores but lower high school class rankings, or test scores equivalent to those listed above but in combination with lower class rankings, usually the top 25%.

Degree of Difference (Honors students/non-honors students): 2.68 on a scale of 5. Some parents and prospective students might prefer an honors program that in many ways stands apart on campus, while others might prefer a program that is more expansive. The rating here tries to provide an indication of where a given honors program is on the stand apart/expansive spectrum. The rating is based on the difference between (1) the average SAT scores for enrolled honors students and (2) the average test scores for all students in the university as a whole *and* for students with scores at the 75% level or above. A score of 3.5 or higher indicates a high degree of difference. A score of 3.2 to 3.49 indicates a relatively high degree of difference. Finally, a score below 3.2 indicates a modest difference. **Please keep in mind that neither the high nor low selectivity of an honors program determines how effective the program is; this rating is merely "cultural" and *not* qualitative.**

NAME: CAMPUSWIDE HONORS PROGRAM, UNIVERSITY OF CALIFORNIA IRVINE

Date Established: 1988

Location: Irvine, California

University Full-time Undergraduate Enrollment: 23,641

Review/Admissions Category--III: Programs with average SAT scores of 1383--1416 for enrolled students. The actual average (mean) three-part SAT for first-year students is 2103, and the *estimated* ACT equivalent is 31.5; the *estimated* high school GPA is 4.2.

Minimum Admission Requirements: "Faculty in UCI's Schools and Majors select incoming freshmen based on the University of California application."

Honors Programs in Admissions Category III (average SAT scores of 1383--1416): Connecticut, Indiana, Kentucky, Miami University, Oklahoma, Penn State, Tennessee, Texas A&M, UC Irvine, and Washington.

Administrative Staff: The CHP has a staff of 4.

FOR ALL "MORTARBOARD" RATINGS BELOW, A SCORE OF 5 IS THE MAXIMUM AND REPRESENTS A COMPARISON WITH ALL 50 HONORS COLLEGES AND PROGRAMS:

PERCEPTION* OF UNIVERSITY AS A WHOLE, <u>NOT</u> OF HONORS: 🎓🎓🎓🎓1/2

OVERALL HONORS RATING: 🎓🎓🎓🎓1/2

Curriculum Requirements: 🎓🎓🎓🎓🎓

Class Range and Type: 🎓🎓🎓1/2

Class Size: 🎓🎓🎓🎓

Adjusted Grad Rate: 🎓🎓🎓🎓1/2

Ratio of Staff to Students: 🎓🎓🎓1/2

Priority Registration: Yes, honors students register for **all** courses, honors and otherwise, with the first group of students during **each** year they are in the program.

Honors Housing: 🎓🎓🎓🎓

Prestigious Awards: 🎓🎓🎓🎓

*Perception is based on the university's ranking among public universities in the 2014 U.S. News Best Colleges report. Please bear in mind that the better the U.S. News ranking, the more difficult it is for an honors college or program to have a rating that equals or improves on the magazine ranking.

Curriculum Requirements (5.0): The CHP completion requirement is rigorous: students must complete a **minimum** of 54 quarter units of honors coursework and at least two quarters of academic research leading to a senior thesis or research project. Counting the research requirement, the minimum quarter units would be 60-62, which converts to approximately 41 semester hours, **one of the highest completion levels of the 50 programs under review.**

CHP students must complete three academic quarters of **honors humanities** core courses, for **24** total quarter units.

Students must also complete three academic quarters in the **social sciences** core sequence, for a total of **18** quarter units.

Non-science majors must also complete three quarters in the **science** core sequence, for a total of **12** quarter units. Science majors who are required by their major to take general chemistry take Honors General Chemistry to meet that requirement, for a total of 21 quarter units.

Finally, CHP students must then complete "two quarters minimum of research with faculty member."

AP/IB Credits: These cannot be used to replace required honors courses.

Range and Type of Honors Courses (3.5): This category brings focus to what prospective students should be looking at: Do you want an established core curriculum that specifies the in-depth, interdisciplinary courses you will take in the humanities, sciences, and social sciences for at least the first two years, or do you want a more wide-open, decentralized program that allows you to take as many departmental and contract courses as you like? Or something in between?

Well if you want an excellent, cohesive core program, here are the humanities, science, and social science courses that are the backbone of the CHP:

Humanities Core--As noted above, all CHP students must take the three-quarter sequence in the humanities. Each academic quarter, 8 units (usually two courses) are offered, and these are team-taught by three professors. During a recent academic year, the theme for the humanities core was **War.** The nine professors who were involved in teaching on this theme for the full three-quarter sequence came from the following academic departments: English (4), comparative literature (2), and history, art history, and European Studies (1 each).

About the theme of **War**: "The course theme, WAR, looks at ways in which people have represented, rationalized, propagandized, memorialized, evaluated, or understood, for themselves or others, the human activity of war that this generation, or indeed humanity, has experienced and must consider. **Texts include classic and contemporary works by Homer, Sun Tzu, Machiavelli, Brecht, Whitman, Dickinson, J.M. Coetzee, Naomi Klein, Cognito Comics, Benjamin Britten, William Wyler, Maya Lin, Stanley Kubrick, Ruth Kluger, and Max Brooks.**

"The course [sequence] efficiently fulfills 6 general education requirements in lower-division writing (2 courses), Arts and Humanities (3 courses), and Multicultural Studies (1 course). Its excellent integrated writing program trains students in multi-modal forms of communication, while giving students the opportunity to work one-on-one with specialists in numerous disciplines."

Science Core--The recent core sequence in science (one 4-unit course each quarter) was centered on the generic course title of **The Idiom and Practice of Science.** In practice, during each quarter the "Idiom" course focuses on a specific scientific discipline. For example, beginning in Fall Quarter 2013, the full course title was The Idiom and Practice of Science—Biology. In Winter Quarter 2014, the subject was physics, and in the Spring Quarter it was chemistry. (The Idiom courses are for non-science majors. Students who are majoring in STEM disciplines that require general chemistry take Honors General Chemistry.)

Let's take a look at **The Idiom and Practice of Science--Physics.** This course had the additional subtitle of "Music, Earthquakes, & Light: Waves in our World." And the following introduction is the reason we chose this course as an example:

"Science is observed truth, tied together by general law, with predictive capability. This [course] emphasizes all three elements. Notice the following description does not approach physics from a give-me-a-formula-to-plug-into-for-answer perspective; **science is not about plug and chug**....

"You will learn to make your own observations and measurements. To have a shared circumstance for these observations, demonstrations will be made in most lectures. You will need to attend every lecture to make and record your observations. Your lecture observations will be important for learning how to do physics and for your exams (which will have problems based on these demonstrations). Your lecture attendance and notes will prove crucial for your course success." Yes, we imagine so. **We find it especially commendable that CHP students receive this inside view of 'doing science' at the same time they are taking traditional lecture and lab science courses.**

The Social Science Core is team-taught by six professors, and includes 6 units each quarter for three quarters. During the 2013-2014 academic year, the course offerings were Naturalized Epistemology and the Social Sciences; Critical Issues in Social Science; and Inequality: Causes, Consequences and Policy. Here we will take a look at **Naturalized Epistemology and the Social Sciences** so we can figure out for ourselves what it's about:

"We will discover that a number of classic findings of the social sciences reveal that the faculties we rely on in the acquisition of knowledge are systematically unreliable, misleading, and subject to deception in myriad ways we never would have anticipated and indeed find hard to believe even when they are demonstrated experimentally....**We will conclude by proposing an alternative picture of human knowledge as an ongoing process of belief revision and problem solving, according to which it is possible to provide justification for many of our beliefs about the world even as we constantly update our assumptions about the nature of our faculties and methods in light of new research in the social sciences."**

Outside of the core, there are Honors Research Seminars offered by the CHP, where a member of the faculty teaches on a topic of their choice that is related to their own research. Topics currently include **Quantum Mechanics, Scientific Realism and Instrumentalism, and Time and Film.** UCI's schools and majors also offer a small number of honors-level lecture or seminar classes in the departments; but like almost all universities, UCI offers departmental research and individual mentoring that lead to a senior honors thesis. And recall that CHP students must spend **a minimum of two academic quarters engaged in departmental research.** Because it is extremely difficult to measure the number of research sections with actual enrollment and because they often do not meet on a regular schedule, we can count them for the curriculum completion requirement (above), but we do not count them in the range and type category.

Average Class Size (4.0): The average honors class has **24.6 students,** with one core science class having a large enrollment. The average class size for all 50 programs under review is 21.2 students.

Adjusted Graduation Rate (4.5): The AGR is not simply the six-year graduation rate of students in the CHP who graduated from the university **(94%),** whether or not the students completed the honors program ("honors completers"). The AGR also reflects the extent to which the honors graduation rate from the university is higher than that for the university as a whole. The **university-wide rate is 86%,** yielding a high AGR of 4.5. The average six-year **honors graduation rate for all 50 programs** under review **is 89%.**

Ratio of Staff to Honors Students (3.5): Our estimate is that there is 1 staff member for every **175** students. (Mean ratio for all 50 programs is 1 staff member for every 159.8 students.)

Honors Residence Halls (4.0): CHP first-year students are not required to live on campus, but many do reside in Loma or Arroyo (Mesa Court community) or the Shire (Middle Earth community). Loma and Arroyo are two of 24 residences in Mesa Court, and the Shire is one of the 29 residences in Middle Earth. Both residence halls feature suite-style rooms with shared baths. Floors are coed with single-sex suites. Neither hall is air conditioned, but there is on-site laundry and convenient dining--Mesa Commons for Loma, and Pippin Commons for the Shire.

Upperclassmen can live in one of four large houses in Arroyo Vista. "Each house is home to 16, 24, or 32 residents who live in **double occupancy rooms** and share a **large kitchen, living room, and study room.** Some houses offer a two-room suite (for 2 students). Academic Theme houses are co-ed, and Greek chapter houses are single gender. Residents prepare their own meals or purchase a voluntary meal plan for use in residence hall dining facilities."

Prestigious Awards (4.0): UCI undergraduates have won 30 Goldwater Scholarships for outstanding promise in the STEM disciplines, along with an impressive number of Gilman Scholarships to assist students of limited means who plan to study abroad. UCI graduates have a solid record of winning National Science Foundation Graduate Research Fellowships, and in the last three years, UCI students have won 15 Fulbright Student Scholarships.

Continuation Requirements: 3.20 cumulative and honors GPA.

Academic Strengths: As previously noted, UCI has one of the most distinguished faculties of any university in the nation, public or private, with 14 of the 15 disciplines we track being ranked in the top 50. Here are the rankings: English (22), sociology (25), chemistry (26), computer science and physics (29), psychology (30), biology and earth sciences (both 34), history (36), education (37), political science (40), math (41), economics (46), and engineering (49).

Undergraduate Research: UCI has an Undergraduate Research Opportunity Program (UROP) that supports undergraduate research opportunities, provides funding opportunities for research, publishes an annual undergraduate research journal, and hosts the UCI Undergraduate Research Symposium each year, where students present their research. The program maintains an electronic database of undergraduate research assistantships, showing the department, area of research, faculty member, and closing date for applications. Another extensive database lists off-campus research, volunteer, and internship positions at scores of major companies and organizations. As noted previously, all CHP students are required to participate in at least two quarters of research under the mentorship of a faculty member.

Study Abroad: UCI does a good job of aligning study-abroad programs with academic majors. For example, students in biological sciences can easily find that they can study at the Bermuda Institute of Ocean Sciences or volunteer for an expedition with the Earthwatch Institute. Physics majors might choose Lund University in Sweden or the National University of Singapore. Engineers can complete their math, chemistry, or physics requirements at the University of Sussex in England, or take upper-division engineering courses in Australia, Singapore, Hong Kong, New Zealand, Ireland, the UK, or Turkey,

According to the CHP, the best times for honors students to study abroad are Fall of junior year; the full junior year; or Fall of the senior year.

"Take Honors Core courses early, before going abroad. Take Social Science Core and Science Core sophomore year--many students already do. Find a research advisor prior to studying abroad, even if you won't do research until you return."

Financial Aid: The most prestigious merit award at UC campuses is the Regents' Scholarship, the amount of which varies each year. The amount can also vary according to the income level of the recipients. For engineering students, there is the Henry Samueli Endowed Scholarship.

Each year, the UCI Alumni Association awards more than $85,000 in scholarships.

Degree of Difference (Honors students/non-honors students): 3.30 on a scale of 5. Some parents and prospective students might prefer an honors program that in many ways stands apart on campus, while others might prefer a program that is more expansive. The rating here tries to provide an indication of where a given honors program is on the stand apart/expansive spectrum. The rating is based on the difference between (1) the average SAT scores for enrolled honors students and (2) the average test scores for all students in the university as a whole *and* for students with scores at the 75% level or above. A score of 3.5 or higher indicates a high degree of difference. A score of 3.2 to 3.49 indicates a relatively high degree of difference. Finally, a score below 3.2 indicates a modest difference. **Please keep in mind that neither the high nor low selectivity of an honors program determines how effective the program is; this rating is merely "cultural" and *not* qualitative.**

NAME: UCLA HONORS PROGRAMS

Date Established: 1979

Location: Los Angeles, California

University Full-time Undergraduate Enrollment: 27,365

Honors Enrollment: approximately 3,000 (mean size of all 50 programs is 1,714)

Review/Admissions Category II: Programs with **average SAT scores of 1343--1382 for enrolled students**. Actual average (mean) SAT three-part score for **enrolled honors students** is 2044, and the average ACT is 30.5 (high end of Category II). The average high school GPA is 4.05, top 5% of high school class.

Minimum admission requirements for **freshman entrants** is an SAT three-part score of 2080 and a capped, weighted high school GPA of 4.1. *The probable reason that the test score requirement for freshman entrants is higher than the average test score for enrollees is that the honors program accepts transfer students with a 3.75 GPA and also allows current UCLA students with a 3.5 GPA to take honors courses. Many of these students are likely to have test scores lower than those of freshman entrants.* (A "capped" high school GPA means that there is a limit to the number of high school advanced class grades that can add "weight" to the overall high school GPA.)

Honors Programs in Admissions Category II (average SAT scores of 1343-1382): Alabama, Delaware, Florida State, LSU, Massachusetts, Missouri, North Carolina State, Ohio University, Temple, Purdue, UCLA, Utah, Vermont, and Wisconsin.

Administrative Staff: The Honors Program have a staff of 10.

FOR ALL "MORTARBOARD" RATINGS BELOW, A SCORE OF 5 IS THE MAXIMUM AND REPRESENTS A COMPARISON WITH ALL 50 HONORS COLLEGES AND PROGRAMS:

PERCEPTION* OF UNIVERSITY AS A WHOLE, <u>NOT</u> OF HONORS: 🎓🎓🎓🎓🎓

OVERALL HONORS RATING: 🎓🎓🎓🎓**

Curriculum Requirements: 🎓🎓🎓🎓

Class Range and Type: 🎓🎓🎓🎓🎓

Class Size: 🎓🎓🎓🎓$^{1/2}$

Adjusted Grad Rate: 🎓🎓🎓🎓🎓

Ratio of Staff to Students: 🎓🎓🎓

**Editor's Note: The overall rating for UCLA Honors would be 5 mortarboards if the program offered priority registration and had designated honors student residence halls, meaning that the academic components of the program are excellent.

Priority Registration: No.

Honors Housing: N/A.

Prestigious Awards: 👕 👕 👕 👕

*Perception is based on the university's ranking among public universities in the 2014 U.S. News Best Colleges report. Please bear in mind that the better the U.S. News ranking, the more difficult it is for an honors college or program to have a rating that equals or improves on the magazine ranking.

Curriculum Requirements (4.0): Freshman entrants *"are automatically placed in Coursework Plan A."* **Plan A** requires a minimum of 44 quarter units of honors credits (converted to semester hours=29.6). Of these, 8 units must be taken in the outstanding Honors Collegium series (see Range and Type of Honors Courses, below) and 12 units must be in honors upper division courses. The additional 24 honors units may be earned by taking pre-approved, rigorous "master list" classes within the departments, additional honors courses, graduate courses, study-abroad courses, research and tutorial classes, or a quarter spent in Washington, DC. Students may also take honors "adjunct" classes (extra work in non-honors classes, typically in a break-out discussion section) or honors contract course that require extra work without a break-out section. (Please note that "adjunct" used here does not mean the discussion sections are taught by adjunct instructors.)

After the sophomore year, when students have settled on a major, they may decide to change from Plan A to Honors **Plan B**. This is essentially a departmental honors plan requiring completion of research and thesis work in addition to the honors courses taken in the first two years. To complete Plan B, the total number of honors units, including thesis and related research, is at least 36 quarter units.

Regarding the opportunity for honors students to take graduate courses, the Director writes that her estimate **"is that about 20% of our students actually enroll in a graduate level course; and about 80% of Honors students in the sciences** will be involved in a research lab alongside grad students and post docs." **Students participating in the Departmental Scholars program (master's and bachelor's) do have enrollment access to graduate level courses.**

 "The Departmental Scholar Program (DSP) allows exceptional juniors and seniors to pursue the bachelor's and master's degrees simultaneously," according to the honors website. "Nomination as a Departmental Scholar is an honor that carries practical benefits--the graduate application process is simplified and students may be admitted to the DSP during any academic quarter. Finally, the Departmental Scholar Program offers advanced students access to graduate level classes and an opportunity to do graduate level research under the direct supervision of UCLA's distinguished faculty."

Eligibility: Students seeking nomination to the Departmental Scholar Program must complete 96 quarter units at UCLA or the equivalent at a similar institution; complete the preparation of their major; have a 3.50 overall GPA; and have a 3.50 GPA in their major.

AP/IB credits are **not** counted as replacements for honors courses.

Range and Type of Honors Courses (5.0): The Honors Director emphasizes to us that "**UCLA's Honors program works by student choice. We give students a vast array of options by which they may receive honors credit for courses taken towards the degree with honors.** So students make choices about how they will accumulate honors credit. We guide them, with counseling, of course, but ultimately they work with what they want to do and what fits in with their other university and major and minor requirements for the degree."

Even if we do not count the hundreds of honors research and tutorial sections at UCLA and honors contract courses, there are still more than 250 honors classes each quarter in every subject area imaginable. There are three main advantages to the UCLA approach:

1. As the Director says, the program works mainly "by student choice." With so much to choose from, flexibility is not an issue. One reason that the program allows such flexibility is that **the university is under a state mandate to graduate as many students as possible in four years. Giving honors students at UCLA--and at many other programs--so many options also makes graduating in four years much more likely.**

2. But it is really **the excellence of the university as a whole**--on anyone's list of the top 3 or 4 public universities in the nation and one of the premier research universities in the entire world-- that allows the luxury of combining so much flexibility with the highest caliber learning environment. Even when taking an adjunct class (contract-type class) or participating in a large mixed section, UCLA honors students will be among some of the best students in the land taught by outstanding faculty. And as for honors research and tutorial classes, there are few better places in the world to be. (It's not just the LA weather that leads to more applicants to UCLA than to any other university in America.)

3. Honors students at UCLA are extremely fortunate to be in what is essentially a very large **blended honors program,** which allows them to explore an extensive range of departmental courses (and graduate courses) at the same time that **they are enjoying honors seminars that are second to none.**

Our estimate is that in the Winter quarter 2014, close to 40 Collegium seminars were presented, along with at least as many seminars at the department level. Of the Collegium classes, about eight are part of the Fiat Lux Freshman Seminar Series. Topics for these include James Joyce's *Ulysses,* Mental Illness and Movies, You Are What You Eat: Food and Chemistry, and **Clones and Zombies: Anxieties around the Human.**

The university says this about the Collegium: "The Collegium is characterized by small classes and individual attention. It encourages intellectual exchange among students, discussion leaders, and professors. Ample opportunity is provided for dialogue and for confrontation of ideas and values within a friendly and informal atmosphere. Students enjoy the advantage of intimate classes and the challenge of an education that strives to connect rather than isolate their studies."

Here are several of the many excellent Collegium courses offered beyond the freshman seminar level: **Psychology of Fear,** Imaginary Women, **Biology and Medicine in a Postgenomic Era**, Past People and Their Lessons for our Own Future, **Future Impact of Nano in New Technologies,** Literature and Political Order: Homer, Shakespeare, Dostoevsky; and **Terrorism, Counterterrorism, and Weapons of Mass Destruction: Practical Approach.**

Many of the departmental classes are also seminars, including several in history; but **the likelihood is that many of the courses taken to fulfill all honors requirements will be in classes on the "master list" of rigorous (but not formally honors) classes within the academic departments.** As noted above, UCLA can make this work because even in large mixed lectures with honors-only breakout sections, both the lectures and the discussion components are likely to be of very high quality. It is also important to keep in mind that there are many seminars that have a discipline-specific focus, and not only the larger departmental classes.

Average Class Size (4.5): This is an excellent rating for a program with so many departmental classes— but it might be a bit generous, as we will explain after summarizing class sizes by type below:

UCLA Honors offers about 70 Collegium seminars each academic year, and the average class size for these is 18 students.

The hundreds of honors seminars offered in the departments during an academic year also average about 18 students each.

About 40 additional departmental courses offered to honors students each year average around 50 students each.

Finally, and somewhat problematically, there are also hundreds of honors "adjuncted" classes, which are really lecture classes with breakout discussion sections. Although these discussion sections average only 13 students each, we have no figures to show how large the main sections are.

UCLA Honors does report an average class size, based on the above but counting only the discussion section enrollment in the adjunct sections: **16.5 students.** The average honors class size for all 50 honors programs under review is 21.2 students.

Adjusted Graduation Rate (5.0): The AGR is not simply the six-year graduation rate of students in the honors program who graduated from the university **(99%),** the **highest of any program**, whether or not the students completed the honors program. The AGR also reflects the extent to which the honors graduation rate from the university is higher than that for the university as a whole. (The **university-wide rate is 92%,** yielding the 5.0 AGR for the college.) The average **honors** six-year **graduation rate for all 50 programs under review is 89%.**

Ratio of Staff to Honors Students (3.0): UCLA Honors is especially decentralized, relying as it does on the student to do much of the planning for his or her honors path. The program does provide counseling, however, and without honors housing, there is no need for staff in that area. Our estimate is that there is 1 staff member for every **300** students. (Mean ratio for all 50 programs is 1 staff member for every 159.8 students.)

Honors Residence Halls (3.0): This is a default rating for programs that do not have separate honors housing. UCLA is one of a few programs--Wisconsin and Illinois are the others--that do not offer separate housing options for honors students. One of the reasons is that all three universities as a whole have talented student bodies, and the other reason is that, from an egalitarian perspective, these schools simply do not want to emphasize the elite status of honors students or have "perks" trump academics.

Prestigious Awards: (4.0) Although the outstanding academic quality of UCLA is not in question, it is true that for much of the history of the Rhodes Scholar awards and a few of the other prestigious scholarships, the UC System in general did not receive the kind of recognition one would expect. In many ways this has changed in recent years.

Now, the Honors Director reports that the "UCLA Honors program looks after the recruitment, selection, and nomination of students for those national and international scholarships which require institutional endorsement. Other scholarships for which the student can apply directly without institutional endorsement are looked after by the Scholarship Resource Center."

One result is that UCLA has now seen its graduates earn 11 Rhodes Scholarships, even after the rough beginning, and **double the average number of** extremely generous and prestigious **Gates Cambridge and Churchill Scholarships** won by public universities. **But the most outstanding performance by UCLA graduates has come in the number of National Science Foundation Graduate Research Fellowships earned during the three-year period 2011-2013, ranking behind only UC Berkeley, UT Austin, Michigan, Illinois, and Washington among public universities. UCLA students have also won almost double the average number of Fulbright Student Scholarships awarded to public university students in the same three-year period.**

Continuation Requirements: 3.50 cumulative GPA for Honors graduation.

Academic Strengths: The UCLA academic departments are recognized as being among the best in the nation among all universities public and private. Across the 14 major academic disciplines that we track and that offer majors at UCLA, the *average* ranking of UCLA departments is better than 13th in the nation, ahead of elite private institutions such as Penn, Johns Hopkins, Duke, Northwestern, Washington University St. Louis, and Brown. Seven of the 14 departments are in the top 10 nationally. (UCLA does not have an undergraduate major in business.) Among the many stellar departments are psychology (2), education and math (both 8), history and sociology (both 9), English and political science (both 10), computer science (14), economics (15), chemistry (16), earth sciences (17), engineering and physics (both 19), and biology (24).

Undergraduate Research: "We are a big research institution and give honors credit for students participating in research in several ways," the Director tells us.

"(1) The Undergraduate Student Research Program: students work in the labs/libraries of professors needing researchers. It is a [pass/no pass] experience and students are usually working on the prof's research, not their own, so we limit the number of units (two units only) that can be applied on the Honors curriculum requirements. **The experience, however, gives students the opportunity to network in the huge research mission and get credit for it. Once the networking has occurred, students can then do their own research.**

"(2) They do this research in very many **upper division courses** numbered 195 through 199. **These are in all disciplines and they allow students to engage in the research mission doing actual projects (often a part of a greater research mission) of their own.** These courses can also be used for credit for research associated with the senior thesis.

Study Abroad: "We ask Honors students on UCLA study abroad or other study abroad experiences to bring back syllabi and evidence of significant project work and we assess courses taken abroad for Honors credit," the Director says. "Students can bring in up to 12 units of honors credit from outside institutions –but **we** assess for honors. (We do not accept the mere declaration of the outside institution that this is an honors class)."

UCLA is ranked 8ᵗʰ among U.S. universities in the total number of students who study abroad and 8ᵗʰ in the number of total students who participate in long-term study-abroad programs. The university is also one of a few nationwide to receive special recognition of its study-abroad programs by *U.S. News.*

Part of the reason is that UCLA students win a high number of generous Boren Scholarships for work and study in foreign countries where the U.S. presence is underrepresented; **UCLA is among national leaders in the number of Gilman Scholarships earned during the last three years, awarded to students of limited means for studying abroad.**

Financial Aid: "UCLA's student body has 70% of students on state and federal financial aid. This includes federal financial aid and Pell grants and Cal grants, and eligible Honors students have access to these, as any other student. **We also have funding from private donations for Honors scholarships with an endowment of about $3 million** and awards from $1,000 to $5,000 dollars."

Degree of Difference (Honors students/non-honors students): 1.00 on a scale of 5. Some parents and prospective students might prefer an honors program that in many ways stands apart on campus, while others might prefer a program that is more expansive. The rating here tries to provide an indication of where a given honors program is on the stand apart/expansive spectrum. The rating is based on the difference between (1) the average SAT scores for enrolled honors students and (2) the average test scores for all students in the university as a whole *and* for students with scores at the 75% level or above. A score of 3.5 or higher indicates a high degree of difference. A score of 3.2 to 3.49 indicates a relatively high degree of difference. Finally, a score below 3.2 indicates a modest difference. **Please keep in mind that neither the high nor low selectivity of an honors program determines how effective the program is; this rating is merely "cultural" and *not* qualitative.**

NAME: HONORS COLLEGE, UNIVERSITY AT ALBANY (THE STATE UNIVERSITY OF NEW YORK)

Date Established: 2006

Location: Albany, New York

University Full-time Undergraduate Enrollment: 12,068

Honors Enrollment: *Estimated* at 550. The mean size of all 50 programs is 1,714.

Review/Admissions Category I: Programs with **average SAT scores of 1235--1342** for enrolled students. The *estimated* average (mean) test scores for honors enrollees are SAT 1299, ACT 29. The *estimated* average high school class graduation rank is 90th percentile.

Minimum admission requirements: The College is somewhat flexible about applying these minimum requirements and will take into account the effect of only one low grade or a modest difference in test scores. The stated minimum SAT is 1250 (ACT 28) and a high school graduation rank at the 90th percentile or higher.

Honors Programs in Admissions Category I (average SAT scores of 1235-1342): Arizona, Arizona State, Arkansas, Colorado State, Iowa, Maine, Mississippi, Oklahoma State, Oregon, Oregon State, Rhode Island, Texas Tech, University at Albany, and Washington State.

Administrative Staff: The Honors College has a staff of 5.

FOR ALL "MORTARBOARD" RATINGS BELOW, A SCORE OF 5 IS THE MAXIMUM AND REPRESENTS A COMPARISON WITH ALL 50 HONORS COLLEGES AND PROGRAMS:

PERCEPTION* OF UNIVERSITY AS A WHOLE, NOT OF HONORS: 🎓🎓[1/2]

OVERALL HONORS RATING: 🎓🎓🎓

Curriculum Requirements: 🎓🎓🎓[1/2]

Class Range and Type: 🎓🎓🎓[1/2]

Class Size: 🎓🎓🎓🎓

Adjusted Grad Rate: 🎓🎓🎓🎓

Ratio of Staff to Students: 🎓🎓🎓🎓[1/2]

Priority Registration: No.

Honors Housing: 🎓🎓🎓🎓

Prestigious Awards: 🎓🎓🎓

*Perception is based on the university's ranking among public universities in the 2014 U.S. News Best Colleges report. Please bear in mind that the better the U.S. News ranking, the more difficult it is for an honors college or program to have a rating that equals or improves on the magazine ranking.

Curriculum Requirements (3.5): In order to graduate with honors, students typically complete 9 credits of honors classes in both the first and second year, for a total of 18 credits (usually six courses). The next two years are devoted to the completion of major requirements, including those for honors in the major. We estimate that most students take a minimum of 9 credits to complete the honors thesis and research related to the thesis. The total of 27 credits does not take into account additional courses that may be required for departmental honors but not for regular graduation in the major. These could add another 6-9 credits, depending on the requirements of a given department.

AP/IB credits: We have not been able to determine whether these credits can replace required Honors courses.

Range and Type of Honors Courses (3.5): We classify the College as a small **departmental honors program,** with a few interdisciplinary honors college classes and considerably more specialized honors classes offered by the various academic departments.

The interdisciplinary courses available in Spring 2014 were five sections of Honors **Writing and Critical Inquiry in the Humanities,** which introduce students to the "study of writing as the vehicle for academic inquiry in the Humanities at the college level. Students will learn the skills necessary for clear, effective communication of ideas through careful attention to the writing process and the examination of a variety of rhetorical and critical practices."

The anthropology honors class was **Critical Thinking and Skepticism,** which asks, "How many people believe most everything they are told, or everything that they read? How can we tell the difference between statements that are based on fact, and those based only on opinion, ideology, error, or falsehood? Why should we care in the first place? This class will help you answer these questions, and hopefully raise many more. We will cover the ways in which your own brain and senses can trick you. We will cover the common mistakes made in reasoning, 'logical fallacies' that can lead even the most critical of thinkers to false conclusions. We will cover several of the most common types of false information that people encounter today, such as psychics, astrology, or complementary and alternative medicine, and will explore why these are problematic."

Genomics & Biotechnology: The Broad Ranging Impact on Mankind presents students the "enormous insights" provided by the sequencing of the genomes of organisms from bacteria to humans. "Almost no aspect of human knowledge has been untouched by the information being compiled. The information gathered has also driven the development of new technologies designed to explore and exploit the information gathered. The goal of this course will be to familiarize students with the nature of the information that can be gathered from genomics and the benefits derived from the new biotechnologies."

The Search for Life Beyond Earth, an honors geology class, explores "how scientists are successfully detecting planets orbiting other stars, determining the environments that led to the origin of life on Earth, and chemical processes and pathways that may have led to the origin of life on Earth and beyond." (Most honors programs do not offer even one geology honors section.) There was one honors section of general chemistry, another in calculus, and an honors physics section. We found one honors psychology class too, Introduction to Behavioral Sciences, but no honors economics section.

An interesting honors political science class was offered by the Rockefeller College of Public Affairs and Policy--**Health and Human Rights,** "an interdisciplinary approach to health and human rights and the contemporary challenges and solutions associated with them. **The course will be taught by physicians and human rights champions Kamiar Alaei and Arash Alaei, with guest lectures from experts in public health, philosophy, social welfare, law, gender studies, public administration and the United Nations, among others.**"

Any discussion of honors programs at UAlbany should also include a summary of the **Financial Analyst Honors Concentration** and the **Honors Program in Criminal Justice.**

UAlbany has the nation's 2nd ranked criminology department, so the honors program in criminal justice is outstanding. **"Students can apply to the Honors Program in the second semester of the sophomore year or the first semester of the junior year.** Minimum requirements for admission include Criminal Justice as a declared first major, an overall GPA not lower than 3.25, and a Criminal Justice GPA not lower than 3.50. Additionally, to remain in the Honors Program, all honors students must maintain a 3.50 GPA in the major."

The **Financial Analyst Honors Concentration** is probably the best of the very few such programs in the nation. "The Financial Analyst Honors Program is **the only honors program in the School of Business.** Outstanding performance in course work is a basic requirement, and you must also demonstrate a passion for finance, attention to detail, strong ethics, and professionalism." The program has a **Boot Camp,** an intensive year-long program to prepare students "for internships and jobs with high-level investment banks and other financial institutions by providing career-focused training, mock interviews and résumé writing." Students are also eligible for selection to the **University at Albany Business Investment Group,** where they can help "manage a diversified investment fund while learning proper research techniques for successful security analysis and portfolio management."

Students in the program also attend a program offered by Training the Street, a Wall Street firm, and are able to visit JP Morgan, Goldman Sachs, Bank of America, and the New York Federal Reserve Bank. The program has an 85% placement rate within three months of graduation. Graduates have gone to work at most of the firms listed above, as well as employment with Siemens, Citigroup, Deutsche Bank, Ernst & Young, IBM, Price Waterhouse, and Berkshire Bank, among many others. Students can compete for scholarships to fund the Level I Certified Financial Analyst Exam. **Completion of the concentration also requires an honors thesis.**

Average Class Size (4.0): Our *estimate* **is that the average honors class size has 22.5** students; the overall average class size for the 50 colleges and programs under review in this edition is 21.2 students.

Adjusted Graduation Rate (4.0): The AGR is not simply the six-year graduation rate of students in the honors college who graduated from the university (*estimated at* **86%**), whether or not the students completed the honors program ("honors completers"). The AGR also reflects the extent to which the honors graduation rate from the university is higher than that for the university as a whole. (The **university-wide rate is 64%,** yielding the 4.0 AGR for the college.) The average **honors** six-year **graduation rate for all 50 programs under review is 89%.**

Ratio of Staff to Honors Students (4.5): Our estimate is that there is 1 staff member for every **110** students. (Mean ratio for all 50 programs is 1 staff member for every 159.8 students.)

Honors Residence Halls (4.0): UAlbany has an architecturally interesting main campus, with four "quads" located at the corners of the Academic Podium, an array of modernist buildings that house many academic departments. Honors students live in State Quad, at either Melville or Steinmetz Hall. The rooms are double suites with a shared living room and bath, but they do not have air conditioning.

Room configurations may include two double rooms, three double rooms, or a combination of two double rooms and a single room. State Quad has many amenities: "its own fitness center, game room, and a newly renovated dining hall."

Prestigious Awards (3.0): UAlbany undergraduates have won 18 Goldwater Scholarships, but the university could benefit from a separate office of prestigious scholarships with the purpose of advising and preparing students for award competition.

Continuation Requirements: 3.25 cumulative GPA

Academic Strengths: In addition to the 2nd ranked criminology program, mentioned above, some of the best departments at UAlbany are sociology, atmospheric science, education, economics, political science, English, and math.

Undergraduate Research: UAlbany has a database called "COS Pivot" that matches students and professors according to their research interests and needs. The university also has an Undergraduate Research Foundation that awards grants for research. Students must provide a letter from their faculty project supervisors in support of the research. The letter must also include a description of the project, a timetable for completion, and a project budget.

Given the quality of the university's program in atmospheric science, students in that department might want to pursue the Ernest F. Hollings Scholarship, an outstanding opportunity for study at a National Oceanic and Atmospheric Administration (NOAA) facility. **The extremely generous Hollings Scholarship** "provides successful undergraduate applicants with awards that include academic assistance (up to a maximum of $8,000 per year) for full-time study during the 9-month academic year; a 10-week, full-time internship position ($650/week) during the summer at a NOAA facility; and, if reappointed, academic assistance (up to a maximum of $8,000) for full-time study during a second 9-month academic year."

Study Abroad: Again, given the strength of UAlbany's criminal justice and atmospheric science departments, students in these majors have some excellent choices for studying abroad (all other majors have great options as well). Criminal justice students can choose one of three universities in the United

Kingdom for study, as well as universities in Copenhagen, Denmark; Nairobi, Kenya; and Cape Town, South Africa. Students in atmospheric science can study at one of two universities in China, another in Seoul, South Korea; and another at the University of Cape Town.

Financial Aid: Many honors students should be eligible for Presidential Scholarships, awarded to the top 10% of UAlbany students. The scholarships are valued at $6,000 for out-of-state students and $3,500 a year for New York residents.

Degree of Difference (Honors students/non-honors students): 3.52 on a scale of 5. Some parents and prospective students might prefer an honors program that in many ways stands apart on campus, while others might prefer a program that is more expansive. The rating here tries to provide an indication of where a given honors program is on the stand apart/expansive spectrum. The rating is based on the difference between (1) the average SAT scores for enrolled honors students and (2) the average test scores for all students in the university as a whole *and* for students with scores at the 75% level or above. A score of 3.5 or higher indicates a high degree of difference. A score of 3.2 to 3.49 indicates a relatively high degree of difference. Finally, a score below 3.2 indicates a modest difference. **Please keep in mind that neither the high nor low selectivity of an honors program determines how effective the program is; this rating is merely "cultural" and *not* qualitative.**

NAME: THE PLAN II HONORS PROGRAM AT THE UNIVERSITY OF TEXAS AT AUSTIN

Date Established: 1935—**one of the oldest honors program among the 50 being reviewed.**

Location: Austin, Texas

University-wide, Full-time Undergraduate Enrollment: 37,083

Honors Enrollment: approximately 700 (mean enrollment of all 50 programs is 1,714).

Review/Admissions Category--IV: Programs with **average SAT scores of 1417 or higher for enrolled students**. Actual average (mean) SAT score for enrolled Plan II students is1423 (721 reading, 702 math; no ACT average is available. High school rank: 70% in top 5%; 17% were Valedictorians or Salutatorians.

Plan II has a holistic admissions process that **requires *two* essays**; credit is **20% for each of the following categories:**

--Personal Essay 1--"Considering your lifetime goals, discuss how your current and future academic and extra-curricular activities might help you achieve your goals."

--Personal Essay 2, Choose A or B--"(A) Describe a setting in which you have collaborated or interacted with people whose experiences and/or beliefs differ from yours. Address your initial feelings, and how those feelings were or were not changed by this experience *or* (B) describe a circumstance, obstacle or conflict in your life, and the skills and resources you used to resolve it. Did it change you? If so, how?"

Essay Criteria are "Content and style; command of language and grace of prose; logical argument and/or creative flair."

--Personal Achievement-- Clubs, community and volunteer service, employment, student government, sports, music, art, religious activities, Scouting, etc., including

- Length and level of commitment
- Breadth and depth, of interests
- Leadership positions and activities
- Awards and honors
- Service to the community and/or dedication to volunteerism
- Work experience

--All quantitative scores and data: SAT, ACT, Class Rank/GPA, AP, IB, SAT Subject tests, dual enrollment credits.

--Breadth & Range: the "Plan II-ness" of the applicant:

--Most subjective criteria

- Broad interests: high school course choices & non-academic choices

• Personal/academic statement (5 sentences in the honors application)
• What will the applicant bring to Plan II?
• Will the applicant make the best use of what Plan II has to offer?

Honors Programs in Admissions Category IV (average SAT of 1417 and higher): Auburn, Clemson, Georgia, Illinois, Kansas, Michigan, Minnesota, North Carolina, Rutgers, South Carolina, UT Austin, Virginia.

Administrative Staff: Plan II has a staff of 7.

FOR ALL "MORTARBOARD" RATINGS BELOW, A SCORE OF 5 IS THE MAXIMUM AND REPRESENTS A COMPARISON OF ALL 50 HONORS COLLEGES AND PROGRAMS:

PERCEPTION* OF UNIVERSITY AS A WHOLE, <u>NOT</u> OF HONORS: 🎓🎓🎓🎓$^{1/2}$

OVERALL HONORS RATING: 🎓🎓🎓🎓🎓

Curriculum Requirements: 🎓🎓🎓🎓$^{1/2}$

Class Range and Type: 🎓🎓🎓🎓🎓

Class Size: 🎓🎓🎓🎓

Adjusted Grad Rate: 🎓🎓🎓🎓$^{1/2}$

Ratio of Staff to Students: 🎓🎓🎓🎓$^{1/2}$

Priority Registration: **No,** but Plan II students have no difficulty registering for Plan II courses, and, as noted below, because they can be in Plan II **and** other outstanding UT Austin honors programs at the same time, they have enhanced access to those honors classes as well.

Honors Housing: 🎓🎓🎓🎓$^{1/2}$

Prestigious Awards: 🎓🎓🎓🎓🎓

*Perception is based on the university's ranking among public universities in the 2014 *U.S. News Best Colleges* report. Please bear in mind that the higher the *U.S. News* ranking, the more difficult it is for an honors college or program to have a rating that improves on the magazine ranking.

Curriculum Requirements (4.5): Plan II is unique in that one of its options is a major and degree in…Plan II. The core curriculum that has always characterized Plan II is more than sufficiently broad and deep to justify a major in its own name. Beyond that, Plan II students can also participate in the university's highly regarded business honors program, can pursue honors engineering simultaneously, and can choose among other, newer options to pursue while remaining in Plan II (see below, Range and Type of Honors Courses). Students cannot, however, participate in both Plan II and the university's liberal arts honors program (LAH).

"Although Plan II Honors is itself a major, almost 75 % of Plan II Honors majors pursue a second (or third) major in the same college (double-majors) or seek simultaneous degrees with a second major in another college (dual-degree). Triple majors are not uncommon. We've seen five majors in four years on more than one occasion (which is certainly not necessary, nor is it necessarily recommended). A dual-degree program means that one of the majors is housed in a different college and they require not only more specific major and college requirements, but additional hours. Dual-degree programs are almost always five-year commitments." **Plan II also provides outstanding preparation for careers in medicine and law. Graduates gain admission to the most prestigious graduate and professional schools in the nation.**

With all these options to consider, we finally concluded that a typical Plan II completion would require a **bare minimum** of about 33 honors credits--though a much higher total is typical. (The curriculum rating is based solely on the total *number* of credit hours required for completion; the *quality* of the courses, however, is reflected in the "Range and Type of Honors Courses" rating below.)

All Plan II students are required to take the core courses in the program: a year-long freshman course in World Literature; a Plan II "signature course" in Fall or Spring of the freshman year; another year-long sequence in the sophomore year, this time in philosophy; Plan II logic or modes of reasoning; two topical junior seminars; Plan II and departmental math, physics, and biology; **and an honors thesis.**

AP credit and high SAT II scores can be applied to some courses, especially the foreign language requirement of four semesters. However, most of the following core requirements listed above "may NOT be satisfied with any AP or SAT II exam."

Range and Type of Honors Courses (5.0): Here is where Plan II, which we classify as a **core honors program,** allows through its flexibility considerable access to many other types of honors courses. (Core honors programs usually do not offer a wide range of departmental or other honors classes outside of their own core requirements.) The other honors programs are business honors, engineering honors, the Health Science Scholars honors program, the Dean's Scholars program in the sciences, the Turing honors program in computer science, and the Polymathic Scholars program, which allows science students to go far beyond their majors to design "a substantial portion" of their curriculum.

Plan II student enrollment in these other honors programs ranges from as low as 8 or 9 to as high as 57(business honors) in any given year. All of these honors programs also have their own honors class sections, and Plan II students with overlapping enrollment (and other Plan II students who talk their way into the classes) may choose some of these excellent additional courses.

A few examples from the Dean's Scholars Program: The End of Us...Rogue Medicine: Groundbreaking or Quackery...and Pseudo-science and the Public: Perception of Science and Scientist. Business honors classes are relatively small and modeled on an MBA-style curriculum. "BHP classes use real-world issues as the foundation, and the case-based curriculum will put you in front of challenges that companies currently face or faced in the past." There are BHP honors sections for finance, statistical modeling, financial accounting, marketing, management, business law and ethics, and many others.

Of the previously mentioned **Plan II core courses**, the year-long freshman course in World Literature (10-11 sections a year) is a rigorous writing-intensive sequence. The "signature courses" emphasize discussion, critical thinking, and (yes, again) writing, and 12-15 of these are offered each year. They include: American Animals: A Cultural History; A History of the Self; Art, Sport, and the Meaning of Life; **and our favorite, College and Controversy: The Histories, Purposes & Cultures of American Universities.**

And let's not forget the **junior seminars, (12-14 each semester)**. Examples:

- The Veil: History, Culture, and Politics
- Plagues, History, Ethics and Literature
- Law, Neuroethics & Brain Policies
- Constitutional Design & the Art and Science of Contracting with Others
- Finally, almost any Plan II student or alum will tell you that **one of the toughest classes you will have at UT Austin will be Plan II advanced theoretical physics.**

Average Class Size (4.0): Most Plan II seminars and year-long series courses meet in small sections that average 14.4 students, but the physics sections might have up to 50 students. The overall class size for Plan II is 23 students per section. However, when we include an estimate of Plan II students in business honors classes, the average rises to **24.4 students per section**. The business honors classes tend to have 25-35 students, although we believe the Lyceum sections are smaller. For all 50 programs in this review, the average honors class size is 21.2.

Adjusted Graduation Rate (4.5): The AGR is not simply the six-year graduation rate of students in the honors program who graduated from the university **(94.0%),** whether or not the students completed the honors program ("honors completers"). It also reflects the extent to which the honors graduation rate from the university is higher than that for the university as a whole. (The **university-wide rate is 79%**, yielding the 4.5 AGR for the college.) *The average six-year* ***honors*** *graduation rate for all 50* **programs** under review **is 89%.**

Ratio of Staff to Honors Students (4.5): Our estimate is that there is 1 staff member for every **100.0** students. (Median ratio for all 50 programs is 1 staff member for every 159.8 students.)

Honors Residence Halls (4.5): The Honors Living Community, comprised of three halls in the "Quad" (Andrews, Blanton and Carothers), houses approximately 500 outstanding students, most of whom are in one of the university's undergraduate honors programs. The dorms are old but remodeled--and they are in the best location possible, close to the west mall and most classrooms.

Both honors and non-honors students can live in the halls, located very conveniently near the "Drag" on Guadalupe Street. The dorms are traditional, with corridor baths. They are air conditioned. "About 45% of Plan II first-years choose honors halls."

Prestigious Awards (5.0): UT Austin is one of the leaders among public universities in the number of prestigious awards won by its students. There is a long and distinguished history of winning postgraduate awards, especially Rhodes, Marshall, and Truman Scholarships (second in Marshall Scholars among public universities, behind only UC Berkeley). We track National Science Foundation Graduate Research Fellowships for the most recent three years, and university graduates are also second nationally behind UC Berkeley in earning NSF grants. UT Austin's record in earning Fulbright Student awards is likewise impressive. During the early years of the Goldwater Scholarship history, UT Austin did not compete as well as its rankings in the STEM disciplines would suggest. In the last decade or so, however, the university has done very well in the Goldwater competition, with multiple winners in several of those years. **Plan II students have won about two-thirds of the UT Truman Scholarships, and more than half of the UT Marshall Scholarships, despite the small size of the honors program.**

Continuation Requirements: 3.25 GPA

Academic Strengths: Along with UC Berkeley, Michigan, Wisconsin, and UCLA, UT Austin has one of the highest rated faculties in the nation among all universities public or private, 5th among public institutions and 14th among all universities. **One of the best things about Plan II and other honors programs at UT Austin is that they concentrate this excellence in the midst of an extremely large campus.** Of the 15 academic departments that we track, **the average national ranking for all 15 disciplines at UT Austin is 14th or higher in the nation.** The very best of the best include business, education, computer science, earth sciences, and engineering, all in the top 10 nationally. In the top 15 nationally are chemistry, math, physics, psychology, and sociology. In addition, English and history are in the top 20 nationally.

Undergraduate Research: The Office of the Vice President for Research awards up to $1,000 for undergraduate research fellowships each semester. The Plan II thesis requirement means that each graduate must do original research, typically in the major department or in a topic approved by Plan II.

Plan II and other university students have access to an excellent research database, called EUREKA, "a searchable database designed to support undergraduate participation in research and creative activity across campus. EUREKA includes profiles for University of Texas at Austin faculty members with information about their research interests and links to their department web pages."

The advantage for undergraduates is that they can readily identify faculty who are doing research that matches their interests and search for research opportunities. Students simply do a search of the database to find faculty members who share your interests.

EUREKA also offers a projects section where research assistant positions are posted by faculty members. "The projects list is by no means comprehensive; faculty members may be willing to work with you even if they have not posted an opening."

Study Abroad: UT Austin has received national recognition for the number of students studying abroad, for the duration of study-abroad experiences, and for the special features of study abroad. **There are more than 600 study-abroad options for students at the university.** More than half of Plan II students study abroad, and the program itself offers information sessions and advising about study-abroad options.

In addition, Plan II offers its own "Maymesters" in Costa Rica and Rome, Italy. In Costa Rica, the Plan II students take a course titled Land Use Issues in Rainforest Conservation. The Rome course, in the history and culture of the Roman Empire, provides credit for a junior seminar **and** an upper-division humanities course.

Financial Aid: Seventeen of the thirty-eight current Forty Acres Scholars are in the Plan II Honors Program. This scholarship program is the premier full-ride, merit-based scholarship at The University of Texas at Austin. All Forty Acres Scholars receive handsome funding. Their tuition, books, and fees are covered, as well as a living stipend. Each scholar also receives financial support for enrichment activities, including a community service project, an internship, and a global experience--or a combination of each. However, UT Austin, along with all of the UC campuses, Washington, Michigan and Virginia appear to have **stopped using their own funds to sponsor National Merit Scholarships**, although all enroll a substantial number of merit scholars, many of whose scholarships are funded by other sources. (Please refer to the introductory sections on National Merit Scholarships.)

There are at least seven Plan II Honors scholarships that are awarded primarily on a financial need-basis; however, some scholarships are awarded strictly for merit. Most awards range from $1,000 to $5,000 for an academic year, although a few larger awards are available.

"Most, but not all, of the Plan II endowed scholarships have a donor specified need-based component. However it's important to make a few strong points: First, applicants with serious financial need usually have that need met through state and federal entitlement programs funding almost all the costs of attendance....Plan II is often unable to give those students a Plan II scholarship without affecting the level of grants and scholarships they have already received."

"Often the admitted applicants and continuing students who are left with 'unmet' need are those who did not qualify for financial aid and those whose families made too much to qualify for entitlement programs." So, a majority of Plan II scholarships are awarded to these families on the basis of their form of "unmet" financial need.

Degree of Difference (Honors students/non-honors students): 2.73 on a scale of 5. Some parents and prospective students might prefer an honors program that in many ways stands apart on campus, while others might prefer a program that is more expansive. The rating here tries to provide an indication of where a given honors program is on the stand apart/expansive spectrum. The rating is based on the difference between (1) the average SAT scores for enrolled honors students and (2) the average test scores for all students in the university as a whole *and* for students with scores at the 75% level or above. A score of 3.5 or higher indicates a high degree of difference. A score of 3.2 to 3.49 indicates a relatively high degree of difference. Finally, a score below 3.2 indicates a modest difference. **Please keep in mind that neither the high nor low selectivity of an honors program determines how effective the program is; this rating is merely "cultural" and *not* qualitative.**

NAME: UNIVERSITY OF UTAH HONORS COLLEGE

Date Established: 1962

Location: Salt Lake City, Utah

University Full-time Undergraduate Enrollment: 17,518

Honors Enrollment: 2,500 students; (the mean size of all 50 programs is 1,714.)

Review/Admissions Category--II: Programs with **average SAT scores of 1343--1382 for enrolled students**. Actual average (mean) ACT score for enrolled honors students is 30, and the *estimated* SAT equivalent would be 1345. The average high school GPA is 3.90 (unweighted).

Minimum Admission: High school GPA 3.50 unweighted. The college is now relying on a more holistic admissions process.

Honors Programs in Admissions Category II (average SAT scores of 1343-1382): Alabama, Delaware, Florida State, LSU, Massachusetts, Missouri, North Carolina State, Ohio University, Temple, Purdue, UCLA, Utah, Vermont, and Wisconsin.

Administrative Staff: The honors college now has a staff of 13.

FOR ALL "MORTARBOARD" RATINGS BELOW, A SCORE OF 5 IS THE MAXIMUM AND REPRESENTS A COMPARISON WITH ALL 50 HONORS COLLEGES AND PROGRAMS:

PERCEPTION* OF UNIVERSITY AS A WHOLE, NOT OF HONORS: 🎓🎓🎓

OVERALL HONORS RATING: 🎓🎓🎓^{1/2}

Curriculum Requirements: 🎓🎓🎓^{1/2}

Class Range and Type: 🎓🎓🎓🎓

Class Size: 🎓🎓🎓🎓^{1/2}

Adjusted Grad Rate: 🎓🎓🎓🎓

Ratio of Staff to Students: 🎓🎓🎓

Priority Registration: No. *(This is the main reason the College does not have 4 mortarboards overall.)*

Honors Housing: 🎓🎓🎓🎓🎓

Prestigious Awards: 🎓🎓🎓🎓

*Perception is based on the university's ranking among public universities in the 2014 *U.S. News Best Colleges* report. Please bear in mind that the better the U.S. News ranking, the more difficult it is for an honors college or program to have a rating that equals or improves on the magazine ranking.

Curriculum Requirements (3.5): The College has two levels of completion, the highest being the Honors Bachelor's Degree. The degree requires a total of 24 credits, as follows:

- Four honors "core" courses, which must include two courses from the honors Intellectual Traditions series, one honors writing course, and one honors science course.
- Three honors elective courses, most of which can be other honors college courses, such as the honors praxis labs, departmental honors classes, study-abroad courses, or internships.
- One 3-credit **thesis** course.

Honors "Praxis Lab" courses typically take a topic and ask students to confront the issues and follow up with solutions or projects that are thoughtful, collaborative, and creative. Recent examples are listed below under the Range and Type of Honors Courses category.

The total honors degree requirement is a minimum of 24 honors credits.

The **honors certificate** requires two Intellectual Traditions courses, one writing course, and two electives from departmental honors courses, internships, study-abroad, or praxis lab credits.

AP/IB credits are **not** counted as replacements for honors courses.

Range and Type of Honors Courses (4.0): Although the College does not specifically refer to most honors courses as seminars, many appear to be interdisciplinary and most are small in class size, so we will go ahead and call most of them **core** classes. Of the 40 honors college sections, five are writing/composition classes, four are research sections, and four more are honors praxis sections. That leaves more than 25 sections spanning the arts, humanities, social sciences, and sciences, including nine sections ("lecture classes") in the Intellectual Traditions series. These are indeed the core of the honors college, and a strong core it is, one of the best among the 50 programs under review. (The 4.0 rating reflects the relative lack of specialized departmental honors sections; the seminar/honors-only lectures and seminars received an excellent rating.) The College does an outstanding job of providing a sweeping intellectual context for its students, teaching them how major ideas have shaped the present world, and will shape the future as well.

Accordingly, there is at least one section of the Intellectual Traditions series for each major topical/chronological period: Antiquity and the Beginning of the Modern Era; Flowering of the Common Era & the Threshold of Modernity; and The Rise of Modernity. Most of the sections focus on topics from the last two periods.

The **Antiquity** course "examines a variety of texts and thinkers from earliest times to the beginnings of the Common Era, with a focus on the ideas that have had an enduring, foundational influence on our understanding of both ourselves and the world in which we live, and that have thereby become canonical works." These may include "Epic of Gilgamesh, Homer, Sappho, Greek tragedy, the philosophy of Plato and Aristotle, Chinese Daoist (Taoist) texts, the Bible, and early Church fathers."

Flowering of the Common Era typically involves readings by or about "St. Augustine, the Qur'an, St. Thomas Aquinas, Dante, Chaucer, Christine de Pizan, Machiavelli, and Shakespeare....Themes that are covered may include: free will and divine justice, the concept of Nature, the Crusades and the conflict between Christianity and Islam, the notion of sin and hell, Renaissance humanism and secularism, and the Reformation."

The Rise of Modernity classes focus on issues such as "the development of modern science and technology, the tension between science and religion, the modern state and totalitarianism, the impact of evolutionary theory and developments in psychology on conceptions of the person....Readings may include Galileo, Descartes, Hobbes, Locke, Rousseau, Jane Austen, Freud, Marx, Virginia Woolf, and Sartre…"

A **heavy writing component** is present in most honors classes, but even so, there are five honors sections focused only on "writing for learning, textual analysis, writing from research, and collaborative writing." In addition, there are four sections of Research University, a 3-credit course "designed to facilitate students' thinking and writing as members of specific disciplinary communities (i.e., engineering, history, psychology, etc.). To do so, students will study and develop different types of thinking and writing skills that are useful across all disciplines, yet are employed uniquely by them." Not only is the writing emphasis commendable in its own right; it is the perfect complement to a curriculum based on sequence and coherence.

Two honors courses in **American Institutions** take up "the idea of equality as a lens to see American history from colonization to the present and explore the emergence and transformations of American democracy and social and political ideals. Equality emerged out of slavery and other harsh inequalities and has always meant different things to different Americans."

Another notable course is **Constructing the Ideal Human Being,** in part an ironic title because the purpose of the course is to explore the dangers of trying to force humans into ideal constructs, such as the "Soviet attempts to create New People, free of selfishness and exploitation, creative and fulfilled. The [course] will examine how all these issues evolved after the horrors of the holocaust and the Stalinist purges, when technologies of the 20th century increasingly fell under question."

Four more honors classes involve science and technology. They include Evidence of Evolution; Exploring Science II; Discovering Complex Systems; and Modern Drug Discovery. And there is the 2-credit **Innovation Roadmap course,** which explores "the big problems and big questions facing the world today. Students will create a personal learning roadmap specific to their individual area of interest. The process of innovation and problem solving will be explored with a panel of interdisciplinary experts. Roadmaps will be designed to enhance academic majors and student interests.

Also highly commendable are the previously mentioned **Praxis Lab** classes. In them, students "work collaboratively to find original solutions to problems our society faces. A faculty member will guide the work of the students participating in the Lab. This experience will greatly enhance students' undergraduate education and prepare them to become leaders in the community upon graduation. Scholarship support will also be available to students participating in the program. **The Praxis Labs are also designed to nurture a new generation of community leaders and intellectuals committed to collaborative thinking and to provide students with practical experience in team research and problem solving."**

When it comes to more specialized honors courses in the academic disciplines, we found about 20 sections offered in Spring 2014, but notably absent were math and physics sections. At least one departmental honors section was offered in biology, chemistry, education psychology, finance, accounting, business, architecture, and art.

"Hinckley Honors Internships are offered through collaboration with the Hinckley Institute of Politics. The Hinckley Institute offers national and international internships to all honors students regardless of major," the Associate Dean tells us.

"The local becomes global in the new 18 credit hour **Ecology and Legacy Honors Integrated Minor, the majority of which will be earned during an intensive six week summer block. The science, arts and humanities minor is strongly place-based with two week sections at the University of Utah and the Great Salt Lake; Centennial Valley, Montana; and the Peninsula Valdez in Patagonia, Argentina."**

Average Class Size (4.5): The **average class size is 19.6 students**, versus the average for all 50 programs under review--21.2 students.
.

Adjusted Graduation Rate (4.0): The AGR is not simply the six-year graduation rate of students in the **honors program** who graduated from the university **(80%),** whether or not the students completed the honors program ("honors completers"). The AGR also reflects the extent to which the honors graduation rate from the university is higher than that for the university as a whole. The **university-wide rate is 59%.** The average honors six-year **graduation rate for all 50 programs under review is 89%.**

Ratio of Staff to Honors Students (3.0): Our estimate is that there is 1 staff member for every **236.4** students. (Mean ratio for all 50 programs is 1 staff member for every 159.8 students.)

Honors Residence Halls (5.0): When the name on the primary honors residence hall is "Marriott," the chances are excellent that the hall will be remarkable--and so it is. The Donna Garff Marriott Honors Residential Community (MHRC) houses 309 honors students, 80% of them in suite-style rooms and the other 20% in traditional double rooms with hall baths.

Freshmen and upperclassmen can choose from **eight living/learning themes in the MHRC:** First Year Experience; Outdoor Leadership and Education; Science and Engineering; Early Access and Leadership; Intellectual Traditions, Business; Engineering; or the Thesis Mentoring Community. The MHRC is fully air conditioned with multiple lounges and on-site laundry. **Each apartment suite also has its own kitchen.** The nearest dining hall is at the Heritage Center, but the MHRC has its own convenience store and deli. Other amenities include cable TV with HBO package, a ski wax room, indoor bicycle storage, an honors library, and high-speed internet.

Twelve honors upperclassmen can live in the **Honors Law House,** a small living/learning community that is half suite-style and half traditional double rooms. Another 12 students can live in the similarly configured **Honors Social Justice House** or the **Thesis Mentoring Community.** Thirty freshmen are also housed in **Sage Point Hall,** featuring suite-style singles and doubles. The nearest dining for all four of these is at Heritage Center.

Prestigious Awards (4.0): University of Utah undergraduates have won a very respectable 31 Goldwater Scholarships awarded to outstanding students in the STEM fields. Most impressive is that university grads have won 22 Rhodes Scholarships and 23 Truman Scholarships, ranking 5th among public universities in Truman awards. The University of Utah is now also eligible to nominate students for the Churchill Scholarship.

In the past year Honors students have received (1 each) Truman, Gates Cambridge, and Udall Scholarships.

Continuation Requirements: 3.50 cumulative GPA

Academic Strengths: The University of Utah has some outstanding academic departments, including five that rank in the top 50 nationally among all universities public and private. The most recognized departments are math (34), chemistry (35), computer science (40), earth sciences (42), and business (47). Additional departments ranked in the top 70 or better include biology (55), engineering (59), English (63), physics (65), and psychology (67).

Undergraduate Research: "Honors students engage in a wide range of undergraduate research as part of their Honors Thesis Project. We have designated faculty in each department who help inform and direct Honors students to research opportunities in their major. Through the University's Undergraduate Research Opportunities Program (UROP) Honors students receive financial support for their research, present their research in a campus-wide Undergraduate Research Symposium and publish their research abstracts in the Undergraduate Research Abstracts Journal."

Study Abroad: The "U" offers 105 study-abroad programs, including **Cuba: Community, Complexity, and Change** during Fall break. Students go to Havana and Cien Fuegos for study. Also notable are the Freshman Business Scholars programs, one each in Paris and London. There are intensive language programs in Kiel, Germany; Grenoble, France; Siena, Italy; Osaka, Japan; Saratov, Russia; and Oviedo, Spain. We also like the summer program **Underground London: Crime and Disorder, 1720-1890.**

The U also offered $220,000 in study-abroad scholarships last year, and other scholarships are available within academic departments and the **Honors College.**

Financial Aid: The Associate Dean tells us that "85% of the students accepted into Honors receive individual scholarships from the University of Utah. Additionally, Honors students have access to approximately $125,000 in achievement and completion-based scholarships through the Honors College."

The **Honors College scholarships** include the following:

George S. and Dolores Dore Eccles Distinguished Scholarship--"This is the most prestigious award offered to incoming freshman at the U…recipients of the award receive a truly transformative educational experience through enrollment in the U's Honors College and guaranteed admittance to the U of U graduate program of their choice upon completion of their Bachelor's degree."

Beck Science Achievement Scholarship--This award is given to students continuing or beginning their education at the University of Utah's Honors College. "Qualified applicants must demonstrate tangible skill and interest in **science-related** areas of study, as well as commitment to attaining an Honors degree and completing their education with high academic standing."

C. Charles Hetzel III Scholarship--"This scholarship fund provides educational assistance to a deserving Honors student who demonstrates high academic achievement. Up to $10,000 may be awarded. The award will be distributed over a period of two semesters toward tuition cost. Half of the scholarship funds will be deposited in the student's tuition account at the beginning of the first semester, and the other half will be deposited in the student's tuition account for use in the second semester."

Duane Harris Butcher Endowed Scholarship--"This scholarship is for students in the Honors College who are descendants of the Utah pioneers who emigrated from 1847-1897. Applicants will demonstrate appreciation for heritage and community through a one-page essay and demonstrate talent or aptitude in a chosen field."

There are about 15 additional scholarships available to honors students at the "U."

Degree of Difference (Honors students/non-honors students): 3.11 on a scale of 5. Some parents and prospective students might prefer an honors program that in many ways stands apart on campus, while others might prefer a program that is more expansive. The rating here tries to provide an indication of where a given honors program is on the stand apart/expansive spectrum. The rating is based on the difference between (1) the average SAT scores for enrolled honors students and (2) the average test scores for all students in the university as a whole *and* for students with scores at the 75% level or above. A score of 3.5 or higher indicates a high degree of difference. A score of 3.2 to 3.49 indicates a relatively high degree of difference. Finally, a score below 3.2 indicates a modest difference. **Please keep in mind that neither the high nor low selectivity of an honors program determines how effective the program is; this rating is merely "cultural" and *not* qualitative.**

NAME: UNIVERSITY OF VERMONT HONORS COLLEGE

Date Established: 2003

Location: Burlington, Vermont

University Full-time Undergraduate Enrollment: 9,956

Honors Enrollment: 826 (mean size of all 50 programs is 1,714).

Review/Admissions Category II: Programs with **average SAT scores of 1343--1382 for enrolled students.** Actual average (mean) three-part SAT score for enrolled honors students is 2066, and the actual average ACT score is 31.2. Average SAT critical reading is 696, math 677. The average (mean) high school GPA is 3.82, and the median high school GPA is 3.94. Vermont Honors College is definitely in the high range for Admissions Category II, and could be in Category III if we used median rather than mean test scores for assigning programs to an admissions category.

Desired Admission Requirements: As the figures above indicate, the **most likely candidates for admission** would have an SAT of 2100 or so, ACT of 32, and would have to be in at least the top 10% of their high school class. The *median* SAT is exactly 2100.

Honors Programs in Admissions Category II (average SAT scores of 1343-1382): Alabama, Delaware, Florida State, LSU, Massachusetts, Missouri, North Carolina State, Ohio University, Temple, Purdue, UCLA, Utah, Vermont, and Wisconsin.

Administrative Staff: The Honors College has a staff of 7.

FOR ALL "MORTARBOARD" RATINGS BELOW, A SCORE OF 5 IS THE MAXIMUM AND REPRESENTS A COMPARISON WITH ALL 50 HONORS COLLEGES AND PROGRAMS:

PERCEPTION* OF UNIVERSITY AS A WHOLE, NOT OF HONORS: 🎓🎓🎓🎓

OVERALL HONORS RATING: 🎓🎓🎓^{1/2}

Curriculum Requirements: 🎓🎓🎓**

Class Range and Type: 🎓🎓🎓🎓^{1/2}

Class Size: 🎓🎓🎓🎓^{1/2}

Adjusted Grad Rate: 🎓🎓🎓

Ratio of Staff to Students: 🎓🎓🎓🎓^{1/2}

Priority Registration: Yes: "The UVM Honors College has a two-tiered system for priority registration. All HCOL students have at minimum in-class priority registration: they have the opportunity to register for all classes half an hour before the standard registration time for students in their class year (based on credits completed at the end of the previous semester). Students in highly structured majors, primarily in the professional programs and sciences, have overall priority registration status: they register the first day of registration week, before all other undergrads at the university, along with a small number of non-HCOL students who also have overall priority registration (some athletes, students with accommodations (ACCESS), etc.)."

Honors Housing: 🎓🎓🎓🎓¹/²

Prestigious Awards: 🎓🎓🎓¹/²

*Perception is based on the university's ranking among public universities in the 2014 U.S. News Best Colleges report. Please bear in mind that the better the U.S. News ranking, the more difficult it is for an honors college or program to have a rating that equals or improves on the magazine ranking.

**Curriculum Requirements (3.0): The relatively modest completion requirement of 21-22 credit hours is the main reason the UVM Honors College does not have an Overall Rating of 4.0. The curriculum metric only reflects the quantity of honors credits required, not the quality of the curriculum or teaching.

"The Honors College experience begins with a Fall semester course, *The Pursuit of Knowledge*, taught in the seminar format to classes of 21 students. In the Spring semester, first-year HCOL students take one section of HCOL 086, *Ways of Knowing*, a selection of special topics courses the majority of which fulfill one course of the University's two-course diversity requirement. Each of these courses applies some of the foundational knowledge learned in the first semester to particular sets of circumstances, often involving race and culture in the U.S. and beyond." The first-year requirement is 6 credits. Incoming students should be willing to participate very actively in the first-year seminars:

"Faculty teaching the first-year courses expect students not only to defend their opinions verbally but also in writing. The courses are designed to be writing-intensive, and to provide specialized writing instruction and support as students make the transition to college."

The work begins even before classes commence. Incoming first-year students receive a book to read at the June Orientation before classes begin. The students must then "**complete a two-page essay that is due on the first day of class in the Fall."**

On most Thursday evenings during regular sessions, all honors students attend a plenary lecture series that is also open to the entire university community.

Each semester, **sophomores** take a three-credit honors seminar, "choosing from an extensive slate of offerings created for Honors College students by schools and colleges throughout the university. Topics vary from year to year."

During their **junior year**, students take a 3-credit honors course along with a 1-credit thesis preparation seminar. Also during their junior year students are required to take up undergraduate research and encouraged to study-abroad. In **senior year,** students complete a 6-credit honors thesis, typically in their major department.

AP/IB credits are **not** counted as replacements for Honors College courses.

Range and Type of Honors Courses (4.5): The UVM Honors College is one of several classic **core honors programs**, normally well below the average size of most programs. Core programs emphasize centralized, small seminars and co-curricular experiences in the first two years and a decentralized approach to the last two years, when students engage in departmental research and thesis work. Upper-division specialization may or may not include departmental honors seminars and lectures.

Similar core programs are at Clark Honors College at the University of Oregon, the Campuswide Honors Program at UC Irvine, the Maine Honors College, the Kentucky Honors Program, the Washington Honors Program, and the Washington State Honors College. With so much focus on seminars, the rating for these core programs depends mostly on the number and variety of the seminar sections and less on the departmental honors classes, often scarce in core program offerings.

The UVM Honors College does an excellent job of summarizing the curriculum requirements and the courses available. The total number of seminars offered in Spring 2014 was 24, including 10 first-year seminars and 14 sophomore seminars, a most impressive number of sections for a relatively small program. In addition, the coherence of the two-year sequence is highly commendable. All in all, the UVM honors seminars rank with the best in the nation.

The Fall first-year courses are topics under the rubric **The Pursuit of Knowledge.** The seminars are organized to address the following questions:

- How do we understand rationalism? How do we understand empiricism? And what about a way of thinking that we might call narrative knowledge--a way of constructing the world through the stories we tell about it and ourselves?
- How do different disciplines and professions (the natural sciences, medicine, literature, etc.) engage in (and sometimes complicate) these different ways of thinking about knowledge--rational, empirical, narrative?
- How might ways of pursuing knowledge that we take for granted (in North America, for instance) be challenged by the way certain non-Western cultures conceive of knowing?

"Students read and discuss challenging and thought-provoking texts such as Descartes' *Meditations*, Hume's *Inquiry Concerning Human Understanding*, V.S. Ramachandran's work on neuroscience, Anne Fadiman's *The Spirit Catches You*, and Mary Shelley's *Frankenstein*." Hume and Descartes for freshmen…now that's about as challenging as it gets.

In the Spring semester, the overriding topic is **Ways of Knowing.** Seminars offered in Spring 2014 included Reading and Writing the Racialized Self; **Religion and Ways of Knowing;** The Construction of Race in American Politics; and **Happiness.**

Reading this list, who wouldn't want to know about **Happiness?** Taught by the college Dean in Spring 2014, the course considers "the theme of happiness from an interdisciplinary perspective, using history, psychology, philosophy, literary analysis, and the scrutiny of current political, economic, scientific and moral questions to illuminate a subject of great personal and public importance. Throughout, a concern will be to consider how the concept of happiness has changed over time and is viewed across cultures."

Religion and Ways of Knowing, "encompasses two related but distinct questions: 'How do religious people know?' and 'How do we know religion?' And of course the distinction blurs if 'we' or any one of us is religious….the problems of defining religion…have engaged many of the great thinkers of the modern West, and continue to challenge our everyday life in a very religiously diverse world." Readings include *When God Talks Back: Understanding the American Evangelical Relationship with God* and *A Radical Jew: Paul and the Politics of Identity.*

The 14 **sophomore seminars** in Spring 2014 are at least as impressive. **The Texture of Memory,** among our favorites that we have reviewed, recognizes that memory is "essential to our understanding of ourselves, of our collective past and present and our existence as humans. But how does memory work? Which parts of our brain are responsible for our memories? What happens when these parts do not function? Can memory be manipulated? What role does memory play for the formation of identity?"

Other sophomore seminars include **The Meaning of Freedom; Ecological Gaming; The Arab Spring; and Imitating Nature.**

Once UVM Honors students complete this excellent two-year sequence, the only remaining Honors College sections are two 1-credit thesis preparation classes. At the departmental level the number of advanced courses preceding the thesis varies, but a total of 3 credits plus a 6-credit thesis is about average. It is not unusual for some of the departmental sections to earn the honors designation through a contract requirement. Very few departmental courses, other than thesis-related sections, have an official "honors" designation. We found a section of honors agricultural life sciences, political science (a senior seminar), a nutrition/sustainability class, and what appears to be one each in mechanical engineering and environmental studies. **Prospective students who want as many *honors* math, science, engineering, economics, and other specialized courses as possible will not find them at UVM Honors College, although certainly the university offers a wide selection of these courses. On the other hand, students *of any major* who want an outstanding college experience that has a very "liberal arts college" feel to it should really enjoy the Honors College.**

Evidence of the liberal arts bent of most Honors College students can be found in the number of students who are enrolled in research/thesis sections in the various academic departments. The majority of senior honors students doing research are in English, history, anthropology, biology, psychology, political science, theatre, and environmental studies.

Average Class Size (4.5): The average UHP honors class has **15.2 students.** The average class size for all 50 programs under review is 21.2 students.

Adjusted Graduation Rate (3.0): The relatively low rating in this category is perplexing, and we do not have an explanation. The AGR is not simply the six-year graduation rate of students in the honors college who graduated from the university **(80%),** whether or not the students completed the honors program ("honors completers"). The AGR also reflects the extent to which the honors graduation rate from the university is higher than that for the university as a whole. (The **university-wide rate is almost as high at 76%,** yielding the relatively low 3.0 AGR for the college.) The average honors six-year **graduation rate for all 50 programs under review is 89%.**

Ratio of Staff to Honors Students (4.5): Our estimate is that there is 1 staff member for every **118** students. (Mean ratio for all 50 programs is 1 staff member for every 159.8 students.)

Honors Residence Halls (4.5): University Heights North houses about 400 honors first-year students and upperclassmen in air-conditioned, suite-style rooms with shared baths between suites. Two laundry rooms are on site. Two dining options are nearby: Harris/Millis Dining Hall with fixed-price menus for every meal, and the University Marché, "a retail venue with multiple dining platforms including an open-concept Euro Kitchen offering plated lunch and dinner entrees, and a great selection of daily offerings from their deli case."

"University Heights North residence hall provides housing for Honors College students in a wide variety of spacious rooms in suite options, as well as single rooms," the Assistant Dean tells us. "In addition, the complex has two classrooms, many study lounges, and a multipurpose room for meetings, lectures, and dinners. Faculty-in-residence play in important role in the HCOL community, leading book and film discussions and serving as advisors to groups of students. Because the HCOL classrooms and administrative offices are also located in UHN, students have easy access to advising and support from the staff and faculty."

Prestigious Awards (3.5): UVM graduates have won 10 Rhodes Scholarships and 10 Truman Scholarships. Given the small size of the university as a whole, UVM students also have a solid record of earning Fulbright Students Scholarships for study and teaching in other countries.

Continuation Requirements: 3.20 cumulative GPA

Academic Strengths: Among the strongest departments at UVM are biology, environmental studies, neuroscience, anthropology, environmental engineering, business, and education.

Undergraduate Research: Each year University of Vermont students are awarded more than 100 undergraduate research grants in nine different award categories from the Office of Undergraduate Research. Awards include the Summer Research Award (a summer award that provides students with research funds and a living stipend to do research full time), the Simon Family Fellowship (for students doing community-based research), and the Public Impact Awards (for students doing research in conjunction with an internship in the public service sector). Grant amounts vary from $250-$5,000. In addition, UVM's Office of Undergraduate Research provides travel stipend and research development funds to students who need to travel to present their research at conferences or to participate in workshops.

The University of Vermont Honors College has additional research grants available to support its students. There are two Honors College-specific award programs in the college: The UROP program and the Reidel Awards. These awards support students in research they are undertaking as a part of their Honors College thesis.

Study Abroad: It is extremely important for UVM students to meet with advisors in their major and minor fields at least 15 months before the study-abroad experience. Honors College students also need to meet with their advisor in the College. UVM has a full range of exchange and faculty-lead programs. UVM and federal financial aid may be available to assist with costs of **Buckham and Oaxaca semester programs and, occasionally, UVM short-term faculty-led programs.**

The **Buckham** Overseas Study Program (BOSP) is for **English majors only** to study at the University of Kent (UKC) in Canterbury in England. BOSP scholars may choose from three different periods to go abroad: the entire year or Period I only (October -December), or Period II only (January -June).

The **Oaxaca semester** offers Spanish Language immersion and three diverse but interrelated academic tracks for students for students majoring in Food Systems, Global Health, Botany, and Music.

Financial Aid: Many honors students would certainly be eligible for Presidential Scholarships, awarded to the most academically talented out-of-state first year students admitted to UVM. Recipients typically rank in the top 20% of their graduating class and have a minimum 1800 SAT CR/M/W, or 26 ACT composite, and are selected based on the application for admissions. They are eligible for a four-year (eight-semester) merit scholarship of up to $15,000 annually. No separate application is required. A cumulative 3.00 grade point average and enrollment in 12 or more credits per semester is required for renewal.

Degree of Difference (Honors students/non-honors students): 3.09 on a scale of 5. Some parents and prospective students might prefer an honors program that in many ways stands apart on campus, while others might prefer a program that is more expansive. The rating here tries to provide an indication of where a given honors program is on the stand apart/expansive spectrum. The rating is based on the difference between (1) the average SAT scores for enrolled honors students and (2) the average test scores for all students in the university as a whole *and* for students with scores at the 75% level or above. A score of 3.5 or higher indicates a high degree of difference. A score of 3.2 to 3.49 indicates a relatively high degree of difference. Finally, a score below 3.2 indicates a modest difference. **Please keep in mind that neither the high nor low selectivity of an honors program determines how effective the program is; this rating is merely "cultural" and *not* qualitative.**

NAME: ECHOLS SCHOLARS PROGRAM, UNIVERSITY OF VIRGINIA

Date Established: 1960

Location: Charlottesville, Virginia

University Full-time Undergraduate Enrollment: 14,928

Honors Enrollment: *Estimated* at 925 (mean size of all 50 programs is 1,714).

Review/Admissions Category IV: Programs with **average SAT scores of 1417 or higher for enrolled students**. *Estimated* average (mean) three-part SAT score for enrolled Echols Scholars is 2240-2260; ACT average is 34. Average high school rank is the top 1-3%.

Honors Programs in Admissions Category IV (average SAT of 1417 and higher): Auburn, Clemson, Georgia, Illinois, Kansas, Michigan, Minnesota, North Carolina, Rutgers, South Carolina, UT Austin, Virginia.

Administrative Staff: For purposes of computing the staff metric for our rating system, **we assigned a full-time equivalent staff of 7 to the Echols Program.** Two administrative staff members are the Echols Dean and the Director--but one of their functions is to assign each Echols Scholar to a faculty advisor, who is often a tenured professor. Twenty faculty advisors from about a dozen departments work with incoming and continuing Echols Scholars.

FOR ALL "MORTARBOARD" RATINGS BELOW, A SCORE OF 5 IS THE MAXIMUM AND REPRESENTS A COMPARISON WITH ALL 50 HONORS COLLEGES AND PROGRAMS:

PERCEPTION* OF UNIVERSITY AS A WHOLE, NOT OF HONORS: 🎓🎓🎓🎓🎓

OVERALL HONORS RATING: 🎓🎓🎓🎓🎓

Curriculum Requirements: 🎓🎓🎓🎓**

Class Range and Type: 🎓🎓🎓$^{1/2}$

Class Size: 🎓🎓🎓🎓

Adjusted Grad Rate: 🎓🎓🎓🎓$^{1/2}$

Ratio of Staff to Students: 🎓🎓🎓🎓$^{1/2}$

Priority Registration: Yes, but only as the first to register with their class. "Incoming first-year Scholars in particular have occasional difficulties in that the current students have already registered for the Fall semester before first-years have even sent their acceptance letters to the Admissions office!

However, during their designated Summer Orientation sessions, Echols Scholars have priority over other incoming first-year students."

Honors Housing: 🎓🎓🎓🎓

Prestigious Awards: 🎓🎓🎓🎓🎓

*Perception is based on the university's ranking among public universities in the 2014 U.S. News Best Colleges report. Please bear in mind that the better the U.S. News ranking, the more difficult it is for an honors college or program to have a rating that equals or improves on the magazine ranking.

Curriculum Requirements (4.0): The Echols Scholars Program could, arguably, not be considered an honors program at all or, plausibly, could be one of the best in the nation. Echols has honors housing and benefits for its scholars, but one of the primary inducements for Echols applicants is that they are not bound by university requirements and can take any course they choose in the College of Arts and Sciences--so **there is no formal honors curriculum. We have excluded from review at least three honors programs that have no formal curriculum, so how can we make an exception for UVA? Our view is, again, that because **UVA students as a whole** have the highest range of test scores (25th-75th percentile scores) of any public university in the nation and an **average (mean) SAT score of 1349,** the entire university is, in a sense, an honors community. And this, in turn, means that all the classes are likely to be appropriately challenging for high level students.

That said, one can argue that the total freedom accorded to Echols Scholars has a downside, for it is conceivable that an Echols Scholar could take most or even all classes without engaging other Echols Scholars in the classroom. True, Echols and Rodman Scholars are housed in the same residence halls; but the free-form nature of dormitory discussions is different from preparing and defending complicated intellectual arguments in a highly competitive classroom under the scrutiny of an outstanding professor (of which UVA has many). On the other hand, one suspects that an Echols, Rodman, or Jefferson Scholar who wears laurels on his or her sleeve will be in for a comeuppance from the "regular" students in the room. In any case, presented with the combination of no formal curriculum but mostly excellent classes, we arrived at a rating of 4.0, based partly on the average *degree* completion requirement of 33 credit hours. **Echols are encouraged to write a senior thesis, but they are not required to do so.**

One thing is certain, the Echols administrators are unfazed about any second-guessing of their program, and if we find it difficult to say exactly what it *is*, they are eager to say exactly what it *is not*. Echols, they assert emphatically, is "*not* a 'college within a college'. The Echols Program does *not* offer a special curriculum with certain 'core' courses or special sections of courses. It does *not* require a thesis or 'capstone' project. We do *not* wish to segregate Echols Scholars from other students in the College or to fit all Echols Scholars into the same academic mold. Rather than placing Scholars into a common introductory course (the 'college within a college' model) we wish to accelerate their progress into upper-level courses and individual areas of interest. The Echols first-year seminar is voluntary rather than mandatory, and is intended to facilitate academic debate rather than achieve a curricular goal." [Emphases added.]

AP credits: UVA typically accepts AP scores ranging from 4 to 5 for credit in a wide variety of courses. **Many Echols students have an abundance of AP credits, giving them the choice to graduate early or take even more advanced classes.**

Range and Type of Honors Courses (3.5): While there are some identifiable undergraduate seminars at UVA, mostly in the humanities, most of the Echols Scholars will probably pursue advanced work in relatively small departmental courses. The availability of these classes may on occasion be problematic because of the impediments facing Echols first-year students (see above, under Priority Registration) and because registering with the first group *in your class* is not as good as full-blown priority registration that allows honors students to register before anyone else or at least as part of the first group overall.

But being able to pick (and generally register for) any class offered by the College of Arts and Sciences at one of the finest universities in the world is a privilege of the highest order.

Average Class Size (4.0): Our *rough estimate* **is that the average** *Echols* **class size is 22.7** students, based mostly on university-wide data listing percentages of class sections within a certain class size range. That Echols Scholars have some form of priority registration to go with their freedom to leapfrog introductory courses allows them to avoid some of the very large sections in the sciences (some with 300 or more students) and some relatively large classes in the humanities. **It is this feature that adds perhaps the most important traditional honors component to the Echols experience-- smaller classes.** The overall average class size for the 50 colleges and programs under review in this edition is 21.2 students.

Adjusted Graduation Rate (4.5): The AGR is not simply the six-year graduation rate of students in the honors college who graduated from the university **(***estimated conservatively at* **95.1%),** whether or not the students completed the honors program ("honors completers"). The AGR also reflects the extent to which the honors graduation rate from the university is higher than that for the university as a whole. (The **university-wide rate is 93%,** yielding the 4.5 AGR for the program.) The average **honors** six-year **graduation rate for all 50 programs under review is 89%.**

Ratio of Staff to Honors Students (4.5): Note: Please see our explanation of this metric above. Our estimate is that there is 1 staff member for every **132.4** students. (Mean ratio for all 50 programs is 1 staff member for every 159.8 students.)

Honors Residence Halls (4.0): In the past, Echols Scholars have resided in Balz-Dobie and Watson-Webb Halls--two of eight "New Dorms" that have been renovated as part of the Alderman Road project, lasting several years. Balz-Dobie and Watson-Webb stand adjacent to each other in the New Dorm area, **but now Balz-Dobie has a new Echols companion dorm--Tuttle-Dunnington--located across a green from Balz-Dobie and beyond a stand of trees.** We do not have any idea why the Echols Program chose a hall farther away from Balz-Dobie than the adjacent Watson-Webb, but at least the renovation of Tuttle-Dunnington is more recent. All dorms are air-conditioned. They are not as convenient to most classroom buildings on "grounds" but they are not all that far away, either. There is a dining commons between Balz-Dobie and Watson-Webb. Echols Scholars share honors facilities with Rodman Scholars (top 5% of UVA engineering students).

Both Scholars' residence halls are traditional in the sense that they feature double rooms with shared baths on the hall--but this communal configuration does not mean that the dorms are not otherwise state-of-the art.

"I have personally been in [Balz-Dobie] and it is a hotel," a student wrote in 2012. "The toilets flush up and down (up for #1, down for #2), have motion-sensitive lighting, and [there are] beautiful lounges. I believe they are LED-certified buildings, and this statement makes me jealous: 'The air handler has an energy recovery wheel that captures the heat from exhaust air and recycles it, and the whole precinct is fed by steam from McCormick Road and chilled water from the Aquatic and Fitness Center.' It's like the environmentally-friendly version of caviar and Perrier."

We always report whether a residence hall has on-site laundry facilities. The answer is yes, but with these added features: a remote sensor can tell the student when a washer is available *and* can let the student know when the clothes are done.

Prestigious Awards (5.0): UVA ranks 1st among all public universities in the number of Rhodes Scholars (50), 3rd in Truman Scholars (28), and is tied for 4th in the number of undergraduate Goldwater Scholars (57). UVA students and graduates also have a strong record of winning Udall Scholarships, Boren Scholarships, Marshall Scholarships, and Churchill Scholarships.

Continuation Requirements: 3.00 cumulative GPA

Academic Strengths: Known as much for the excellence of its undergraduate teaching as for its academic research, the average UVA ranking of the 15 academic departments that we track is around 30 among all universities public or private. Although the departmental rankings are not quite as high as those at much larger and more research-oriented institutions such as UC Berkeley, Michigan, UCLA, Wisconsin, and UT Austin, UVA has 11 departments that rank in the top 40 nationwide, most notably, perhaps, business ("commerce" at UVA) ranked number 5. Other highly-respected departments include English (10), history (20), education (22), sociology and psychology (both 26), computer science (28), economics (30), engineering (35), political science (36), and physics (40).

Undergraduate Research: UVA's **Harrison Undergraduate Research Awards** are among the most generous that we know of among the 50 universities whose honors programs are under review. Harrison Awards fund "outstanding undergraduate research projects to be carried out in the summer following application for the award and the subsequent academic year. **Approximately forty awards of up to $3,000 each** will be granted on a competitive basis to current first-, second-, and third-year undergraduate students."

Another key element of the awards is that Harrison faculty advisors "receive research support in the amount of $1,000."

Study Abroad: UVA ranks 29th nationally in the total number of students studying abroad and 40th nationally in the percentage of undergraduates who study abroad, the latter ranking especially notable because many of the universities and colleges who do well in this category are selective private institutions that have much smaller student bodies.

More than one program offers study at Oxford University. One of these is the very British (indeed) sounding "Visiting Student Programme," which offers "suitably qualified students the opportunity to come to Oxford as members of Mansfield College and Registered Visiting Students of the University of Oxford. **We normally admit 35-40 VSP students per year, from Ivy League and other top US institutions** and a few from other non-EU countries. Students study arts, humanities, and social science subjects for one year."

The "UVA in Paris" program adopts a polished travelogue approach in its description: "Students will consider the ghosts of history that haunt, yet continue to shape, the spaces and places of France's majestic capital city. For Paris is like a massive palimpsest, made up of multiple layers of memories. Our itinerary will include a number of places that reveal traces of these layers and provide a deeper, more complete, and decidedly more panoramic understanding of the city."

Financial Aid: Echols Scholars can also be selected as **Jefferson Scholars,** an extremely fortunate group of about **31-36 students each year who receive one of the most generous merit awards in the nation.**

"No one may apply for a Jefferson Scholarship directly. For the regional competitions, a prospective Jefferson Scholar must be nominated by his/her school (eligible schools may nominate one or two students per year from the senior class). Currently, over 3,900 secondary schools are eligible to nominate in the regional competitions.

"Once nominated, students are placed into regional competitions which will determine the 120 finalists who will be invited to Charlottesville for the Jefferson Scholarship Selection Weekend in late March." Students offered the scholarships must accept by mid-April.

The rewards are huge.

Total value of the scholarship exceeds:
- **$240,000** for non-Virginian students
- **$125,000** or Virginian students

The Jefferson Scholar Stipend in 2014-15 will exceed:
- **$56,000** or non-Virginian students
- **$26,000** for Virginian students
- Jefferson Scholars' stipend includes tuition, fees, books, supplies, room, board, and personal expenses.

Here are some representative statistics from a recent year, when 31 Jefferson Scholars enrolled:

- 2260 average SAT
- 23 scholars had a perfect score of 800 on at least one section of the SAT
- 88 scores of 5 on AP exams
- 16 varsity athletes

297

Degree of Difference (Honors students/non-honors students): 2.62 on a scale of 5. Some parents and prospective students might prefer an honors program that in many ways stands apart on campus, while others might prefer a program that is more expansive. The rating here tries to provide an indication of where a given honors program is on the stand apart/expansive spectrum. The rating is based on the difference between (1) the average SAT scores for enrolled honors students and (2) the average test scores for all students in the university as a whole *and* for students with scores at the 75% level or above. A score of 3.5 or higher indicates a high degree of difference. A score of 3.2 to 3.49 indicates a relatively high degree of difference. Finally, a score below 3.2 indicates a modest difference. **Please keep in mind that neither the high nor low selectivity of an honors program determines how effective the program is; this rating is merely "cultural" and *not* qualitative.**

NAME: UNIVERSITY HONORS PROGRAM, UNIVERSITY OF WASHINGTON

Date Established: 1961

Location: Seattle, Washington

University Full-time Undergraduate Enrollment: 26,021

Honors Enrollment: Approximately 1,500 in three types of honors options (mean size of all 50 programs is 1,714)

Review/Admissions Category III: Programs with average SAT scores of 1383--1416 for enrolled students. Mean average for three-part SAT is 2125 and for ACT it is 32; the average high school GPA is 3.92.

Minimum Admission Requirements: "We do a holistic review and there is no minimum requirement. Students are evaluated on the basis of GPA, SAT and/or ACT, activities, essays, and one letter of recommendation."

Honors Programs in Admissions Category III (average SAT scores of 1383--1416): Connecticut, Indiana, Kentucky, Miami University, Oklahoma, Penn State, Tennessee, Texas A&M, UC Irvine, and Washington.

Administrative Staff: The honors program has a staff of 7.

FOR ALL "MORTARBOARD" RATINGS BELOW, A SCORE OF 5 IS THE MAXIMUM AND REPRESENTS A COMPARISON WITH ALL 50 HONORS COLLEGES AND PROGRAMS:

PERCEPTION* OF UNIVERSITY AS A WHOLE, <u>NOT</u> OF HONORS: 🎓🎓🎓🎓¹ᐟ²

OVERALL HONORS RATING: 🎓🎓🎓🎓¹ᐟ²

Curriculum Requirements: 🎓🎓🎓🎓🎓

Class Range and Type: 🎓🎓🎓🎓¹ᐟ²

Class Size: 🎓🎓🎓¹ᐟ²

Adjusted Grad Rate: 🎓🎓🎓🎓¹ᐟ²

Ratio of Staff to Students: 🎓🎓🎓

Priority Registration: No.

Honors Housing: ♟♟♟ⁱ/²

Prestigious Awards: ♟♟♟♟♟

*Perception is based on the university's ranking among public universities in the 2014 U.S. News Best Colleges report. Please bear in mind that the better the U.S. News ranking, the more difficult it is for an honors college or program to have a rating that equals or improves on the magazine ranking.

Curriculum Requirements (5.0): The UHP has three options for honors students:

"Interdisciplinary Honors students are asked to think intentionally about education, knowledge and interdisciplinarity. They take a majority of their general education requirements in Honors-specific courses, complete experiential learning requirements, and maintain a portfolio throughout their participation in this curriculum." **This option is available to freshman honors entrants only.**

Completion of Interdisciplinary Honors requires nine 5-unit honors core courses **(quarter system)** plus two 1-unit honors sections. (To convert quarter units to semester hours, multiply the quarter units by two-thirds. In this case, 47 quarter units=31.3 semester hours.) In addition, completion requires students to participate in two honors experiential learning projects and maintain a continuing portfolio of their work and their reflections on what they have learned. Experiential projects "should involve activities in the areas of leadership, research, service or international engagement."

"Students will be introduced to the Honors Portfolio in HONORS 100, when they will be given practical and theoretical tools to create and compile this electronic portfolio of their academic and experiential work. With the help of their Honors peers, advisers and faculty, students will continue to contribute to their portfolios throughout their time at UW and in Honors. **Students will polish and present their portfolios in HONORS 496**."

"Departmental Honors allows students to explore their majors in greater depth by completing upper-level electives, research, or an extended thesis. Departmental Honors also exposes students to a close working relationship with faculty mentors. **Admission to Interdisciplinary Honors does not guarantee admission to Departmental Honors.** Admission procedures are specific to each department; students should consult with an academic adviser within their department for more information.

Departmental Honors completion requirements vary, "but usually constitute an additional 10-15 credits of upper-level coursework, additional research or an extended thesis.

"Departmental Honors can be completed alone to graduate with Honors in [the major].

"Typically, students apply for departmental admission in their junior year of college, although some majors have earlier entrance options. For admission into a Departmental Honors program or details about the process, please speak with a departmental adviser."

College Honors, the completion of **both Interdisciplinary Honors and Departmental Honors,** allows students to experience both Honors general education and the deeper understanding of their chosen focus. College Honors completion is one of the most rigorous in the nation, combining the unsurpassed excellence of the UHP core seminars with the research and thesis demands within the academic disciplines. Completion requires 57-62 honors quarter units (equivalent to 38-42 semester hours).

Range and Type of Honors Courses (4.5): The UHP is a **core honors program,** meaning that its mission is to develop well-honed critical thinking skills in combination with an interdisciplinary approach to learning. Although there are some departmental honors classes and seminars as well that are more narrowly focused on the disciplines (especially in math and the sciences), the highest level of excellence is most evident in the honors seminars that are shaded toward five general subject-area categories: Arts and Humanities; Interdisciplinary; Natural Sciences; Social Sciences; and Special Topics.

In the Humanities category, there is a seminar titled **Vladimir Nabokov,** which studies "the works of [the author], from his early novels written in Europe to his later masterpieces, including *Lolita, Pnin, Pale Fire,* and *Ada.*" Another Humanities offering in Spring 2014 was the History of Modern Architecture, "a survey of architecture from 1750 to the present (primarily, but not exclusively, in Europe and North America). Emphasis is placed on the development of the architecture of this period including significant buildings and projects, important theories and critical writings."

One of the Interdisciplinary classes is among our favorites from all the honors programs we have reviewed: **Plato's Timaeus: Physics for the Sake of the Self.** Is the course as demanding and intriguing as its title suggests? You decide. "Within this study, our primary aim will be to demarcate disparate disciplines such as theology, history, rhetoric, mathematics, astronomy, psychology, medicine, and botany while at the same time making sure not to unravel them from the controlling context into which they are woven, the study of kosmos, or what arguably amounts to, a cosmology or even physics of the self. Second, this course is a study in how to read and write about books." No easy voyage through the "kosmos" here.

The Natural Sciences were impressively represented in Spring 2014, featuring Honors Biochemistry, Honors Chemistry, and Honors Organic Chemistry--along with Computer Science and **The Neuroscience of Sex,** and several others.

In the Social Sciences, we have Who Should Know What and Why? The Political and Moral Context of Education and Schooling; and **Geographies and Politics of Poverty and Privilege.**

Our favorite among several in the Special Topics category: **Buddhist Biology: Ancient Eastern Wisdom Meets Modern Western Science.**

The departmental honors classes included at least three sections of honors math—calculus with analytical geometry, accelerated calculus, and advanced calculus, all carrying 5 units of credit, and a physics class on wave theory. Again we say it—the core classes offer the best, and in them the disciplines find creative expression.

Average Class Size (3.5): The average UHP honors class has **25.86 students, making good on the UHP commitment to keep classes below 30-35. Many of the seminar sections are much smaller.** The average class size for all 50 programs under review is 21.2 students.

Adjusted Graduation Rate (4.5): The AGR is not simply the six-year graduation rate of students in the CHP who graduated from the university **(94%),** whether or not the students completed the honors program ("honors completers"). The AGR also reflects the extent to which the honors graduation rate from the university is higher than that for the university as a whole. (The **university-wide rate is 80%),** yielding the AGR rating of 4.5. The average **honors** six-year **graduation rate for all 50 programs under review is 89%**.

Ratio of Staff to Honors Students (3.0): Our estimate is that there is 1 staff member for every **214.3** students. (Mean ratio for all 50 programs is 1 staff member for every 159.8 students.)

Honors Residence Halls (3.5): The UHP is as good as it gets when it comes to the fundamentals of honors education, but the relative lack of perks--priority registration and state of the art residence halls--is what keeps the overall UHP rating from being 5 mortarboards. As noted above, there is no priority registration for honors students, and the UHP position on this perk seems firm, in the interest of not fostering an atmosphere of elitism.

And in the two older residence halls set aside at least in part for honors students, there are only 150 honors spaces combined. Neither is air conditioned, although the absence of this amenity--many would say an absolute necessity in a hot climate--is likely not much of a negative in Seattle.

The two residence halls currently housing both honors first-year students and upperclassmen are Haggett Hall and Poplar Hall. The nearest dining to Haggett is The 8; the closest dining to Poplar is Eleven 01 Café. Both residence halls have on-site laundry.

Prestigious Awards (5.0): Now we are in UW's wheelhouse: the university ranks 7th out of the 50 universities we are reviewing for this edition in the total number of prestigious awards its students and graduates have earned. **Most impressive is that UW ranks 3rd among all public universities in the number of Rhodes Scholarships its graduates have won--37.** UW grads have also earned 13 Truman Scholarships, five Marshall Scholarships, four Gates Cambridge awards, and three of the rare Winston Churchill Scholarships. Reflecting the strength of its faculty and programs in the sciences, **UW ranks 3rd among all public universities in winning National Science Foundation Graduate Research Fellowships** during the three-year period 2011-2013, and **6th in the number of Fulbright Student Scholarships.**

Continuation Requirements: 3.30 GPA

Academic Strengths: UW has an outstanding faculty, with its **lowest-ranked** department listed at **number 34 in the nation** among all universities public or private. The average department rankings are just behind those at Johns Hopkins and Northwestern and ahead of those at Duke. All of the 15 most recognized academic disciplines are excellent at UW, led by: computer science (7), education (12), earth sciences (13), psychology (14), biology (15), physics (19), sociology (20), business (22), chemistry and engineering (both 26), math (27), and political science (28).

Undergraduate Research: The Honors Director tells us that "All students in the Interdisciplinary and College Honors programs are required to complete two of four experiential learning requirements, one of which is research. Students in Departmental Honors and College Honors must complete a research project. **Each year the UW offers an Undergraduate Research Symposium at which around 1,000 undergraduates present their research.**"

The university has a very active Undergraduate Research Program, which sponsors the symposium mentioned above. In addition, the **Levinson Emerging Scholars Program** offers funding for highly talented undergraduate students to do research in biology, biochemistry, bioengineering, bioinformatics, chemistry, genetics, neuroscience, and related fields.

Washington Research Foundation Fellowships for advanced undergraduates support promising students who work on creative and sophisticated science and engineering research projects under the guidance of UW faculty. The foundation targets undergraduates who have already participated in undergraduate research for at least three quarters and who are working beyond an introductory level in a project that requires creativity and advanced knowledge.

"Undergraduates who are interested in devoting a significant portion of time to research, which both complements their coursework and furthers their professional goals, are especially encouraged to apply."

The **Washington Research Foundation** generously supports fellowships "to recognize and support undergraduates who achieve a high level of accomplishment in research, particularly in areas relevant to the development of new technologies" in the fields of science and engineering. **Fellows may receive up to $6,000, disbursed "in the amount of $2,000 at the beginning of the Autumn, Winter, and Spring Quarters."**

Through endowments and other funding sources, UW also provides funds to undergraduate researchers for expenses and registration fees at academic conferences around the nation.

Study Abroad: UW ranks 18th among all U.S. universities in the total number of students who study abroad and 11th for the number of students involved in long-term study abroad.

Financial Aid: There are many scholarship opportunities at UW, many specifically for honors students. The UHP Director sent us the following information:

First year scholarships:

> Stamps Scholarship (4 year package, but this may not continue)
> Mary Gates Endowment Scholarship (2 year tuition for in-state students)
> Honors Undergraduate Scholar Award (4 year tuition waiver for in-state students)
> Honors Achievement Award (one-time partial tuition waiver for out-of-state students)
> Campbell Scholarship (one-time award of $3,000 for first generation student)
> Eberharter Scholarship (four-year $3,000 award for student interested in international studies, with support for study abroad.
> Clack Scholarship (one-time award of $3,500 for in-state resident from Spokane County with financial need)

Honors also has a number of one-time awards for continuing students:

Bordeaux Scholarship (rising juniors in Interdisciplinary/College Honors; $1,500)
Dilman Scholarship (rising seniors in Interdisciplinary/College Honors; $1,500)
Friedman-Hechter Scholarship (Any year in Interdisciplinary/College Honors; $500)
Honors Program Scholarship (Any year in Interdisciplinary/College Honors; $500)
Greene Scholarship (Any year in Interdisciplinary/College Honors; one year of in-state tuition)
Hennes Scholarship (Any year in Interdisciplinary, Departmental, or College Honors; $5,000)
Mary Gates Achievement Scholarship (rising sophomores in Interdisciplinary/College Honors; one year of in-state tuition)
Gerberding Scholarship (rising seniors and above in Interdisciplinary, Departmental, or College Honors; $1,500)
Wang Scholarship (Any year in in Interdisciplinary, Departmental, or College Honors; $2,000)

Degree of Difference (Honors students/non-honors students): 2.75 on a scale of 5. Some parents and prospective students might prefer an honors program that in many ways stands apart on campus, while others might prefer a program that is more expansive. The rating here tries to provide an indication of where a given honors program is on the stand apart/expansive spectrum. The rating is based on the difference between (1) the average SAT scores for enrolled honors students and (2) the average test scores for all students in the university as a whole *and* for students with scores at the 75% level or above. A score of 3.5 or higher indicates a high degree of difference. A score of 3.2 to 3.49 indicates a relatively high degree of difference. Finally, a score below 3.2 indicates a modest difference. **Please keep in mind that neither the high nor low selectivity of an honors program determines how effective the program is; this rating is merely "cultural" and *not* qualitative.**

NAME: THE HONORS COLLEGE, WASHINGTON STATE UNIVERSITY

Date Established: 1960

Location: Pullman, Washington

University Full-time Undergraduate Enrollment: 20,082

Honors Enrollment: 612 (mean size of all 50 programs is 1,714)

Review/Admissions Category--I: Programs with **average SAT scores of 1235--1342 for enrolled students**. The **actual average** (mean) test scores for enrollees at the honors college are SAT 1270 (math 640, verbal 630), ACT 28.1. The average high school GPA is 3.84.

The **minimum** requirements are not listed, but an essay is required.

Honors Programs in Admissions Category I (average SAT scores of 1235-1342): Arizona, Arizona State, Arkansas, Colorado State, Iowa, Maine, Mississippi, Oklahoma State, Oregon, Oregon State, Rhode Island, Texas Tech, University at Albany, and Washington State.

Administrative Staff: The Honors Program has a staff of 6.

FOR ALL "MORTARBOARD" RATINGS BELOW, A SCORE OF 5 IS THE MAXIMUM AND REPRESENTS A COMPARISON WITH ALL 50 HONORS COLLEGES AND PROGRAMS:

PERCEPTION* OF UNIVERSITY AS A WHOLE, <u>NOT</u> OF HONORS: 🎓🎓 1/2

OVERALL HONORS RATING: 🎓🎓🎓 1/2

Curriculum Requirements: 🎓🎓🎓 1/2

Class Range and Type: 🎓🎓🎓 1/2

Class Size: 🎓🎓🎓🎓 1/2

Adjusted Grad Rate: 🎓🎓🎓 1/2

Ratio of Staff to Students: 🎓🎓🎓🎓 1/2

Priority Registration: Yes, honors students register for **all** courses, honors and otherwise, with the first group of students during **each** year they are in the program.

Honors Housing: 🎓🎓🎓🎓

Prestigious Awards: 🎓🎓🎓

*Perception is based on the university's ranking among public universities in the 2014 U.S. News Best Colleges report. Please bear in mind that the better the U.S. News ranking, the more difficult it is for an honors college or program to have a rating that equals or improves on the magazine ranking.

Curriculum Requirements (3.5): "To graduate from the Honors College…

- a minimum 3.2 GPA must be maintained;
- a minimum of 15 graded Honors credits in Honors College courses in social science, arts and humanities, and interdisciplinary science are required, plus the Honors Thesis;
- you must demonstrate an intermediate level of competency in a foreign language, as evaluated through the STAMP test."

Note: The College Dean estimates that the language requirement adds an average of 8 credit hours to the completion requirement. We estimate that the average total hours required for completion is 27-29.

AP/IB credits are **not** counted as replacements for Honors College courses.

Range and Type of Honors Courses (3.5): The Honors College is very much a **core honors program,** and, as such, most of the courses are honors seminars and small lectures that meet university Gen Ed requirements in science, arts and humanities, and social sciences. One noteworthy feature of the College is its insistence on considering these subject areas in the context of **Global Issues,** two words that precede the Gen Ed seminar titles (e.g., Global Issues in the Arts and Humanities).

Two honors seminars illustrate the global emphasis: Drug Abuse: A Global Perspective, and **Pearls of Global History.**

In this cleverly metaphorical course description of **Pearls,** we find that "students will actively engage in humanities case study research, probing a pocket of history linked to period art. Perhaps your team will investigate the finely crafted samurai swords, art of the Mughal Empire, Goya's art during the Napoleonic wars, fresco painting and the Mexican revolution, or Zambian Masquerades. **Art is the pearl. Through research, you will strive to understand the structural cultural clamshell and the historical machinations that produced the visual pearl."**

There are many interesting seminars that we could choose to include in our summary, but these will have to do: **Being Human: An Introduction to Greek Literature and Culture;** DNA as a Language of Information; Energy and Society; Music and Your Brain; Art & Theory of Art; **Pursuits of Happiness: The Hollywood Comedy of Remarriage;** Representations of Childhood and Adolescence in Spanish Peninsular Film; and two sections of **Science as a Way of Knowing.**

So, we know we can't get away without summarizing **The Hollywood Comedy of Remarriage:** "There was a time when most of our big ideas came from books. Sometime early last century this changed: a lot of our big ideas now come from films. This is perhaps most evident in our ideas of romance, marriage, love. We will work through several issues in philosophy and film. And in particular we will work through the films in *Pursuits of Happiness: The Hollywood Comedy of Remarriage*."

In **Science as a Way of Knowing,** we encounter a dramatically different view of **truly BIG ideas**: namely, "the development of the scientific method as manifest in the history of western astronomy from the ancient Greeks to the time of Sir Isaac Newton. The course is in three sections: motion in the sky, history of astronomy, and a dramatic reading of the play, *Life of Galileo* by Bertolt Brecht."

The core sections also include two classes in Honors English, open to students who have an appropriate Honors College Writing Diagnostic scores. These classes are in fact sophisticated explorations of rhetoric and its uses and require frequent journeys into the rarefied world of literary jargon.

Also requiring a qualifying Writing Diagnostic score is **Examining the American West.** More, well, down to earth, this class asks students to study the "environmental, political, historical and literary studies of the American West. Articles and books are coming out every which way with fascinating stories to explore: the ship of orphans and nuns who brought small pox inoculations, body by body, across the Atlantic; the migration of the horse; the pre-Lewis and Clark West; the nature of native nutrition, and the chance to explore it right in our own backyard, at an uncultivated 30-acre prairie slope (Virgin Palouse Prairie) just south of Pullman."

As for **honors departmental honors classes**, the best are in math (advanced calculus, linear algebra, each with 30 students), and the sciences, which are offered in small or relatively small sections: honors chemistry II in Spring 2014 had 48 students but two labs for more individualized work; honors biology for non-science majors had only 22 students; and honors physics for scientists and engineers had only 24 students. Other departmental sections are in psychology, economics, and geology.

Average Class Size (4.5): The average honors class size is 18.2 students; the overall average class size for the 50 colleges and programs under review in this edition is 21.2 students.

Adjusted Graduation Rate (3.5): The AGR is not simply the six-year graduation rate of students in the honors college who graduated from the university **(84.2%),** whether or not the students completed the honors program ("honors completers"). The AGR also reflects the extent to which the honors graduation rate from the university is higher than that for the university as a whole. The **university-wide rate is 67%,** yielding the 3.5 AGR for the college. The average honors six-year **graduation rate for all 50 programs under review is 89%.**

Ratio of Staff to Honors Students (4.5): Our estimate is that there is 1 staff member for every **102** students. (Mean ratio for all 50 programs is 1 staff member for every 159.8 students.)

Honors Residence Halls (4.0): The **Honors Hall** houses first-year students and upperclassmen in suite-style rooms with shared baths. The rooms are not air conditioned, but that is not a significant problem in eastern Washington. The nearest dining is Hillside Dining Hall. There is on-site laundry in Honors Hall, three honors lounges, and a kitchen.

"Honors Hall is the home of 118 students," the Associate Dean tells us. "The 1st floor of the building houses the Honors College and the 1st floor lounge is the meeting place for the Honors Student Advisory Council (HSAC). This allows for much overlapping for programming, discussions, presentations, seminars and events put on by the residence life staff, Honors College, and HSAC. This maintains a strong academic environment within the hall.

"WSU also has another residence hall that is considered a Scholars Hall (Scott-Coman), but it is not part of the Honors Hall or College."

Prestigious Awards (3.0): "In 2010, a new Distinguished Scholarships Office was created at WSU and, since that time, WSU has worked to encourage high-achieving students to pursue prestigious awards," the Associate Dean tells us. "Additionally, in 2012, WSU administration signed a contract with a private consultant to support efforts towards that goal. Scholarships from the Public University Honors list for which WSU students have competed successfully in the past decade are the Goldwater, Boren, and Gilman Scholarships and the Fulbright Fellowship. In most cases, the rate at which WSU students have won these two awards has increased in recent years."

WSU students have already won 10 Rhodes Scholarships, and the total of Goldwater Scholars has risen to a total of 22. **WSU students have won 4 Boren Scholarships in the last three years, placing them in the top 10 among public universities during that period. Boren Scholars receive $20,000 to work or study abroad. The Global (and language) focus of the Honors College is a likely contributor to this success.** The Distinguished Scholarships Office should go a great way toward increasingly better achievement in winning other prestigious awards.

Continuation Requirements: 3.20 GPA

Academic Strengths: The most recognized academic departments at WSU are sociology, engineering, earth sciences, physics, chemistry, and computer science.

Undergraduate Research: "All Honors College students, except those majoring in engineering, are required to complete an Honors thesis that involves research directly under the supervision of a faculty mentor. The students have to complete a written thesis and defend it orally in front of a faculty committee that includes at least one external examiner (i.e., not from the student's home department/college) and one faculty member from the Honors College. For students majoring in engineering (about 20% of our students) their capstone project (part of the ABET requirement) is counted in lieu of the Honors thesis. However, many of the engineering students in Honors also do undergraduate research."

Study Abroad: The Associate Dean reports that **"45.3 % of our May 2013 graduating class studied abroad at some time during their college career;** 27.9% studied for full summer, semester or year, while 17.40% went on faculty led trips.

"The Honors College has three Honors Exchanges: two Universities in Wales (Aberystwyth and Swansea), and Southeast University in Nanjing, China.

"We offer 2-3 faculty led trips every summer, offered by Honors faculty. Honors has led the university in providing this type of experience since 1996.

"Scholarships are available specifically for study-abroad programs. These are provided by Honors, the Office of International Programs, and through the academic degree-granting colleges."

Financial Aid: "The Honors College at Washington State University (WSU) is very proud to have many alumni, friends, and programs dedicated to helping our students meet the financial demands as they earn their education in Honors and at WSU," says the Associate Dean. "Honors scholarships and awards for Honors College students are awarded based on or to support incoming freshmen, merit for outstanding grades and achievements, financial need as determined by FAFSA, diversity, study-and research-abroad experiences including foreign language immersion programs, undergraduate research, and pursuit of a specific major. Most scholarships go into student accounts and are used for tuition and/or fees. Each of our scholarship awards requires that applicants be current Honors students and have a WSU cumulative grade point average of at least 3.20.

"For the 2013-2014 academic year, of the 612 Honors students, 532 of them (87%) received scholarship support from the University. In addition to these scholarship awards, **the Honors College awarded 164 scholarships to 302 eligible Honors students, with awards ranging from $500 to $2,000. This equates to 54% of our eligible students receiving scholarship awards from the Honors College.** Of these awards, 25 were given to incoming freshman; 4 awards were given to students for their Honors thesis research or who needed financial help to attend a conference.

Degree of Difference (Honors students/non-honors students): 3.62 on a scale of 5. Some parents and prospective students might prefer an honors program that in many ways stands apart on campus, while others might prefer a program that is more expansive. The rating here tries to provide an indication of where a given honors program is on the stand apart/expansive spectrum. The rating is based on the difference between (1) the average SAT scores for enrolled honors students and (2) the average test scores for all students in the university as a whole *and* for students with scores at the 75% level or above. A score of 3.5 or higher indicates a high degree of difference. A score of 3.2 to 3.49 indicates a relatively high degree of difference. Finally, a score below 3.2 indicates a modest difference. **Please keep in mind that neither the high nor low selectivity of an honors program determines how effective the program is; this rating is merely "cultural" and *not* qualitative.**

NAME: UNIVERSITY OF WISCONSIN-MADISON LETTERS AND SCIENCE (L&S) HONORS PROGRAM

Date Established: 1958

Location: Madison, Wisconsin

University Full-time Undergraduate Enrollment: 28,188

Honors Enrollment: 1,200 (mean size of all 50 programs is 1,714)

Review/Admissions Category II: Programs with **average SAT scores of 1343--1382 for enrolled students**. Actual average (mean) SAT score for enrolled honors students is 1344, and the average ACT is 30.3. The average (mean) high school GPA is 3.76, but the median is 3.91.

Minimum Admission Requirements: "There is no test score or GPA requirement for admission to the Letters & Science Honors Program at UW-Madison. The standards of admission to the University of Wisconsin College of Letters & Science are sufficiently rigorous that every admitted first-year student is invited to apply."

Honors Programs in Admissions Category II (average SAT scores of 1343-1382): Alabama, Delaware, Florida State, Massachusetts, Missouri, North Carolina State, Ohio University, Temple, Purdue, UCLA, Utah, Vermont, and Wisconsin.

Administrative Staff: The honors program has a staff of 6.

FOR ALL "MORTARBOARD" RATINGS BELOW, A SCORE OF 5 IS THE MAXIMUM AND REPRESENTS A COMPARISON WITH ALL 50 HONORS COLLEGES AND PROGRAMS:

PERCEPTION* OF UNIVERSITY AS A WHOLE, <u>NOT</u> OF HONORS: 🎓🎓🎓🎓¹ᐟ²

OVERALL HONORS RATING: 🎓🎓🎓¹ᐟ²**

Curriculum Requirements: 🎓🎓🎓🎓

Class Range and Type: 🎓🎓🎓🎓

Class Size: 🎓🎓🎓

Adjusted Grad Rate: 🎓🎓🎓🎓

Ratio of Staff to Students: 🎓🎓🎓¹ᐟ²**

Priority Registration: No. *

Honors Housing: NA**

Prestigious Awards: 🎓🎓🎓🎓🎓

*Perception is based on the university's ranking among public universities in the 2014 U.S. News Best Colleges report. Please bear in mind that the better the U.S. News ranking, the more difficult it is for an honors college or program to have a rating that equals or improves on the magazine ranking.

Editor's Note: *The L&S Honors Program at UW Madison is unique. In our opinion, no other program has been so determined in combining an open, egalitarian philosophy with the high expectations of honors education. The result is a program that lacks some honors features--especially what many would call "perks"--in order to minimize the separation of honors and non-honors students and, perhaps incidentally, to allow the university to use its resources more to the benefit of the student body as a whole. One major example is that there is no separate housing for honors students; another is that honors students do not have the perk of priority registration. The majority of honors classes are "honors-option" classes rather than small honors-only sections, and this allows academic departments to maintain higher levels of students taught per instructor. It also results in a lower than average staffing level for the L&S Honors Program. In addition, some of the courses that carry honors credit for all students who enroll in them may be open to non-honors UW-Madison students. Yet another example is that the L&S Honors Program abandoned the use of threshold test scores and even high school GPAs about six years ago, saying that such metrics "correlate directly with family social status and income." We hope that recognizing these characteristics of L&S up front will help focus attention on the most substantial components of the program, while realizing that L&S Honors exists within one of the best public universities in the nation.* **The overall mortarboard rating for L&S Honors would be 4.0 or 4.5 were it not for the absence of the perks mentioned above.

Curriculum Requirements (4.0): L&S has three options for completion, as outlined below:

Honors in the Liberal Arts--Students must complete 24 credits of honors courses, including "6 Honors credits in each breadth category: Science, Social Science, and Humanities (and another six in an area of their choice)." Honors course credits can come from **(H)** courses, which are all-honors classes, most of them smaller than other classes that may be taken. Credits may also be earned through advanced or accelerated **honors-level** courses, coded **(!)**, also called "unrestricted" courses because they are open to non-honors students. Finally, credits may come from courses coded **(%)**; these are non-honors classes where an extra component is required for honors credit.

Honors in the Major--This option requires at least 6 credits, depending on what the student's major department requires for research and thesis credit. **A thesis is required.**

Comprehensive Honors--The highest option, Comprehensive Honors requires completion of requirements for **both** Honors in the Liberal Arts and Honors in the Major, or at least 30 semester hours of honors work. **A thesis is required.**

AP/IB credits are **not** counted as replacements for honors courses.

Range and Type of Honors Courses (4.0): Counting the **(%)** classes each term, which are listed formally on the university class schedule, honors student have as many as 200 sections to choose from each term. Fewer than half of these are in honors-only and honors-level sections, however. (One of the programs most comparable to L&S in this category is the University of Delaware Honors Program, in which the L&S **(%)** type courses are referred to as Add-Ons. These differ from contract courses in that they are lined up in advance and more prepared to handle honors student participation rather than being mostly arranged after a student's enrollment.) L&S is certainly a **department-based** program, as there are no honors courses offered directly by honors with a separate honors departmental code. (Again, this is a big reason that the L&S Program may not need a larger staff.)

Even though the L&S Program does not itself offer honors seminars, many are offered directly by the academic departments. Most prominent in this group are the history and psychology departments, with 11 advanced history seminars in Spring 2014, and 13 more in psychology.

History seminars included On the Road: Wandering, History, and the U.S.; Foundations of Modern Political Thought; Feudal Society in the Crusader States; Genocide, Justice, and Postwar Human Rights; and one of our favorites, **Historical Memory.** All of the history seminars require "**intensive writing and small group discussion** [resulting] in a project demonstrating original or creative analysis of primary and secondary sources."

The psychology seminars cover a wide spectrum of topics: Psychology of Religion; **Psychopathy and Conduct Disorder;** Legal Psychology: Criminal and Civil Issues; Psychology of Stress and Coping; Mood Disorders; **Psychology of Juvenile Delinquency**; Epigenetics and the Brain; and The **Psychology of Technology.**

When it comes to math and science, relatively few sections are **(H)** classes restricted to honors students. For example, there is only one honors-level advanced section in math--differential equations. There are, however, more than a dozen honors option classes **(%)**, and while a couple of these may have 45-50 students, there are others (analysis II, introduction to stochastics) that have enrollments of 8-15. The same holds true for physics, where the lecture sections in general physics may have almost 300 students, along with breakout discussion sections of 20-25 students, including sections for honors students that are led by the faculty member teaching the course rather than by a teaching assistant. But the more specialized honors option classes--modern physics, atomic/quantum physics--have 30 students or less.

The university is renowned for its excellence across the academic disciplines, and there are honors option courses in everything from Asian art and anthropology, to Hebrew and Dutch, to Scandinavian literature and all of the Romance languages, to math and chemistry, and multiple courses in sociology offered by one of the premier departments in the nation.

Average Class Size (3.0): Although the *estimated* average honors class size of **36.2** is high compared to most other programs under review, the aforementioned history and psychology seminars average only 11.5 and 22 students, respectively. Still, especially for intro science classes, some lecture sections are quite large, though the smaller breakout sections offset that. The average class size is 21.2 among all 50 programs under review.

Adjusted Graduation Rate (4.0): The AGR is not simply the six-year graduation rate of students in the honors program who graduated from the university **(89.9%),** whether or not the students completed the honors program ("honors completers"). The AGR also reflects the extent to which the honors graduation rate from the university is higher than that for the university as a whole. (The **university-wide rate is 83%,** yielding the 4.0 AGR for the college.) The average six-year **honors graduation rate for all 50 programs** under review **is 89%.**

Ratio of Staff to Honors Students (3.5): Our estimate is that there is 1 staff member for every **200** students. (Mean ratio for all 50 programs is 1 staff member for every 159.8 students.)

Honors Residence Halls (3.0): This is the default rating for programs with no separate honors residence halls. There are, however, at least 11 Living/Learning Communities to choose from at UW-Madison, including the International Learning Community (with seven language houses); Open House (a gender learning community); WISE House (Women in Science and Engineering); Bio House; Green House; and the ERLC (Entrepreneurship Residential Learning Community).

Prestigious Awards (5.0): The undoubted excellence of UW-Madison shines through in this category, with the university in the top five of the 50 under review when it comes to its undergraduates and graduates earning prestigious scholarships. UW-Madison grads have achieved a record that ranks 6th among all public universities in the total number of Rhodes, Marshall, Gates Cambridge, Churchill, and Truman Scholars, including 31 Rhodes Scholarships, 19 Marshall Scholarships, and 19 Truman Scholarships. University graduates are also among public university leaders in winning generous National Science Foundation Graduate Research Fellowships. UW-Madison undergraduates have won 55 Goldwater Scholarships, ranking 6th among all public universities.

Continuation Requirements: 3.30 cumulative GPA for graduation.

Academic Strengths: UW-Madison has an outstanding faculty that is among the top three among all public universities, with only UC Berkeley and Michigan having higher departmental rankings across the 15 academic departments that we track. The university's faculty also ranks with those at elite private institutions such as Cornell, Yale, Chicago, Penn, Columbia, Northwestern, and Johns Hopkins. *Every* department at UW-Madison that we track is ranked 18th in the nation or higher among all universities public and private: sociology (1), chemistry (7), psychology (9), education (10), computer science (11), earth sciences, economics, and engineering (all 13), history (14), biology and political science (both 15), English and physics (both 17), and business and math (both 18).

Undergraduate Research: From the Honors Director: **"Each year, roughly 60 Honors Program undergraduates receive funding from the Honors program to support their research**. Students also pursue research opportunities outside of our aegis through formal programs for undergraduate research that are available to Honors and non-Honors students. In addition, a number of our Honors students pursue research through less formal mechanisms.

"There are several formal programs for undergraduate research. The most obvious is funding for senior thesis research. We have a number of named scholarships available for students to do that type of research: the Trewartha Award, the Summer Senior Honors Thesis Grant, the Ann Haney Infinite Boundaries Award, and the Mark Mensink Scholarship. We also provide funding for a Welton Sophomore Summer Apprenticeship Program, where students collaborate with a faculty mentor on a research project. This experience serves as a learning tool for our students, and the students who complete the apprenticeship program produce stellar senior theses, and have high success rates for research funding later in their undergraduate careers."

Study Abroad: UW-Madison ranks 6th among all major universities in the total number of students who study abroad and 5th in the number of students engaging in long-term study abroad. "There are three different Honors-only grants available to Honors students for studying abroad," the Honors Director tells us. "The University of Wisconsin as a whole has many affiliated study abroad programs. **Two have been designated as Honors-level: one in Utrecht, The Netherlands; and one based in Quito, Ecuador. We also recognize studying abroad as an Honors-like experience, and have ways in which students can bring back some credit from their time abroad to count towards their Honors degrees."**

The honors site has great information about the Quito program. **"Students participating in the program receive a total of eleven Honors credits:** Conservation Biology (three credits), Tropical Ecology I: Terrestrial Ecosystems (four credits), Tropical Ecology II: Marine Ecosystems (four credits). "Students take classes for the first month of the semester at the Universidad San Francisco de Quito (USFQ). **While at USFQ, students take intensive Spanish language classes as well as introductory classes on the ecology of Ecuador. The Spanish course helps students acquire the Spanish language skills that are necessary to build relationships with their Quito and Galapagos host families,** and effectively communicate during fieldwork projects and internship placements. All other courses are taught by ecologists with over thirty years of experience in the tropics."

Students choosing the Utrecht program study at **University College Utrecht (UCU),** the international Honors College of Utrecht University. "The college's special characteristics include an **international student body, students' freedom and ability to compose their own curriculum, small classes and individual attention. UCU specializes in the liberal arts and sciences and contains four departments: Academic Core, Humanities, Science and Social Science.**

"Courses are available in a variety of subjects. UCU is a residential college, and all students live on campus in one of the multiple UCU residence halls around the main campus area."

The Abraham S. Burack and Kurz Scholarships can provide $1,000 to honors students who study-abroad.

Financial Aid: The Director tells us that "The Honors Program has a number of grants and scholarships available to honors students. Several grants are merit-based scholarships given to students to enhance their undergraduate research. **There is also a service-based scholarship called the Leadership Trust Award that provides tuition and funding for a student to pursue a community service project of his/her design.** The Honors Program also has merit-based funds for value-added experiences such as travel to conferences and for studying abroad."

The university provides little or no university sponsorships for National Merit Scholars, although scholars qualify for corporate NMS awards. Many of the merit-based scholarships at UW-Madison are connected to academic majors and departments.

Degree of Difference (Honors students/non-honors students): 1.83 on a scale of 5. (The L&S egalitarian approach is evident here.) Some parents and prospective students might prefer an honors program that in many ways stands apart on campus, while others might prefer a program that is more expansive. The rating here tries to provide an indication of where a given honors program is on the stand apart/expansive spectrum. The rating is based on the difference between (1) the average SAT scores for enrolled honors students and (2) the average test scores for all students in the university as a whole *and* for students with scores at the 75% level or above. A score of 3.5 or higher indicates a high degree of difference. A score of 3.2 to 3.49 indicates a relatively high degree of difference. Finally, a score below 3.2 indicates a modest difference. **Please keep in mind that neither the high nor low selectivity of an honors program determines how effective the program is; this rating is merely "cultural" and *not* qualitative.**

REGIONAL HONORS PROGRAMS

NAME: SANDRA AND JACK PINE HONORS COLLEGE, EASTERN ILLINOIS UNIVERSITY

Date Established: 1982

Location: Charleston, Illinois

University Full-time Undergraduate Enrollment: 7,906

Honors Enrollment: 456 (mean size of 50 national university programs is 1,714)

Admissions: EIU Honors relies almost entirely on ACT scores, and the average (mean) score of enrolled students is 27. The average high school GPA is 3.78.

The **minimum** requirements are ACT 26, and a high school GPA of 3.50. Top 10% of high school class.

Administrative Staff: The Honors Program has a staff of 4.

Priority Registration: Yes, honors students register for **all** courses, honors and otherwise, with the first group of students during **each** year they are in the program.

Curriculum Requirements: University Honors Program completion requires 25 honors credits and a capstone course or project. "Students may complete all 25 hours through completion of Honors versions of general education coursework, if doing so is both possible and most appropriate to their personal, academic, and professional goals. Students may be selective in determining which courses to take, based on their programmatic needs and personal interests. **The only specific courses for which credit must be earned include: the 4-hour Honors Senior Seminar required of all students; the Honors First Year Seminar required of Presidential Scholars; and the Honors Forum required of all first-term freshmen not part of the Presidential Scholars Program.**

"Students who have compelling reasons for doing so may, with administrative approval, complete alternate activities for University Honors credit. **Alternate activities which may earn a University Honors student up to 6 hours of credit include: Departmental Honors coursework in the major or minor; graduate coursework in the major; Honors reflective projects related to study abroad, National Student Exchange, REU, professional internship, or extended distant service experiences.**"

Completion of **Departmental Honors** requires 12-15 credits, including the thesis, dependent on discipline or school. "Currently, twenty-four disciplines/schools are supported by Departmental Honors programs. These include: Applied Engineering and Technology; Biological Sciences; Business (School of); Chemistry; Communication Disorders and Sciences; Communication Studies; Economics; English; Family and Consumer Sciences; Foreign Languages; Geography; Geology; History; Journalism; Mathematics; Music; Philosophy; Physics; Political Science; Psychology; Recreation Administration; Sociology; Special Education; Theatre Arts. An additional two disciplines are currently developing Departmental Honors Programs: Health Studies; Secondary Education and Foundations."

"Departmental Honors is notable for its focus on independent research and research writing. Theses are required in all Departmental Honors programs. Many Departmental Honors programs include special topics seminars that may, or may not, be related to students' research topics; several Departmental Honors programs require or strongly encourage the completion of graduate level courses. The Departmental Honors program in the School of Business is unique in requiring the completion of either an Honors internship or an Honors study abroad experience."

AP/IB credits are **not** counted as replacements for required Honors courses.

Range and Type of Honors Courses: Honors students are fortunate to have an excellent range of Gen Ed and other courses available that are all-honors courses. (A few Spanish sections have honors and non-honors students.) A commendable emphasis on writing skills is evident in the three honors composition sections offered in Fall of 2014. There were three speech classes, six in the humanities (not counting Spanish), and two in fine arts.

The science offerings were excellent as well: three in biology and one each in chemistry, physics (astronomy), and environmental sciences (weather and climate). Also offered were one or more sections of political science, psychology, philosophy, geography, sociology, education, and music. There was also one section of finite mathematics.

Our favorite seminars include Literature, Self & the World; World History: The Age of Sail; and Roots of the Modern World: Society and Religion; and The Good Life: An Introduction to Ethics.

In **Literature, Self & the World,** students learn how science fiction "tends to complicate the distinction between self and other, to unsettle the relationship of self to world. In this course, we will consider science fiction stories, novels, and films that raise questions about selfhood and identity in precisely these terms. Commercialism and the media, gender and sexuality, science and technology, and race and colonialism will be among the many topics we explore. **Roots of the Modern World: Society and Religion** "explores the historical origins of the world's great religions including Hinduism, Buddhism, Confucianism, Judaism, Christianity, and Islam. We will study the lives of the 'founders' of each faith, learn the central beliefs of each group, and analyze the conflicts (spiritual and political) that promoted changes of belief and practice over time."

The 14th through 19th centuries are the focal point of **World History: The Age of Sail**, for that was "when global history was marked by the use of sailing ships for war, trade, exploration, and piracy. This course examines how seas acted as bridges and barriers between civilizations. It focuses on the motivations and experiences of common individuals from across the globe who traveled long distances and periods and seeks in these global lives the roots of the modern world."

"A critical examination of a variety of contemporary issues such as abortion, euthanasia, animal welfare and capital punishment," **The Good Life: An Introduction to Ethics** offers students "Ethical theories such as Utilitarianism, Kantianism, Relativism, Egoism and Natural Law." The **senior seminars** in Fall 2014 were **Film and Contemporary Society** and **The Holocaust.** In the former, students are acquainted with "the theory, aesthetics, history, and cultural contexts of film, concentrating on the relationships among film, literature, popular culture, music, and the plastic arts." **The Holocaust** covers the period from 1933-1945 and examines "the many factors that led to the institutionalized destruction of European Jewry."

Average Class Size: The average honors class size is less than 15 students; the overall average class size for the 50 national university colleges and programs under review in this edition is 21.2 students.

Honors Graduation Rate: The six-year graduation rate of students in the honors college who graduated from the university, whether or not the students completed the honors program ("honors completers"), is **75%. The university-wide rate is 60%.** The average six-year honors **graduation rate for the 50 national universities under review is 89%.**

Ratio of Staff to Honors Students: Honors has 1 staff member for every **114** students. (Mean ratio for all 50 national university programs that we rated is 1 staff member for every 159.8 students.)

Honors Residence Halls: The Honors Theme communities are in Thomas Hall--1 South for men and 2 South for women. Thomas Hall features traditional double rooms and shared hall baths. There is on-site dining and laundry, but the rooms are not air conditioned.

Prestigious Awards: "The Honors Academic Advisor also serves as Coordinator of Eastern Illinois University's National Scholarships and Fellowships Program. Both of Eastern Illinois University's Goldwater Scholars were Honors students. Mr. Jonathan Jones was named a Goldwater Scholar in 2012, for his work in Physics. He completed both the University Honors Program and the Departmental Honors Program in Physics. Mrs. Rebecca (Grove) Laird was named a Goldwater Scholar in 2008, for her work in Chemistry. She completed the University Honors Program."

Completion Requirements: 3.50 GPA

Academic Strengths: EIU is known for its programs in education, biological sciences, and communications disorders.

Undergraduate Research: "The Honors College offers undergraduates the opportunity to apply for competitive funding to promote their research, scholarship, and creative activities. Applicants must be undergraduate students in good standing with a minimum 3.00 GPA and enrolled full-time for the current semester AND the semester in which the research/creative activity is to be conducted: for summer awards students must be enrolled in at least one class. Research must be completed and the summary reflection submitted to the Honors College prior to the end of the semester following the one for which the grant was awarded.

"Student research and creative activity that has been funded has gone on to be presented at regional and national discipline-specific meetings or at meetings of the National Conferences on Undergraduate Research (NCUR). In 2014, the Honors College sponsored 43 students' attendance at the annual NCUR meeting."

Study Abroad: "EIU is a partner with the University of Evansville's Harlaxton campus in the U.K., and Honors students (along with some EIU faculty) regularly spend a semester there. The Honors College supports student study abroad with special scholarships that help defray the costs: some preference is given to students studying for a semester or more."

Financial Aid: "The Honors College also offers several named awards, including the Charles Austin Scholarship (for study abroad), as well as the Dorothy Davis Bunge, the Rachel Richardson, the First

Neighborhood Bankshares, the Margaret Schmidt, the President Doudna, and the John L. Whisnand scholarships.

"In addition the Honors College awards $70-100,000 worth of Continuing Student scholarships and Study Abroad Scholarships annually: these awards vary in value."

Degree of Difference (Honors students/non-honors students): The average ACT for the top quarter of EIU students is 24; the average ACT for honors students is 27.

NAME: FREDERIK MEIJER HONORS COLLEGE, GRAND VALLEY STATE UNIVERSITY

Date Established: 1973

Location: Allendale, Michigan

University Full-time Undergraduate Enrollment: 21,627

Honors Enrollment: 1,600 (mean size of 50 national university programs is 1,714)

Admissions: GVSU Honors uses ACT scores more than SAT scores, and the average (mean) score of enrolled students is 29.44 (SAT equivalent is about 1315). The average high school GPA is 3.904, and GPA, motivation, and applicant responses to an essay prompt, are the most important factors.

The **minimum** requirements are ACT 28 (SAT 1240) and a high school GPA of 3.50.

Administrative Staff: The Honors Program has 6 full-time equivalent staffs.

Priority Registration: Yes, honors freshmen select their honors courses as soon as they like, and their place is held with a permit in our registration software until they register; they do not, however, have priority registration for non-honors courses.

Curriculum Requirements: Except for engineering majors, most honors students must complete 29-33 credits designed to fulfill university Gen Ed requirements as well. The honors options are highly commendable for providing excellent variety along with a strong degree of coherence within the options.

Option I: Twelve credits in a sequence--four courses taken over two semesters. Students can choose from eight sections of American, Asian, Classical, Islamic, European Civilization, and history of science classes; yet another class is titled **Big History.**

Option II: Nine academic course credits over two semesters, plus the 3-credit **Honors Live, Learn, and Lead** course in Fall. The three courses other than Live, Learn, and Lead are *not* the same courses offered in Option I; rather they cover national security, urban issues, **World Construction of Religion and Society;** theories of rights, social product innovation, and **Food for Thought.**

Option III: This is the option for engineering students and requires completion of 12 credits over **four semesters** instead of two. Students complete a four-course sequence: one section of **Making Europe** each semester for two years or one section of **How to Love the World** each semester for two years.

In the **sophomore year,** students usually take two 3-credit social sciences honors courses, one 3-credit course in life science, and one 4-credit course in physical science with a lab.

The **junior year** usually brings an end to many Gen Ed requirements, but honors students take a 3-credit junior seminar, with half a dozen choices, most with a "World Perspective" or "U.S. Diversity" theme.

The **senior project** can be from 1-4 credits. It can be a thesis in the major or a project begun in another course. Students "may study an area of interest in a sustained and in-depth exploration; learn more about their chosen field; make stronger connections with professionals in the field; do a project while studying abroad; hone research, writing, and critical thinking skills; or create a tangible, substantive accomplishment they can feel proud about and can discuss in job interviews, letters of application, and graduate school applications." Students can even provide future employers or educators with online access to the project itself.

AP credits can substitute for some honors composition, math, and science courses.

Range and Type of Honors Courses: The honors Gen Ed courses at GVSU, especially those in the **Foundational Interdisciplinary Sequence,** are outstanding. Many of these are classes taken as part of the **Option I requirements listed above.** Of the dozen courses in the sequence, we will single out two as emblematic of the quality of these courses.

In **Big History,** students "examine the past on the largest possible time scale: [the course] begins with the origins of the universe, and goes on to tell a series of linked stories about the origins of stars and planets, of life on earth, the emergence of human beings, and the various types of human societies that have existed up to the present day." **Big History** is an emerging field of its own within the history profession, one that **"weaves evidence and perspectives from many scientific and historical disciplines into a single, accessible origin story--**one that explores who we are, how we got here, how we are connected to everything around us, and where we may be heading."

We must offer a description of **How to Love the World,** one of the classes required under **Option 3** for engineers. "The premise of this course is that if we look closely at some artists (poets and painters) who profess to love the world--and we study the intimate details of their work--how they think, act, and create, as well as how they and others talk about their work-- we will learn something about ourselves, and how we can engage meaningfully with 'the world'--our lives; the beings, human and otherwise, around us; our professions."

Average Class Size: The average honors class size is about 20 students, with some of the **Foundations** classes reaching 25 or so, and a few of the other sections enrolling only 10-12 students; the overall average class size for the 50 national university colleges and programs under review in this edition is 21.2 students.

Honors Graduation Rate: The six-year graduation rate of students in the honors college who graduated from the university, whether or not the students completed the honors program ("honors completers"), is **83.3%.** The **university-wide rate is 62%.** The average six-year honors **graduation rate for the 50 national universities under review is 89%.**

Ratio of Staff to Honors Students: Honors has 1 staff member for every **266.7** students. (Mean ratio for all 50 national university programs that we rated is 1 staff member for every 159.8 students.)

Honors Residence Halls: The Glenn A. Niemeyer Living/Learning Center is as good as any honors residential community that is a part of the 50 national university honors programs we have reviewed. Home to 450 honors first-year students and upperclassmen, **the LLC offers apartment-style living with either 4-bedroom or 2-bedroom air-conditioned apartments, each with its own kitchen.**

Located on the south side of the campus, the LLC also houses the offices of the Honors College. Convenient dining is available at **Connections,** where students can choose from three options: **Engrained** serves entrees, salads, and deli selections; **P.O.D.** a convenience store and coffee shop with late-night service and grab and go panini sandwiches; and a **Papa John's Pizza.**

About 110 first-year honors students live in the Hills Honors Residence, which features traditional double rooms and shared baths, and 60 more first-year students live in Pickard Honors Residence with the same room styles. Neither dorm is air conditioned. The nearest dining is at Kleiner Commons.

Prestigious Awards: GVSU students have won both Goldwater and Boren Scholarships for undergraduates. In 2011, GVSU received recognition as a top producer of Fulbright Student Scholars among universities whose highest level of degree is a master's.

Continuation Requirements: 3.20 GPA

Academic Strengths: GVSU is third among Michigan universities in the number of graduates who go into health sciences fields. Strong departments include nursing, occupational therapy, physical therapy, physician's assistant, public affairs, social work, and business. There is also an early assurance program in partnership with the Michigan State University College for Human Medicine for top GVSU pre-med scholars who are also first-generation college students.

Undergraduate Research: The Honors Director reports that "freshmen are introduced to research in their freshman seminar or interdisciplinary sequence. Further, they are encouraged to seek out faculty to work with in labs and special projects.

"We have a freshman research paper competition, and invite those who are nominated by faculty to participate in a local Honors conference. We then encourage upper-classmen to present at a regional conference, and then as juniors or seniors to participate at a national or discipline-specific conference."

Study Abroad: The Director tells us that in the college's exit survey "we ask about study abroad, and each of the last few years approximately 30% report studying abroad in a long-term experience. **The university was recognized as being in the top 10 for universities of its size and type for the number of students who study abroad, and has partner institutions in many places around the world (including Ghana, India, South Africa, Mexico, Spain, etc.)** The college has its own faculty-led programs, including a service-learning program to Ghana and another program in Nicaragua."

Financial Aid: GVSU offers several merit awards, some of them for honors students only:

The Award of Distinction--Faculty Award requires a minimum 30-31 ACT and a 3.6 High School GPA. The value is $500-$3,000 per year for as many as four years (on top of $1,500 Award of Excellence given to anyone who has a 26 ACT or above);

Students may also be eligible for the Zukaitis Scholarship, for those accepted into Honors; the value is up to $2,000 additional per year;

The Award of Distinction--Presidential Award requires a minimum 32 ACT and a 3.8 High School GPA; the value is $3,000-$7,000 per year for as many as four years (on top of $1,500 Award of Excellence given to anyone who has a 26 ACT or above);

Students may also be eligible for the Lubbers Scholarship, for those accepted into Honors; the value is up to $2,000 additional per year.

The Meijer First Generation Scholarship is a full tuition scholarship awarded to select first generation students who compete in the Scholarship Competition.

Degree of Difference (Honors students/non-honors students): The average ACT for the top quarter of GVSU students is 26; the average ACT for honors students is 29.44.

Student Testimonials:

--"Through the Honors College, I also had the life-changing opportunity to study abroad in Ghana for two months on a service-learning trip. This unique experience brought students from various disciplines together to work toward one common goal: eliminating child trafficking in West Africa and beyond. Each summer, a group of students, faculty, and staff travel to Ghana to engage in non-profit development courses, and to work hands-on with Challenging Heights, a world-renowned anti-human trafficking non-government organization."

--"Due to the small class sizes and unique learning opportunities found in Honors (such as a class that simulates a counter-terrorism organization), I have been able to develop a meaningful academic relationship with every instructor I have had. These relationships and learning opportunities have shaped my education, as well as my career path; I am now pursuing a law degree as a way to enter the counter-terrorism sector."

--"Two of the defining experiences of my college career were a direct result of the relationships I was able to build with honors faculty. One of those experiences was that I was able to study abroad in China on a trip led by honors faculty. This trip helped to develop my critical thinking skills and challenged some of the traditional viewpoints I held."

--"With the encouragement from Honors Director, Dr. Jeff Chamberlain, and other honors faculty, I developed a more effective mentoring program for incoming honors freshmen. To help ensure that all new incoming students transition smoothly into the honors community and receive the help they need, I formed a mentor council. The mentor council is a group of experienced mentors who help and guide new mentors with their responsibilities and make sure that all the incoming honors students receive the attention and guidance they need."

NAME: UNCW HONORS SCHOLARS COLLEGE

Date Established: 1965 first departmental honors graduates at UNCW; 1994- Honors Scholars Program (4 year honors curriculum implemented); 2011-transition to Honors Scholars College (HSC)

Location: Wilmington, North Carolina

University Full-time Undergraduate Enrollment: 11,295

Honors Enrollment: 671 (mean size of 50 national university programs is 1,714).

Admissions: The average (mean) scores of enrolled honors students are SAT 1310 (critical reading and quantitative only), ACT 29 composite; the average high school GPA is 4.3 (weighted).

The **minimum** requirements are SAT 1240, ACT 28, and a high school GPA of 3.50 (unweighted) or 4.0 (weighted).

Administrative Staff: The Honors Program has a staff of 5.

Priority Registration: Yes, honors students register for **all** courses, honors and otherwise, with the first group of students during **each** year they are in the program.

Curriculum Requirements: The HSC offers several honors completion options, providing an unusual degree of flexibility that very likely leads to high levels of completion.

University Honors with Honors in the Major requires a minimum of 29 semester hours of honors credit, or 23.4% of the 124 hours required for graduation. Of the 29 honors credits, at least 23 must be in honors Gen Ed courses or seminars, with the honors thesis counting for the remaining 6 credits.

- 12 credits must be in honors Gen Ed courses;
- 8 hours must be in honors seminars (includes honors freshman seminar, two honors experiential seminars, and one honors interdisciplinary seminar);
- Typically, no more than 3-4 honors contract credits can be used for the above;
- Up to 3 credits of the above requirements may be met through studying abroad;
- 6 credits of honor thesis (departmental honors).

Departmental Honors in the Major requires the completion of a 6-credit honors thesis, usually in the student's major.

Note: Students may also be recognized as UNCW Undergraduate Research Scholars if they complete University Honors or Departmental Honors and present research at an approved off-campus conference or other venue.

Honors Global Citizen Recognition is the only option of its kind among the 50 national and 6 regional university honors programs reviewed in this publication, and a highly commendable option it is.

Students must (1) meet the requirements for University Honors or Departmental Honors; (2) complete an honors thesis or project on an approved topic "emphasizing global engagement"; (3) complete at least 12 study-abroad credits; (4) demonstrate language competency; and (5) complete at least 12 credits of courses with a global theme.

AP credits cannot be used to replace required honors courses.

Range and Type of Honors Courses: After studying university-wide and honors program class schedules for months, it is a great relief to find that the HSC course information--listed by discipline, class type, credit hours, instructors, and *course descriptions*--is presented in one location: http://www.uncw.edu/honors/academics/curriculum.html

In Fall 2014, there were seven 3-credit, first-year honors seminars; five 1-credit, first-year honors enrichment seminars; two 1-credit enrichment seminars open to higher level students; four 3-credit interdisciplinary seminars for higher level students; and twenty 3-4 credit honors sections of Gen Ed courses in various academic disciplines. We classify the HSC as a **blended honors program**, which presents an excellent combination of interdisciplinary seminars along with a representative range of more specialized courses in the academic disciplines.

Of the seven first-year seminars, we will focus on two of our favorites: **Smart People, Strange Ideas** and **Animal Einsteins--or Not?**

The **Smart People** description is an attention-grabber: **"Stevie Wonder said it best, 'When you believe in things that you don't understand you suffer. Superstition ain't the way.'** Are all claims to knowledge equal? How do we distinguish between valid scientific research and assertions that are founded on opinion, stories, or just plain nonsense? We'll explore some of the weird things some smart people believe and learn how to distinguish the truth from truthiness."

Animal Einsteins, taught by the Honors Director, strives to answer questions that almost everyone has asked: "How do we know what animals know? Are animals intelligent or just trainable? Or are those the same? In this seminar, we will explore the field of animal cognition. We will use the book *Animal Wise* to explore what we know or think we know about the minds of animals such as ants, birds, fish, rats, elephants, dolphins, chimps, and canids. Are humans smart enough to design studies to test for animal intelligence?"

First-year enrichment seminars include Leadership: Theory and Practice; The Politics of 2014; Survey of Professional Nursing; Art in the Capital; and Prosecuting Capital Crimes: Death Along the Cape Fear. Open only to students who have completed core courses in the disciplines are two enrichment seminars, **Survey of Biological Research** and **Survey of Business Research.**

Notable interdisciplinary seminars are **Evolution and Literature** and **The Geology of National Parks.** The former "investigates the varied effects Charles Darwin's 1859 publication *The Origin of Species* has had on literature over the last 150 years." The Geology seminar focuses on "the history of the Earth, from the big bang to today to understand how these amazing National Park locations in the U.S. came to be. We will then complete several case-studies, investigating different aspects of National Parks."

More specialized classes in the academic disciplines are well represented: sections in microeconomics, biology, chemistry, calculus/analytical geometry, history, psychology, English (several), music, speech, international studies, and oceanography were offered in Fall 2014. We found no honors sections in physics or anthropology, although the latter is offered in other semesters.

Average Class Size: The seminars are capped at 20 students, and some have 10-15 students enrolled. **Impressively, the sections in the disciplines are also small, 20-24 students**. We estimate that **the average honors class size is 18-20 students**; the overall average class size for the 50 national university colleges and programs under review in this edition is 21.2 students.

Honors Graduation Rate: The **six-year graduation rate** of students in the honors college who graduated from the university, whether or not the students completed all honors program requirements ("honors completers"), is **82.4%**. The **university-wide rate is 68%**. The average six-year honors **graduation rate for the 50 national universities under review is 89%.**

Ratio of Staff to Honors Students: The HSC has 1 staff member for every **134.2** students. (Mean ratio for all 50 national university programs that we rated is 1 staff member for every 159.8 students.)

Honors Residence Halls: About 96 HSC first-year students live in Honors House, a coed residence hall with traditional double rooms and hall baths. Honors House is air-conditioned, has a kitchen and on-site laundry facilities, and offers convenient food service at Wagoner Hall. The Honors Director tells us that "we have additional designated 'honors space' in a residence hall adjacent to Honors House so **all freshmen who are in Honors and live on campus are in Honors community."**

Sixty honors upperclassmen live in nearby Seahawk Hall, an air-conditioned residence with suite-style rooms and shared baths. The most convenient dining is also at Wagoner Hall.

Prestigious Awards: "The Honors College is the umbrella for advising for Major Fellowships and Scholarships," the Director reports. "We have a half-time faculty member who is our Coordinator of National Fellowship Advising. UNCW has produced several Fulbright Student Scholars (one in 2012-13) and several NOAA Hollings Scholars (three in 2012-13; two in 2013-2014). We also have several current Gilman Scholars. Past recipients also include Madison awardee and Phi Kappa Phi Study Abroad Scholarships. A new program for a small cohort of Honors students is the Wilmington Fellows mentoring program. These first-year students make an early commitment to become strong candidates for national fellowships and graduate schools. They are then mentored for early engagement in undergraduate research as well as invited to participate in honors and undergraduate research conferences.

Continuation Requirements: 3.30 GPA by 27 credits, and 3.50 GPA by 58 credits and thereafter.

Academic Strengths: Business, nursing, education, biology, psychology, English, creative writing and film studies attract the most students at UNCW.

Undergraduate Research: The Honors Director reports that "The Center for the Support of Undergraduate Research and Fellowships (CSURF) is under the umbrella of the Honors College. This is the centralized support service to promote undergraduate research for all undergrads (not honors students only)."

Aside from having the best name we have seen for an undergraduate research program, CSURF does an excellent job of qualifying students for the extremely generous Hollings Scholarships. As noted above, five UNCW students won the awards in the past two years.

Study Abroad: As part of the Honors Global Citizen Recognition program, honors students can enroll in an honors semester at University of Swansea (Wales) every spring. "With the Swansea program it is also possible to experience a professional internship. For an intense three-week period, or longer as a part-time intern when classes begin, you can gain valuable professional experience," according to the Swansea site. "UNCW students have worked in health care, legal services, early childhood education, journalism--you can be placed into an internship that fits your particular goals.

"Another attractive feature of the Swansea program is the opportunity to travel around Europe. Spring vacation at Swansea lasts for three weeks, so it can be a very good value to see many appealing sites across Europe while you are there."

Financial Aid: "Competitive honors merit scholarships are available to honors students regardless of need," the Director tells us. **About half the honors students have an honors merit scholarship.** Students may also apply for need based scholarships separately. They may also apply for departmental scholarships separately.

"Honors also hires honors students as work assistants and places honors students who have federal work study."

Degree of Difference (Honors students/non-honors students): The average SAT for the top quarter of UNCW students is 1250; the average SAT for honors students is 1310.

NAME: THE HONORS COLLEGE AT WESTERN KENTUCKY UNIVERSITY

Date Established: 1963 as honors program; 2007 as Honors College

Location: Bowling Green, Kentucky

University Full-time Undergraduate Enrollment: 13,868

Honors Enrollment: 1,301 (mean size of 50 national university programs is 1,714).

Admissions: The average (mean) scores of enrolled students are ACT 30.24, SAT 1350; the average high school GPA is 3.94 (unweighted).

The **minimum** requirements are 27 ACT, 1210 SAT composite, *or* a 3.8 unweighted high school GPA, *or* a ranking in the top 15 percent of the high school class. "Students must have one of the three of these criteria to be eligible to apply," according to the Executive Director of the program. "Included in the application are essays, a résumé of activities, a leadership portfolio, service and honors, as well as letters of recommendation. Additionally, there are 'bonus points' that are available based upon Honors College priorities: ethnic diversity, regional diversity (i.e., out of state/international students), first generation, students with passport or international experience, studying a critical language, etc."

Administrative Staff: The Honors College has an administrative staff of 11 and 6 honors academic faculty. We estimate that the full-time equivalent staff is 14.

Priority Registration: Yes. "Priority Registration is not restricted to honors courses; it is available for all of the scholars' courses. Additionally, scholars have Priority Registration as long as they remain in the College in good standing."

Curriculum Requirements: "Honors scholars admitted to the Honors College as first-year scholars must earn at least 33 hours of honors credit by taking unique honors courses in general education, upper-division courses in their major, special Honors Colloquia, and electives. These scholars have the option of completing their undergraduate experience through a six-hour Honors Capstone Experience/Thesis…or by earning six additional Honors hours in their major." The honors completion requirement represents a very substantial 27.5% of the total hours required for university graduation.

Thesis Option--Students must complete the 3-credit Honors 251, **Citizen and Self;** 9 credits in honors lower-division courses (earned in at least three separate academic colleges other than the Honors College); 6 credits in honors upper-division electives; 6 credits in honors upper-division in the major field; and 6 credits in honors thesis or capstone project.

Non-Thesis Option--The same total requirement of 33 credits, but instead of a 6-credit thesis/capstone, students complete 6 additional credits of honors coursework, based upon original research or creative endeavors.

Honors in the Major: Total of 18 credit hours of courses including a three-credit hour Capstone Experience/Thesis (CE/T) Project. "Honors in the Major" is designed for community college transfers and current WKU students with at least 45 hours completed. The 18 credit hours can come from any combination of Honors College Seminars, honors contract, honors study abroad, or honors departmental courses. However, at least three of the credit hours must be CE/T research credits.

AP credits cannot be used to replace required honors courses.

Range and Type of Honors Courses: The Executive Director provided this excellent summary:

"Honors courses are offered by departments in all academic colleges on the lower and upper-division levels, ensuring that Honors scholars can complete the honors curriculum regardless of their major...The Honors College gets to have a strong influence in faculty selection, because the College buys out faculty time to teach select stand-alone honors courses to ensure that the most appropriate faculty are offering the honors courses that our scholars need most."

Editor's Note: We counted **69 stand-alone sections offered in Spring 2014**, not including individual research and directed study sections. Eight of these were Citizen and Self classes, and another five were honors seminars. There were nine honors English stand-alone classes; four in computer science; and an extremely impressive 10 in mathematics (calculus I, II, and Advanced Problem Solving). It is also commendable that political science and psychology offered three honors-only sections each--many programs do not have that many, even counting "embedded" or mixed sections.

(**Citizen and Self** challenges first-year honors students to conduct independent research projects that focus on their community, along with emphasizing writing intensive-assignments, and spirited class debates. "The course helps teach honors scholars skills and academic 'habits of mind' that they will use in the rest of their honors courses.")

"*Honors Enriched Embedded Courses*: To increase curricular flexibility, departments offer Honors **Enriched Embedded Courses (HEECs) for select upper-division courses.** In a HEEC, two sections (honors and non-honors) meet together with the same professor; however, the 'embedded' honors section has additional opportunities and responsibilities to provide honors scholars an enriched honors experience. Many of these HEEC sections have additional meeting time with the faculty or involve independent research....The average number of scholars in a HEEC is less than eight scholars." Note: We found about **59 "embedded" sections in Spring 2014.**

One significant measure of the Honors College embedded courses is that, unlike most honors programs with embedded (add-on, mixed, stacked) sections, the average size of the College's mixed sections, including both honors and non-honors students, is not all that large. Indeed, many have fewer than 35 students, some as few as 15-20. The largest mixed sections are, unsurprisingly, in chemistry and biology, but even these are not really large: one biology section had 53 total students, 23 of them honors; one chemistry section had 49 total students, of whom 24 were honors. The honors organic chemistry II class did have 57 total students (33 honors), but by most measures these are actually small for science sections. Biology also had several smaller sections, including at least two stand-alone of 30 students or less.

"*Honors Self-Designed Major/Minor:* Scholars within the College have the opportunity to design their own major. **If WKU does not offer the major or minor the scholar seeks, then they can work with a**

small committee of faculty and design the major or minor suited for their unique educational and/or professional goals." The Self-Designed Major requires a 6-credit thesis or capstone project."

"Masters of Philosophy Degree (Starting Fall 2015): The Honors College will be able to even better prepare its scholars for advanced graduate and professional study through offering the Masters of Philosophy Degree (M.Phil.). The M.Phil. will be a 30-hour JUMP (Joint Undergraduate Master's Program), allowing undergraduate Honors College scholars to use up to twelve hours of graduate credit within an approved concentration toward both undergraduate and graduate degrees, thus both strengthening the baccalaureate degree and accelerating their time to earning the M.Phil. degree. *Honors scholars who complete the M.Phil. program will earn two degrees from WKU in four years*--their core undergraduate degree (e.g., BA, BS, BFA, BNS, etc.) from an academic college and the M.Phil. degree from the Honors College."

"Chinese Flagship Program: **The Chinese Flagship Program at WKU is one of only eleven such programs in the nation and the only Chinese Flagship Program (CFP) embedded in an Honors College.** Therefore, all of the Chinese Flagship scholars are members of the Honors College. The goal of the CFP is to develop the scholars' Chinese language skills to the superior level of fluency in 4-5 years. **On average, our scholars study abroad in China 3-4 times during their undergraduate careers,** and thanks to generous funding from The Language Flagship, the Honors College at WKU and nationally competitive scholarships, the majority of these experiences have been funded from external sources."

Average Class Size: Our estimate is that the average honors class size, *even if the total enrollment of mixed sections is counted,* is still **an outstanding 16.6 students per section;** the overall average class size for the 50 national university colleges and programs under review in this edition is 21.2 students.

Honors Graduation Rate: The **six-year graduation rate** of students at the Honors College at WKU who graduated from the university, whether or not the students completed the honors program ("honors completers"), is **75%.** The **university-wide rate is 50%.** The average six-year honors **graduation rate for the 50 national universities under review is 89%.**

Ratio of Staff to Honors Students: The HSC has 1 staff member for every **92.9** students. (Mean ratio for all 50 national university programs that we rated is 1 staff member for every 159.8 students.)

Honors Residence Halls: About 360 **first-year honors students** live in **Minton Hall**, which has traditional double rooms and shared hall baths. Rooms are coed by floor. Minton is air conditioned with an on-site laundry and kitchen, and convenient dining at the Downing Student Union is only about 40 meters away.

Just over **130 upperclassmen live in Bates-Runner Hall**, housed in suite-style rooms with shared baths. Rooms are coed by floor. The residence is air conditioned with laundry and kitchen facilities and, like Minton Hall, is located only 40 meters away from the Downing Student Union.

Another 106 honors students reside in **McLean Hall,** configured in the same way as Bates-Runner Hall. The Downing Student Union is still a short walk away—80 meters or so.

Prestigious Awards: "Since 2008, WKU students and recent alumni have earned over $3 million in national scholarship competitions." **WKU students have won a total of 16 Goldwater Scholarships for**

outstanding students in the STEM fields, and what is most impressive is that 8 of those have been won in the last three years. Few national universities, public or private, have a better record during the period. WKU students also have a strong record of winning Gilman Scholarships for study abroad, Fulbright Student Scholarships (16), and Boren Scholarships for extended work and study abroad.

One reason for WKU's success in winning Goldwater Scholarships is the **Gatton Academy of Mathematics and Science,** a state-supported residential high school "for students interested in pursuing advanced careers in science, technology, engineering, and mathematics. **Instead of spending their junior and senior years in traditional schools, 121 students take all their coursework through Western Kentucky University with regularly enrolled college students."** Gatton has been ranked the number 1 public high school by Newsweek/The Daily Beast. WKU is the number 1 destination of Gatton graduates, who become members of the Honors College if they choose WKU.

Continuation Requirements: 3.20 GPA

Academic Strengths: WKU has an outstanding journalism and broadcasting program, ranked in the top 8 nationally for 17 consecutive years. WKU students do extremely well in national forensics (debate) competitions, and the Honors College offers several sections in forensics. Other popular majors are education, biology, management, agriculture, and engineering.

Undergraduate Research: Again, the Executive Director has provided excellent information:

"WKU funds 100 Faculty Undergraduate Student Engagement (FUSE) Grants (and international version known as iFUSE grants) annually. FUSE grants are substantial ($5,000 per award) and designed to support undergraduate students' intellectual development by fostering active engagement in the areas of research, creative and scholarly activities, and/or artistic performances. Although all undergraduate students in good academic standing who will reach at least sophomore status at the time of award may apply, **honors scholars earn a majority of the awards. FUSE grants are intended for sophomore and junior level undergraduates. The timing of these grants fits perfectly with most students [thesis and capstone] timelines.**

"Another source of funding, albeit available only to Honors College scholars, is the Honors Development Grants (HDG). The HDG is designed to support honors scholars' intellectual development by providing awards up to $500 to offset costs for traveling to professional conferences, presenting academic papers, conducting research, or acquiring tangible items to support intellectual and creative endeavors. Additionally, Capstone Experience/Thesis Excellence Grants offer up to $1,500 to scholars to enrich their Capstone Experience/Thesis projects in preparation for submission to publication or other national recognition."

Study Abroad: The Executive Director presents a strong argument that WKU, and the Honors College, rank with the best when it comes to the percentage of students studying abroad. He writes that he has "compared the Honors College to the top private liberal arts colleges in the United States over the past five years. Based on [the Institute for International Education] *Open Doors* data and definitions, the Honors College at WKU has a higher 'undergraduate participation rate' than any private liberal arts college over the past five years."

"Regarding semester or full-year study abroad participation… nearly half of all the WKU students who studied abroad for a full semester or longer were enrolled in the Honors College. Additionally… nearly half of all Honors College scholars who studied abroad in 2012-13 did so for at least a full semester."

"WKU has begun construction on a new $22 million, 67,000 square foot Honors College and International Center. We expect to move into our new building August 2015. The combination of international programs (e.g., Study Abroad and Global Learning, Kentucky Institute for International Studies, Cooperative Center for Study Abroad, International Student Office) and units with the Honors College (e.g., Office of Scholar Development, Chinese Flagship Program) is conscious and shows the importance of continuing the internationalization of the College in terms of both study abroad and international diversity within the College."

Financial Aid: "All WKU students who are awarded the university's top two scholarships--'Henry H Cherry Presidential Scholarships (tuition, room, board, and book stipend) and the "1906 Founders Scholarships" (tuition, room, and book stipend)--are required to be in the Honors College. On average, the 300 Honors College first year students are awarded [a total of] approximately $2.5 million in renewable scholarships for WKU. **On average, nearly 70% of our incoming 300 first year scholars are awarded at least a renewable tuition scholarship."**

Degree of Difference (Honors students/non-honors students): The average ACT for the top quarter of Honors College students is 25; the average ACT for honors students is 30.24.

NAME: UNIVERSITY HONORS PROGRAM, UNIVERSITY OF WISCONSIN-EAU CLAIRE

Date Established: 1983

Location: Eau Claire, Wisconsin

University Full-time Undergraduate Enrollment: 9,605

Honors Enrollment: 652 (mean size of 50 national university programs is 1,714)

Admissions: The average (mean) ACT score for honors enrollees is 29.4, and the average high school graduation level of enrolled students is the 94th percentile (median is 96th percentile).

"There are several ways to gain admission to the University Honors Program":

Automatic invitations are issued to students with ACT composites of 28 and up (SAT 1280, 1880), and high school class rank in the top 5%; **or** 29 ACT composites (SAT 1300, 1940) and top 10%; **or** 30 ACT (SAT 1340, 2000), top 15%.

Students admitted to UW–Eau Claire with a 26 ACT or up composite (SAT 1190, 1770), high school class rank of top 10% or higher, or 3.75 high school GPA may be considered for holistic admission. In past semesters, invitations have been issued to approximately 20% of students considered holistically. The Honors Director tells us that "We in the University Honors Program and at the University of Wisconsin–Eau Claire are very proud and excited about our multi-faceted approach to Honors admissions. **Our holistic admissions process, which involves a large team of application readers from across our campus, enables us to search for and find Honors students in our University applicant pool whom our automatic admissions procedures had been missing. Similar review processes also enable us to evaluate and invite international and non-traditional students into Honors." The program received an award from the UW System for its holistic approach.**

Second- and third-semester invitations may be offered to students with an ACT composite score of 26 who have completed at least 15 academic credits at UW–Eau Claire, provided the students have demonstrated "excellent academic performance, including attaining an "A-" average (3.67 GPA)."

Transfer students from other university Honors programs are admitted on request. Honors courses taken at accredited institutions of higher education are accepted toward meeting the requirements of UW-Eau Claire's Honors Program.

Petitioning the University Honors Council is an option for students who are highly motivated to do Honors work, including transfer and non-traditional students.

Administrative Staff: The Honors Program has a staff of 4.

Priority Registration: Yes. "The privilege of Early Registration is granted to University Honors students who successfully complete a minimum of one 3-credit Honors course, seminar, or experience in each regular university semester (fall, spring). Honors students engaged in off-campus study or experiences (study abroad or away, National Student Exchange) retain the privilege for the semester they return to campus."

Curriculum Requirements: The Honors Director has done an exceptionally fine job of describing program completion requirements….

"To graduate with University Honors at the University of Wisconsin–Eau Claire, Honors students complete at least **26 credits of Honors courses and Honors experiences**, or at least 22% of their total undergraduate credits.

"Students at UW–Eau Claire may earn departmental or college Honors in 20 different programs to date, with several more such programs in the development and approval pipeline.

"University Honors students also pursuing departmental Honors may count up to 9 credits of their departmental Honors courses and experiences toward the 26 credits required to graduate with University Honors. This gives them the opportunity to undertake 4 years of Honors work, starting in general education (GE) and ending in high-level work in their major fields.

"This fall, I am happy to report, the University catalog will list 13 newly approved Honors umbrella courses, including 3 levels of Honors directed study, Honors independent study, Honors study abroad, and Honors internship courses, and 1-6 credits of Honors thesis. We are quickly transforming the program through these and other steps from a '[Gen Ed] replacement' program to a 4-year, scaffolded, developmental Honors program that welcomes entering students at all levels and from all disciplines and enables them, in collaboration with Honors and disciplinary advisors, to map and undertake a challenging, rewarding, individualized educational odyssey. Our very first honors thesis will be completed in Academic Year 2014-2015 in Forensic Anthropology."

The flexible University Honors completion requirement allows up to 9 honors credits from contract courses and up to 9 credits from honors experience courses.

An AP score of 4 or an IB score of 5 can be substituted for one honors course (maximum of 5 credits).

Range and Type of Honors Courses: We commend the UHP Director and staff for putting together a remarkably complete and accessible honors class schedule!

Honors sections may be honors colloquia, which are interdisciplinary classes that typically earn 3 credits; sections may also be 1-credit honors seminars; honors electives are actually what in this edition we refer to as **departmental honors** classes that are more specialized and discipline-specific; and honors experiences may be directed study, independent study, internships, or study-abroad courses, all of which may be from 1-4 credits.

As the Honors Director noted above, the UHP is in now transitioning from what has been mainly a **core program** fulfilling Gen Ed requirements, to a more **blended program,** which combines the outstanding colloquia and seminars of the core curriculum with an increasingly wide range of departmental honors courses.

In Fall 2014, we counted 13 of these departmental sections, representing an excellent range of academic disciplines: accounting, chemistry, communications (speech), economics, geography, geology, history, math, psychology, political science, sociology, women's studies, and composition. Most are 3-credit courses, but chemistry (including the lab) is 6 credits, math (calculus) is 4 credits, and composition is 2 credits.

Some of our favorites among the colloquia and seminars include **American Decades: the 20's;** Game Analysis & Design; **Voices of Color in America;** Science Fiction & Film; **Political Islam;** Hmong Culture, History & Language; and **Introduction to Ancient Greek Literature**.

The **Greek Literature** colloquium, taught by the Honors Director, explores "some of the most influential works of ancient Greek literature and history, by Homer, Aeschylus, Herodotus, Sophocles, Euripides, Thucydides, Aristophanes, and Plato. We shall read them, not as monuments of some 'superior' cultural tradition, but as explorations--often tentative, critical, and contradictory--of what it meant to the Greeks to be human, and what it meant to the Greeks to be Greek."

In **Political Islam,** a topical course indeed, students examine "the many faces of political Islam, and how Islam, as a social and political force, shapes politics in North and East Africa, the Middle East, and Central, South and Southeast Asia. The course will center on key topics such as social movements, party politics, political economy, and gender studies."

Other colloquia and seminars include **Civic Agency: From Health Care to Life Care;** Community Leadership: Moving from Talk to Action; **Tracking the Campus Carbon Footprint;** Global Cultural Relations; **Recovery, Restoration & Reform in Christianity;** and World Cinema: 21st Century Latin American Film.

Average Class Size: The average honors class size is about 23 students counting a few departmental sections that have honors and non-honors students (these also have separate honors discussion sections with fewer students). But most of the classes are colloquia and seminars that average 18-20 students. The average class size for the 50 national university colleges and programs under review in this edition is 21.2 students.

Honors Graduation Rate: The six-year graduation rate of students in the UHP who graduated from the university-- whether or not the students completed the honors program ("honors completers")--is **84.5%.** The **university-wide rate is 66%.** The average six-year honors **graduation rate for the 50 national universities under review is 89%.** The Honors Director also reported that **the UHP four-year graduation rate is an extremely high 77.4%.**

Ratio of Staff to Honors Students: Honors has 1 staff member for every **163** students. (Mean ratio for all 50 national university programs that we rated is 1 staff member for every 159.8 students.)

Honors Residence Halls: Between 35 and 60 honors students choose to live in **Bridgman Hall,** which features traditional double rooms and shared corridor baths. Bridgman is not air conditioned, but there is on-site laundry and convenient dining at the Riverfront Café in Hilltop Center.

Prestigious Awards: UW-Eau Claire students have done remarkably well in winning prestigious Goldwater Scholarships (5 so far), awarded to outstanding undergraduates in the STEM disciplines. University students have also won 16 Fulbright Student Awards, and one student has won a Rhodes Scholarship.

Honors Graduation Requirements: 3.50 GPA

Academic Strengths: The most popular majors at UW-Eau Claire are business/marketing, health professions, education, biology, communications, and psychology. "As the UW–System school best known for the Liberal Arts, UW–Eau Claire also has especially strong programs in the humanities, including Music and Theater Arts, Languages, and English, enhanced by a vibrant city and regional arts community."

Undergraduate Research: The Honors Director reports that "The University of Wisconsin–Eau Claire is the University of Wisconsin System Center of Excellence for Student-Faculty Research Collaboration. We have a well-developed culture of student-faculty research collaboration, and excellent funding mechanisms to support the work. The University Honors Programs invites and encourages students in Honors to apply for Honors course credits for substantial faculty-student collaborative research projects in their individual disciplines. In addition, an increasing number of Honors courses engage students in research experiences and projects in and out of the classroom." The university has a very high number of undergraduate students engaged in research--as many as 700.

Study Abroad: The university is regularly recognized as being in the top 10-15 for universities of its size and type for the number of students who study abroad. The Director's response for this publication bears that out: "The University of Wisconsin–Eau Claire is a national leader in study abroad: 25% of our undergraduate students study abroad. Exciting news: as of fall 2014, Honors students who study abroad may earn Honors credit for some academic work done abroad by arranging Honors contracts supervised by a UW-Eau Claire faculty member."

Financial Aid: "All students admitted to the University Honors Program are eligible for a one-time Honors Scholarship of $1,000. Honors students are also eligible for all other University, College, and Departmental scholarships and other forms of financial aid."

Most honors student should qualify for some university merit award. The university Admission page says that "freshmen scholarship applicants must have an ACT score of 25+ and be in the top 25 percent of their high school class (or if class rank is unavailable, a GPA of 3.5+ on a 4.0 scale) to be considered."

Degree of Difference (Honors students/non-honors students): The average ACT for the top quarter of UW-Eau Claire students is 26; the average ACT for honors students is 29.4.

Faculty Testimonial:

Dr. Marty Wood, Professor of English and former Dean, College of Arts and Sciences--"There is nothing quite like the camaraderie, collegiality, and enthusiastic sense of community I've experienced among our Honors students in the Honors colloquia we offer. Those of us who have been lucky enough to teach these special classes have entered into a vibrant, sparkling collection of eager minds at work and play. Or work *as* play! These remarkable students quickly learn that everyone in this Honors community supports a shared pursuit of academic excellence. If you long to join a group of hard-working, voracious learners who do not know what it means to hide their whole-hearted embrace of the intellectual life, who cannot comprehend what it would be like to duck a cognitive challenge, an Honors colloquium is the place for you. In nearly every colloquium class period, I witness 'that continual and fearless sifting and winnowing' in pursuit of truth championed by our University of Wisconsin Board of Regents more than 100 years ago. Indeed I am delighted and enriched to experience the excitement of this pursuit, alive and immediate, in the passion and commitment of the students in my Honors colloquia."

Public University Press publishes the *Review of Fifty Public University Honors Programs* and operates the website PublicUniversityHonors.com.

The editor of both is John Willingham, who began researching and writing about public university honors colleges and programs in 2011, a time when many states had already made several annual cuts in funding for higher education. Some political leaders had become so focused on applying business models of "productivity" and "efficiency" to state universities that they lost sight of the critical need to offer the highest levels of quality. As a way of exemplifying the excellence that can and should be sustained in public universities, the editor compiled a comprehensive review of the honors programs in major state universities, hoping that readers would not only gain some comparative knowledge about the programs but also develop a greater awareness of the value that they all offer to highly talented students.

The *Review* is the work of the editor, an assistant editor, and a Ph.D. statistician, all in Portland, Oregon. The editor's background includes years of work in journalism and public administration, mostly in Texas. For three years, he was a regular contributor to the History News Network (HNN.us), writing several articles that covered the controversy in Texas over the adoption of social studies and science textbooks and curricula. His education includes a BA, with honors, from the University of Texas at Austin, and an MA in history from UT Austin, including graduate minors in education and journalism.

Made in the USA
Lexington, KY
12 March 2015